Lesley Adkins is well known as an archaeologist and author of several books on archaeology and history, including the acclaimed *The Keys of Egypt*. She is a Fellow of the Society of Antiquaries of London and lives in Devon.

By the same author

The Keys of Egypt:
The Race to Read the Hieroglyphs

Empires of the Plain

HENRY RAWLINSON AND THE LOST LANGUAGES OF BABYLON

Lesley Adkins

HARPER PERENNIAL

Harper Perennial
An imprint of HarperCollins*Publishers*
77–85 Fulham Palace Road
Hammersmith
London W6 8JB

www.harpercollins.co.uk/harperperennial

This edition published by Harper Perennial 2004
9 8 7 6 5 4 3 2 1

First published by HarperCollins*Publishers* in 2003

A catalogue record for this book is
available from the British Library

ISBN 0 00 712900 9

Set in Photina MT by
Rowland Phototypesetting Ltd,
Bury St Edmunds, Suffolk

Printed and bound in Great Britain by
Clays Ltd, St Ives plc

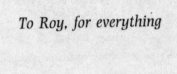

To Roy, for everything

Contents

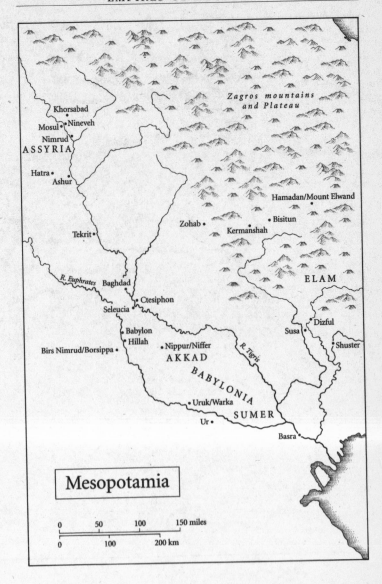

Zagros mountains
and Plateau

Khorsabad

Mosul • Nineveh
Nimrud
ASSYRIA

Hatra
Ashur

Hamadan/Mount Elwand

Zohab • • Bisitun
Kermanshah

Tekrit •

R. Euphrates
Baghdad

ELAM

• Ctesiphon
Seleucia

• Babylon
• Hillah

Birs Nimrud/Borsippa •   • Nippur/Niffer

AKKAD

BABYLONIA

Susa •   • Dizful

• Shuster

R. Tigris

• Uruk/Warka

SUMER

Ur •

Basra •

Mesopotamia

0   50   100   150 miles

0   100   200 km

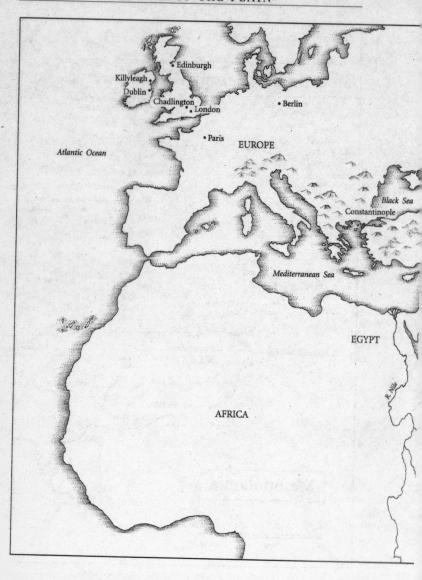

Edinburgh

Killyleagh
Dublin
Chadlington
London

Berlin

Paris

EUROPE

Atlantic Ocean

Black Sea
Constantinople

Mediterranean Sea

EGYPT

R. Nile

AFRICA

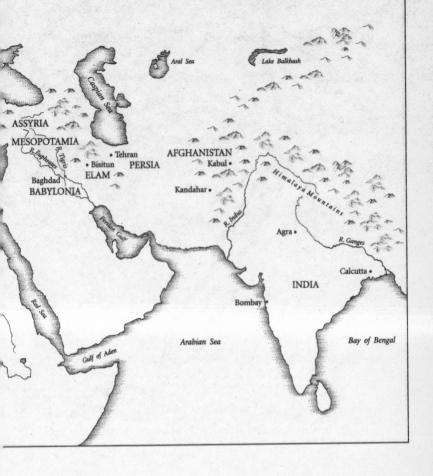

Great Britain, Europe, Africa and Asia

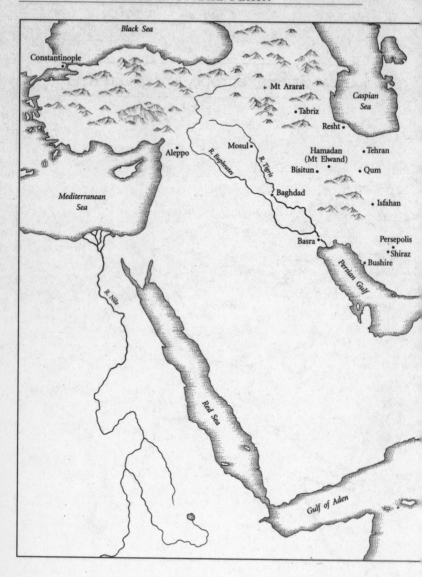

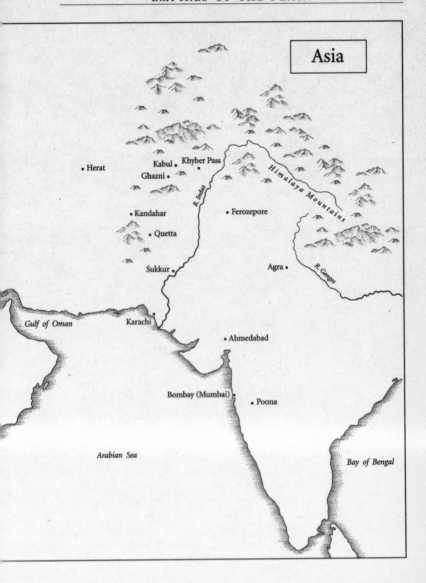

Asia

Herat
Kabul
Khyber Pass
Ghazni
R. Indus
Himalaya Mountains
Kandahar
Ferozepore
Quetta
Sukkur
Agra
R. Ganges
Karachi
Gulf of Oman
Ahmedabad
Bombay (Mumbai)
Poona
Arabian Sea
Bay of Bengal

Empires: Key Events

The following list gives often approximate dates to show the order of events, mainly occurring in Mesopotamia and Persia:

Dates BC

8000	First use of clay tokens
3600	Cylinder seals appear
3500	Numerical clay tablets appear
3300–2900	Proto-cuneiform clay tablets
3100–2700	Proto-Elamite cuneiform
3000–2300	Sumerian civilization
2800	Sumerian is first written down (not technically as cuneiform)
2600	Possible date for Gilgamesh as king of Uruk
2600	Sumerian is written using a true cuneiform script
2500–2000	Old Akkadian cuneiform
2300	Elamite cuneiform begins
2300	Akkadian Empire begins under King Sargon
2200	Akkadian Empire collapses
2000	Sumerian ceases as an everyday language
2000–1600	Old Babylonian cuneiform
2000–1500	Old Assyrian cuneiform
1792–1750	Hammurabi is king of Babylon
1600–1000	Middle Babylonian cuneiform
1500–1000	Middle Assyrian cuneiform
1400	Babylonian cuneiform becomes the lingua franca
1235	Assyria sacks Babylon

1115–1077	Tiglath-Pileser I is king of Assyria: first use of clay prisms
1000–600	Neo-Assyrian cuneiform
1000–600	Neo-Babylonian cuneiform
930	Neo-Assyrian Empire begins
883–859	Ashurnasirpal II is king of Assyria and builds a palace at Nimrud
878	Nimrud becomes the capital city of Assyria (moved from Ashur)
858–824	Shalmaneser III is king of Assyria and builds a new palace at Nimrud
825	The Black Obelisk is erected at Nimrud by Shalmaneser III
800	Aramaic language and script begin to spread in Mesopotamia and Persia
753	Mythical foundation of Rome
713	Sargon II of Assyria founds Khorsabad as his capital city (moved from Nimrud)
704–681	Sennacherib is king of Assyria and moves the capital from Khorsabad to Nineveh
668–627	Ashurbanipal is king of Assyria
612	Nineveh is sacked: collapse of the Neo-Assyrian Empire
605–562	Nebuchadnezzar II is king of Babylon
600 BC–AD75	Late Babylonian cuneiform
559–530	Cyrus the Great is king of Persia and founder of the Achaemenid dynasty
555–539	Nabonidus is king of Babylon
530–522	Cambyses II is king of Persia
522–486	Darius the Great is king of Persia
520	The Bisitun monument is started and Old Persian cuneiform is invented
486–465	Xerxes I is king of Persia
401	Cyrus the Younger is killed at the battle of Cunaxa
336–331	Darius III is king of Persia
333	Alexander the Great of Macedonia defeats Darius III at the battle of Issus
331	Persepolis is destroyed by Alexander the Great
330	Babylon is taken by Alexander the Great

330	Darius III is murdered: end of the Achaemenid (Persian) Empire, which now comes under Macedonian Greek control
323	Alexander the Great dies at Babylon
238	The Parthians (nomads from central Asia) begin to take over the former Persian Empire
141	Seleucia on the Tigris is taken by the Parthians

Dates AD

75	The last known use of cuneiform (at Babylon)
224	Sasanians conquer the Parthian Empire
240	Shapur I becomes the second ruler of the Sasanian Empire
260	The Roman emperor Valerian is captured by the Sasanians
594–628	Khusro II is ruler of the Sasanian Empire
651	The Sasanian Empire falls to the Arabs
762	Baghdad is founded by al-Mansur
1258	Baghdad falls to the Mongols
1299	Beginning of the Ottoman Empire
1588–1629	Shah Abbas I is ruler of Persia
1600	The East India Company is formed
1602	Cuneiform is observed for the first time at Persepolis
1623	Shah Abbas I of Persia captures Baghdad
1638	Baghdad is taken by Murad IV of the Ottoman Empire
1661	Bombay is ceded to Britain by Portugal
1722	Afghans besiege Isfahan
1789	Tehran becomes the capital of Persia
1792	Edward Hincks is born
1798–1834	Fath Ali is Shah of Persia
1802	The first cuneiform decipherment by Grotefend
1810	Henry Rawlinson is born
1815	Battle of Waterloo (final defeat of Napoleon)
1817	Austen Henry Layard is born
1827	Rawlinson goes to India
1829	First ascent of Mount Ararat
1833	Rawlinson leaves India for Persia
1834	Fath Ali Shah of Persia dies

1838   Coronation of Queen Victoria
1839   Layard leaves England for Ceylon
1839–42   First Anglo-Afghan War
1848   Revolutions in Europe
1849   Rawlinson and Layard meet at Nimrud
1849–51   Rawlinson is in England
1855   Rawlinson leaves Baghdad for good and returns to
            England
1857   The cuneiform competition is held
1859   Rawlinson goes to Tehran as Envoy
1860   Rawlinson resigns from his post at Tehran
1862   Rawlinson marries
1866   Hincks dies
1872   Discovery of the Flood tablet
1887   Discovery of the Amarna Letters
1889   Rawlinson's wife dies
1894   Layard dies
1895   Rawlinson dies

Rawlinson's Rock

Henry Rawlinson was hanging by his arms, watched in horror by his two companions. What had stopped him plunging to his death was the grip of his hands on the remaining length of wood that bridged the gap in the ledge – the ledge beneath the great cuneiform inscription cut into the side of a mountain at Bisitun in Persia. Years before, Rawlinson had thought nothing of climbing up and down this perpendicular rock with nobody to help him, defying the intentions of Darius the Great, King of Persia, who more than two thousand years earlier had ordered the cliff face below his monument to be cut back and smoothed to prevent anyone climbing up and vandalizing it. Rawlinson was no longer an agile young soldier, but a thirty-four-year-old diplomat in Baghdad, yet he had lost none of his mountaineering expertise and remained physically fit through horse riding and hunting. He had made the long journey on horseback to Bisitun with ropes, ladders and men to try to copy much more of the inscription, as well as the enormous relief sculpture itself.

It was only for a few moments that Rawlinson clung to the piece of wood across the break in the ledge. More than 200 feet above the boulders strewn at the foot of the mountain, the ledge was for much of its length hardly 2 feet wide, but occasionally it increased to 5 feet. In places it petered out altogether, with a sheer drop to the rocks below. Above rose the huge inscription, surrounding the sculptured scenes of Darius and the rebel leaders he had defeated. Overall, the monument measured nearly 25 feet high and 70 feet wide, with line after line of strange cuneiform signs, the earliest form of writing in the world. Although finely cut, many signs had been virtually obliterated by weathering and so required the closest examination to make an accurate copy.

Ladders had never been used on the ledge before, and Rawlinson found the ones he had brought were too long – when propped against the inscription, the angle was too steep to climb up without toppling over backwards and plunging down the cliff. The only solution was to shorten his ladder, which worked well for the middle of the inscription, but for the upper lines it meant standing on the very top rung, clinging to the rock face with one hand, while struggling to copy the signs with the other, a task that required total concentration and commitment, an unshakeable nerve and the muscle-control of an athlete.

Despite the danger, Rawlinson and his companions made good progress until they reached a point where the ledge was missing. Rawlinson intended laying his ladder flat across the gap, but because he had shortened it, the ladder would only reach the opposite ledge close up to the rock face. Away from the cliff, the gap was wider than the length of the ladder, and barely three out of the four ends could rest flat on the ledge at any one time. Because this makeshift bridge would have tilted over if Rawlinson had stood on it, he decided to turn the ladder on its side, so that one long side firmly spanned the gap and the now-vertical rungs supported the other long side suspended beneath. He began to edge along this bridge, with his feet on the lower side and his hands on the upper side to steady himself, but he had only gone a short distance when the ladder suddenly disintegrated. The rungs had not been securely fixed, and Rawlinson was left hanging by his arms from the upper side of the ladder. Fortunately it did not snap with the sudden jolt, and he was able to inch his way back to his companions, who recovered from their shock and hauled him to comparative safety on the narrow ledge once again.

The next attempt to make a bridge was done with a longer ladder laid flat across the gap, so that Rawlinson could reach the ledge beyond and also stand on this ladder bridge to copy the inscription above. In order to reach the upper lines, there was no choice but to prop a vertical ladder precariously on the rungs of the horizontal ladder bridge. Standing at the top of this ladder to copy the cuneiform signs was the most dangerous task of this perilous project, but Rawlinson achieved it without further accidents. By the end of the work in the intense summer heat of 1844, much of the relief sculptures and inscription had been successfully copied, but one part of the inscription proved impossible to reach and would have to be tackled in a further expedition a few years later.

What Rawlinson was copying at Bisitun was the most important trilingual inscription of the ancient world – the same message written three times, in three different languages and three different types of cuneiform script. The importance of the inscription lay in its considerable length, because although short trilingual inscriptions had already been copied, a much longer example was needed as an aid to the decipherment of cuneiform. Bisitun has the longest trilingual cuneiform inscription known, which eventually provided many clues to unscrambling the various types of cuneiform writing. It proved far more important than Egypt's Rosetta Stone.

The monument at Bisitun was carved to exalt the triumphs of the Persian king Darius the Great, beginning with the words, 'I am Darius, the great king, the king of kings, the king of Persia, king of countries, son of Hystaspes, the grandson of Arsames, an Achaemenian'. In the three decades before the inscription was cut, the Persian Empire had expanded rapidly and ruthlessly under King Cyrus the Great, who overwhelmed great tracts of land from the Indus River to the Black Sea. He was killed in battle against a remote tribe east of the Aral Sea in 530 BC, but the war machine continued under his son and successor Cambyses II, who captured Egypt, the greatest prize of all. Here the good fortune of the Achaemenid dynasty failed, as Cambyses's campaign was beset by problems and his army perished in the desert. When news reached Cambyses that a priest by the name of Gaumata had seized the throne in Persia, he hurriedly left Egypt, only to die on the journey – from blood poisoning caused by accidentally wounding himself with his own sword. This was the year 522 BC, and Darius, who may have been one of the king's courtiers and a distant relation, seized the initiative by executing Gaumata and declaring himself king. He went on to brutally suppress the many rebellions that erupted throughout his empire.

His triumphs were recorded on the mountainside at Bisitun, forming a landmark along the important caravan route through the Zagros mountains between the two ancient cities of Babylon and Ecbatana. The monument fulfilled an important propaganda role by proclaiming that Darius was the true king of Persia and by acting as a warning to other would-be usurpers of the throne. In the relief sculpture Darius is shown as the tallest and therefore most important figure, with an imposing long rectangular beard, wearing the full, pleated Persian costume, armed with a bow and with his right foot on the helpless body of Gaumata. Nine diminutive rebel leaders stand before Darius, roped together at the neck and with their hands bound behind their backs, and the scene is watched over by the winged figure of the great Persian god Ahuramazda.

The Bisitun inscription was carved entirely in cuneiform, which was not a language but a means of writing using signs made up of combinations of strokes and arrows. The remarkable aspect of the inscription is that Darius invented a simplified form of cuneiform specifically for Old Persian, the formal language of his court that had never before been written down. He even boasted in the inscription that he distributed copies to each province of his empire, a statement that has been verified by duplicate versions found as far afield as Babylon and southern Egypt. That Darius chose to invent a form of cuneiform for writing down the Persian language was not a strange act, because for centuries cuneiform had been the universal writing system for international relations: diplomatic correspondence between the great civilizations of Mesopotamia, Asia Minor, Palestine, Syria and even Egypt (with its own hieroglyphic writing system) was all written in cuneiform on clay tablets.

Unlike Egyptian hieroglyphs, cuneiform was not a single system

of writing representing just one language – it was used for numerous languages over 3,000 years and varied from language to
language. Three languages were present in the Bisitun inscription
– Old Persian, Elamite and Babylonian. Although it was the Babylonian that Rawlinson failed to copy on this occasion, at the risk
of his life he had obtained the full Old Persian and Elamite texts:
over 650 lines of cuneiform signs written in eight columns. He
not only had the dedication and skill to copy the inscription, but
he also possessed the linguistic abilities to tackle the decipherment,
impelled by an unquenchable thirst for knowledge of history and
ancient geography and a driving ambition to be first in anything
he undertook.

Having copied parts of the Old Persian inscription on previous
occasions, Rawlinson had already made significant progress in the
decipherment of that particular script and language and now
knew what Darius had written at Bisitun. On his return to Baghdad, Rawlinson forged ahead with unravelling Babylonian, his
ambition now further fuelled by competition from an increasing
number of rivals. This was a critical time, because the mounds of
Mesopotamia, once ancient cities, were just starting to be explored,
with exciting discoveries of palaces filled with astonishing finds.
Rawlinson was in a prime position to examine the cuneiform
inscriptions covering the relief sculptures and colossal statues, as
well as the thousands of cuneiform tablets that had belonged to
the palace libraries.

Following in Rawlinson's footsteps, other cuneiform scripts
have since been successfully deciphered, and it is now known that
cuneiform was used within an area of at least 600,000 square
miles for writing documents as diverse as diplomatic correspondence, accounts, mathematics, legal contracts, astronomy and
astrology, as well as history, medicine, magic and religion, epic
stories and political propaganda. The decipherment of cuneiform
literally revealed a completely undiscovered and unsuspected
dimension of the ancient world, not only betraying the long-
forgotten secrets of cities like Babylon, Nineveh and Nimrud, but
other civilizations whose very names had been lost long ago.

One: Into India

A few days before Henry Creswicke Rawlinson's fifth birthday, he watched the Royal Scots Greys in their magnificent dress uniforms marching out of Bristol. Reputedly the finest cavalry in Europe, though few had seen active service, these troops and their splendid grey horses were heading from their winter quarters to fame and glory at the Battle of Waterloo, where Napoleon Bonaparte was defeated on 18 June 1815. Many of them would not return from the slaughter. The sight of the cavalry parading down the steep hill of Park Street in Bristol was Rawlinson's earliest distinct memory – and perhaps his first encouragement to be a horseman and a soldier.

Nearly five years earlier, despite the chill of gloomy, showery spring weather, Wednesday 11 April 1810 had been a day of rejoicing for Abram and Eliza Rawlinson, when their second son was born at Chadlington in north Oxfordshire. Henry's birth came at a time of continuing upheaval and worry in Europe. That same month Napoleon's troops began to annex Holland, and the Emperor himself married Marie-Louise, Archduchess of Austria, while France headed towards deep economic crisis. As the year wore on, the Napoleonic Wars were concentrated in Spain and Portugal, where the British troops fought the French under the command of Wellington. In Britain King George III's mental condition deteriorated, and the following year he was declared insane; his son the Prince of Wales, the future George IV, ruled in his stead as the Prince Regent.

The Rawlinson family had already grown many branches, but their roots were in Lancashire in northern England – respectable but hardly noteworthy members of the gentry, who owned land mainly in the isolated Furness area. The derivation of the surname remains uncertain, possibly 'son of Roland', as in the associated surnames Rowlinson and Rollinson, yet these names occur in Lancashire only from the sixteenth century, decades later than Rawlinson. One of Henry's ancestors was Daniel Rawlinson, a wealthy London vintner, tea merchant and keeper of the Mitre Tavern in Fenchurch Street, much frequented by his friend and neighbour Samuel Pepys until its destruction in the Great Fire of 1666. Daniel's son Sir Thomas Rawlinson, who inherited his estates and businesses, was Lord Mayor of London in 1705–6. His own eldest son Thomas developed a passion for books and manuscripts, amassing over 50,000 volumes and 1,000 manuscripts that were eventually sold to settle his debts. This unpalatable task was forced upon his younger brother Richard, himself a book collector and antiquary, who in 1750 set up an endowment for a professorship of Anglo-Saxon at Oxford University. Now called the Rawlinson and Bosworth Chair of Anglo-Saxon, its most notable incumbent was J. R. R. Tolkien. Another Anglo-Saxon scholar was Henry's ancestor Christopher Rawlinson, born in 1677, who is most famous for having prepared and published an Anglo-Saxon edition of King Alfred's translation of Boethius's *Consolation of Philosophy*.

Although Henry was not directly descended from Daniel and Christopher, they could all trace their roots back to two brothers, William and John, in the reign of Henry VIII. Earlier still the family tree lacks detail, but ancestors certainly served at the Battle of Agincourt in 1415 under Henry V, who awarded the Rawlinson coat-of-arms that has three silver-bladed swords with gold hilts on a sable ground, and for the crest a lower arm sheathed in armour, with the hand grasping a sword. Henry's own father, Abram Tyzack Rawlinson, was the elder of the twin sons of Henry Rawlinson, a merchant and Member of Parliament for Liverpool who married a Newcastle upon Tyne heiress, Martha Tyzack. The twins' father died in 1786 when they were nine years old, but they continued to live at Caton near Lancaster, in the ancestral home of Grassyard (now Gresgarth) Hall. Here Abram and his twin Henry Lindow were raised by their mother and subsequently educated at Rugby School and Christ Church, Oxford, where they concentrated on sporting, not educational attainment. On inheriting Grassyard Hall and its estate, Abram promptly sold up and began to look for an estate 'in the more civilised part of England',[1] having come to despise northern England 'for its roughness, its coarseness, and its "savagery"'.[2] In August 1800 at St George's Church in Hanover Square, London, he married Eliza Eudocia Albinia Creswicke, who had inherited the enormous sum of £20,000 from her deceased brother Henry.

Six years after his marriage to Eliza, Abram bought a 700-acre agricultural estate at Chadlington, an ancient pre-Domesday village just south of Chipping Norton and 13 miles north-west of Oxford – close to his wife's former home at Moreton-in-Marsh. The spacious L-shaped manor house at Chadlington, where Henry Creswicke Rawlinson was born and spent his childhood, was built of Cotswold stone and was separated from the medieval church of St Nicholas and the village to the north by a belt of trees, while in front was a lawn terrace, a ha-ha and a hay meadow. The extensive view across the Evenlode Valley first took in clumps of elms and oaks in the meadow, with fields and copses beyond as far as the river, while the extensive Wychwood forest covered the hillside in the distance. It was a perfect place to live.

For much of the day Abram rode from field to field, watching over the running of his largely arable farm, talking to the labourers and discussing business matters with his bailiff. The months of September and October were occupied by shooting and the rest of the autumn and winter by riding with the Duke of Beaufort's hunt. Another of Abram's passions was the breeding and training of racehorses, in which he had several successes, and he was also involved in civic duties as a Justice of the Peace and a Deputy-Lieutenant of Oxfordshire.

When Henry was born, he was the seventh, but not the last,

of Abram's children – he and his older brother Abram and sisters Anna, Eudocia, Maria, Georgiana and Caroline were soon joined by four more brothers – Edward (who died only a few months old), George, Richard and, three months after the Battle of Waterloo, another Edward. At a time when a farm labourer was earning less than £30 per year, the income of the Rawlinson family in good years was around £2,000, partly from property Abram had inherited in the West Indies, but primarily from the farm. The ending of the Napoleonic Wars in June 1815, though, witnessed a period of severe agricultural depression in Britain that affected income from the land, and freak weather the following year led to harvest failures, starvation, unemployment, bankruptcies, increased emigration, demonstrations and riots. Although Abram sent his eldest son to Rugby School, he was forced to economize on the education of the other boys during this period of financial uncertainty, and so up to the age of eleven Henry attended a day school at Chadlington and was also educated at home by his mother, learning Latin, English grammar and arithmetic, supplemented by lessons from his sisters' governesses.

Not only did Henry spend his early years in rural Chadlington, but also in the contrasting environment of the city of Bristol. For over five years, from the time the Royal Scots Greys marched to Waterloo, he often lived with his maternal aunt Anna and her husband Richard Smith, in their elegant terrace house at 38 (now 80) Park Street, and for a short while attended a day school in the city. Richard Smith was a surgeon to the Bristol Royal Infirmary, and he successfully treated his nephew's serious eye condition that had threatened his vision, so that in the end only his left eye was partially impaired. When Henry was seventeen years old, he was told a story about 'good Aunt Smith's marriage', that she was engaged to Henry Pelly, but he went to sea to make his fortune, and on returning discovered that Anna, like Henry's own mother, had inherited a fortune. He was too proud to approach her, and because she was annoyed at being ignored, Anna eloped with another admirer, Richard Smith. In view of Henry's sight being saved, this was a happy outcome, and he himself noted:

'Who that has seen *their* perfect content and happiness will ever believe in the *inevitable miseries* of an elopement.'[3]

At Bristol, Henry came under the influence of his aunt's wide literary circle, including Hannah More, a poet and playwright who had achieved great success in London and whose hugely popular religious tracts aimed at the reform of conditions for the poor had led to the founding of the Religious Tract Society in 1799. She was then living at Wrington in Somerset, to the south-west of Bristol, where Henry's maternal grandmother also had her home. From 1813 his aunt's closest companion was Mrs Mary Anne Schimmelpenninck, an author of popular religious and educational works and a campaigner for the abolition of slavery. She often talked to Henry, who recorded that she 'took a great interest and taught me scraps of Hebrew',[4] which she herself was studying with his aunt.

In January 1821, eight months after the death of his eleven-year-old sister Caroline, Henry was sent to a boarding school at Wrington. He later condemned his two-and-a-half years there as of limited use, because he 'got well grounded in Latin and Greek. Also in General History but learned no Mathematics'.[5] Much more influential for him must have been spending nearly every Sunday in the company of Hannah More and her supporters. A few weeks after starting this school, just before Easter, Henry undoubtedly heard about his uncle's involvement with John Horwood, hanged at Bristol's New Gaol on Friday 13 April for murdering a woman who had rejected him. By order of the court, Horwood's body was released to Richard Smith at the Bristol Royal Infirmary for dissection, which was carried out before a large audience and was followed by several lectures. Smith had an account of the trial, execution and dissection bound into a book that was covered by Horwood's own tanned skin – a macabre volume now held in the Bristol Record Office.

Henry's older sister Anna Maria died in 1823, and in August the following year he was moved to the much larger Great Ealing School, then considered to be 'the best private school in England'.[6] Although now swamped by the suburban spread of London, the village of Ealing was predominantly agricultural, dotted with fashionable country houses. Henry judged his two-and-a-half years at this school to have been crucial, because for the first time he developed a desire to excel in academic studies rather than just in sports. He acquired such a good command of Classical languages that by the time he left he was first in Greek and second in Latin within the entire school, a substantial accomplishment considering his previous piecemeal education. Even so, he had no intention of going to university, as he had long cherished an ambition to seek adventure by entering the army; apart from his nickname of 'Beagle', from an early age his brothers and sisters called him 'the General'.[7]

Although diligent in his school work, Henry was a strong character, not above breaking the rules when it suited him. On one occasion he was caught with another boy, Frank Turner, after they had walked to and from London to see an opera. The penalty for such a premeditated breach of the school's strict discipline could be harsh – flogging or expulsion. Instead they were set the task of learning by heart, in the original Latin, all 476 lines of the *Ars Poetica*, written by the Roman poet Horace around 19 BC in the form of a letter giving views on the nature of poetry. After a fortnight, Henry completed the task and recited the lengthy poem without a flaw, but the other boy failed and was expelled.

As might be expected from a family background so steeped in field sports, Henry had a natural talent for all the games played at the school: prisoners' base, cricket, football and fives. He was exceptionally gifted at fives, a rough ball game that required great physical endurance, using the hands rather than bats or rackets. He spent the school holidays at Chadlington entirely immersed in the outdoor pursuits of hunting, shooting and fishing, and at times was invited by Lord Normanton to attend shooting parties with his father in the woods east of Chadlington that formed part of the Ditchley Park estate. On his first occasion Henry shot and killed every pheasant before Lord Normanton had taken aim, and so he had to be advised of the correct etiquette. He then held back,

only to prove himself the best shot after Lord Normanton had
fired – in the sporting slang of the time, 'wiping his lordship's
eye'.[8]

In December 1825, Henry's older sister Eudocia died at Bristol
at the age of twenty-three. Five months later, when he was sixteen
years old, Henry left school with a nomination to a cadetship in
the East India Company, a position he owed to the influence of
his mother's half-brother, although his formal nominator was
William Taylor Money, one of the Company's directors. Henry
was now 6 feet tall (6 inches above the average height at the
time) and was 'broad-chested, strong limbed, with excellent thews
and sinews, and at the same time with a steady head, a clear
sight, and a nerve that few of his co-mates equalled'.[9] In fact,
with all the qualities of a young soldier.

For the sons of gentry, entering the British army as an officer
meant buying a commission and having a private income to supplement the low pay, but this burden could be avoided by entering
the army of the East India Company as a cadet and rising through
the ranks by promotion – which Henry Rawlinson proposed to
do. Granted a charter on the last day of December 1600 by Queen
Elizabeth I, the East India Company (more correctly 'The Governor
and Company of Merchants of London, Trading into the East
Indies') had exclusive rights to trade with the 'East Indies', a
term covering the entire south-east expanse of Asia. Initially, the
Company competed with the Dutch for the Indonesian spice trade,
but after the 'Massacre of Amboyna' in 1623 when Company
merchants and their servants were tortured and executed by the
Dutch, the Company turned to the subcontinent of India.

In the mid-eighteenth century the East India Company was still
a purely commercial company, importing and exporting goods
from its bases at Bombay on the west coast, Madras on the east
coast and Calcutta on the Hooghly River in the north-east. So
successful was its business that it was able to loan money to the
British government, but all this began to change, because conflict
with the French and the crumbling of the Mughal Empire provoked
the Company's intervention in political and military struggles in

India, initially in the south and east. In 1756 the new nawab (ruler) of Bengal captured Calcutta, where scores of his prisoners suffocated in an airless room, an incident dubbed 'the Black Hole of Calcutta'. In revenge, the Company's army, led by Robert Clive, recovered Calcutta and took control of the entire province of Bengal. The land tax revenue from this new territory enabled the Company to build up a sophisticated civil service and an extensive army, which gave them the means to conquer further territory and defeat the French.

By this time, many Company employees found themselves able to amass huge fortunes, often by unscrupulous means, while soldiers and officers were eager for further military campaigns because of the resulting opportunities to acquire loot and prize money. These 'nabobs' (a corruption of nawab) would retire to Britain with their new wealth, causing much resentment of their lavish lifestyles and their efforts to gain political advancement. Perceived as being answerable only to its shareholders, the Company was the target of several hostile government reports, and with mounting debts, the Company's Board of Directors was obliged to accept a degree of government control under Acts of Parliament in 1773 and 1784.

The East India Company, also known as John Company, became primarily an administrative rather than a commercial body, acting as an agent of the government and no longer relying on trade, but on the collection of land taxes from the territories it ruled. The Governor of the Bengal Presidency, based at Calcutta, was now also the Governor-General of India, exercising superiority over the Bombay and Madras presidencies. By the time Henry arrived in India, large swathes of the area now divided into India and Pakistan were ruled by the Company through conquest, or indirectly through alliances with hundreds of small states ruled by Indian princes. The Company's army was 300,000 strong and was split between the three presidencies; it accounted for over three-quarters of the Company's expenditure. Most of the East India Company troops were native sepoys (from the Persian word *sipahi*, 'soldier') and their officers were mainly British, but all were regarded as inferior to the regular British army, a judgement based on class rather than efficiency.

Having been nominated directly, Henry could have sailed for India immediately, as he was not obliged to attend the Company's Military Seminary at Addiscombe, near Croydon. Instead, he chose to receive private tuition from Thomas Myers, a mathematician and geographer and formerly a professor at the Royal Military Academy in Woolwich. Myers was now living and teaching at Blackheath village, a small and affluent suburb just over 5 miles south-east of London. 'Here', Henry noted, 'I learned Hindestanee and Persian, surveying, advance Mathematics, Military drawing, fencing and all other requisites for an Indian soldier's life.'[10] Numerous languages were spoken throughout India, but it was important to have some knowledge of the Hindustani language (known today as Urdu), because it was the main language of communication between East India Company officials and the natives. It had its origins in the Muslim courts and cities of northern India. For hundreds of years Persian had been the language of administration in India, although by the nineteenth century the version of Persian used in India was very different to the language used in Persia. In Persian, Hindustan meant 'land of the Hindus'.

Impatient to embark on his new career, Henry regarded the six months spent at Blackheath with Myers as wasted. By the end of 1826 he was ready to leave on the first available ship for India, but was destined to be disappointed, because early in the new year he fell ill of typhus fever during an epidemic at Bristol when he was staying with his aunt and uncle. He was looked after by his beloved sister Maria and for that reason he later remembered this moment as one of his happiest. Spring and summer 1827 were spent in convalescence at Chadlington in the continuous company of his three younger brothers George, Richard and Edward, who were also home from school following a bout of the fever. Henry ordered them to do constant broadsword exercises, while he entertained them with tales of the war with Burma and graphically hacked the trunk and lower branches of a tree near the house in imitation of the terrible wounds he intended inflicting on his barbarian opponents. This was an idyllic time for Henry and his younger brothers, all innocent of the fact that one of them would be dead and the rest grown men before Henry set foot in England again.

After the long months of waiting, the seventeen-year-old nearly missed setting sail for India. Thinking there was time to spare, he had gone to see one of his father's horses win in the races at Cheltenham, but a messenger rushed up to him with the news that the ship was about to leave London Docks for Portsmouth. Hurrying back to London, Henry managed to get kitted out and rapidly purchased around one hundred books. Even without the necessity of buying a commission, it was still an expensive under-taking to send Henry as a cadet to India, as his passage alone cost over £100, while his father spent a further £500 on his kit, and he himself would only be paid from his arrival at Bombay. Henry managed to reach the south coast just before the 644-ton chartered ship *Neptune* set sail for Bombay from Portsmouth harbour on 6 July 1827. An old East Indiaman vessel built in 1815, it was captained by its owner John Cumberlege.

The *Neptune* followed the fastest route available, around Africa's Cape of Good Hope, but even so the journey lasted four months. From the outset Henry was desperately homesick, missing above all else his two surviving sisters, Maria and Georgiana. Having promised Maria that he would keep a journal to send home, he often recorded his adolescent feelings of misery and anxiety in a style that was intimate, spontaneous, often poetic and lacking the polished structure and formality of his later writing. He began the journal on his very first day: 'Shook hands with my brother Abram and stept into the boat at Portsmouth which was about to bear me from my native shore, to exchange the society of parents, friends, brothers and sisters whom I love with an affection never to be shaken for a life of misery and sorrow among strangers and barbarians. During my crossing over to the ship the beautiful blue waves, glittering beneath a July sun and placid as the calm I once enjoyed, lulled my feelings into something like repose, and

I reached the ship Neptune in a species of mental stupefaction . . .
The calling of the sea makes any head so giddy that I can hardly
tell what I am about, and my fellow passengers so disturb my
attention that it is only when I sit by myself on the poop and view
the moon beams glancing on the silvery sea that I can believe I
am wretched, miserable, alone, in one word that I am an exile.'[11]

Three days later, he felt no better: 'It is now Saturday July 7th
6 o'clock in the evening and I am sitting alone in my cabin writing
this commencement to my journal. Maria, if your bright blue eyes
should ever chance to rest on these promised pages, know that I
am now thinking of your lovely face which, perchance, I never
may behold again, and I swear that I may be destined to pass the
remainder of my days in banishment and misery. Whenever the
natural instability of my disposition may bring me to engage in
a quarrel, I will think of your angelic form, and I shall be the
coolest of the cool, and though you seem to think that I shall
never remember you, be informed that not a day or an hour will
ever elapse without your sweet face being presented to my
memory, and whatever may be my fate, prosperous or unhappy,
good or bad, I never never will forget you. I think I have been
writing a great deal of nonsense which can be of no interest to
anyone, but I was alone, I was unhappy, the bitterness of my
feelings seemed to overpower my understanding, and I have shed
tears of the bitterest anguish. We are now sailing down the channel at the rate of 9 knots an hour, but every league I proceed
adds but another link to the chain of my misery, for I am sailing
farther and farther away from everything which I love in this
world. I intend commencing hard fagging [hard work] as soon as
this cabin, which I have with another man of the same following,
is in tolerable order . . . now for a tune on my flute and then a
walk upon deck.'[12]

The next day, Sunday, Henry wrote: 'I am in rather better
spirits today, I am come down to my cabin to proceed with my
journal. We are sailing down the channel at a tolerable pace and
they say today we shall pass Land's End.'[13] Although less homesick, he was awkward and unhappy in his relationships with the

other passengers, being constrained by etiquette in approaching them. He felt especially ignored by Sir John Malcolm, who was on his way to Bombay to take up the governorship: 'Sir John now speaks to every other passenger on board except me, and as I cannot get introduced to him I see no probability of our ever conversing.'[14] Misery again overwhelmed Henry: 'I am sure I shall hate India and [wish] that I was once more in England – could I but once more see Georgiana and Maria, there is no situation however menial that I feel at present I had not rather undergo in my native land than be a private among strangers and savages . . . the rest of my life will be merely a mechanical employment of the body . . . I cannot write without becoming unhappy so I had better conclude for the present and read Scott's Life of Napoleon.'[15]

The advice given in *The Cadet's Guide to India* was to pass the time usefully and 'to devote two or three hours in the morning to the study of the Hindoostan language; then let reading, or drawing, fill up the space after dinner, after which he [the cadet] will be at leisure and like to walk the quarter-deck with his companions, or partake of their rational sports'.[16] Henry began to follow this advice, as seen in his journal entry for 9 July: 'It has been a very uncomfortable day and I have been all day in my cabin reading, fagging and playing the flute. Begin to get rather more comfortable, though I cannot as yet reflect with any comfort on my future destiny. Until I become tolerably habituated to banishment, I should deem it best to think as little as possible of my former happiness . . . Maria and Georgiana – I still think of you, and whatever pain the thought may cost me, the recollection of my home and infancy shall never be forgotten.'[17]

Henry's ambitions began to stir when he was finally noticed: 'Sir John drank wine with me at dinner . . . it will be no very difficult thing to bring myself into his notice as most of my fellow passengers are sad stupes. He scribbles poetry so I'll try an ode . . . We have been crossing the Bay of Biscay these last two days and I have hitherto escaped sickness. I think myself pretty safe now for the rest of my voyage.'[18] But for 11 July he recorded: 'Rather stormy and very heavy sea which made me a little sick but nothing to signify – have been talking to Sir John Malcolm – shall never persuade myself to cringe and toad-eat him as some of the fellows do ... indeed I cannot think he likes it as he is a very clever man himself and often says that everyone's promotion must depend on his own talents and he will never give a place to any one unfit for it, however strongly recommended – can get no one to join me in my Hindoostanee as they are all only just beginning. Played some whist ... and by a continued run of good cards cleaned them out of 14 shillings. I have now, Maria, written one sheet of my promised journal and will send it by the first conveyance.'[19]

The next day a severe storm threatened: 'We have now passed the Bay of Biscay and they say the coast of Spain was to be seen ... After dinner there was a tolerable commotion as the Captain ... prognosticated a hurricane. The sails were all taken down or furled, the decks were cleared and we all waited in anxious suspense. The stormy Petrel skimmed along the waves, the sky became covered with lurid and spiral clouds and the waves rose portentously – however like the fable of the mountain and the mouse, while we were thus all raised to the highest pitch of expectation, a few gulls huddled fitfully among the shrouds, a few large heavy drops descended upon the deck and it was gone. The waves again subsided, the sails were unfurled and we soon left far behind us the boisterous and uneasy waters of the Bay of Biscay. This is my first adventure and I flatter myself I have described it very prettily.'[20]

A week into the voyage brought better weather, but Henry's mood remained melancholy: 'This has been the first warm day. The evening was delightful – the blue expanse of heaven where the stars glittered with ethereal splendour was lighted occasionally by gleaming meteors, and the silent and placid water over which we glided appeared frequently ignited. The luminous nature of the phosphorus sometimes sparkling and sometimes winding in wreaths of transient light around the vessel occasioned this extraordinary appearance ... had I been in the company of Georgiana or Maria, I had [would have] been happy – but real pure happiness

I have lost for at least 10 years if not for ever. In future every pleasure I enjoy must be embittered with the reflexions that I have no one who loves me to share it with me, and what are all the delights and enjoyments of the body compared with pure genuine and unsophisticated love!'[21]

The next day, Henry suffered his first proper bout of seasickness: 'Very high sea and the waves were really for some time beautiful, but the ship rolled so, that I was for the first time sea sick and so was deprived of the pleasure of viewing them – however after I had slept for an hour, eaten a hearty dinner and drank lots of wine I was quite well.'[22] He went on to regret the lack of women on board – these was only one (Sir John's daughter), and she was married. Gradually, Henry became more confident with the people on board and professed admiration for Sir John, who 'must be an exceedingly clever person, and he seems possessed of such a fund of anecdotes that though he has been unremittingly employed in telling stories ever since he came on board, he still goes on at such a rate as to keep the whole table in a continual roar in which he himself always heartily joins'.[23] Many of his tales were of Persian history and literature, which inspired Henry to resume studying Persian when he reached India. Sir John also believed it his duty to urge all the cadets on board to strive for the greatest success, encouraging them throughout the journey by lending them books and giving them tasks to perform, such as copying out his manuscripts.

At last Henry was enjoying himself: 'After tea we have plenty of amusements beginning with fencing and singlestick – afterwards dancing and music and finishing with chess, cards, backgammon &c. We have a little band on board belonging to the ship consisting of clarionets, fifes, trumpet, violin and drum, which they play reels, waltzes, the quadrilles as much as we like. Sir John goes on laughing, talking and story telling as much as ever . . . I have not yet given way to my temper at all, notwithstanding I have had many provocations.'[24] Henry also recorded that he was now 'quite an expert sailor, having been up higher [in the rigging] than any of the Passengers except McDougal, who is a regular dab at it.

All laugh at him about his foolhardiness, but I must own that I admire it.'[25] His own bravado and agility would later serve him well when climbing the rock face of Bisitun.

What Henry regretted was his tendency to drink too much wine, and after one particularly heavy session drinking punch, he felt quite unwell and was 'determined to be abstemious',[26] though soon after he was drinking his brother Abram's health on his birthday 'in a bumper of claret'.[27] He might try to be abstemious, but he could not avoid wine and beer altogether, for the water on board was so bad that Henry refused to drink it. Personal hygiene must also have been sparing, to judge from the advice given to cadets: 'Washing of linen is not permitted at sea, as the fresh water cannot be spared for it. Hence it will be proper for the Cadet not to change his linen oftener than is absolutely necessary to his own comfort and decent appearance before other persons.'[28] The cadet manual set great store by proper appearance, but said nothing about smell, although now they were in a warm climate, the cadets could bathe in a sail filled with sea water. On one occasion in a dead calm, they ignored the advice of the *Neptune*'s crew concerning sharks and dived into the sea for a swim, until a cry of 'War Shark' caused a frantic rush for the ship, with Henry being first to haul himself up on a rope. The crew caught the huge shark, and Henry recorded that 'they then cut a slice out of his Cheek and gave us shark cutlets for breakfast, which I beg to state were extremely tasty'.[29]

After only a fortnight into the voyage, Henry was already overcoming his homesickness, as he admitted to Maria: 'this sheet is written in a different tone from the last, but my dearest Maria, though I am now tolerably comfortable, I still and ever shall think of my absent sisters with the deepest affection and hoping they will not forget me'.[30] Towards the end of August, he published his first issue of *Herald of the Deep*, a weekly newspaper, copied out by hand, for the amusement of the passengers, in which he included anonymously poems that he had written. Amusements aside, Henry could not avoid the reality that he was travelling to India to join the army, whose discipline was made apparent towards the end of the journey when a private of the Dragoons was court-martialled for impudence to his corporal and received a sentence of one hundred lashes. 'The flagillators would not cut it in tight,' Henry noted, 'so that the fellow got tolerably well off, never uttering a sound during the process – the punishment was nothing to what I had been led to expect.'[31]

On Friday 26 October 1827, Bombay came into view, and from now on Henry regarded the date of 26 October as very special, 'my fatal day during all the early part of my life – especially in cycles of 6 years'.[32] As the ship approached the coast of India and the view of Bombay grew steadily clearer, Henry wrote an excited journal entry, the last of the voyage: 'I cannot be melancholy now, but Oh! How I wish you were here to enjoy my pleasure with me – the picture is beautiful – islands, mountains, boats, ships, tents, blacks, whites, browns, greens, Oh it is lovely after 4 months of sea and sky.'[33]

Two: From Poona to Panwell

The low-lying fortified island of Bombay (now called Mumbai) was known as Bom Bahia ('good bay') when it was a Portuguese possession. In 1661 it became British when ceded to Charles II as part of the dowry of his Portuguese wife, Catherine of Braganza, and seven years later it was leased to the East India Company for an annual rent of £10. The city with its sheltered harbour developed rapidly as more islands were reclaimed from the marshland, and apart from the fort and esplanade, there was an extensive native town. Over two decades before Henry Rawlinson's arrival, a fire broke out in the fort, which led to the destruction of many houses, but allowed improved rebuilding along wider streets.

Rawlinson initially attended cadet classes, but was soon attached as ensign, the lowest-ranking officer, to the 2nd European Infantry Regiment, known as the Bombay Buffs. His first military duty was Saturday 1 December 1827, when he attended the early morning muster of the regiment. The next day he agreed to accompany a shooting party, explaining to his sisters that Sundays were not regarded as a holy day of rest: 'This day is considered here as no more than any other day with respect to shooting, playing billiards &c. Indeed it is generally pitched upon us an excursion day; notwithstanding how much your ideas of propriety may be shocked, you must not consider us at anything particular in us rising at 2 in the morning, and having sent our servants on before with lots of tuck, in starting with guns, powder and shot on a shooting excursion to Kourlee in Salsette.'[1] They arrived just as it was light enough to begin shooting, and, wrote Rawlinson, 'No sooner had we began to beat than four quails got up, at which of course I immediately blazed away, and running to pick up my game was rather astounded at perceiving the effect of my shott in a group of beaters . . . lying prostrate and bleeding on the ground – they had just left the road to begin beating, and being hidden from my sight by a thin bush received the whole contents of my charge to their no slight confusion and dismay – only one was hurt at all seriously, who had about a dozen shot a few inches in his legs and face – however he was speedily reconciled to his condition by a douceur of 2 rupees.'[2]

This was the first time Rawlinson had seen anything of the Indian countryside, which to him appeared 'extremely prepossessing. The woods were filled with birds of the brightest colours and butterflies of a magnitude which [would] rather surprise Georgiana.'[3] Wildlife abounded, and conservation was never an issue, only the sport. The day's shooting was fairly successful, and Rawlinson told his sisters: 'The following items compose my days sport – 6 beaters, more or less damaged, 3 black pigeons, one splendid kingfisher, one muena (a most beautiful blue and scarlet bird), one hoopooe, 2 quails both lost in the long grass, one hawk, one rook, one gull, one paddy bird and eight sand snipers – we were much disappointed at not meeting with any partridges . . . We had lots of beer and returned home very merry at about 9 oclock at night racing our buggies all the way.'[4] At the age of seventeen he found himself in an exotic world where he wielded power even as the lowest-ranking officer and, compared to the indigenous population, immense riches – for an immature young man it was intoxicating.

Military activities for Rawlinson in India were not onerous, though he studied with a native language teacher (a *munshi*). The day after his excursion he declared himself 'too lazy to do much with my moonshee'.[5] Instead, he went pigeon shooting with his friends Hogg and Philipps: 'I backed every shot of mine against theirs at a rupee a shot and after about two hours shooting I came off a winner of fifteen rupees . . . I rode my horse in the evening being the first time for this last week as he has been in physick – saw a good many cronies on the Esplanade and dealt out a little nonsense to my friend Mrs Hull, by far the prettiest lady there.'[6]

Next occurred an event that threatened his future in the army: 'Met Brown who asked me to dine with him at seven which I accordingly did, found a party of 8 jolly fellows assembled at dinner and spent the pleasantest evening I ever did since I have been here – lots of Claret, Beer, Punch – and sallying out for a lark at about 10 oclock, commenced levelling all the tents in the vicinity – it was glorious fun, but I am afraid we shall get into a terrible row about it. I am always exceedingly sorry after such parties that I have made myself such a fool, yet I have not sufficient resolution to resist the temptation of attending them.'[7] The following day an official complaint was made of their behaviour, and Rawlinson was dismayed at the possible outcome: 'there seems every probability of our being brought to a Court Martial and dismissed the service. I am really quite disgusted with the world now – if I am now really cashiered for such a trifling offence, I shall immediately tell the fellows who prosecute that they are no gentlemen and if they shoot me they may – if I survive I shall enter into the King of Persia's services and try if I cannot make some figure in the world there. India is too narrow a field for my ambition – everything here goes by interest and it is impossible to get into notice unless patronized by some of the Grandees. I cannot bear the idea of creeping unknown through the world.'[8] To his relief, no more was heard of the court martial and he vowed never to get drunk again.

By now Rawlinson was hoping to receive letters from home, but was bitterly disappointed when the *Upton Castle* came in. 'Out of sight, out of mind,' he complained, 'I suppose I am now entirely forgotten by all my friends in England ... I have [made] minute enquiries and find that there is no letter, packet or parcel of any description, come out for me by the Upton Castle, which has not only surprised but greatly annoyed me as I did not expect to be forgotten quite so soon as it appears I am.'[9]

The following Sunday he marched to church with the regiment, but was not impressed with the service: 'Carr the clergyman gave us a terrible long sermon about Serjeant Tedman who has lately "*gone out*". The deaths here are really quite awful.'[10] Among Europeans in India the death rate was especially high, from causes such as malaria, cholera, dysentery, smallpox, dog bites, snakes and scorpions. Because of these threats, Rawlinson considered a new career in England: 'I am frequently resolved to adopt an entirely new course of life, to give up all the future prospect of glory and delight, which I have so often and so fondly pictured to my ardent mind, and turn religious. I used at one time certainly to be really pious and in a fit state to be called into the presence of my maker, but I was then a child, I was then a stranger to the temptations of the world and had then never experienced what I am afraid I shall never have sufficient strength and resolution to withstand.'[11] He had little regard for Carr, adding: 'I am not as yet sufficiently under the influence of the Spirit of God to relish three hours prosing controversy on disputed texts . . . I hope and trust I may in time acquire the power of abstracting my mind in prayer which for any length of time, I find at present particularly difficult.'[12] The subject of religion was a recurring topic in Rawlinson's early journals, and it obviously bothered him that, as a Christian, his beliefs were not as strong as he wished.

He was now hard at work studying Hindustani and in mid-December wrote: 'I was obliged to go to Fort George to meet my new Moonshee at 10 oclock. I like him much better than the last; tho' he is a little high and connected, he is certainly very clever and I stand a much greater chance of improving under his tuition.'[13] Three days later he was less happy, writing that he 'waited for my moonshee till 10 oclock – blew him up sky high for not coming earlier – he tells me I shall not pass unless I fagg very hard – now as it is impossible to fagg even tolerably hard in this climate, I shall give up all ideas of passing this examination and not try until the next.'[14]

A mood of depression set in, fuelled by unhappiness at receiving no word from England on the arrival of two more ships, especially as all the other officers received letters, 'which makes my disappointment more cutting'.[15] On Sunday 16 December, Rawlinson marched to church early in the morning with his regiment, but was suffering from a bad cold and sore throat, so did not go out again afterwards: 'I have been very low all day. I neither like the climate, country, inhabitants or profession and shall be most heartily glad to get back to England again. If an officer has neither a regimental, nor general staff appointment his life here must be the idlest, and least profitable, occupation in the World – far from being able to lay by money, his pay will be inadequate to his expenses, especially if at a dear station like Bombay – my mind is I think extremely fickle. I am sometimes elated with ideas of wealth, glory and happiness, and again if anything should happen to depress my spirits (such as those bitter disappointments in not hearing from England) I can see nothing before me but want, penury and distress. Oh money, money, how vain and yet how indispensable thou art in a great measure to human happiness.'[16]

To add to his mood, on Monday he received 'another blowing up ... for not attending parade at gunfire, for which however I had never received any orders ... I am in future to attend all parades'.[17] He had, though, decided to take his Hindustani examination in the new year after all, even though it was difficult to work: 'Fag a little now and then with my moonshee; I am fully aware of the necessity of the most assiduous study, if I hope to be ready for the next examination, yet such is the relaxing nature of the climate, that it is with the utmost difficulty I can bring myself to get even a page of the Bagh & Buhar [a story written to teach students Hindustani] ready for my moonshee – there is consequently very little if any chance of my passing in January ... I really must fagg ... these lazy habits will not do. I must study 4 hours a day at least ... I have not been out to a party this age – it is really very stupid here and if I can but pass next month, get posted to a regiment and start off up the country, why I may perhaps be a little more comfortable.'[18] He had now been in Bombay just fifty-two days.

Rawlinson still indulged in shooting, going to dinner, drinking tea, writing poetry and a play, and singing at parties, even though he claimed not to have attended any party recently. On 22 December his first poem was published in the *Bombay Courier*. Eleven verses long and entitled *On the first sight of land*, the poem appeared 'with a most insulting Editor's note'.[19] Wisely, Rawlinson used a pseudonym, because reaction was not favourable: 'With respect to the poetry in the Courier, there are various opinions concerning it, and as it is considered by the majority to be trash, I have not ventured to avow the authorship except to a few of my particular cronies.'[20] Further disappointment occurred when another ship came in with no mail, but Rawlinson was now somewhat happier. On 24 December he noted: 'The parade bugle sounded at gunfire and we marched out to a grand Brigade parade – there were four regiments consisting altogether of about 3000 men . . . I know enough of the drill now to manoeuvre with any company and got through the parade without a single blunder.'[21]

On Christmas Day, he admitted: 'I begin to like my situation a great deal better than I have done as I am getting better acquainted with my fellow officers. I used to fancy that they treated me particularly coldly, which I supposed had arisen from the row I had got into about the tents . . . I have in fact hardly any doubt that this was the case. I am fully resolved now never to indulge in future at any of the mess parties so as to get in the least inebriated. I do it chiefly out of my love of fun and jollity and certainly not out of any fondness for liquor, as with the exception of a few wines I absolutely hate.'[22]

In late January 1828 he was working hard for his examination, as he explained to Maria in his journal: 'I . . . really do begin to have some hopes of success in the examination which takes place on Feb^ry 15. The Regiment is to start for Deesa on the 5th of February (your birthday). I have not made up my mind as yet to what course I shall adopt with respect to stopping in Bombay after the Corps is gone, but rather think I shall apply for leave to pitch my tent on the Esplanade and do nothing until the Examinations . . . My Monshees encourage me and tell me that there is a very good chance of my passing, but I am by no means confident of any knowledge as I find myself woefully deficient in the Colloquial examination which we have to undergo.'[23] Due to a scarcity of officers, Rawlinson's application to remain in Bombay and work for his examination in two weeks' time was refused, but when he found himself called as a witness in a court case at Bombay, he transferred to the 7th Native Infantry Regiment: 'I am at present living in a tent in the seventh lines, that is with the officers of the Seventh Reg., with which corps I am now doing duty. My old Corps the Europeans left Bombay for Deesa about a week ago and I got myself removed from them to the seventh in order to wait for the examination.'[24]

On Saturday 16 February, the examination over, Rawlinson wrote: 'I was called up the very first which is a great disadvantage, and my examination did not last more than half an hour during which time however they kept me pretty well close at it – Courts Martial to be translated, General Orders to be read off in Hindoostanee, Bagh & Buhar, Idiomatical Questions and Conversations by a Moonshee (who by the bye happened rather fortunately to be my own private Moonshee) formed the Ordeal – and as I got through them all pretty tolerably, if I have not passed I am close upon it.'[25] Should he fail, Rawlinson was determined not to give up: 'I shall go up again in May when I think I shall be pretty sure of passing – if they give me an affirmative I shall immediately begin to study Persian in readiness for the Russian Invasion.'[26]

'My old Moonshee has just entered with the news – I have *not* passed,' continued Rawlinson's journal, 'I was within an inch of passing and in fact ought to have passed. There are five members, two of whom voted for me and 3 against – my translations both from Hindostanee into English and from English into Hindoostanee were actually the best of the whole lot.'[27] One reason for failure was not being sufficiently acquainted with idiomatic expressions, or 'the manners of the natives',[28] but the examiners also thought Rawlinson too young and immature. Had he been in India two or three months longer, they would have passed him, even without doing as well. Sensitive to failure, Rawlinson wrote that 'they mentioned all this in the report which was sent to the Commander in Chief, but he did not think fit to publish it in General Orders, as recommended by the Committee, which I consider a great shame. There were only 4 passed out of 10. I consider myself perfectly sure of it next May – and as I am subpoened to Hockin's trial at the end of April, it will be no inconvenience to me stopping here.'[29] He was heartened by the support of the governor Sir John Malcolm: 'I went out to breakfast with him and he talked to me a good deal about it, advising to fag hard to be ready for the next time.'[30]

Rawlinson also continued his Classical studies, as he reminisced years later: 'I kept up my Latin and Greek and translated Greek Chorusses for the Bombay Gazette . . . I was a fair classic in those days – and when an Inscription was wanted I remember being asked to write it for the Municipality of Bombay.'[31] Indulging as well his love of writing, he was thrilled to be published again, as he noted in mid-March: 'I have again appeared in print – my muse this time has taken a classical flight and I have translated a Chorus from Aeschylus. I had the satisfaction to hear one day at dinner a Captain of the 7th – who is considered a clever man, say in reading it – "This is very very good only a little too long to be read". This is the delight of anonymous publication – that single sentence of accidental praise was worth to me a month of labour.'[32]

He was less happy with news about Maria that he heard when dining with an officer newly arrived from Bristol: 'he is a relation of the Brook Smiths and knows Abram a little, he said he had heard *young Brooks was to be married* and was very anxious to know *who the lady was to be*'.[33] Rawlinson knew it was Maria: 'I wish I could hear something from you – it really does seem very odd to be hearing news of my own family from strangers. He and young Brown are the only people whom I have heard speak of young Brooke and they both call him a most insufferable dandy. I myself really think that *you are a great deal too good for him*.'[34] He continued bitterly: 'I have now given up all hopes of hearing from you at all, I have been waiting nearly 5 months now in expectation of a letter. I had fondly hoped I had friends in England to whom I was so dear as they are and ever will be to me – what can be the reason for your not writing yourself? I cannot understand it at all – it is now nearly 9 months since I left England and I have not heard a syllable from any of you – what changes and revolutions may have happened since that time! I rather expect you and Georgiana are both married. I feel a presentiment that you will be sooner or later Mrs B Smith.'[35] His presentiment was right, although Maria did not marry Brooke Smith for another four years.

At the beginning of May, Rawlinson sat the Hindustani examination again and wrote excitedly in his journal: 'I have just passed an Examination in Hindoostanee and am reported qualified to act as Interpreter in that language.'[36] In Bombay he had also developed a particular passion for reading about history and was buying increasing numbers of books. 'I seldom went to bed,' he commented, 'without being conscious that I had gained some information in the course of the day of which I had been ignorant when I arose – there is something extremely gratifying in being conscious of continual progression in knowledge.'[37] His thirst for learning led him into debt: 'The Borkas are a class of men who go about selling mostly books, and of them I bought most of mine, especially oriental works. The only time I ever got into trouble for debt was with one of these Borkas, a pock marked brute with big turban. I had a row with him and refused to pay him, and he had me arrested. I was on the point of starting up the country to Ahmedabad and Guzerat, and I owed him 75 Rupees – but with expenses the sum amounted to double and then other claims came in upon me.'[38] He was loaned £50 to help settle his debts, and towards the end of his life noted that apart from a further £50 borrowed from his father, he never owed money again.

On 1 June 1828, Rawlinson travelled over 300 miles north to join his new regiment, the 1st Grenadier Native Infantry, at Ahmedabad, the capital city of Gujarat that had been founded in the fifteenth century. Here he remained desperately unhappy that he had heard nothing from his family, noting sadly in his journal on 6 July: 'On this day twelvemonth I bade adieu to the fair, the lovely shores of Albion. I have since never passed a day, I might almost say an hour, without thinking of my early friends, of sisters who in days of yore protested that they loved me – but mark their conduct – they have let me languish on a foreign shore, unnoticed and uncheered by one single line or token of recollection for a *long lonely year*. They have forgotten me and I *will* forget them . . . I am resolved. I will forget you all, until I again believe you worthy of my regard. I am wretched, I am miserable, but I swear – never to think on you again . . . henceforward my thoughts shall be of myself, my mind shall rest upon the future. I have set the stamp of everlasting misery on my brow – but *I swear, I swear, I swear* would that I would die.'[39]

Rather than admit he was miserable, Rawlinson resorted to pleasure and neglected his studies, about which he was later ashamed: 'my days were spent in gambling, my nights in drinking – the billiard table and the Mess room were my only supports.'[40] It was not until 21 October that he received 'a very nice long letter from Abram',[41] but still nothing from his sisters. Three days later came the long-awaited news from Maria, and with great relief Rawlinson wrote: 'now indeed that I have received your journal I feel a pleasure in sitting down in the evening and recording my adventures (such as they are)'.[42] What he did put in his journal was the routine of his life at Ahmedabad: 'Saturday [25 October]. The days all pass much in the same manner. Parade at sunrise, they last until 7 – breakfast at 8 – study more or less till 11 – write, play billiards, go out visiting, idle or sleep until ½ past 2, dress for dinner at 3 – pool or billiards afterward, then out riding until dark, and in the evening sometimes cards, but generally we retire quietly to our respective domiciles and pass the evening as best we may, not but that it is far from unusual to have a bit of supper swilled down with a pint or two . . . and sometimes too we go so far as to indulge in a bit of a spree in the bazaar afterwards – this you must allow is a most monstrous course of life even when compared with yours at Chadlington – I am really quite sick of it.'[43]

From now on he was more relaxed and less than a week later he fell in love with a young widow, Mrs Doherty: 'I mustered courage to go up and have a chat – she was rather entertaining, and I of course was immediately over head and ears in love – this seldom lasts more than a day or two.'[44] After only two days he commented: 'it cannot be said that I am at all seriously committed, but really a pretty woman is such a scarcity here that we transform her into an angel.'[45] Over the following days the eighteen-year-old ensign did his utmost to accept invitations where she would be present and was extremely happy when 'she evidently showed a decided preference for my conversation above the others'.[46] By late November he admitted that he was totally lovesick. He obviously considered marrying her, but his regiment soon left for Bombay, and she later married a judge.

The regiment was back in Bombay on 1 December, and by now Rawlinson had received two more family letters – one from Georgiana and the other from his younger brother George. He resumed his studies, concentrating on Marathi, the language of the Maharastra state in which Bombay is situated. The following year, 1829, he 'worked like a horse at languages',[47] then passed his Marathi examination, and in July gained the post of Quarter-master, Paymaster and Interpreter with his regiment. He resumed a vigorous social life, being 'Steward of the Balls, Manager of the theatre, head of the Billiard & Racquet Rooms'.[48] In addition, he was involved in hunting, shooting and horseracing and was constantly trying to impress the women in Bombay, where 'I do flatter myself that I cut no very disreputable figure'.[49] In private, though, Rawlinson noted that 'I was educating myself by an extensive course of reading . . . From this time dates my passion for books.'[50]

In 1830 the regiment moved to Poona (now known as Pune) in the Western Ghats mountain chain, a march of nearly 100 miles south-eastwards from Bombay. Poona acted as a refuge from the summer heat for those in Bombay, with an extensive military camp about 2 miles from the town. Here Rawlinson remained for over three years, another militarily inactive period, but one that continued to be highly enjoyable. Years later he wrote that this period was 'the most enjoyable of my life. I had excellent health, was in the heyday of youth, tremendous spirits, was celebrated in all athletic amusements, riding, shooting and especially hunting, and with the whole world before me.'[51] He was so busy that he did not resume his journal until 11 April 1831, his twenty-first birthday, evidently irritated that nobody had marked the occasion, which recalled 'more forcibly to my mind the loss I experienced in being thus far absent from the bosom of my family'.[52] In years to come he kept returning on his birthday to this same journal entry in order to add comments on the progress in his life.

At Poona, Rawlinson's maxim was: ' "never engage in anything unless there is every chance of becoming first in it" – if I did not think I could be first I gave it up.'[53] He was so good at sports that nobody would accept his challenge to compete for the considerable stake of £100 in a combined competition of 'running, jumping, quoits, racquets, billiards, pigeon-shooting, pig-sticking, steeple-chasing, chess, and games of skill at cards'.[54] In November 1831 at Newmarket in England, George Osbaldeston undertook a momentous horseracing match, completing 200 miles in less than eight hours using twenty-eight horses. It received massive attention, and the officers in Poona debated how they could emulate this success. It was Rawlinson who accepted a wager to race from Poona to Panwell, the mainland port of Bombay. The distance was 72 miles and the stake was £100, with a forfeit of 4 rupees to be paid for every minute over the four hours and the same amount to be paid to the rider for every minute under that time. 'The general opinion,' Rawlinson noted, 'was that the match would not be won.'[55]

At quarter-past-five in the morning of 22 May 1832, the 6-foot tall, 12-stone, twenty-two-year-old rider set off, dressed in 'hunting costume, jockey cap, thick ticking jacket, with a watch sewn into the waistband, samberskin breeches, and a pair of easy old boots'.[56] He encountered numerous setbacks, from being forced to scramble with his horse over the backs of bullocks that were obstructing his way to descending the precipitous Ghats with his horse out of control. He changed horses ten times, on the third occasion being forced to abandon the exhausted animal and run uphill for a quarter of a mile to meet his next mount, because it had been stationed in the wrong place. Thousands of villagers lined the last three miles, and to the incredulity of the umpires he rode into the compound of Panwell tavern after a ride of just three hours and seven minutes, soundly winning the wager. Riding back to Poona in the afternoon with the same horses and in almost the same time, he 'appeared at a party the same evening apparently as fresh as a lark but this was swagger!'[57]

So remarkable was Rawlinson's achievement that it was reported in newspapers in both India and England, yet in spite of these diversions he still found time for study and wrote in his journal: 'I read a great deal, and passed a first-class examination in Persian, and in fact I believe I was a general favourite.'[58]

Three: In the Service of the Shah

Having arrived in Bombay as a raw and immature East India Company cadet in 1827, on his 'fatal day' of 26 October, Rawlinson left India exactly six years later, a more mature and experienced officer, especially competent in the Hindustani, Marathi and Persian languages. His destination was Persia, known today as Iran.

The East India Company's interest in Persia was originally commercial, but over the previous three decades every diplomatic effort had been made to maintain the country's independence so that it could not be used as a base by Russia, Afghanistan or France for an invasion of British India, a threat that was felt to be very real. Fath Ali Shah, the ruler of Persia ('Shah' being the Persian title given to the country's king), had made alliances with Britain and then France, but turned to Britain again in 1809. The following year British officers began to train the Shah's army and accompany it into battle, but once peace was established between Britain and Russia in 1813 and Napoleon was defeated at the Battle of Waterloo two years later, this military presence was largely withdrawn.

By the early 1830s, Russian influence in Tehran began to alarm the British to such a degree that the Company formed a new military detachment, drawn from all over India. Under the command of the forty-four-year-old Cornishman Colonel William

Pasmore of the Bengal Native Infantry, the detachment consisted of native troops, eight officers, fourteen sergeants and an assistant apothecary. Rawlinson was chosen because of his proficiency in Persian, a language he was inspired to pursue by Sir John Malcolm, who had died of influenza in England a few months earlier. That inspiration caused 'the most momentous change in his whole life'[1] and would have a profound impact on the study of ancient cuneiform writing.

The military detachment sailed from Bombay on 26 October 1833 and completed the 1,700-mile journey to Bushire in early November. Known today as Bushehr, this Persian Gulf port is situated at the northernmost end of a narrow promontory, and the East India Company set up a factory there in 1763, although it was of little use as a port because ships had to drop anchor 2 to 3 miles offshore and transfer cargo in small boats. Rawlinson and his fellow officers were heading for Tehran and so needed to cross the coastal strip and make their way through the formidable Zagros mountains, rising to over 13,000 feet in height. News that the narrow mountain passes were already blocked with deep snow forced them to remain nearly three months in Bushire, considered 'a most wretched place',[2] but their stay did at least coincide with the cooler weather and enabled sufficient baggage animals to be organized for the long trek ahead.

At the beginning of February 1834 Colonel Pasmore at last ordered his men to leave Bushire, and after a climb of 120 miles up through the mountains they reached Shiraz. This city is at an altitude of 5,000 feet and it became the capital of the province of Fars in the late seventh century, after the Arab conquest. From the thirteenth century it was renowned as a literary centre, especially because of two poets who were born and buried there: Sa'di (died 1292) and Háfez (died 1390). To the north of Shiraz the mountains rise steeply, and deep snow in the passes brought a halt to their journey.

Rawlinson made use of his enforced stay at Shiraz by immediately riding out to the ruins of Persepolis, some 30 miles away. Known now as Takht-i Jamshid (Throne of Jamshid) after a mythical king of Persia, Persepolis lies on the edge of a wide plain. It was Darius the Great, soon after his accession as King of Persia in 522 BC, who decided to build an impressive new capital city there, which he called 'Parsa'. The city had monumental palace buildings constructed on a huge artificial stone terrace overshadowed by a fortified hill. The ancient Greek name of Persepolis may be a contraction of 'Persai polis' (meaning 'the city in Persis'), or it can be translated as 'destroyer of cities', a more apt phrase for the site because nearly two centuries later, in 331 BC, it was looted and burned to the ground by Alexander the Great and his troops who had set out from Greece to conquer the Persian Empire. The destroyed city was abandoned and never rebuilt, but great stone columns, gateways, staircases and impressive relief sculptures remained standing, and Rawlinson spent many hours examining these ruins and copied some of the cuneiform inscriptions – strange writing with abstract, geometric signs. Though this site had been visited and recorded by many European travellers, he had not encountered such inscriptions before and was fascinated.

Still unable to move on to Tehran, Rawlinson made a further trip with two other officers and his head groom back into the mountains, this time to explore the deserted ruins of Bishapur – 'The Beautiful [City of] Shapur' – a city that had been founded nearly eight centuries after Persepolis. It took its name from the second Sasanian ruler of Persia, Shapur I, who ruled for over three decades from AD 240. He belonged to the Sasanian (or Sassanian) dynasty that was founded by Ardashir, supposedly a descendant of the legendary ruler Sasan. Shapur himself was particularly successful in battle against the powerful Roman Empire, defeating two of its emperors and even capturing Valerian in AD 260 – the only time a Roman emperor was taken prisoner. At Bishapur Shapur's victories were commemorated in three sculptured reliefs on the rock faces of a river gorge, showing the king on horseback trampling and receiving in submission his Roman enemies, while beyond the gorge at the foot of a mountain he built the royal city of Bishapur.

Rawlinson had been warned that 'a notorious Robber chief had possession of the whole country and it was as much as my life was worth to venture into his lands. I also learnt from my servant who had been in his service, that Bakir Khan the son was in reality a very good fellow, smoking his segar [cigar], and taking his glass of wine as kindly as any English gentleman – he was also a very good rider and first rate shot . . . I took the precaution therefore before starting to take a few presents, on the chance of meeting Bakir Khan, and above all I put aside a few bottles of sherry and brandy.'[3]

After some hours sketching ruins and copying inscriptions, they rode on a few miles and agreed to climb a steep mountain to look for the famous Cave of Shapur with its colossal statue of Shapur I, once over 20 feet high, but now collapsed. 'Up to this time,' Rawlinson recorded, 'we had not seen a single soul in any part of the ruins and so hoped to escape all observation of the robber tribes who lived near.'[4] Leaving their horses with the groom, they began the difficult climb in the sweltering heat. Although they were all capable, resourceful soldiers, only Rawlinson had the nerve and climbing ability to reach the cave: 'The ascent of the mountain was exceedingly difficult, and my two companions . . . gave in before reaching the summit. I went on, found the cave and carved my name on the statue.'[5] Some years later he was told that 'some travellers, penetrating to the statue and imagining they were the first Europeans to visit the spot, were misdeceived and astonished by finding it'.[6]

For two hours Rawlinson stayed in the cave, while his companions returned to camp, so when he returned to his groom, he was alarmed to be surrounded by Persian horsemen, followers of Bakir Khan, who was himself visible in the distance. In order to avert a potentially dangerous situation, Rawlinson rode straight up to him and greeted him in Persian. Although he was reproached for coming to the area like a spy, a friendly conversation followed, ending with Bakir Khan asking for something to drink. Rawlinson's groom filled up a drinking cup with half a bottle of brandy, which Bakir proceeded to drink rather rapidly until he staggered about and collapsed. Immediately Bakir's men aimed their long matchlock guns at Rawlinson, who seized the cup and drank the remaining liquid in case it was thought to be poisoned. While they hesitated to fire, Bakir Khan showed signs of recovery and asked: 'Sahib, what was that liquid fire you gave me? It was very good but awfully strong. I thought it was sherry, but it was the father of all sherries, where did it come from?'[7] Rawlinson diplomatically replied that he had given him brandy, the strongest of all liquors, having heard he could drink anything. Before leaving, Bakir promised 'to take care of any travellers who might bring letters from me, and I believe he acted up to this promise [and] always behaved well to Englishmen'.[8] Rawlinson was saddened a few years later when Bakir Khan was killed by government forces 'for some banditti proceedings'.[9]

With weather conditions improving, the detachment set off from Shiraz towards the end of February and managed to travel 250 miles until hampered by deep snow in the mountain passes beyond Isfahan. From the late sixteenth century, Isfahan had been transformed into one of the most magnificent cities of Persia by Shah Abbas I (ruler from 1588 to 1629), who made it his capital. Its splendour was short-lived, as the Afghans invaded Persia and besieged the city in 1722, massacring most of its inhabitants, and it never recovered its former glory. After a week, the British detachment advanced as far as Qum (pronounced Ghom in Persian), one of the most sacred places of pilgrimage for the Shi'ite Muslims.

In AD 817, Fatima al-Ma'suma died on a journey to her brother, Imam Ali Reza, and was buried at Qum, where her shrine became a site of pilgrimage. Imam Ali Reza died a year later and was buried at Messed in north-east Persia, the country's holiest city. Both the shrine of Imam Reza and that of Fatima were restored some eight hundred years later by Shah Abbas I and, not long before Rawlinson's visit, the reigning Shah, Fath Ali, had repaired Fatima's shrine and embellished the dome with gilding. The shrine was strictly barred to non-believers, but Rawlinson was determined to be the first European to gain entry, even though it was 'whispered that instant death would be the portion of the audacious infidel who should be found intruding into its hallowed precincts'.[10] Over fifty years later, he wrote that 'I visited the sacred shrine in the disguise of a pilgrim, a visit of great danger which has never been repeated by any one up to the present time'.[11] Thrilled to be inside, he was nearly detected by turning his back on the holy spot as he viewed everything around him, but realized his error in time – and came out alive.

The detachment continued northwards from Qum for another 90 miles and finally reached Tehran in mid-March. The city lies in the foothills of the Elburz mountains, a snowy backdrop dominated by the dormant volcano Damavand, which is the highest mountain in Persia at 18,600 feet. It was only a modest trading town when it became the capital city of Persia in 1789, but over half a century later Tehran's population had risen to around 50,000. A near-contemporary description of the city was uncomplimentary, reckoning that the 'streets swarm in the day time with beggars from every region in Asia, their attire as diversified as their extraction . . . The Bazaars of Teheran are constructed in the form of long, covered corridors, lighted from above. On either side of the interior, are ranges of shops, occupied by dealers and working people, each quietly plying his avocation . . . The Bazaar is both a market and a factory . . . The streets of Teheran have never been cleaned since the place was built . . . The public ways are infested with the remains of camels, apes, mules, horses, dogs and cats; and here they lie, until some starving dog strips the bones of their flesh, and leaves them to the gradual corrosion of time'.[12] The detachment remained at Tehran for several months 'studying Persian and becoming acquainted with the country'.[13]

To emphasize his importance, Fath Ali Shah, the second ruler of the Qajar dynasty, kept the officers of the detachment waiting a few weeks before receiving them, and Rawlinson's own observations of the occasion indicate his opinion of the absurd pomp and rigid etiquette. In order to impress the Persians, Rawlinson and the other officers formed a glittering and gaudy spectacle as they set out on their horses from the residence of the British Envoy in the south of the city. 'A party of two-and-twenty Europeans thus brilliantly attired,' Rawlinson noted, 'is a spectacle to which the eyes of the Teheranees are but little accustomed.'[14] Riding through the narrow streets and bazaars, they reached the Golestan Palace, dismounted and were led through courtyards and gloomy passages to the splendid Golestan Garden. The Shah was in an adjoining audience room, 'but, it being utterly inconsistent with etiquette that we should proceed thither by the direct route, we were paraded half round the enclosure before being permitted to approach the throne'.[15] Seated on a throne in one corner of the room overlooking the garden, the Shah was surrounded by sword and shield bearers and miscellaneous princes, who were attired in expensive robes and equipped with jewel-encrusted weapons. The throne, Rawlinson observed, 'was shaped much like a large high-backed old-fashioned easy chair, and, though made of gold, and studded throughout with emeralds and rubies, appeared a most strange ungainly piece of furniture'.[16]

This display of wealth contrasted with the simplicity of the room and with the appearance of the elderly Shah (then sixty-four years of age). Although portrayed in numerous flattering paintings gorgeously attired and with a beard down to his waist, Rawlinson thought him a person of 'a plain and almost mean appearance. The old man's beard is still of prodigious length, but its claim to supremacy in this respect may, I think, be fairly questioned. His face is dark and wrinkled; his teeth have all fallen out from age; and he retains not a trace of that manly beauty which is said to have distinguished him in former days, and which characterizes even now the pictures which are daily taken of him.'[17] In a polite conversation lasting just fifteen minutes, the Shah expressed the value he placed on the detachment, and they were then dismissed with the greatest honour.

As his son Crown Prince Abbas Mirza had died the year before after a long illness, Fath Ali now appointed as his successor his twenty-six-year-old grandson Muhammed Mirza ('Mirza' being a Persian title meaning 'born of a prince', given to those of good birth), who was one of the twenty-six sons of Abbas Mirza. This announcement dashed the hopes of Fath Ali's other sons and grandsons, who, according to Rawlinson, numbered nearly three thousand, 'and every Persian in consequence felt a pride in being the subject of such a king. The greatest misfortune, indeed, that can befall a man in Persia is to be childless. When a chief's *"hearthstone,"* as it was said, *"was dark,"* he lost all respect.'[18] Summoned from his military campaigns beyond the north-eastern border of Persia, Muhammed Mirza lifted his siege of the Afghan city of Herat and entered Tehran in a grand procession on 14 June. He was proclaimed Crown Prince straightaway, and the British detachment was transferred to him as a bodyguard, accompanying him at his investiture a few days later.

Because the city of Tabriz, capital of the province of Azerbaijan, was also the official residence of the heir-apparent, Muhammed Mirza was sent there as governor by the Shah. Situated in the far north-west of Persia, this was strategically important territory as it bordered Russia and the Turkish Ottoman Empire. Tabriz had been captured by Russia as recently as 1827, after provocation by Persia, although it was restored the following year. The city was located in a valley at the foot of the mountains, and had over the centuries been battered by invading armies, epidemics and devastating, frequent earthquakes, as well as bitterly cold winters with heavy snowfall and hot, dry summers. Accompanied by Colonel Pasmore's British detachment, Muhammed and the Persian army from his Herat campaign set off from Tehran on 4 July after delays finding sufficient transport animals for the journey of over 300 miles.

Most of the British officers suffered from illness on the march, including Rawlinson who had to be carried for much of the way in a palanquin (a covered litter). 'Prostrated by fever and ague',[19] he was most likely suffering from malaria, although it was only towards the end of the nineteenth century that the cause of the illness was found to be a microscopic parasite transmitted through mosquito bites. The symptoms of malaria include violent shivering, followed by a fever with very high temperature, then profuse sweating, as well as headaches and vomiting, culminating in a period of fatigue. Such symptoms caused Rawlinson to spend several days in bed when they reached their destination towards the end of July.

Throughout August and September 1834 the British officers relentlessly trained the Persian troops, stationed on the disputed frontier region. In mid-October Rawlinson and two colleagues obtained a few days' leave and headed across the border towards Bayazit, a town of about three thousand Armenian inhabitants, 20 miles south-west of Mount Ararat, where a Turkish force was encamped. In the nearby village of Ahura, on the south-eastern slope of Mount Ararat, a legend persisted that a shepherd had once seen a great wooden ship on their mountain, which was believed to be none other than Noah's Ark of the Old Testament book of Genesis. Today three main controversies still surround Noah's Ark. Where did it land? Could it have survived to the present day? And did it ever exist? As related in Genesis, God decided to destroy everything living on earth with a catastrophic flood because wickedness among people was so great, but Noah, a righteous man, was told to build an ark (a box-like boat) to protect himself, his family and a pair of every bird and animal. Of enormous size (300 cubits long, equivalent to 450 feet), the ark was equipped with three decks and took over one hundred years to build. The flood, caused by relentless rainfall for forty days and forty nights, did not begin to subside until after a hundred and fifty days, and the tops of mountains only began to be visible after a further two months.

Genesis, originally written in Hebrew, does not say that the ark came to rest on a specific peak, but on the 'mountains of Ararat', and for believers in the literal story of the ark, the imposing Mount Ararat has been favoured as the resting place since medieval times. The mountain actually has two peaks 7 miles apart, the highest being Great Ararat, which rises to 16,945 feet and has a permanent ice cap and glaciers. It was not originally known as Ararat, but as Masis to the Armenians and Ağri Dağ in Turkish. The reference in Genesis is probably to Urartu, a very powerful state in the Lake Van area in the eighth and seventh centuries BC, extending into what is now Iran, Iraq, Turkey, Armenia and Azerbaijan. The name Urartu is found in the cuneiform inscriptions of Assyria, its great rival to the south, although the people of Urartu actually called their own land Bianili.

From the mid-nineteenth century there have been over forty claims of spotting the ark on Mount Ararat, at times seen embedded in ice or submerged in a lake, since when about 140 expeditions have attempted to find the ark. Ancient wood can survive for thousands of years in very dry or in waterlogged conditions, but Mount Ararat is a large and inhospitable dormant volcano, although no known eruptions have occurred in historical times. There is no evidence of marine deposits from a flood, and the volcano has probably erupted within the last 10,000 years, since any Biblical flood. The ice cap, hundreds of feet thick, is thought to be the most likely hiding place for the ark, and yet the movement of the glaciers would pulverize a wooden vessel.

The summit of Mount Ararat was reached for the first time, on his third attempt, in October 1829 by a German professor of natural philosophy, Friedrich Parrot, only five years before Rawlinson's visit. Rawlinson was unaware of Parrot's success, and although he believed in the ark story, he was less certain that Ararat was its resting place. Nevertheless, it was an irresistible, formidable challenge: 'I should enter on the attempt with sanguine expectations, and if ever I have an opportunity for putting my wishes in execution during my residence in the North of Persia, I shall certainly avail myself of it in the middle of August as the most favourable time for the ascent.'[20] The opportunity never arose, but years later the search for Noah's Ark was overshadowed by the decipherment of similar flood stories from earlier civilizations written in cuneiform on clay tablets.

On 10 November news reached the British camp of the sudden and unexpected death three weeks earlier of Fath Ali Shah at Isfahan and his burial at Qum in the shrine of Fatima. With the Persian troops, Rawlinson marched back to Tabriz, where the Scottish General Henry Lindesay-Bethune had just arrived to take over from Colonel Pasmore. Lindesay-Bethune was an impressive figure 'six foot eight inches in height (without his shoes), and thus realized, in the minds of the Persians, their ideas of the old heroes of romance'.[21] Fath Ali may have been poisoned, and the delay in Muhammed Mirza hearing about the death had allowed his position as heir to the throne to be disputed by other claimants. Muhammed was unable to advance on Tehran in force because his Persian troops had not been paid for four years, and so Russia and Britain agreed to ensure his succession, with the British Envoy providing funds for the soldiers' pay. A few days later Lindesay-Bethune set off with the troops for Tehran and on the way forced the surrender of the army of one of Muhammed's uncles who had proclaimed himself Shah. Tehran was reached in late December, and on 2 January 1835 Muhammed, as the new Shah, entered the city. Lindesay-Bethune marched the Persian troops to Isfahan and Shiraz to put down further resistance, after which Muhammed Shah had various uncles, brothers and nephews exiled, imprisoned or blinded.

In mid-January Rawlinson and some of his fellow officers met Muhammed Shah for the first time in the main reception room of the palace, but Rawlinson's verdict, recorded in his private journal, was damning: '[he] has little appearance of Eastern sovereignty about him. Instead of a fine, bold, manly bearing, with the gleam of intellect upon his brow . . . he possesses a gross, unwieldy person, a thick, rapid, unimpressive utterance, an unmeaning countenance, and a general bearing more clownish and commonplace than is often met with even in the middle ranks of Persian society. There is in his appearance no spark of grace, dignity, or intelligence.'[22]

By contrast, the palace reception room was considered by Rawlinson to be 'probably the most splendid apartment in Persia',[23] the focus being the magnificent seventeenth-century Peacock Throne with its 26,000 emeralds, rubies, diamonds and pearls. Commissioned by the Mughal Emperor of India, Shah Jehan, for his Red Fort at Delhi, it had been brought back to Persia by Nadir Shah in 1739 as part of the treasure he had looted from the city after massacring some 20,000 of its citizens. Muhammed Shah, who had chosen not to sit on the throne but on more comfortable velvet cushions, firmly announced his wish 'to have an army of 100,000 disciplined troops, and – Inshallah – to revive the days of Nadir in Iran. Otherwise the conversation related chiefly to the wonders of European science – balloons, steam guns, Herschel's telescope, and the subject of aerolites were successively touched upon.'[24]

The coronation of the new Shah took place on the last day of January, and those attending included 'the chief executioner and his establishment, who, with their very red robes and turbans and axes of office, presented a very imposing appearance'.[25] Rawlinson had not changed his opinion of the Shah, who 'waddled in his usual undignified manner across the chamber to the foot of the throne, clambered up the steps, and sat himself down at the further end, leaning against the richly carved marble back. His appearance was rendered more ludicrous on this occasion than I ever previously beheld it, by his being obliged to keep one hand up at his head in order to preserve the ponderous top-heavy crown, which he wore, in its place . . . It appeared to be made of white cloth, and owed its weight, of course, to the vast quantity of jewels with which it was adorned.'[26]

Rawlinson, newly promoted to Lieutenant, evidently impressed the Shah, however, as he was chosen to raise and train troops from Kurdish tribes in the province of Kermanshah for the Governor Bahram Mirza, who was the Shah's own brother. Accompanied by one other European – Sergeant George Page – Rawlinson left Tehran on 10 April for the town of Kermanshah (today renamed Bakhtaran), 300 miles to the south-west in the Zagros mountains. The following day was his twenty-fifth birthday and he made an extremely brief journal entry: 'The year has evolved and brought no material change, either in my fortune or my feelings.'[27]

Kermanshah was on the main trade route between Tehran and Baghdad, in a region rich in ancient rock-cut reliefs and inscriptions of varying dates. Just over halfway there, Rawlinson passed the large town of Hamadan at the foot of Mount Elwand (or Alvand), once the ancient city of Ecbatana, which was founded as the capital of the empire of the Medes in the eighth century

BC. At an altitude of 5,900 feet in the mountains, Ecbatana controlled the major east–west route from the plains of Mesopotamia to the central Iranian plateau. Famous in ancient times for its vast wealth and architectural splendour, Ecbatana became part of the Persian Empire when it was conquered in 550 BC by King Cyrus the Great, who used it as his summer capital. Passing through this area so rich in the remains of ancient and largely unknown civilizations, Rawlinson was in his element, appealing as it did to his flair for exploration and linguistics, and his growing interest in ancient history.

A detour was made to find cuneiform inscriptions Rawlinson had heard about a few miles away along a wooded gorge of Mount Elwand, aware that other travellers had seen them but unaware that copies had been done as recently as 1827 and subsequently given to Friedrich Edward Schulz. A German professor of philosophy, Schulz had himself been recording inscriptions and other antiquities for the French government in the Lake Van area, until he was murdered by Kurds in 1829. His papers passed to Antoine-Jean Saint-Martin, an Oriental scholar in Paris who had been a great friend of Jean-François Champollion, the decipherer of Egyptian hieroglyphs, until politics tore them apart. Although Saint-Martin intended to publish these inscriptions from Mount Elwand, he died of cholera at the age of forty-one in 1832, only months after Champollion's death. Saint-Martin's papers passed to Eugène Burnouf, another Oriental scholar in Paris who had replaced Champollion as a member of the Academy of Inscriptions and became Professor of Sanskrit at the College of France. While Rawlinson was copying the Elwand inscriptions, Burnouf was preparing them for publication.

In the Elwand Gorge, two adjacent square panels of trilingual cuneiform inscriptions, one slightly higher than the other, had been cut into the steep rock face, praising Ahuramazda (Persian for 'Great God') and recording the lineages and prowess of the Persian king Darius the Great in one panel, and his successor Xerxes I in the other. The site became known as Ganj Nameh (Tales of a Treasure) in the belief that the strange inscriptions described the location of a large treasure hidden during the campaigns of Alexander the Great. Rawlinson spent some time carefully copying these inscriptions, unaware that the real treasure they contained were clues to the decipherment of cuneiform, because they were trilingual inscriptions; like those at Persepolis and Bisitun, they had been carved in the three ancient languages of Old Persian, Elamite and Babylonian. Rawlinson later recorded that the 'first materials which I submitted to analysis were the sculptured tablets of Hamadán [Mount Elwand], carefully and accurately copied by myself upon the spot, and I afterwards found that I had thus, by a singular accident, selected the most favourable inscriptions of the class which existed in all Persia for resolving the difficulties of an unknown character'.[28]

Four: The Cuneiform Conundrum

Before the decipherment of cuneiform, stories in the Bible and those of Greek and Roman writers were the only written record of the ancient history of the Middle East. Genesis, the first book of the Hebrew Bible, is an explanation of the origins of heaven and earth, the very name Genesis being derived from the ancient Greek word for 'origins'. It relates that after the Flood, Noah, his wife, his sons Shem, Ham and Japeth and their wives were the only people in the world. God spoke to Noah and his sons: 'Be fruitful, and multiply, and replenish the earth'.[1] Noah died at the ripe old age of 950, and his sons had numerous descendants. Nimrod, a great-grandson of Noah, was supposedly the initial ruler of Shinar and Assyria, which made up Mesopotamia, stretching from the Taurus mountains of Anatolia southwards to the Persian Gulf and encompassing much of modern Iraq. Shinar was the Hebrew name for Babylonia (southern Mesopotamia), while Assyria was the name given to northern Mesopotamia. The name Mesopotamia is itself an ancient Greek term, 'between the rivers', referring to the Tigris and Euphrates. Genesis records Nimrod as the founder of the first cities after the Flood, including Babel, Nineveh and Calah – better known today as Babylon, Nineveh and Nimrud.

As all the people of the world descended from Noah and his sons, only one language should have been spoken, and so the author of Genesis tried to explain that the confusion of many languages was yet another punishment from God. Of those people who had migrated to Shinar, Genesis records: 'they said to one another, "Come, let us make bricks, and bake them thoroughly." And they used brick instead of stone and bitumen for mortar. Then they said, "Come, let us build ourselves a city and a tower whose top reaches to the heavens; and let us make a name for ourselves, so that we are not scattered over the face of the whole earth." And the LORD came down to see the city and the tower that the sons of men had built. And the LORD said, "Behold, they are one people speaking the same language. This is the beginning of what they will do and nothing they plan to do will be impossible for them. Come, let us go down and confuse their language so that they will not understand one another's speech." So the LORD scattered them all over the earth, and they left off building the city. That is why its name was Babel – because the LORD there confused the language of all the earth'.[2] This story refers to the building of the fabled city of Babylon that grew up alongside the Euphrates, 55 miles south of the later city of Baghdad. Although supposedly one of the first cities after the Flood, archaeological excavation has shown that Babylon was not one of Mesopotamia's oldest cities, but that it only developed around 1800 BC and that there are many older cities along the banks of the Tigris and Euphrates.

The main natural resources of ancient Mesopotamia were clay, silt and mud, as well as bitumen, which seeped to the surface in many areas. Buildings were constructed primarily of bricks manufactured by mixing together mud, straw and water and shaped in wooden moulds, after which they were left to dry hard in the sun, and only rarely baked in a kiln. Mortar was unknown, but mud bricks were bonded together with mud and also bitumen. Bricks were entirely coated with bitumen as a protection against damp when it was necessary to waterproof the foundations of buildings, because such bricks rapidly revert to mud when wet. Even with normal wear and tear, mud bricks gradually turn to dust, so that collapsed buildings would form a layer of soil over which new buildings were constructed. With the accumulation of rubbish and decomposed bricks, mounds (called tells) were formed and have become a distinctive feature of the Mesopotamian landscape.

The Genesis story relates that at Babylon a mud-brick tower – the Tower of Babel – was constructed with the intention of reaching heaven, which incurred the displeasure of God. The story may have been inspired by Babylon's immense ziggurat known as Etemenanki ('Foundation of Heaven and Earth'). Like other ziggurats, Etemenanki was a solid stepped pyramid with a monumental exterior staircase and a temple on top. The reason for God's displeasure is not given in Genesis, but instead of sending another flood, the punishment this time was to disperse the inhabitants of Babylon far and wide and to 'confuse their language',[3] so that they spoke different languages and could no longer communicate and cooperate. Because the similar-sounding Hebrew word *balal* means 'confuse' (and therefore a confusion of languages, or babble), the Genesis writer believed that this was why the city was called Babel, but it was actually due to the much earlier name of *Babilu*, which means 'gate of the god'. Later on, the ancient Greeks called the city Babylon. The origin of the city's name had nothing to do with why many languages are spoken throughout the world, but referred to the impressive gates of this fortified city.

The lack of stone and the abundance of mud not only determined building methods in Mesopotamia, but also its very writing system. With no other suitable material for writing, the ubiquitous mud was used to make rectangular, square or occasionally oval tablets. From a ball of damp clay, tablets were flattened into a shape that fitted in the hand, though some could be far larger, and they generally had one convex and one flat side. Writing on the tablet was done with a special implement (stylus) when the clay was still damp, first on the flat side, then the convex side. Styli have not survived as they were made from perishable materials, primarily reeds that grew abundantly in the marshlands: the Babylonian word for a stylus was *qan tuppi*, 'tablet-reed'. Writing was not normally done by incising or scoring lines with the stylus, but by making impressions in the damp clay of the tablet, and so it was easier to make straight rather than curved lines. Because one end of the reed stylus was cut at an angle, signs were made up of lines or strokes that had one end wider than the other, displaying a characteristic wedge or tapering shape. The system of writing is known today by the clumsy word 'cuneiform', which is literally 'of wedge-shaped form', from the Latin word *cuneus*, meaning wedge. Mistakes were erased by smoothing the clay surface with the stylus; after writing, tablets were left to dry hard in the sun, or occasionally fired in a kiln.

Cuneiform was not a language, but a script or writing system that was used to convey several different spoken languages. In Egypt, hieroglyphic writing was used only to write down the ancient Egyptian language, so hieroglyphs tend to be considered as both a writing system and the ancient language, but cuneiform is more like the later Roman script, which was first used at Rome to write down the Latin language. With modifications, this Roman script has continued to be a writing system for over two thousand years and is used today to write down numerous languages worldwide, such as English, German and Spanish.

Cuneiform is similar to the Roman script in that it too was used for a long period to write down different languages, evolving to suit each language and also evolving over time. For around three thousand years it was the writing system that recorded the many languages spoken across an extensive area, from Iraq to Syria, central Turkey, Palestine and south-west Iran. These languages included Sumerian, Akkadian, Urartian, Elamite and Old Persian. The last known use of cuneiform was in AD 75, on a clay tablet about astronomy found at Babylon. Because the system of cuneiform varied from language to language and changed over time, decipherers had a twofold problem: working out the particular writing system and translating the language in question. With the resulting tangle of multiple languages and varying versions of cuneiform script, decipherment could never be a single landmark achievement. The prize was not the knowledge of a single ancient civilization, but the knowledge of many ancient cultures, and the challenge was too much work for one person – too much for a single lifetime. Those attempting the decipherment of cuneiform had no concept of the enormous task ahead.

The very first writing evolved in Mesopotamia from the need of accountants and bureaucrats to keep a visual check of goods entering and leaving temples and palaces. Small clay tokens dating from 8000 BC appear to have been an early tally system and a precursor of writing. They have various geometric shapes, such as spheres, cones and discs, perhaps representing different commodities. In the mid-fourth millennium BC, tokens were sometimes placed inside hollow clay balls or envelopes and were sealed with cylinder seals.

Used in Mesopotamia for over three thousand years, cylinder seals were invented around 3600 BC as an aid to bureaucracy in the vast city of Uruk in southern Mesopotamia. These seals are small cylinders, usually made of imported stone and carved with intricate designs, especially scenes of everyday life. When rolled across damp clay, they left a continuous impression, and both seals and clay sealings have been found. As well as on clay balls, seals were used on clay tablets and on lumps of clay attached to cords securing door-bolts, bags, sacks, boxes, jars and other containers, as a deterrent against theft. The sealed clay balls may have accompanied deliveries of merchandise (acting as bills of lading), whose contents could be checked by breaking open the balls to reveal the tokens. Some balls have marks on the outside that seem to indicate the number and type of tokens they contained, but this information could also be recorded on flat clay tablets, and the earliest ones – termed numerical tablets – date from 3500 BC and had impressions of tokens and cylinder seals similar to those on the clay balls that they replaced.

The most primitive form of recognizable writing was a bookkeeping system done on clay tablets, with simple signs for numbers and pictorial signs (pictographs) to represent what was being counted or listed, such as oxen or barley. At this stage, the wedge-shaped stylus producing distinctive 'cuneiform' writing had not come into use. Instead, signs were written with a stylus that had a circular end to make impressions representing numbers and a pointed end to draw linear pictorial signs, and this writing is termed 'proto-cuneiform'. Tablets with a proto-cuneiform script date to 3300–2900 BC. Since signs were written on damp clay, scribes could only produce stylized sketches rather than the realistic images used in Egyptian hieroglyphs. Two wavy lines, for example, represented water, while the outline of a head of an ox represented an ox. Pictorial signs were also used as ideograms, to represent an associated idea. For example, a picture of a mouth might also mean 'to speak'. About 1,200 signs are known, but many are not understood today. On the clay tablets, groups of proto-cuneiform signs were written relatively randomly within square or rectangular boxes. The boxes themselves were arranged in horizontal rows that were read from top to bottom and in a right to left direction.

The amount of information that could be expressed by this sort of writing was severely limited – most proto-cuneiform tablets were concerned with book-keeping, although about 15 per cent of the surviving tablets are lists of words, such as the names of animals and cities, and were probably used in the training of scribes. As each pictograph or ideogram represented an entire word that could be understood universally, like those used today at airports, the language spoken by the people who made the pictographs is uncertain, but was probably Sumerian. In south-west Iran, once known as Elam, a script composed of numerical and other signs has been found on similarly early clay tablets dating to 3100–2700 BC. It seems to be more developed than simple picture signs, but remains poorly understood. It was originally labelled proto-Elamite on the assumption that it was an early form of the Elamíte language that was written down a few hundred years later.

The next development was to write words using the sounds of syllables, a more sophisticated method that enables specific languages to be identified. The earliest language to have been written on clay tablets and the earliest known language in the world is Sumerian, dating from at least 2800 BC – or several centuries earlier if proto-cuneiform is accepted as Sumerian, and so earlier than Egyptian. Sumer was the southern part of Babylonia in the period 3000–2300 BC, and stretched from Nippur (south of Babylon) to the Persian Gulf. The Sumerians called their territory *kiengir* ('homeland'), but later their Akkadian neighbours called it *Shumeru*, from which the modern name Sumer is derived. Sumerian is not related to any known family of languages, and it was possibly the only one of its family to have been written down, with the others dying out before writing was invented. Nothing is known about languages before Sumerian.

By 2600 BC major changes had taken place with the signs used to write Sumerian. They were now written as if turned 90 degrees to the left, so that the outline of a head of an ox was turned on its side and the two horizontal wavy lines representing water became vertical lines. They were also now written from left to right, not right to left. The other major change was that signs were no longer incised in the clay, but were impressed using a reed stylus with an angular end, forming the distinctive cuneiform ('wedge-shaped') signs. This was a more rapid way of writing, with the stylus being pushed into the damp clay rather than used to incise lines. Because of this change, signs became much more stylized, so that the sign for an ox was composed of a few impressed lines, barely resembling the original abstract outline of the head of the ox.

These cuneiform signs could still be used as pictographs, so that the stylized sign for a mouth meant 'mouth' (*ka* in Sumerian), and they could still be used as ideograms, so that the sign for a mouth also meant 'tooth' or 'word' (*zú* and *inim* in Sumerian). Many Sumerian words had only one syllable, such as *ud*, 'day', and sometimes even a single vowel, such as *a*, 'water'. The signs for these words began to be used phonetically to spell out syllables of different words, regardless of the original meaning of the sign, such as the sign for barley, pronounced *she*, being used where the syllable *she* was required. In English an example would be a picture of a ring used to spell the 'ring' sound values of 'bring', 'ringleader' and 'daring'. As words could now be spelled with syllables, there was no longer a need to have a separate sign for every Sumerian word, and so the number of signs dropped to around six hundred. This was still a very complicated system when compared with modern alphabets of around twenty-five or twenty-six letters, and so knowledge of writing was restricted to specially trained scribes, with the rest of the population remaining illiterate.

On the early Sumerian tablets, the cuneiform signs were grouped randomly in boxes, which were arranged in horizontal rows that were read from the top of the tablet to the bottom, but each box was now read from left to right, not right to left. With the increased use of signs for syllables, the written language became more structured, and grammatical elements developed. More complex words could be expressed, and because word order became important, signs began to be written in a single horizontal line, from left to right. Even so, there was no punctuation, nor any spaces between words.

Because Sumerian cuneiform signs started off as pictographs that were subsequently used as ideograms and syllables as well, almost every sign acquired several different functions. Many signs (termed polyphones) had several alternative sounds. For example, the sign ⟪ is *du*, meaning 'leg', but the same sign can have other associated meanings with different pronunciations, such as *gub*, 'to stand', *gin*, 'to go', and *túm*, 'to bring'. To get around this problem, the correct reading could be emphasized by adding another cuneiform sign, called a phonetic complement, comprising the final consonant and a vowel (usually a). This sign was not pronounced, but indicated what word was meant. For example, when this particular sign was to be read as *gin*, a sign for *na* was added, which cuneiform scholars write as gin(na) or gin^{na}.

Several Sumerian signs were pronounced the same way (like flour and flower in English). These signs are termed homophones – having the same sound. For example, there were ten different signs for the word or syllable pronounced *tum*. In modern transcriptions the particular word meant is shown by the addition of accents and numbers (diacritic signs). For example, several different signs were pronounced *gu*. The one meaning 'ox' is written in transcriptions as gu$_4$. Scribes also added signs called determinatives (or classifying signs) before or sometimes after a word to indicate the category to which a word belonged, so that its meaning was clarified. The sign *ki*, for example, indicated that the adjacent word was a place-name and *dingir* the name of a god. These determinative signs were not pronounced, but were present merely to show the meaning of the words.

Sumerian ceased to be an everyday spoken language by about 2000 BC, but scribes continued to copy out texts and word lists, often with Akkadian translations, because Sumerian became a prestigious and scholarly dead language, like Latin in the Middle Ages. Akkadian, the oldest known Semitic language, belonging to the same family of languages as Hebrew and Arabic, had become the everyday spoken language. The term Semitic was coined in the eighteenth century because the speakers of these languages were believed to be descendants of Noah's son Shem or Sem. Originally used alongside Sumerian, Akkadian was first written down from around 2500 BC. Although a Semitic language, the cuneiform writing system for Akkadian was based on Sumerian, despite the two languages being vastly different. Early cuneiform decipherment did not tackle Sumerian, as its existence was not initially recognized. Akkadian ('the tongue of Akkad', *lishanum akkaditum*) takes its name from Akkad (or Agade), which was founded as the capital city of the new empire of Akkad around 2300 BC by King Sargon, after he united several independent city-states in northern Babylonia and Sumer. The city of Akkad has not yet been discovered, but it probably lay north of Babylon.

Most Akkadian words had more than one syllable, and the cuneiform signs used to spell out words phonetically were either single vowels such as *a*, consonant-vowels such as *tu*, vowel-consonants such as *an* or consonant-vowel-consonants such as *nim* – never single consonants. Sumerian signs were frequently adopted as syllables or to represent entire Akkadian words. For example, the Sumerian sign ➤➤⊤ *an*, meant 'sky' or 'heaven', and this same sign was adopted for Akkadian, but in that language was pronounced as *shamu*. The same Sumerian sign could mean a god, *dingir*, which was also adopted in Akkadian, but pronounced *ilu*. Signs taken from Sumerian are now called Sumerograms. Cuneiform scholars today write Sumerian words in lower-case Roman script, Akkadian words borrowed from Sumerian in UPPER-CASE Roman script and Akkadian words in *italics* in an attempt to lessen the confusion.

As in Sumerian, a few Akkadian signs were used as determinatives and placed before or after words to clarify the type of word (such as a place, woman, god), and these signs were not pronounced. Phonetic complements functioned in a similar way to those of Sumerian cuneiform, but were not so widely used.

By 2000 BC about six hundred Akkadian signs were used, but most signs had two or more values or readings, representing a syllable, an entire word or a determinative. Some signs (the polyphones) had more than one phonetic value or syllable, such as the sign 𒌷, which can represent the syllables *ur*, *lig* or *tash*, and several different signs (the homophones) shared the same sound, such as

𒌷 𒄯 𒌋 𒌝 𒀉 𒅕 𒈘 𒂟

which all represent the sound *ur*. As with Sumerian, scholars today show a sign's value by a system of accents and numbers: the most common homophone in a group has no notation, the second an acute accent over the vowel, the third a grave accent, and the fourth and following have numbers, as in ur, úr, ùr, ur₄ and ur₅, called ur-one, ur-two, ur-three, ur-four, ur-five and so on. They are all pronounced in the same way.

Sumerian had a great influence on the written form of Akkadian, such as the verb occurring at the end of the sentence, which does not happen in other Semitic languages. However, verbs in Akkadian were not constructed like those of Sumerian (which had a fixed root word to which prefixes or suffixes were added). Instead, they had a root of three consonants (triliterals), which changed internally according to the meaning, mainly with the addition of different vowels. This is similar to English: the verb 'to write' can have various forms, such as written, writes and wrote – but w, r and t remain constant. Many Akkadian nouns ended in 'm', such as *sharrum* (king), but this ending was dropped towards the end of Old Assyrian and Old Babylonian, so that the word became *sharru*. There were no spaces between words, but there was occasional punctuation, such as an upright wedge 𒑱 to indicate the beginning of a sentence. The writing was read from left to right, and larger clay tablets could be divided into columns, like a modern newspaper, which were also read from left to right. On the reverse of tablets, though, the order of the columns could be left to right or right to left. Horizontal lines often separated each line of cuneiform writing.

There were three main Akkadian dialects, known today as Old Akkadian, Babylonian and Assyrian, and all used slightly different cuneiform scripts. In reality they were so similar that the terms tend to be interchangeable, and today they are studied as a single language. As with any other language though, Akkadian changed over the centuries. The Old Akkadian dialect dates to 2500–2000 BC, and under King Sargon it replaced Sumerian as the official language of administration. Only a century after its foundation, the Akkadian Empire collapsed, and for the next few centuries southern Mesopotamia experienced incursions from neighbouring tribes and was ruled by dynasties from cities such as Ur and Babylon, even though the kings still described themselves as rulers of the lands of Sumer and Akkad.

From 2000 BC it is possible to distinguish between the dialects of southern Mesopotamia (Babylonia) and northern Mesopotamia (Assyria). Babylonia incorporated what was formerly Sumer and stretched from the Persian Gulf northwards to the present city of Baghdad. Babylonian, the dialect of this region, is usually subdivided into Old Babylonian (2000–1600 BC), Middle Babylonian (1600–1000 BC), Neo-Babylonian (1000–600 BC) and Late Babylonian (600 BC to AD 75), while the term Standard Babylonian is used for the version of Old Babylonian that was preserved after

1500 BC by scribes in Babylonia and Assyria. From 1400 BC cuneiform, especially Babylonian, became the international language, the lingua franca, of diplomatic relations and trade over a vast area from Asia Minor to Egypt. Literacy rates within the population were still low, as the written language remained difficult.

The Assyrian dialect of the Akkadian language was contemporary with Babylonian, but was spoken in northern Mesopotamia. This region, known as Assyria (after the town of Ashur or Assur), stretched from what is now Baghdad northwards to the Anatolian mountains. Its main towns were Ashur, Nineveh, Nimrud, Khorsabad and Arbela, and at first Assyria was a collection of independent city-states. It became a powerful military state, expanding its territories and even invading Babylonia and sacking Babylon in 1235 BC. After 1100 BC Assyria went into decline, but from 930 BC the Neo-Assyrian Empire emerged as the dominant force in the region, conquering and annexing territory as far as Israel, Judah and Egypt. Many cuneiform inscriptions from this period have been found in vast library archives of clay tablets. In 612 BC the empire collapsed when Nineveh fell to the Babylonians and Medes.

The Assyrian dialect is usually subdivided into Old Assyrian (2000–1500 BC), Middle Assyrian (1500–1000 BC) and Neo-Assyrian (1000–600 BC). From the eighth century BC, Aramaic – the Semitic language of the Aramaeans, a nomadic tribe from the Syrian desert – became widespread as a spoken language, gradually replacing languages such as Akkadian. Scribes of cuneiform and Aramaic are depicted in sculptured reliefs working side by side at this time. The Aramaic writing system, based on the Phoenician alphabet, was much more simple and could be written with pen and ink on materials such as parchment and papyrus. It soon began to be adopted in place of cuneiform, and Aramaic became the international language of diplomacy and administration, while Akkadian became a literary and scholarly language.

From the sixth century BC Persia (modern-day Iran) began to expand its already immense empire westwards, first into areas like

Elam and Babylonia where cuneiform was used and later as far as Egypt and Greece. Elamite, a non-Semitic language not closely related to any other, is first seen around 2300 BC and became an official language of the Persian Empire. It is known mainly from hundreds of clay tablets found at Susa, the city that became the summer capital of Darius the Great, and also at his new capital Persepolis, as well as on monumental inscriptions such as at Bisitun. Not content with adopting Babylonian and Elamite cuneiform, Darius also invented a system of cuneiform for writing down his own language of Old Persian, which had never before been written down. This was the first time in antiquity that a complete writing system had been invented, rather than gradually evolved. Old Persian cuneiform began to be used from early 520 BC in the inscription at Bisitun, and Darius and his successor Xerxes had many of their achievements recorded in other trilingual inscriptions in Elamite, Babylonian and the newly invented Old Persian cuneiform.

Loosely based on the signs used for Sumerian and Akkadian, Old Persian cuneiform was a far simpler system, since it followed the alphabetical principles of Aramaic. There were thirty-six signs in all – signs for the three vowels *a*, *i* and *u*, twenty-two signs for consonants usually linked to the vowel *a*, four linked to the vowel *i* and seven to the vowel *u*. Two simple signs were used as word dividers, which was to prove a valuable aid to decipherment, and single signs represented the words king, land, earth, god and Ahuramazda, as well as numerals. Unlike other types of cuneiform, the invented Old Persian cuneiform is rarely found on clay tablets, but normally as inscriptions on rock faces, metal plaques, vases, stone buildings and stone monuments. Old Persian cuneiform was in use for less than two centuries, having been abandoned by the time the Macedonian Greek conqueror Alexander the Great defeated Darius III in 333 BC, overran the Persian Empire and sacked Persepolis.

After Alexander the Great, the Persian Empire came under Hellenistic Greek rule, until it was conquered a century later by the Parthians, nomads from central Asia, around 238 BC. The

Parthians and their empire survived for more than four centuries, before being overthrown in AD 224 by the Sasanians under their first king Ardashir. It was the son of Ardashir, King Shapur I, who built the city of Bishapur that Rawlinson visited in 1834 while staying at Shiraz. The Sasanian Empire also lasted over four centuries until the Islamic conquest of Persia in AD 651.

Just before his trip to Bishapur, Rawlinson had visited the ruins of Persepolis and seen for the first time trilingual cuneiform inscriptions carved in the three scripts of Old Persian, Babylonian and Elamite, but at this stage he had no idea of their significance. The obsession of the Persian kings for inscriptions carved in three languages on rock faces and buildings ensured that those inscriptions remained visible to early European travellers, whereas most inscriptions in Mesopotamia were hidden from view, awaiting discovery in archaeological excavations. Because Europeans had greater contact with Persia at an earlier date than with Mesopotamia, it was inevitable that attempts at deciphering cuneiform began here, most notably at the ruins of Persepolis. Old Persian became crucial in understanding all other cuneiform scripts, and when Rawlinson achieved his first breakthrough in the decipherment of cuneiform, it was Old Persian that was to provide the first clues.

Five: Discovering Darius

Over two centuries before Rawlinson arrived in Persia, European courts had been attempting to establish trading links with Shah Abbas I, and while on a mission to the Persian court on behalf of Philip III of Spain and Portugal, Antonio de Gouvea visited Persepolis in 1602. He found the writing of the inscriptions very strange: 'there is no one who can understand it, because the characters are neither Persian, Arabic, Armenian, nor Hebrew, the languages now in use in the district.'[1] Back at the Spanish court, Antonio de Gouvea met Don Garcia Silva Figueroa, who was himself inspired to visit the site in 1618 when in Persia as ambassador. Don Garcia was the first person to identify the ruins as Persepolis, but was equally puzzled by the sight of the inscriptions: 'The letters themselves are neither Chaldaean, nor Hebrew, nor Greeke nor Arabike, nor of any other Nation which was ever found of old, or at this day to be extant. They are all three cornered, but somewhat long, of the forme of a Pyramide, or such a little Obeliske as I have set in the margin.'[2]

Pietro della Valle, a traveller from Rome, became acquainted with Don Garcia at Isfahan, and when della Valle left the city towards the end of 1621, he spent two days at Persepolis and the neighbouring ruins. Like Don Garcia, he noted: 'One cannot tell in what language or letters these inscriptions are written, because the characters are unknown.'[3] He was unsure of the direction of writing, 'whether the characters are written from right to left as is the Oriental custom, or the opposite, from left to right as with us',[4] but because of the way the signs were constructed, he correctly deduced from left to right. He copied five of the most common cuneiform signs, and even though publication of the account of his journey was delayed until 1658, these were still the first cuneiform signs ever to be published.

Dutch, English, French and German travellers and artists were in turn drawn to Persepolis, many publishing engravings of the inscriptions, although these were often inaccurate. Samuel Flower, an agent of the East India Company, copied several trilingual inscriptions, from which a random selection of twenty-three cuneiform signs from the three scripts, each one divided by a full-stop, was published in 1693. Scholars were misled into believing that this random selection represented a full inscription with punctuation, a confusion that lasted for over one hundred years. Thomas Hyde, a Professor of Hebrew and Arabic at Oxford, studied Flower's so-called inscription and wrote in 1700 that the signs were purely decorative and could not represent writing, not least because they were all different and divided by full-stops. Although led astray by this composite inscription, he described the signs as *ductuli pyramidales seu cuneiformes*, so coining the term 'cuneiform'.

The next significant advance was by Carsten Niebuhr, a Danish scholar and explorer who spent several days at Persepolis in 1765. When the account of his travels was published a few years later, his drawings of inscriptions at last provided reliable material for scholars to use in their attempts at decipherment. Niebuhr was the first to realize that the inscriptions comprised three different scripts and therefore probably three different languages. He misleadingly referred to each script as an alphabet, although only the Old Persian was an alphabet. Referring to the scripts as classes I, II and III, he thought that class I (recognized later as Old Persian) was more simple than the other two and had forty-two alphabetical signs (there are actually even fewer – thirty-six). He confirmed della Valle's view that the writing was done from left to right, after observing that in two identical inscriptions the line endings were not in the same position. It did not seem to occur to Niebuhr that the three different scripts each reproduced the identical text.

Two decades later, in 1798, Oluf Gerhard Tychsen, a Professor of Oriental Languages at Rostock, published a paper wrongly alleging that the inscriptions at Persepolis were of Parthian date and claiming to make out the name of the first Parthian King, Arsaces ('Aksak'), in a recurring group of signs. He did correctly identify one diagonal sign ◣ in the Old Persian script as a word divider, although he was incorrect to claim it could also signify the conjunction 'and'.

That same year Frederik Münter, a Professor of Theology at Copenhagen, read two papers to the Royal Danish Society of Sciences that were published in 1800 (and translated into German in 1802). In his opinion the ruins and inscriptions could only belong to the Achaemenid kings, and among his many observations on the inscriptions he correctly concluded that the diagonal sign was only ever a word divider. He rejected Tychsen's reading of the name Aksak and rightly suggested that it might be a Persian title, such as 'king of kings'. However, he incorrectly suggested that the languages of the three scripts were Avestan (or Zend as it was then called), Pahlavi and Parsi.

The known languages of Persia are divided into Old Iranian (in use up to Alexander the Great's conquest), Middle Iranian (used up to the Islamic conquest) and New Iranian. The Iranian language belongs to the Indo-Iranian branch of Indo-European languages, and around 1000 BC Iranian speakers spread from central Asia into Afghanistan and Persia (Iran). Old Iranian comprised two known languages, Old Persian and Avestan, and the former was the everyday speech of the Achaemenid kings and was probably the spoken language of south-west Persia. It is represented by a limited number of cuneiform inscriptions, as at Bisitun and Persepolis. At the same time, Avestan was spoken in north-east Persia and became the language used to compose the Avesta or Zend-Avesta, the holy texts of Zoroastrianism that became the state religion from the time of Cyrus the Great. The Avesta was originally handed down from one generation to another by word of mouth, but was written down for the first time in the Sasanian era, probably in the sixth century AD, long after cuneiform had gone out of use. The earliest surviving manuscripts date from the thirteenth century, just as most Latin texts from the Roman Empire survive only as medieval copies.

In 1771 Abraham-Hyacinthe Anquetil Duperron published the first translation, into French, of the Zend-Avesta. Because Avestan was similar to Old Persian, knowledge of this language was to prove invaluable as it enabled decipherers to work out the vocabulary of Old Persian. Münter at Copenhagen tried to compare the frequency of cuneiform signs in the Old Persian inscriptions with the frequency of letters in Avestan texts, and although his method did not succeed, it led him to suggest correctly that the other two scripts in the trilingual inscriptions from Persepolis were translations of the first.

In July 1802, Rafaello Fiorillo, secretary of the Imperial Library at Göttingen in Germany, was out walking with the twenty-seven-year-old schoolteacher Georg Friedrich Grotefend, a man 'possessed of an extraordinary memory and excellent health, which allowed him to study from the earliest morning until late at night, without stint or relaxation ... although he was considered by persons not in his intimacy, to be of a cold and reserved character, wholly occupied with his recondite studies, and uninterested in anything beyond them, this learned man was really full of feeling, and endowed with an almost child-like simplicity, which endeared him to all those who were of the circle of his friends.'[5] Fiorillo asked if it could ever be possible to understand cuneiform inscriptions, when both the alphabet and the language were absolutely unknown. Rising to the challenge, Grotefend chose two trilingual inscriptions copied by Niebuhr at Persepolis that looked very similar, examining in each the most simple of the three scripts (the Old Persian). Just a few years earlier, Silvestre de Sacy, an Oriental scholar in Paris, had worked out the meaning of Sasanian (Middle Persian) inscriptions from Naqsh-i Rustam near Persepolis, using the aid of identical inscriptions in ancient Greek. Because they contained the names and titles of kings, Grotefend thought that his cuneiform inscriptions from Persepolis might be similar, but perhaps dating to the time of Xerxes. From these suppositions, he thought that the inscriptions would include the formula 'Xerxes, great king, king of kings, son of Darius, great king, king of kings, son of Hystaspes'.

Using this method, Grotefend successfully identified the groups of signs for Xerxes, Darius and Hystaspes and also the group of signs for 'king', but did not work out all the individual cuneiform signs correctly. Using versions of the names derived from ancient Greek, Hebrew and Avestan, he thought that the cuneiform signs 𐎭 𐎠 𐎼 𐎲 𐎢 𐏁 𐎰 for Darius represented d-a-r-h-e-u-sh (darheush), although in fact they spell da-a-ra-ya-va-u-sha (darayavaush). The cuneiform signs for Xerxes 𐏂 𐎠 𐎴 𐎤 𐎭 𐎠 𐏁 were identified by him as kh-sh-h-e-r-sh-e (khshhershe), but they are actually xa-sha-ya-a-ra-sha-a (xashayarasha).

The group of signs 𐏂 𐎠 𐏁 𐎴 𐎡 𐎠 𐎴 that Grotefend believed meant 'king' gave him kh-sh-e-h-?-?-h, when looking at identical signs within darheush and khshhershe. From the Avesta, he knew that khsheio was a royal title, so he deduced that the missing signs were i and o, to give khshehioh, although the word is actually xa-sha-a-ya-tha-i-ya (xashayathaiya). By working out the values of the signs 𐎻 𐎡 𐏁 𐎫 𐎠 𐎿 𐎱 that he thought represented the name Hystaspes, and by filling in the gaps, Grotefend arrived at g-o-sh-t-a-s-p (goshtasp), although it is now spelled vi-i-sha-ta-a-sa-pa (vishatasapa).

From identifying these names, Grotefend next worked out part of the alphabet for Old Persian, not realizing that many signs represented syllables, not single alphabetical letters. Despite many errors, he had achieved the first steps in decipherment, and his remarkable results were announced to the Academy of Sciences at Göttingen in four papers from September 1802 to May 1803 and published in 1805 within a book by Arnold H. L. Heeren – *Ideen über die Politik, den Verkehr und den Handel, der vornehmsten Völker der alten Welt* (Ideas on the politics, communication and trade of the first peoples of the ancient world).

Grotefend's results were applauded in Paris by de Sacy, whose own pupil Saint-Martin tried to improve on the alphabet, but with minimal success. Just before his death in 1832, Saint-Martin was studying copies of the trilingual Elwand inscriptions, which were subsequently handed to Burnouf, who was working on Avestan and Sanskrit, two closely related ancient languages. Burnouf's *Commentaire sur le Yaçna* was published from 1833 to 1835 – the Yasna was part of the Zend-Avesta, and this commentary far outstripped Duperron's earlier translation of the Zend-Avesta. It was while Burnouf was preparing the Elwand inscriptions for publication that Rawlinson was carefully copying the very same inscriptions on his way from Tehran to Kermanshah in April 1835.

Towards the end of April, Rawlinson reached Kermanshah, where he would become well acquainted with the town and its people. Situated at an altitude of over 4,000 feet, on the edge of an extensive plain and at the foothills of a range of the Zagros mountains, Kermanshah controlled trade between the surrounding region and Baghdad to the south-west in Turkish territory. A fortified mud-brick wall, roughly circular in plan and with five gates, surrounded the town's flat-roofed mud-brick houses, extensive covered bazaars, palace, baths, caravanserais and mosques, although imposing domes and minarets were noticeably lacking, in spite of Shi'ite Muslims being in the majority. Equally obvious was the sparse population, which had more than halved to around 12,000 after a recent plague epidemic. Five years later, in 1840, the adventurer Austen Henry Layard (a future collaborator with Rawlinson on cuneiform) travelled to Kermanshah and gave his initial impressions: 'It stands in a fine, well-watered plain, surrounded by lofty serrated mountains towering one above the other, with high precipitous peaks, then still covered with snow. It is a place of considerable size, in the midst of gardens, vineyards, and orchards, amongst which are wide-spreading walnut trees and lofty poplars. An abundant supply of water descended from the mountains, divided into numerous canals, irrigated the lands, and rendered them bright with verdure. Altogether I was very favourably impressed with the appearance of the place from a distance. I thought it one of the prettiest and most flourishing towns I had seen in the East.'[6]

Finding himself in this mountainous region with many tantalizing inscriptions, Rawlinson was instantly lured to nearby Taq-i
Bustan, with its Sasanian rock-cut reliefs and grottoes, several
centuries later in date than those trilingual cuneiform inscriptions
at the foot of Mount Elwand that he had recently copied. The
Taq-i Bustan reliefs included one of King Khusro II, who was a
contemporary of the Prophet Muhammed and ruled from AD 594
to 628. The king, seated on his favourite horse Shabdiz, is in full
armour and helmet, holding a lance and looking very much like
the knights of medieval Europe. Throughout Persia, sculptured
reliefs of Fath Ali Shah and his court had been carved next to
Sasanian reliefs, including one here at Taq-i Bustan, so continuing
a long tradition.

What really gripped Rawlinson's attention, though, was hearing about another trilingual cuneiform inscription, located at
Bisitun, 20 miles from Kermanshah. Frustratingly, no sooner had
he discovered the inscription than his work as a soldier demanded
his total commitment. Within weeks of arriving he had gained
Bahram Mirza's trust to such an extent that it was laid down that
Persian soldiers of all ranks would take orders from him, while
he himself would only take orders from the prince. 'The Prince',
he recorded, 'took to me, was very kind and gave me the practical
command of the Province'[7] – including arms, equipment, stores,
and the recruitment and training of the troops.

Having put cuneiform inscriptions out of his mind for now,
Rawlinson's first concern was the raising of troops from local
Kurdish tribes. Wild in their ways of living and independent in
their attitude, the Kurds only felt allegiance to their own tribe
and resented being ruled by Persians. In his journal at this time,
Rawlinson set out his rules for his own conduct, demonstrating
his grasp of the fragility of the situation: 'Create business for yourself. Lose no opportunity of making yourself useful, whatever may
be the affair which may happen to present the chance. Grasp at
everything, and never yield an inch. Above all, never stand upon
trifles. Be careful of outward observances. Maintain a good establishment; keep good horses and showy ones; dress well; have good

and handsome arms; in your conversation and intercourse with the natives, be sure to observe the customary etiquette.'[8] In this way, by unceasing work and tactful persuasion, Rawlinson succeeded in recruiting and training three regiments.

In mid-August Bahram Mirza ordered Rawlinson to assist Suleiman Khan, the governor of Kurdistan to the north of Kermanshah. Suleiman was, Rawlinson thought, 'a regular tyrant, but made great friends with him'.[9] Rawlinson took control from the governor of raising and training a regiment of troops from among the Guran Kurds, a most unruly mountain tribe. About six weeks later he was recalled to Kermanshah by Bahram Mirza, and that same day the Guran Kurds mutinied, murdered Suleiman Khan and headed off westwards towards the frontier, with the intention of crossing into Turkish territory where they would be safe from Persian reprisals. News of the revolt compelled Bahram Mirza to send Rawlinson straight back to the mountains to try to quell the rebellion. He managed to rescue Suleiman Khan's son Muhammed Wali Khan, proclaimed him governor and began rounding up the less disaffected troops. Hurrying towards the border, Rawlinson persuaded those who had not reached it to accept Muhammed as their new leader and reaffirm their oath of allegiance to the Shah. Inevitably, many mutineers escaped into Turkish territory, but in the space of a few days Rawlinson's military skills and diplomacy had put down the rebellion and restored peace.

After ten days of 'continual excitement and very hard work'[10] Rawlinson was struck down by 'bed fever', probably malaria from which he had last suffered over a year previously at Tabriz, and was forced to complete the journey back to Kermanshah in a litter. After trying all types of remedy, he was getting no better, so 'made them cut the fever by bleeding me till I fainted – rather severe treatment'.[11] Remaining extremely weak and unable to face the long trek to Tehran for treatment, he chose to be transported along the shorter and easier route westwards out of Persia to Baghdad, in what was then Turkish territory, where he could be cared for by a European doctor. He reached Baghdad on 29 November 1835 and placed himself in the hands of Dr John Ross, the thirty-year-old surgeon to the British Residency. Under Ross's treatment Rawlinson recovered rapidly.

A whole month was spent on sick leave recuperating at Baghdad, but ever anxious not to be idle, Rawlinson set about learning Arabic and 'made the acquaintance of Colonel Taylor and was initiated into Arabic lore'.[12] Colonel John Taylor, the East India Company Resident at Baghdad, was an antiquarian and 'so good an Arabic scholar, that when the Cadi or the Mufti met with a difficult passage in some old manuscript and were not sure of the correct reading, they sent or went to him. He never left his house and was always to be found in his study poring over Arabic books. Unfortunately he never wrote anything.'[13]

At the end of December, Rawlinson was sufficiently recovered 'in health and spirits'[14] to ride from Baghdad to the Persian town of Zohab at the foot of the Zagros mountains, at that time 'a mass of ruins, with scarcely 200 inhabited houses'[15] because of constant wars between Persia and Turkey. Here he met up with Bahram Mirza early in the new year and stayed for six weeks, training the Guran regiment, 'until he had brought his new corps into a state of perfection almost unknown in these regions'.[16] All the while, Rawlinson wrote down his observations of the district and took delight in the scenery, such as at the source of the Holwan River, which 'rises in the gorge of Rijáb, on the western face of Zagros, about 20 miles E. of the town of Zoháb. It bursts in a full stream from its source, and is swollen by many copious springs as it pursues its way for 8 miles down this romantic glen. The defile of Rijáb is one of the most beautiful spots that I have seen in the East; it is in general very narrow, scarcely 60 yards in width, closed in on either side by a line of tremendous precipices, and filled from one end to the other with gardens and orchards, through which the stream tears its foaming way with the most impetuous force until it emerges into the plain below.'[17]

In a mountain gorge north of Zohab, Rawlinson copied a small sculptured relief with a cuneiform inscription, noting that it was 'divided into three compartments of four lines each, and written perpendicularly in the complicated Babylonian character, which

I had never before seen, except upon bricks and cylinders'.[18] He had in fact already seen Babylonian at Bisitun, but did not yet realize it was the same script used on baked clay objects such as bricks, because without careful study they appeared so different. Just south of Zohab, at a place called Sarpol-i Zohab, as well as 'Gates of Asia', he recorded a sculptured relief on another rock face: 'It represents a figure in a short tunic and round cap, with a shield upon his left arm, and a club resting upon the ground in his right, who tramples with his left foot upon a prostrate enemy; a prisoner with his hands bound behind him, equal in stature to the victor, stands in front of him, and in the background are four naked figures kneeling in a suppliant posture, and of a less size, to represent the followers of the captive monarch; the platform upon which this group is disposed is supported on the heads and hands of a row of pigmy figures, in the same manner as we see at the royal tombs of Persepolis. The face of the tablet has been much injured by the oozing of water from the rock, but the execution is good, and evidently of the same age as the sculptures of Bísutún and Persepolis.'[19]

This remarkable monument that Rawlinson had discovered was just over 100 miles due west of Bisitun, but he misinterpreted the sculpture, because the prisoner with the same stature as the victor did not have bound hands and was in fact the warrior goddess Ishtar, the most important female deity in Mesopotamia. She is shown offering King Anubanini the royal diadem, while he stands on a prisoner, with other captives shown around him, all of a smaller size. The relief dates to about 2000 BC, one thousand five hundred years earlier than that at Bisitun, but it must have been copied by Darius the Great, as he is shown at Bisitun in virtually identical pose, with the goddess Ishtar transformed into Ahuramazda.

Bahram Mirza next ordered Rawlinson to take the regiment on an expedition southwards through the Zagros mountains into Luristan and Khuzistan (the area in south-west Persia that was once ancient Elam) to suppress increasing trouble with the powerful and fiercely independent Bakhtiari mountain tribe. Rawlinson

knew that the area 'had seldom, if ever, before been trodden by
the foot of an European',[20] and recognizing this as an opportunity
for pioneering exploration, he kept copious notes of everything of
geographical and historical interest on the journey.

The expedition set off on 14 February 1836, with Rawlinson
leading 3,000 Guran troops and their artillery southwards
through the mountains. They marched between 20 and 40 miles
a day, and Rawlinson met and talked with the chiefs of various
local tribes through whose territory they passed. He often left his
men to march to their overnight camp while he went ahead on
horseback to explore the antiquities of the region, which were
mostly Sasanian, ranging from ruined cities, temples, bridges and
fortifications to small rock-cut inscriptions. Four days on he
explained: 'I halted to-day at Chárdawer, to enable the troops to
come up and rest, after their very fatiguing march. I was in some
apprehension at first; for there was blood between the Gúráns and
the followers of Jemshíd Beg, the latter having joined the Kalhur
tribe in their last foray on the Gúrán lands, and having lost several
men in the skirmish which ensued. "Had they slain, however, a
hundred of my men," said Jemshíd Beg, "they are your sacrifice;
the Gúrán having come here under your shadow, they are all my
guests;" and he insisted, accordingly, in furnishing the regiment
with supplies, as a part of my own entertainment. Neither could
I prevail on him to accept of any remuneration.'[21]

The next day they marched 15 miles to the camp of another
leader, Ahmed Khán, whose family, Rawlinson recorded, 'are
notorious for their intolerant spirit; and I should recommend any
European traveller visiting the province of Pushti-kúh, in order
to examine its remarkable antiquities, to appear in the meanest
guise, and live entirely among the wandering I'liyát, who are
mostly 'Alí Iláhís, and are equally ignorant and indifferent on all
matters of religion.'[22] Rawlinson added: 'In my own case, of
course, I had nothing to apprehend, as I was marching at the
head of a regiment, and the rulers of the province were anxious
to propitiate the favour of the prince of Kirmánsháh, in whose
service I was known to be; but I saw enough on this journey, and

upon subsequent occasions, of the extreme jealousy and intolerance of the Wáli's family, to feel assured that the attempt of an European to explore the country in an open and undisguised character, with any less efficient support, would be attended with the greatest danger.'[23]

On 4 March they reached Dizful at the foot of the mountains, the chief city of the province of Khuzistan and with, Rawlinson reckoned, about 20,000 inhabitants. After five days camped here, he rode over 20 miles south-westwards to the ancient city of Susa (or Shush), on the edge of the great alluvial plain of Mesopotamia. Although it had been the summer capital of Darius the Great, it had been founded as far back as 4000 BC and became the principal city of Elam. 'At the tenth mile from Dizfúl,' Rawlinson wrote, 'the river makes an abrupt turn to the S.E., and the road then leaves it, and stretches across the plain to the great mound of Sús, which is, from this point, distinctly visible on the horizon. As I approached the ruins, I was particularly struck with the extraordinary height of this mound, which is indeed so great as to overpower all the other ruins in the vicinity.'[24] Rawlinson described his first discovery: 'Upon the slope of the western face of the mound is a slab with a cuneiform inscription of thirty-three lines in length engraved on it, and in the complicated character of the third column of the Persepolitan tablets.'[25] What he had found was an inscription in the Elamite script, and he was told that the slab was 'part of an obelisk, which existed not many years ago, erect upon the summit of the mound, and the broken fragments of the other parts of it are seen in the plain below'.[26]

At Susa he had hoped to be able to find and record an inscribed stone nearly 2 feet high, apparently written in cuneiform on two sides and Egyptian hieroglyphs on one face, that previous travellers had been prevented from removing. He felt that such a bilingual inscription would be an asset in decipherment, as hieroglyphs had been deciphered thirteen years previously by Champollion, but he was bitterly disappointed: 'I visited at this spot the pretended tomb of the Prophet Daniel; but the famous black stone, with the bilingual inscription, cuneiform and hieroglyphic, which formerly existed here, and by means of which I trusted to verify or disprove the attempts which have been made by St. Martin and others to decipher the arrow-headed character, no longer remains. It was blown to shivers a short time ago by a fanatical Arab in hopes of discovering a treasure; and thus perished all the fond hopes that archaeologists have built upon this precious relic.'[27] Though this was a setback, Rawlinson found the place idyllic: 'The ruins of Sús and the surrounding country are celebrated for their beautiful herbage: it was difficult to ride along the Shápúr [river] for the luxuriant grass that clothed its banks; and all around, the plain was covered with a carpet of the richest verdure. The climate too, at this season, was singularly cool and pleasant, and I never remember to have passed a more delightful evening than in my little tent upon the summit of the great mound of Sús – alone, contemplating the wrecks of time that were strewed around me, and indulging in the dreams of by-gone ages.'[28]

In mid-March they continued their trek and came to the banks of the Kuran River, where the town of Shuster was visible on the other side, its population drastically reduced after the devastation of the plague four years earlier. That same year the bridge across the river had been swept away by floods, 'and, not having been repaired when I was there,' Rawlinson noted, 'we were obliged to bring the troops and guns across the river upon rafts, or kalaks, as they are called, supported on inflated skins. We pitched our camp along the pebbly beach, in the bed of the river; a most unsafe position, as a sudden rise of the waters would have swept it away bodily; but there was positively no other ground available.'[29]

A week later they began a five-day march towards the principal fortress of the Bakhtiari tribe, and after a halt of two days, 'I accompanied the Prince a distance of 3 farsakhs [about eleven miles], to Khári-Shutur-zár, where he received the submission of the Bakhtiyárí chief, against whom our expedition was directed'.[30] The leader was Mohammed Taki Khan, and he held such power that he could 'at any time, bring into the field a well-armed force of 10,000 or 12,000 men'.[31] Of the Bakhtiari tribe, Rawlinson observed that their 'language is a dialect of the Kurdish, but still differing in many respects, and more particularly in their method of pronunciation, from any of the other modifications of that tongue which are spoken by the different tribes extending along the range of Zagros. I believe them to be individually brave, but of a cruel and savage character; they pursue their blood feuds with the most inveterate and exterminating spirit, and they consider no oath nor obligation in any way binding, when it interferes with their thirst of revenge; indeed the dreadful stories of domestic tragedy that are related, in which whole families have fallen by each others' hands . . . are enough to freeze the blood with horror . . . Altogether they may be considered the most wild and barbarous of all the inhabitants of Persia; but nevertheless, I have passed some pleasant days with their chiefs, and derived much curious information from them.'[32]

Returning to Shuster, Rawlinson wrote to his brother George of his disappointment at the lack of military action: "I have marched to this place (Shuster) in command of a force of three thousand men, intending to attack and plunder the country of a rebellious mountain chief; but now that we are near his fort he shows the white feather, and wants to come to terms.'[33] He acknowledged to his brother that the time nevertheless passed pleasantly, because he could indulge two of his passions – shooting game and visiting antiquities: 'I am in a country abounding both with game and antiquities, so that, with my gun in hand, I perambulate the vicinity of Shuster, and fill at the same time my bag with partridges and my pocket-book with memoranda.'[34]

It had been nearly nine years since Rawlinson had left England, and at times he felt isolated and missed the close relationship with his family, as he confided gloomily in the long letter to George: 'The only evil is the difficulty of communicating with any other civilised place from this said province of Khuzistan; it is nine months since I heard from England, and three since I heard from either Teheran or Baghdad, so that I am completely isolated and utterly ignorant of what is going on in any of the other regions of the globe. News from England I am particularly anxious for.'[35] Moreover, friendships with other soldiers were proving to be ephemeral: 'India has now ceased to be of any interest to me. I have few correspondents there, and each letter that I receive tells me a fresh tale of the worthlessness of worldly friendships. C—, who was wont to call himself my particular friend and chum, has never once written to me since he returned to India; and all my other quondam cronies have equally fallen off. But "out of sight, out of mind" is an old proverb, and I have no right, therefore, to complain of any particular grievance in my case.'[36]

Rawlinson wrote to members of his family constantly, but whether or not they received his letters seemed a matter of chance. He explained to his brother how his latest letter would, if it survived, make its way to England: 'From Shuster my letter is to be conveyed to Bussorah [Basra], from thence to Baghdad by another courier, then to Constantinople, and then put in the Vienna post-bag, so that, if the document reaches you safe and sound after all this chopping and changing, you must consider that Mercury [messenger of the Roman gods] has an especial favour for you.'[37] All Rawlinson wanted to do now was to return to England on leave once he had served ten years with the East India Company, intending to immerse himself in study at Oxford and Cambridge for three years: 'Next year [1837], however, when my ten years expire, I shall certainly come home on furlough, unless in the interim some kind angel slips me into a caldron, like Medea's, and wipes off the corrosion of nine glowing summers. So look out for a nice cheap lodging at Oxford, where (and at Cambridge) I think I shall pass most of my three years for the sake of consulting the classical and Oriental works which are there alone procurable, and a reference to which is absolutely necessary before I can prepare for publication my papers on the comparative geography of the countries which I am now visiting.'[38] His longing to return home came to nothing, as he became too immersed in affairs in Persia.

Six weeks were spent in the vicinity of Shuster and Dizful, but in mid-May Rawlinson left the regiment and returned to Kermanshah using a shorter, more difficult route through the mountains of Luristan, accompanied by only a few other soldiers on horseback, without the burden of baggage mules. At one point they passed a 'very lofty range, called Sar Kushtí, where the Lurs suppose the ark of Noah to have rested after the Flood'.[39] After eleven days, dogged by attacks of fever, they reached Bisitun, from where it was a short ride back to Kermanshah.

For the next few weeks Rawlinson applied himself to his cuneiform studies, looking first at the Elwand inscriptions, but he soon realized that, with only these short inscriptions to work on, he was unlikely to make much progress. He therefore made the decision to try to copy the trilingual inscription at Bisitun.

Six: Bewitched by Bisitun

The imposing appearance of Bisitun greatly impressed Rawlinson, who considered it 'a very remarkable natural object on the high road between Ecbatana and Babylon ... The rock, or, as it is usually called by the Arab geographers, the mountain of Behistun, is not an isolated hill, as has sometimes been imagined. It is merely the terminal point of a long, narrow range which bounds the plain of Kermanshah to the eastward. This range is rocky and abrupt throughout, but at the extremity it rises in height, and becomes a sheer precipice.'[1] It is, in fact, the end of a ridge of peaks of the Zagros mountain range, where the limestone rock rises dramatically to a height of 1,700 feet above the plain, with the inscription of Darius the Great carved at a height of over 200 feet. The monument appears small in relation to the mountain, yet it is over 25 feet tall and 70 feet wide, and the panel of relief sculptures alone is nearly 18 feet wide and 10 feet high.

The massive monument was made as an extensive inscription surrounding relief sculptures of Darius and his defeated prisoners. Although the inscription was trilingual (written in three scripts and three languages) it was not originally designed as such. The inscriptions Rawlinson had already seen at Persepolis were intended to be trilingual from the outset, as was the Rosetta Stone in Egypt with its three different scripts (although technically bilingual, with just two languages), whereas the Bisitun monument evolved gradually. The monument did not overlook the plain, but was carved on the south-facing wall of a cleft in the mountain. A natural pathway originally led to the spot chosen by Darius, and once the rock surface was cut back and dressed smooth with iron chisels, the work of carving and engraving could begin.

At first, Darius intended the relief sculpture as the centrepiece, with inscriptions placed symmetrically round the figures. For the inscriptions, the rock face was lightly engraved with guidelines about 1½ inches (possibly two fingers' width) apart. The sculptured panel was started early in 520 BC, and four columns of Elamite cuneiform inscription, a total of 323 lines, were added to the right. Because Rawlinson did not know the origins of this type of cuneiform, he used the term 'Median', after the Medes who once inhabited this area, as well as 'Scythic', thinking it may have originated with the Scythic tribe of the Russian steppes. 'Susian' replaced these terms, after the city of Susa that Rawlinson had recently visited. Finally, 'Elamite' was introduced after the earliest known name for the region, and that term is still used today.

In 519 BC, only months after the carving of the relief sculpture and Elamite inscription, a Babylonian inscription was added to the left, on an overhanging rock face. It was carved in a single column nearly 14 feet high and consisted of 112 lines of cuneiform, some of which are themselves over 13 feet long: the engraver clearly misjudged this task, as it should have been split into two columns. Later that same year the Old Persian inscription was added, in four columns of cuneiform, totalling 378 lines, which were engraved immediately below the relief sculpture, although the fourth column extended beneath the Elamite inscription, perhaps where the engraver misjudged his calculations in laying out the text. Although this was a translation of the Elamite text, minor changes and omissions were made, and an additional paragraph was incorporated towards the end, which related how the Old Persian cuneiform was a new form of writing, that this was the first time it had ever been used, and how copies and translations of the Bisitun text were being circulated throughout the Persian Empire. No room was available to add this extra paragraph to the main body of the Elamite inscription, but instead it appeared as a detached inscription above the relief sculptures. It was never added to the Babylonian, even though there was room.

Another figure of a defeated rebel, Skunkha, was added to the relief sculptures in 518 BC, necessitating the obliteration of part of the first column of the Elamite text. Incredibly, Darius ordered a copy of the entire Elamite inscription to be meticulously carved to the left of the Old Persian inscription, below the Babylonian, this time as three columns totalling 260 lines. At the same time a short fifth column giving an account of his new military victories was added to the end of the Old Persian, and the rock surface with the first Elamite inscription was smoothed so that it was barely visible.

Once all the inscriptions were finished, the monument was made as inaccessible as possible, including quarrying away the mountain path, to reduce the risk of vandalism. From the plain below, the inscriptions were too far away to be read, and through succeeding generations the meaning of the monument was lost. In ancient Greek times it became known as Bagistanon, 'a place of the gods', which gave rise to its Persian name of Bisitun (or Bisotun or Behistun), meaning literally 'without columns'.

Early European travellers noticed the site, but did not understand it. Over a decade before Rawlinson arrived at Kermanshah, the artist and traveller Robert Ker Porter made the first recorded ascent, though seemingly not to the actual ledge below the inscriptions: 'I could not resist the impulse to examine it nearer ... To approach it at all, was a business of difficulty and danger; however, after much scrambling and climbing, I at last got pretty far up the rock, and finding a ledge, placed myself on it as firmly as I could.'[2] He was initially interested in the relief sculptures, not the inscriptions beneath, commenting: 'but still I was farther from the object of all this peril, than I had hoped; yet my eyes being tolerably long-sighted, and my glass [telescope] more so, I managed to copy the whole sculpture.'[3] Porter's drawing was reasonably accurate, and he also made notes about the inscriptions beneath the sculptures: 'the excavation is continued to a considerable extent, containing eight deep closely written columns [the Elamite and Old Persian] in the same character. From so much labour having been exerted on this part of the work, it excites more regret that so little progress has yet been made towards deciphering the character; and most devoutly must we hope that the indefatigable scholars now engaged in the study of these apparently oldest letters in the world may at last succeed in bringing them to an intelligible language. In that case what a treasure-house of historical knowledge would be unfolded here.'[4]

To copy the inscriptions at Bisitun would be, Porter believed, an enormous undertaking: 'to transcribe the whole of the tablets, could I have drawn myself up sufficiently high on the rock to be within sight of them, would have occupied me more than a month. At no time can it ever be attempted without great personal risk; yet I do not doubt that some bracket on the surface might be found, to admit a tolerably secure seat for some future traveller, who has ardour and time, to accomplish so desirable a purpose.'[5]

In the early summer of 1836, Rawlinson used every spare minute to make repeated climbs up to the narrow ledge below the inscriptions and copy the initial lines of the first column of the Old Persian. He had deduced that there were three different types of cuneiform, as on the Elwand inscriptions, and he chose to start with the Old Persian script that appeared the most simple. Nobody had ever before managed to climb right up to these inscriptions, let alone record them, and even four years later the artist Eugène Flandin found the task virtually impossible. He and an architect, Pascal Coste, had been instructed by the French government to copy all the ancient monuments and inscriptions of Persia, and in July 1840 Flandin went on his own to Bisitun. He managed to climb to the ledge, but once there he found it impossible to move. His description of the ascent and descent is in stark contrast to Rawlinson's understated record of the climb, and highlights Rawlinson's nerve and mountaineering skills: 'Mount Bi-Sutoun rises up in a pyramidal shape, black and savage,' began Flandin. 'It is one of the highest summits of the chain. The bas-relief, set in a reflex angle of the mountain ... is only seen with great difficulty from below. In order to draw it, it is necessary to get close up by climbing some of the blocks that litter the foot of the mountain, which can be done up to a certain height. There then remains quite a great height still, so that it is necessary to use a telescope. The steep rock slope below this sculpture makes access almost impossible, so aiding its preservation ... I wanted to try to get to the inscriptions that I had only been able to see from the foot of the mountain ... I folded up my tent in the evening and I left for Bi-Sutoun [from Taq-i Bustan] ... and crossed the lonely plain, and, keeping straight ahead, I went alongside the foot of the mountains. The day had been very stormy. The summits of Mount Bi-Sutoun were covered with great reddish clouds ... The thunder rumbled across their thick layers ... the flashes of lightning were recurring like prolonged echoes.'[6]

The moon then rose, dispersing the clouds and, Flandin wrote, 'its silver light, spread over the mountain, changed the savage and sad colours that the leaden clouds had given to the rocks of Bi-Sutoun into fantastic and strange effects. I had returned to Bi-Sutoun with the intention of copying the inscriptions. I was hoping to succeed by using two ladders that I had brought from Kermanshah and was counting on putting the two together. By placing them as high as possible on the rocks, I was hoping to reach a little ledge that was at the level of the engraved tablets. But a vain hope ... What to do? It was absolutely impossible without a specially constructed scaffolding, and positioning it would have encountered great obstacles. Besides ... I had no wood, no ropes, and the region had no workman who could put it together.'[7]

Nevertheless, Flandin was determined to reach the inscriptions. 'I wanted to make an attempt', he explained, 'to try to climb the polished and perpendicular rocks by the aid of some fissures that afforded a means of support. I left my shoes, so as not to slip, I hung on by my hands and feet to all the rough patches that I was able to seize hold of. In this way I climbed the rock with difficulty, stopping after each burst in order to prepare for a new exertion, and fearing, with every movement, that I would be hurtled to the bottom. I don't know how long it took to get to my goal, but it seemed to me to be a long time, and I was fearing I would not succeed when I felt under my hand the edge of the ledge. Not before time, because my tired, grazed fingers had no more strength to haul me up . . . I had bloody feet and hands. At last I was on the projecting rock, below the inscriptions that I could clearly see. I took a quick breath, after which I examined the engraved tablets. What sorrow I had, after going to so much trouble, on realizing that it was impossible to take a copy. This impossibility resulted from the height that they were still at, as well as the narrowness of the ledge on which I found myself forced against the rock, without being able to move back a single inch. I had therefore climbed the mountain for nothing, and the reward for my troubles was that I could only state simply that the inscriptions are all cuneiform, engraved in seven columns, each containing 99 lines, and that above the figures, there are several more little groups of similar characters.'[8]

Flandin might have been even more despondent if he had known that Rawlinson had already recorded all this information – and much more besides. 'But that wasn't all,' Flandin complained, 'the most difficult thing was to return back down. I was at a height of 25 metres, and I could not think of any way of climbing down other than backwards, taking hold of and gripping the rock with my fingernails, as I had done in climbing up: this was really like the gymnastics of a lizard. I was therefore very happy to reach the bottom, but wounded, cut by the sharp angles of stones, completely torn and bloody.'[9]

Several years later, in 1850, Rawlinson recorded that the task of climbing this precipice was not especially challenging: 'Notwithstanding that a French antiquarian commission in Persia described it a few years back to be impossible to copy the Behistun inscriptions, I certainly do not consider it any great feat in climbing to ascend to the spot where the inscriptions occur. When I was living in Kermanshah fifteen years ago, and was somewhat more active than I am at present, I used frequently to scale the rock three or four times a day without the aid of a rope or ladder:

without any assistance, in fact, whatever.'[10] With the age-old rivalry between the French and English, Rawlinson was doubtless playing down the daunting task, but the very fact that he had the skill and stamina to repeat such a climb, day after day, speaks for itself.

By mid-summer 1836, Rawlinson had sufficient cuneiform copied to be able to compare the Elwand and Bisitun inscriptions. Although he had not yet seen Grotefend's publication, he later realized that he followed the same method of analysis of working out values of cuneiform signs, because he deduced that the Persian equivalents of the names Hystaspes, Darius and Xerxes would be present in the inscription: 'It would be fatiguing to detail the gradual progress which I made . . . The collation of the two first paragraphs of the great Behistun Inscription with the tablets of Elwend supplied me, in addition to the names of Hystaspes, Darius, and Xerxes, with the native forms of Arsames, Ariaramnes, Teispes, Achaemenes, and Persia, and thus enabled me to construct an alphabet which assigned the same determinate values to eighteen characters that I still retain after three years of further investigation.'[11]

He wrote to his sister Maria in early July of his ambitions and progress: 'My antiquarian studies go on quietly and smoothly, and despite the taunt which you may remember once expressing of the presumption of an ignoramus like myself attempting to decypher inscriptions which had baffled for centuries the most learned men in Europe, I have made very considerable progress in ascertaining the relative value of the characters.'[12] Since his stay in Baghdad a few months earlier, he no longer felt so isolated: 'Now that I am assisted by the erudition of my neighbour Colonel Taylor of Baghdad, the best scholar living probably in the ancient languages of the East, I aspire to do for the cuneiform alphabet what Champollion has done for the hieroglyphics – when you hear the archaeologists of Europe enquire who this Rawlinson is who has shed so extraordinary a light over ancient history both sacred and profane, you will probably feel a thrill of greater pleasure than in acknowledging yourself the sister of the madcap . . . My character is one of restless, insatiable ambition – in whatever sphere I am thrown my whole spirit is absorbed in an eager struggle for the first place – hitherto the instability of youth has defeated all my ends, but now that advancing years are shedding their quietizing influence over my mind, I trust to be able to concentrate my energies as to proceed steadily and surely to the goal ... I am now therefore compelled to rest upon my oars until the arrival of the works I have commissioned from England opens a new field to my enquiry or I can steal a fortnight's leave to gallop to Baghdad and cull fresh honey from the treasures of Col. Taylor's library.'[13]

His studies were brought to an abrupt halt in the late summer when he was ordered to march his regiment of Guran Kurds to Tehran to join Muhammed Shah's forces, who were ready to subjugate unruly tribes in the north-east. He left Kermanshah in August, and at the Shah's camp near Tehran he was allowed to retain command of the Gurans: 'I paraded the new Regiment before the Shah to his extreme delight as it was composed of good fighting Kurds – who had never before been at the Royal head Quarters.'[14] The army moved on to the frontier with Afghanistan, but it was discovered that the Shah's real intention was to besiege the Afghan city of Herat once again – his earlier siege having broken up after the death of Fath Ali Shah. An outbreak of cholera provided the excuse for the British detachment to withdraw immediately.

Rawlinson made his way to Tehran where he spent a few days, until ordered to rejoin Bahram Mirza who was camped near Isfahan. Shortly afterwards they returned to Kermanshah, reaching the town in late November, and the following month his sergeant, George Page, was married with Rawlinson's consent to an Armenian woman by the name of Anna. Because his troops were sent back to their homes for the winter, Rawlinson was now able to concentrate on his cuneiform studies. With access to a library at Tehran he had managed to become acquainted for the first time with the research of Grotefend and Saint-Martin and was fairly dismissive of their work. 'I found the Cuneiform alphabets and translations which had been adopted in Germany and France,' he noted, 'but far from deriving any assistance from either of these sources, I could not doubt that my own knowledge of the character, verified by its application to many names which had not come under the observation of Grotefend and Saint Martin, was much in advance of their respective, and in some measure conflicting, systems of interpretation.'[15]

Unfortunately, rather than announce his own results on Old Persian, Rawlinson admitted he did not feel sufficiently confident to do so: 'As there were many letters, however, regarding which I was still in doubt, and as I had made very little progress in the language of the inscriptions, I deferred the announcement of my discoveries, until I was in a better condition to turn them to account.'[16] So far, he had worked out the values of eighteen signs, using proper names such as Darius, but had not managed to translate anything. The decipherment of cuneiform was a twofold process: transliteration and translation. First of all, it was necessary to work out what the signs meant – did they represent a single alphabetical letter, a syllable or a whole word? Once this was established, they were converted or transliterated to a Roman alphabet, and the resulting foreign words could be translated, but for this a knowledge of related languages, dead and living, was essential. The process is the same as, for example, the ancient Greek πεντε being transliterated to *pente* and then translated as 'five'.

By now, Rawlinson knew enough about the problems of cuneiform decipherment to realize that what was hindering progress was the lack of a long inscription; the obvious solution was to copy as much as possible of the nearby Bisitun monument. Early in 1837 he began to make daily visits there from Kermanshah to gather more lines of the Old Persian inscription. He was unable to copy every line, because parts were severely eroded or inaccessible, but while perched on the narrow ledge on the cliff face he did succeed in copying the entire first column, the opening paragraph of the second, ten paragraphs of the third column, and four separate inscriptions accompanying the relief sculptures – in all, over two hundred lines of Old Persian cuneiform. At this stage, Rawlinson may have used a telescope to help copy the upper parts of this 12-foot-high inscription, as he does not mention ladders.

This work was brought to a halt again because Bahram Mirza, under whom Rawlinson had been serving for nearly two years, fell out of favour with his brother the Shah and was recalled to Tehran, to be replaced in February by a Georgian eunuch called Manuchar Khan. Problems immediately arose from the appointment of this new governor, who was hated and feared for his cruelty. In March, Rawlinson was ordered by the Persian government at Tehran to prepare five regiments, each with over a thousand men, in readiness for service, and so he wrote to Manuchar Khan for assistance and support in recruiting, drilling, clothing and equipping troops. Receiving only evasive replies and being pressed by the Prime Minister, he complained directly to Tehran, sending copies of his correspondence. Manuchar Khan was reprimanded, and Rawlinson was ordered by the Shah himself to despatch two regiments to the capital when ready.

Although Rawlinson appeared to be hard-working and professional, he held a harsher view of himself, as seen in his private journal entry written at Kermanshah on 11 April, his twenty-seventh birthday. 'Let me probe my soul to the quick,' he began. 'What am I and what am I likely to become? In character, unsteady, indolent but ambitious – in faith – a direct infidel – in feelings callous as a stone – in principle like my neighbours, neither too good nor too bad – with some talent and more reputation for it – culpably wasteful and extravagant and incapable of forming and adhering to any fixed purpose on a single subject.'[17] It is noticeable, though, that in assessing his prospects, his army career was not mentioned, being evidently of far lesser importance to him than his studies. 'I am now engaged in a circle of study so vested with Oriental literature and archaeology, but I suspect I am too volatile to enable me to distinguish myself in a faith which of all others requires clever and diligent attention ... I have no fixed aim for myself, but I write and read with a sort of instinctive longing to do something to attract the attention of the world.'[18] Far removed from the eyes of his superiors, Rawlinson noted in this journal entry that a female companion (certainly a local woman) 'enlivens my solitude, and I have never yet even put it to myself whether such a connection is criminal or not'.[19]

In mid-May Rawlinson left Kermanshah for the hills to assemble troops from the Guran inhabitants, but only a few days later was ordered by Manuchar Khan to engage in military action on the Turkish border near Zohab, as Persian merchants had been attacked by marauding tribes. With 1,500 cavalry and foot soldiers, he headed into a difficult situation, and after some exchange of fire and loss of life, Rawlinson was forced to remain there for three weeks to attempt to resolve the problem diplomatically. Impressing on Manuchar Khan that the British government did not allow him to fight Turkish subjects, he was instructed to return to Kermanshah, and for the last two weeks of June he prepared one new regiment for departure to Tehran. He repeatedly warned Manuchar Khan that the troops should be paid, but to no avail, and it was no surprise when they deserted and returned to their homes in the hills and mountains. The tribal chiefs were induced by Manuchar Khan to send back the recruits, and Sergeant Page was ordered to accompany them to Tehran two weeks later, with the expectation of appealing to the Shah for settlement of their arrears of pay. On arriving at the capital, the Shah had already left for his campaign, so once again the troops mutinied and returned to their homes.

Rawlinson had remained in Kermanshah to collect together the second regiment, but warned Manuchar Khan that these troops were disaffected because they had been badly treated when serving with the Shah in north-east Persia the year before. At a critical moment, Rawlinson went down with an attack of malaria, and the troops took a solemn oath not to march to Tehran, and then deserted. He was sent to bring them back, but once aware of their oath, he realized it was an impossible situation. On 1 September he received an order from the Shah to join the royal camp immediately, but for Rawlinson, now obsessed with cuneiform, the first priority was 'spending my last week at Bisitun completing my copy of the Inscriptions'.[20]

Seven: Royal Societies

On his arrival at Tehran, Rawlinson learned that Muhammed Shah had already left with his army for the planned expedition to the north-east. Because the British were alarmed that the Shah was being urged by the Russians to resume their attack on Herat, just over the border in Afghanistan, the British Envoy at Tehran, John McNeill, had prevented any of the British detachment from accompanying the Shah. Known as the 'Gateway to Afghanistan', Herat was also a gateway to India, and there was fear that its capture would enable the Russians to expand their influence throughout western Afghanistan and threaten British interests in neighbouring India.

In the eighteenth century, the Afghan Empire extended into parts of modern-day Iran, Pakistan and India – including Kashmir, Punjab, Baluchistan and Sind. Ruled by the Sadozai dynasty, this powerful empire controlled trade routes between Persia, India, Turkestan and central Asia, but by the early nineteenth century the empire had shrunk and fragmented through civil war into several independent regions. When Muhammed Shah was planning to capture Herat, that city was still under the Sadozai ruler Shah Kamran, while Muhammedzai rulers had seized control elsewhere, with Dost Mohammed Khan at Kabul and three half-brothers (the 'Dil' brothers) at Kandahar. At the same time that Rawlinson was ordered to the royal camp by the Shah of Persia, Lord Auckland, the Governor-General of India, had sent a mission to Kabul under Captain Alexander Burnes in an attempt to persuade Dost Mohammed to act in the British interest. A few years older than Rawlinson, Burnes was similar in many ways, having entered the East India Company army as a cadet at Bombay at the age of sixteen, with an enthusiasm and mastery of Hindustani, Persian and Arabic that enabled his career to progress rapidly. With the British involved with both Persia and Afghanistan, a complex situation was developing.

As Russian influence in Persian affairs was suspected, McNeill found it useful to allow Rawlinson to catch up with the Shah, as originally directed, and so he rode night and day on virtually unserviceable post-horses. After a week, on 8 October 1837, Rawlinson stumbled across the first evidence of a Russian connection with the Shah of Persia and with Dost Mohammed at Kabul: 'Our whole party were pretty well knocked up; and in the dark, between sleeping and waking, we managed to lose the road. As morning dawned, we found ourselves wandering about on the broken plain . . . and shortly afterwards we perceived that we were close to another party of horsemen . . . I was not anxious to accost these strangers, but on cantering past them, I saw, to my astonishment, men in Cossack dresses . . . I thought it my duty, therefore, to try and unravel the mystery. Following the party, I tracked them for some distance along the high road, and then found that they had turned off to a gorge in the hills. There at length I came upon the group seated at breakfast by the side of a clear, sparkling rivulet . . . I addressed him [the officer] in French – the general language of communication between Europeans in the East – but he shook his head . . . All I could find out was, that he was a *bona fide* Russian officer, carrying presents from the Emperor [Tsar Nicholas I] to Mohammed Shah.'[1]

That evening Rawlinson met up with the Shah in his new camp close to the Afghan border. Rawlinson was completely exonerated for the dispute with Manuchar Khan, and the Shah appointed him to the post of Custodian of the Arsenal at Tehran, with responsibility for training new recruits. On mentioning that the Russian officer was bringing him presents, the Shah exclaimed: 'Bringing presents to me! Why, I have nothing to do with him;

he is sent direct from the Emperor to Dost Muhammed of Cabul, and I am merely asked to help him on his journey.'[2] Two days later, the Russians turned up at the camp, and the officer Rawlinson had met on the road was introduced as Captain Vitkievitch, who now managed to converse in fluent French. In order to warn McNeill of the ominous mission of the Russians to Kabul, which would prove an even greater threat to India than the capture of Herat, Rawlinson returned to Tehran a few days later in what became a famous epic ride of 750 miles accomplished in 150 consecutive hours. His discoveries would precipitate the first Anglo-Afghan War.

At the end of the year Vitkievitch reached Kabul only to find that Burnes had for the last few weeks been in talks with Dost Mohammed. Three years earlier the Sikh army of the Maharajah Ranjit Singh had captured the city of Peshawar, incorporating it into his Punjab Empire. He now threatened to march up the Khyber Pass and take Kabul, so Dost Mohammed wanted the support of the British to regain Peshawar and also to prevent his half-brothers at Kandahar entering into an alliance with the Shah of Persia, who had begun to besiege Herat in November and was promising them that city in return for their support. Because Vitkievitch was also offering Dost Mohammed financial aid to regain Peshawar, Burnes advised the British government that they should do everything possible to assist Dost Mohammed in Afghanistan in order to keep the Russians at bay, while McNeill in Tehran largely supported these views, believing that a united Afghanistan would be better security against Persia and Russia.

Newly promoted to the rank of Major, Rawlinson was now involved with duties at the Arsenal at Tehran, but the task was not running smoothly. When recalled from Kermanshah by the Shah, Rawlinson had sent a copy of the order to his commanding officer, Lieutenant-Colonel Benjamin Shee, who had replaced Lindesay-Bethune the year before. On Rawlinson's return to Tehran from the royal camp in late October, he found a letter from Shee asking for an explanation of his activities in Kermanshah over the last few months. In the ensuing exchange of correspondence, Shee accused Rawlinson of wrong-doing and disobedience, and objected especially to his appointment at the Arsenal. Rawlinson was furious, and on 10 January 1838 Shee informed him that 'the whole of this correspondence will form the subject of my next Report to India'.[3] It must have been very satisfying to receive notification from Shee on 16 February that: 'I have the honor to send you a Royal Firman transmitted to me by the Military Secretary of Her Britannic Majesty's Embassy at the Court of Persia – appointing you to the superintendence of the Arsenal and to drill recruits in Tahran.'[4]

Rawlinson's duties were nevertheless not onerous, leaving him much time for studying. His first task was to compose a formal account of his Zohab to Susa expedition, which was published by the Royal Geographical Society at London in their journal for 1839. He also began to look at cuneiform again. Although he had copies of far more inscriptions than any other researcher, he had no access to the most recent research: 'I was still under the impression that Cuneiform discovery in Europe was in the same imperfect state in which it had been left at the period of Saint Martin's decease [in 1832].'[5] Without full knowledge of what other scholars had subsequently done, Rawlinson was working in a vacuum, but he did succeed in translating several paragraphs of the Bisitun inscription. His method of working was to transcribe the Old Persian signs into Roman characters, and then translate this version into English.

On 1 January 1838, at the age of twenty-seven, Rawlinson sent the translation of the first two paragraphs of Bisitun to the Royal Asiatic Society in London, with an accompanying letter in which he explained: 'I avail myself of the kindness of my friend Mr McNeill [the Envoy] in giving me a note of introduction to you to open a correspondence on the subject of some very interesting researches in which I am now engaged in this country and the results of which I am anxious to communicate to the world thro the Journal of the Royal Asiatic Society. On my arrival in Persia about four years ago, I applied myself with diligence to the study of the history, geography, literature and antiquities of the country. The latter field of research as being the least cultivated I found possessed of the most interest, and at an early stage of my enquiry, I could not of course but recognise the great importance of the Arrow headed inscriptions, the most ancient historical records that we possess in Persia . . . If you consider the subject of sufficient interest to be laid before the Society in its present incomplete state, I shall have much pleasure, when I receive your answer, in forwarding a statement of my researches as far as at the time they may extend. I anticipate the most extraordinary results, as far as the elucidation of ancient history is concerned from the interpretation of these inscriptions.'[6]

Rawlinson also explained in his letter that he had seen the results of Grotefend and Saint-Martin, but that much of the work of these two scholars was flawed, and that out of forty Old Persian cuneiform signs, he had discovered the meaning of around thirty and was also analysing the language, using clues from Zend and Sanskrit. He went on to describe how the inscription at Bisitun related the eastern victories of Darius and said that he was working on its most simple script. For now, he sent the society a transcription and translation of the opening two paragraphs (the titles and genealogy of Darius the Great), with a promise to send much more if they were interested.

The long letter was received in London in March. While other scholars in Europe were unknown to Rawlinson, he himself was unknown in England. The reply to him in early April by Major-General John Briggs, Secretary of the Royal Asiatic Society, demonstrated the genuine interest and enthusiasm of the society and a willingness to encourage and guide this young scholar 'removed from the information which European libraries and scholars might afford you if on the spot'.[7] Briggs first of all emphasized 'that the Society is extremely happy to learn from you that there is a prospect of obtaining the contents of the cuneiform tablets . . . and it will thankfully receive and publish anything new which you may have the goodness to send on the subject'.[8] Briggs went on to say that he had written to Dr Julius Mohl of Paris, an Oriental scholar who had been acquainted with Saint-Martin, entreating him to contact Eugène Burnouf, 'one of the most profound Oriental scholars in Europe, and I believe the last who has occupied himself in translating the cuneiform character. He has succeeded in making out (according to his own alphabet, and from his thorough acquaintance with the Sanscrit and Zend languages) two inscriptions, one procured at Murghab, near Hamadan [Elwand], and the other at Van ... His alphabet differs from that of Professor Grotefend and M. St. Martin, and, as you have both these, I believe, I now send that of Burnouf, showing the differences between it and those of his predecessors in the same study.'[9]

There was a genuine sense of excitement as word about Rawlinson's achievements spread through the academic community, and a few days later his translation was exhibited to the Société Asiatique in Paris. His work was perceived to be so pioneering that, on 21 April, the Royal Asiatic Society informed him that he had been elected an honorary Corresponding Member, and the Société Asiatique did the same soon after. Mohl and Burnouf also sent copies of additional relevant publications to London for the Royal Asiatic Society to forward to Rawlinson.

At a meeting in London in May, the Royal Asiatic Society recorded: 'Among other subjects of congratulation the Council cannot refrain from noticing the discovery made by our countryman, Major RAWLINSON, (at present in the army of the King of Persia) of vast tablets existing in various parts of that country, covered with cuneiform inscriptions, some of which contain a thousand lines each. The Society is aware of the efforts which have been made by some of the most learned Orientalists in Europe to decipher these inscriptions – efforts in which they have only partially succeeded hitherto, but which, through the energy of Major Rawlinson, and the aid of which he will be able to avail himself in the published Transactions of Messrs. Grotefend, St. Martin, Klaproth, Müller, Rask, Bellino, and Eugene Burnouf, may, it is hoped, be crowned with success.'[10]

Their report continued with the significance of Rawlinson's discoveries: 'A remarkable feature in the translation of a portion of one of these inscriptions, sent to the Society by Major Rawlinson, is the fact that the genealogy of a race of kings found on a tablet (which records, as he informs us, the conquests of Darius Hystaspes), corresponds very closely with the list of the same line of monarchs given in the seventh chapter of the second book of Herodotus. It is not, therefore, too much to hope that at no distant period, the mysteries of these inscriptions may be developed, and it seems probable these interesting monuments may throw additional light on the ancient history of Persia, beyond what has been transmitted to us by Greek authors.'[11]

Scholars were especially willing to extend every assistance to Rawlinson, because of the prospect of verifying Herodotus and increasing their knowledge of ancient Persia. They had no idea that the decipherment of cuneiform would also lead to momentous revelations about virtually unknown civilizations in Assyria and Babylonia. The society announced that Rawlinson had been urged 'to devote himself, in the first place, to obtain copies of all the cuneiform inscriptions which are procurable in Persia, and to send one set for deposit in this Society'.[12] A long relationship with the society developed, with Rawlinson frequently communicating his latest results by letter.

That summer, on 28 June 1838, the coronation of Queen Victoria took place in London, while in Tehran, Rawlinson received Burnouf's report on the Elwand inscriptions, *Mémoire sur deux Inscriptions Cuneiformes trouvés près d'Hamadan*, that had been published two years earlier. He was disappointed to discover that he was not the first to copy and study this inscription and that Burnouf had pre-empted his own work. In the report, Burnouf discussed the work of other scholars on Old Persian cuneiform and reproduced the alphabet that Saint-Martin had worked out, commenting: 'M. Saint-Martin assured me more than once that he believed his system of decipherment beyond criticism, at least in its general results. According to him, what still needed to be made clear were both the language in which these inscriptions was written ... and the two other systems of writing to which he had given the names *Median* and *Assyrian*.'[13] Nevertheless,

Burnouf suggested a new alphabet of his own, thirty letters in all with three uncertain ones.

Rawlinson's own work did not completely coincide with Burnouf's, and he disputed several points: 'The memoir of M. Burnouf on the Inscriptions of Hamadán [Elwand] . . . showed me that I had been anticipated in the announcement of many of the improvements that I had made on the system of M. Saint Martin, but I still found several essential points of difference between the Paris alphabet and that which I had formed from the writing at Behistun, and my observations on a few of these points of difference I at once submitted to M. Burnouf.'[14] On 30 July Rawlinson wrote again to the Royal Asiatic Society, enclosing a long letter to Burnouf in Paris, which gave his own Old Persian alphabet and extensive copies of the cuneiform inscription at Bisitun. He explained to the Royal Asiatic Society that he was waiting to receive Burnouf's report on the Yasna 'before I forward you my copy and attempted translation of the great Bisitoon inscription. I have still thought it advisable to lose no time in putting myself in communication with that gentleman with a view to defining the exact points of coincidence and variance between our respective alphabets of the Cuneiform character. I have therefore written him a letter upon the subject which I forward to your address, and as it is possible that discussions may hereafter arise regarding the priority of claim to the determination of certain characters, perhaps you will kindly allow the letter to be copied and preserved among the records of your society.'[15] Rawlinson explained that once he had received the Yasna and tested various points, 'I trust to be able to bring my remarks on the Bisitoon Inscription to a state that will enable me to send off a considerable portion of the copy and translation by the next courier'.[16]

In fact, Burnouf's *Commentaire sur le Yaçna* arrived that same day, and later Rawlinson wrote that 'I there, for the first time, found the language of the Zend Avesta critically analyzed, and its orthographic and grammatical structure clearly and scientifically developed'.[17] While he concentrated on Avestan (what he called Zend), Rawlinson learned much more about the language of Old

Persian, appreciating that Avestan would give clues about vocabulary and grammatical structure. He began to progress beyond Burnouf's achievements and seriously confronted Old Persian as a language, not just as a cuneiform script.

A few months earlier McNeill had gone to the Shah's camp outside Herat in Afghanistan in an effort to persuade him to lift the siege and, Rawlinson noted, 'left the confidential direction of the Legative affairs in my hands'.[18] Having failed in his mission, McNeill returned to Tehran in June and subsequently led the British detachment to Tabriz near the Turkish frontier, with a view to quitting Persia. At the same time Lord Auckland sent a force from India, which occupied the strategically important island of Karak in the Persian Gulf and was threatening to invade the Persian mainland. The siege at Herat dragged on, with the Persian army making little progress, but when news of the British threat reached Herat in mid-August, the Shah was so alarmed that he abandoned the ten-month siege in early September. No good reason remained for the British to intervene in Afghanistan, especially as any real threat from Russia had now evaporated under British pressure. The Russians recalled their agent Vitkievitch, officially reprimanding him, and Rawlinson recorded that 'not having accomplished all that had been expected of him, [he] was disavowed on his return to St Petersburg, and blew his brains out'.[19]

Although the problem had been resolved, Lord Auckland was intent on interfering in Afghanistan. Earlier in the year he had ignored the advice of Burnes to support Dost Mohammed at Kabul, but instead followed the advice of William Macnaghten, who was Chief Secretary of the Calcutta government. Support was guaranteed for the exiled Sadozai ruler of Afghanistan, Shah Shuja, and a treaty was signed between Shah Shuja, the Sikh leader Ranjit Singh and the British, with Shah Shuja agreeing to cede all territories that were once held by Afghanistan but were now occupied by the Sikhs, including Peshawar. At the summer capital of Simla in northern India, in the foothills of the Himalayas, Lord Auckland issued on 1 October 1838 what was in effect a declaration of war on the states of Kabul and Kandahar. It became known as the Simla Manifesto and was an attempt to justify an invasion of Afghanistan.

While based at Tabriz, Rawlinson received permission to undertake an expedition to explore north-west Persia that he had planned, but first of all he sent a letter to the Royal Asiatic Society apologizing for not sending the Bisitun inscription, but the troubled state of Persia made it too difficult. On 16 October he left the camp, and his journey over the next few weeks took him south and south-east of Tabriz, constantly compiling notes on the antiquities, villages, tribes and countryside. This time he was on his own, without the backing of an army of a few thousand men – a hazardous undertaking in which he relied on local guides. After two days he stopped at a village near Lake Urmia, where 'Melik Kásim Mírzá, a son of the late Sháh of Persia . . . has built himself a palace in the European style near the village . . . To great intelligence and enterprise he unites a singular taste for the habits of European life, and the cultivation of many useful arts which belong to European civilization.'[20]

The following day was spent with the prince, 'giving him such information and assistance as I was able in his various objects of pursuit. His acquaintance with European languages is extensive. Of French he is a perfect master; and in English and Russian he converses with much fluency. His habits of domestic life are also entirely European: he wears European clothes, breakfasts and dines in the European style; and, as far as regards himself, has adopted our manners, to the minutest point of observance; and this singular transition – a change which a person accustomed to the contrasts of European and Oriental life can alone appreciate – has arisen entirely from his own unbiased choice, and without his having had either means or inducement to effect it beyond his occasional intercourse with European society at Tabríz.'[21] Rawlinson confessed that the village 'presents a phenomenon in social life, which I should little have expected to meet with in Persia; and when I reflect that moral development can alone proceed from an improvement in the social condition, I fervently hope that the prince may have many imitators, and that a brighter day may thus be opening upon Persia.'[22] Like many Victorians, Rawlinson believed that the adoption of European values could only bring about an improvement in the way of life.

The region south-west of Lake Urmia, near the Turkish border, had seen very few Europeans, and Rawlinson noted that its Kurdish tribesmen 'are a remarkably fine, active, and athletic race, and are, perhaps, the most warlike of the many warlike clans who inhabit this part of Persia. From their exposed position, indeed, upon the immediate frontier of Turkish Kurdistán, they are constantly engaged in frays with the wild tribes who inhabit the neighbouring mountains; and I saw several of the chiefs who wore their shirts of mail day and night, and always kept their horses ready saddled, not knowing at what moment they might be called on to sally forth and repel a foray. Their common weapon is a spear, and they are loth to give it up; but finding that the mountain clans with whom they engage have almost universally adopted the use of fire-arms, they are beginning gradually to follow their example.'[23]

In the mountains of this border region, Rawlinson was held up for two days by bad weather. He wanted to climb to the highest point of the Kal-i Shin mountain, where he had heard of an inscription on a pillar of rock, 'the stories of which had long excited my curiosity'.[24] His efforts to reach the monument indicate his complete dedication and his physical skill. Because of the region's warlike tribes, it was only possible to reach the spot when they had moved away from the area and before winter weather set in: 'The only times at which the mountain can be ascended in safety are the first fortnight in October, and the last in March. I was now ten days too late in the season, and the Khán strove hard to dissuade me from making the attempt; but as I had come so great a distance for the express purpose, I was determined that nothing should stop me but the absolute impracticability of the ascent. This morning accordingly, when the weather fortunately cleared, and the wind, which had been blowing furiously for the two preceding days, appeared to have exhausted itself, I set out, attended by two horsemen, well mounted, well wrapped up, and with every defence against the snow-drift, which I was told I should certainly encounter at the summit.'[25]

After 5 miles, they entered the snow, and 'the difficulties commenced: the ravines which indented the face of the shoulder became, as we ascended higher, choked with snow, and in one of them we narrowly escaped being engulphed.'[26] Alternately riding and walking for four hours, they reached the famous pillar, and Rawlinson found it to be dark blue in colour, about 6 feet high, with a cuneiform inscription of forty-one lines on one face. 'I had come prepared to take a copy of the inscription,' he related, 'but, much to my regret, I found this now to be quite impracticable. On breaking away the sheet of icicles with which the surface of the stone was covered, the upper half of the inscription was shown to be irrevocably obliterated, and the lower half also to be so much destroyed that, except under a very favourable aspect of the sun . . . it would be impossible to distinguish half a dozen consecutive letters: an impression on moist paper was also of course impracticable, when the thermometer stood at 20 degrees below freezing point; so I could do nothing more than copy a few characters, to determine the class of writing to which the inscription belongs, and measure the dimensions of the pillar.'[27] The pillar was in fact set up in the late ninth century BC by Ishpuini, King of Urartu, and his co-regent and son Menua, not long after cuneiform had been adopted for the Urartian language. The inscription was bilingual, in Urartian and Assyrian cuneiform.

The danger of reaching the monument, Rawlinson explained, 'arises not so much from the depth of snow (for an active mountaineer, by threading his way along the most exposed points, can generally avoid this difficulty), as from the violent and deadly drifts which keep continually sweeping over the face of the mountains during the greater part of the winter months . . . a winter is never known to elapse without several persons being lost here in the snow. From the frequency of these accidents an extraordinary degree of dread and mystery is attached to the pass; and in the superstition of the Kurds, this feeling connects itself with the talisman of the Keli-Shín [the pillar with its inscription], which is supposed to have been created by some potent magician, to afford the means of protection against danger, but which, its use being now unknown, only serves to lure fresh victims to destruction.'[28] Anxious for their safety, Rawlinson's guide was urging him to hurry, 'for the wind had been gradually rising; and another half hour, he assured me, would bring on one of the fatal drifts. I thus only delayed to take a few bearings, and have one glimpse from the point of the pass of the magnificent mountain scenery.'[29]

Rawlinson was not the first European to have reached the monument, because he learned that Schulz, who had been recording inscriptions for the French government, had copied much of the inscription on his final journey, shortly before he was murdered. Because the area was so remote and the warlike tribes especially menacing, Rawlinson noted that 'no other European has, I believe, seen this singular relic of antiquity'.[30] He offered some advice to future travellers on how to avoid being attacked: 'Much curiosity, I am aware, is alive at present regarding the antiquities and geography of Kurdistán . . . I consider attempting to visit Kurdistán in any disguise as quite impracticable, the protection of a government, either Turkish or Persian, is fraught also with danger rather than advantage. The most safe, and at the same time the most agreeable way of travelling in Kurdistán would be to visit, in the first place, a frontier chief, whose connexion with his government, either Turkish or Persian, would oblige him to assist and protect the European recommended to his care; this chief then would be able, from his connexion with the tribes in the vicinity to pass the traveller on to another chief in the interior, and from thence, availing himself of the same means of protection, he might penetrate to still more remote regions . . . indeed, I was assured at Ushneï that the tragic death of the lamented Schultz was owing entirely to this cause – when he visited Ushneï, Semed Khan, the Governor, offered to send an escort of his own Zerzá Jurds with him to Júlámerik, detaining a nephew of the Hekárrí chief, who was with him at the time upon a visit as security for his safe return: Schultz unfortunately declined this offer, and preferred the direct protection of the Persian government through the Afshár chief of Urumíyah; he consequently returned to that place, and took with him as his guide an Afshár soldier, hateful to the Hekárrís, as well from being the servant of the Persian government, as from belonging to a tribe opposed to them in nation, in language, and in religion, and with whom they were constantly at feud. Schultz was thus regarded by the Hekárrís as a government emissary, and his enquiries about antiquities were explained by his supposed errand to survey the country and discover the best route for the Persian guns.'[31]

Rawlinson had developed a deep understanding of the social structure of the tribes in these remote regions and an increasing knowledge of their dialects, which eased his passage through unfamiliar territory. He much preferred to be in their company than in the cities: 'I had no reason to complain of want of courtesy, but, I confess, the rough sterling kindness of the tribes has always pleased me far better than the jaunty bearing of the city fashionables.'[32]

Having reached the border with Turkish Arabia, Rawlinson headed back eastwards, taking a different route, and after twelve days, on 8 November, he reached the ruins of Takht-i Suleiman, overlooking a lake that legend declared was bottomless. This was one of the most important late Sasanian religious centres of Zoroastrianism, with a fire temple where a fire for the warriors burned constantly. Rawlinson found out that 'the common popular tradition regarding the ruins of Takhti-Soleïmán ascribes the foundation of the palace to Solomon, the son of David. He is believed to have here held his regal court, and to have invited the queen of Sheba, whom the easterns name Balkís, to visit him at the Takht, from her palace in the city of Ushneï.'[33]

A few miles further on, Rawlinson recorded: 'I heard wonderful accounts of an inscription in an unknown character, which was to be found upon a neighbouring hill, and the clue to which was kept with the greatest secrecy, as it was supposed to contain a talisman for discovering the entrance to some inexhaustible mine in the vicinity . . . my curiosity was not, I confess, a little excited when I found that some Feringí [foreign] traveller, who, from the description, I at once recognised to be Schultz, had been actually detained here for three days searching for the tablet; and after every endeavour to obtain a sight of it by bribes and persuasion, had at last left the place without being able to effect his purpose.'[34]

Rawlinson discovered the whereabouts of the inscription from an old holy man, but claimed he was not especially interested in seeing it, thinking that Schulz had doubtless appeared too eager. The next day he wandered about the hillside looking in vain for the inscription among many disused mine shafts, but eventually the old man revealed its location, and 'when I was at last summoned to behold and explain the talisman, I found it to be mere common Arabic writing, very rudely cut, and so nearly obliterated as to have appeared to the ignorant Afshárs like an unknown character'.[35] Rawlinson recorded this story 'as a lesson to travellers in Persia, to be very cautious in trusting to the hearsay evidence of their guides; it is impossible to feel any certainty, with regard to inscriptions or other remains of antiquity, without personal examination'.[36]

Safely back at Tehran after his expedition, Rawlinson was summoned in mid-November 1838 to Resht on the Caspian Sea by McNeill, who was there conducting negotiations with the Persian Court following the Shah's abandonment of the siege of Herat. The discussions came to nothing, and McNeill formally broke off diplomatic relations with Persia and left for Constantinople, while Rawlinson accompanied the other officers of the British detachment to Baghdad, in Turkish territory, arriving there early in 1839 after a difficult winter journey through the mountains. He had been in Persia for over five years and had made a considerable impact. A report in *The Times* observed that travellers to that country a few years later 'found that one Englishman had left such a name among every class of society that a letter from him would have been a passport throughout the whole of Persia. That gentleman was Major Rawlinson, of Bagdad, who was supposed to be gifted with almost supernatural powers, as he could dispute with the Mollahs of Ispahan, could write and speak the Persian tongue, was deeply skilled in the poetical learning of that country . . . there was no European who had made such an impression on the population of Persia, and that not merely on the learned societies or the higher and polished societies, which had been aptly called 'the French of the East,' but his influence extended to the wild chiefs of Koordistan, who respected him as the best shot and the boldest rider they had ever seen.'[37]

Rawlinson and a few other officers remained in Baghdad for many months, expecting to be recalled to Tehran. With nothing else to do, Rawlinson was able to spend much of the year in 'lettered seclusion',[38] resuming his study of Arabic and writing three papers for publication. The first was his 'Memoir on the Persian Cuneiform Inscription at Behistun' written for the Royal Asiatic Society's journal, the original intention being to combine his drawings from Bisitun with a commentary on points of interest relating to ancient Persia, such as philology, history and geography. As one who had chosen a military and not a university career, Rawlinson had few scholarly connections, and his eleven years spent in India and Persia had increased his isolation. Although he had become acquainted with the work of some other scholars, most notably Burnouf in Paris, he was still much in the dark as to what else was happening in Europe in the field of cuneiform decipherment. In April, on the eve of completing his Bisitun report and claiming the honour of being the first to decipher Old Persian cuneiform, he received a long letter from the Norwegian scholar Christian Lassen. Ten years older than Rawlinson and a professor at Bonn University, Lassen specialized in Sanskrit and Indian literature. The letter had been written many months ago in August 1838 and had been forwarded to Persia by the Royal Asiatic Society, just when Rawlinson was leaving the country. It finally caught up with him in Baghdad.

Not only had Lassen worked out the meaning of the Old Persian cuneiform signs using a very limited number of inscriptions, but Rawlinson learned that he had even published his results. Lassen explained that he was writing to Rawlinson to share information, 'not from any expectation that you would derive any great benefit from this brief sketch, being yourself so far advanced in the study of the arrow-headed characters, but merely with the hope that it might be agreeable to you to learn the state of the question as it now stands on the continent of Europe'.[39] Although this news must have been a terrible blow to Rawlinson's hopes, an exchange of amicable correspondence began. Lassen sent a summary of his own research and a detailed commentary on Burnouf's work, and Rawlinson soon saw that Lassen's decipherment 'coincided in all essential points with my own'.[40] Rawlinson was convinced that, working independently, both he and Lassen had made the breakthrough and had worked out the alphabet of the Old Persian form of cuneiform. Regrettably, Rawlinson had delayed his own publication, while Lassen had gone ahead, and Rawlinson conceded that 'I cannot pretend to contest with him the priority of alphabetical discovery'.[41] He greatly admired the work of Lassen, 'who with such very limited materials as were alone at his disposal in Europe, has still arrived at results so remarkably correct'.[42]

Undaunted, Rawlinson decided to rewrite his own report, but as he needed several books to be sent to him from England, he turned instead to writing an extensive paper on his recent expedition. This was completed in late May and published in the Royal Geographical Society's journal in 1841. His exploration and geographical research were so acclaimed that in 1840 the society awarded Rawlinson the prestigious Gold Founder's Medal. Their decision was influenced 'not merely by the zeal, perseverance, and industry with which that officer has successfully explored the provinces of Luristan, Kusistan, and Azerbijan, and the valuable additions which, in his Memoirs published in our Transactions, he has thrown on our knowledge of the physical geography of that large and important portion of the mountain-ranges which divide the basin of the Tigris from the elevated plains of Central Persia; but they have wished more particularly to give this mark of approval and regard to the vast extent of learning and historical research which Major Rawlinson has brought to bear on the objects of his geographical memoirs.'[43]

Returning to his Bisitun report, Rawlinson made contact once again with the Royal Asiatic Society on 25 July 1839, attributing his long silence to travelling in Persia and waiting for books to be sent from England, so that he could do further research on Old Persian in the light of receiving Lassen's letter. Rawlinson enclosed a draft version of his précis, or introduction, which gave a summary of large parts of the Old Persian inscription. 'Of course, I can have no objection to your reading the precis . . . to the Society,' he remarked, 'but it is written hurriedly, as you will see, without any view to publication, and before I lay myself open to Continental criticism, I am desirous to work out the enquiry in a full and satisfactory manner.'[44] He added a note that he was also looking with intense interest at the other alphabets. A month later he sent an update on his progress, that 'the intolerable heat of the Baghdad dog-days has prevented me working as steadily during the past month as I would have wished, but still I have completed a fair copy and translation of all the inscriptions'.[45] He had also completed many notes and reckoned that 'if I keep my health, I think I shall certainly be able by the next post to send the packets off to you'.[46]

This was the last time the society heard from Rawlinson for nearly six years. Of his report, he later commented: 'I might have still hoped to publish the Memoir in its amended form in the spring of 1840, had not circumstances, over which I had no control, and which I could neither have desired nor foreseen, arrested my inquiries in mid-career and superseded for a long period the possibility of their resumption.'[47] He was about to become embroiled in the First Anglo-Afghan War.

Eight: An Afghan Adventure

Tired of waiting for orders from India, Rawlinson left Baghdad on 26 October 1839 – setting out once again on his 'fatal' day and arriving at Bombay at the beginning of January 1840. He spent the following two weeks in routine duties, waiting to be recalled to Tehran, although his greatest desire was for the East India Company to give him a political appointment back in Baghdad where he could continue his cuneiform studies, so completely absorbed had he become by this pursuit over the last few months. 'I hate a Bombay life,' he wrote, 'it has not the quiet for literary work, nor sufficient excitement to afford me any gratification.'[1] To his astonishment, he was informed on the evening of 16 January that he was to go immediately to Kandahar in Afghanistan.

Over a year previously, not long after Persia gave up besieging the western Afghan city of Herat, a huge 'Army of the Indus' had set off from northern India to invade Afghanistan, with the intention of deposing Dost Mohammed and installing the exiled ruler Shah Shuja. It had been anticipated that the Sikh ruler Ranjit Singh would allow them to march across the Punjab to Peshawar, then up the Khyber Pass to Kabul, but he proved less than enthusiastic. Instead, virtually the entire army marched from Ferozepore across the harsh Sind desert to Sukkur, northwards through the Bolan Pass to Quetta, and then through the Kojuk Pass into Afghanistan. They were heading for Kabul, on a journey over twice as long as that originally planned through the Khyber Pass.

The army comprised 6,000 soldiers hired by Shah Shuja, 9,500 Bengal and 5,600 Bombay army troops (Europeans and sepoys, mostly Hindus) and forty-two artillery guns. There were huge numbers of cattle and horses, as well as a vast quantity of baggage transported on 30,000 camels, animals that were wholly unsuitable for Afghan territory, all accompanied by a staggering number of camp followers – 38,000 men, women and children. The instructions to the army had been to travel light. 'It is no unusual circumstance for subalterns, in time of war,' observed one young officer, 'to have five or six camels for the carriage of their baggage; and when such is the case, and other ranks travel in a proportionate degree of grandeur, it is easy to conceive what an unwieldy mass the baggage of an Indian army becomes.'[2]

By March 1839, while Rawlinson was immersed in his studies at Baghdad, the army reached the Bolan Pass, then advanced to Quetta and in April reached the city of Kandahar, where Shah Shuja was proclaimed ruler. The ill-conceived campaign had insufficient supplies of food and water, so that the soldiers starved and thousands of animals perished. Instead of pushing on to Kabul, the army ground to a halt at Kandahar through a lack of provisions and money and an outbreak of disease and dysentery. In June it set off again, leaving a garrison at Kandahar and a small contingent at Herat. Some 230 miles north-east of Kandahar, the virtually impregnable fortress of Ghazni (or Ghuznee) was stormed and captured – an action celebrated as a notable victory in Britain. Kabul was reached in August, but Shah Shuja was not welcomed with enthusiasm. That summer, Ranjit Singh died, and a Sikh army of 5,000 men and a force of 6,000 led by Shah Shuja's son Timur subsequently fought its way up the Khyber Pass, to join the forces in Kabul in early September. Now that Shah Shuja was installed, the Bombay army was recalled to India, but much of the Bengal army remained at Kabul under the command of Sir Willoughby Cotton.

In mid-February 1840, Rawlinson set out from Bombay by sea to Karachi, then rode to Sukkur and briefly met up with his regiment, the 1st Bombay Grenadiers. From here he travelled through the Bolan and Kojuk Passes, where the bottoms of the ravines and slopes were 'lined with the skeletons and bones of camels and horses'[3] lost by the army the year before. Due to increasing disaffection among the tribes, the countryside was very unsettled. Between Herat and Kandahar the Durrani tribes were originally supporters of Shah Shuja (because the previous ruler, Dost Mohammed, had removed many of their privileges), but their enthusiasm had turned to rebellion when his promises to them remained unfulfilled. Between Kandahar and Ghazni, the Ghilzye tribes had never accepted Shah Shuja and were waiting for a suitable moment to rebel, and in the far west, Herat remained the stronghold of the independent but elderly ruler, Shah Kamran. The Durranis and Ghilzyes were encouraging his powerful Vizier, Yar Mohammed, to revolt and attack Kandahar. Around Kabul, other tribes were in a state of ferment, and even communications with India were under threat.

When Rawlinson reached Kandahar, he stayed for a while with Major Robert Leech of the Bombay Engineers, who was the city's Political Agent (or Resident), equivalent to a diplomat, but a few weeks later Rawlinson was ordered to Kabul by the British Envoy, Sir William Macnaghten. The city of Kabul was reckoned at the time to be 'one of the most delightful in the world ... situated on a large well-watered plain, 6000 feet above the level of the sea, over which are scattered innumerable villages, the Cabùl river and three rivulets running through it. Cabùl is a busy bustling city, and boasts of a bazaar almost unrivalled, for it contains no fewer than 2000 shops ... The town is encompassed on three sides by hills, and on one of these ... is the palace of Dost Mohammed Khan ... East of Cabùl is an almost circular plain ... surrounded by the Hindoo Koosh and Soliman mountains.'[4]

The garrison at Kabul carried on their lives much as they had done in India, oblivious to the unrest around them. Many officers sent for their wives and children and, depending on the season, conducted a vigorous social life of cricket, fishing, ice skating, wrestling, cock fighting and theatrical entertainments. In addition, the 'troops were reviewed; and the officers rode races; and the Shah, ever delighting in pageantry and parade, established an order of knighthood, and held a grand Durbar, at which the ceremony of investure was performed with becoming dignity and grace. And the officers, happy in the belief that they were soon about to turn their backs on Afghanistan for ever, went about purchasing memorials of their visit to Caubul, or presents to carry back to their friends.'[5] Rawlinson cannot have failed to observe that the garrison was in a highly vulnerable position. The original plan had been to house the troops at the Bala Hissar citadel, overlooking the entire city and suburbs, but Shah Shuja had objected, so instead they were camped outside the city in extremely poorly defended cantonments.

Macnaghten ordered the thirty-year-old Rawlinson to accompany Captain Arthur Conolly, a fervent Christian, on a mission across the Hindu Kush into central Asia, where they were to visit the courts of rulers and the camp of the Russian troops, who were moving into the territory, much to the alarm of the British. When news arrived that the Russians had retreated after suffering terrible losses during dreadful winter weather, the British mission was reduced in size. Rawlinson was sent instead, at the end of June, to replace Leech as Political Agent at Kandahar. In late August, just before his departure, Conolly wrote eagerly to Rawlinson about his mission: 'It is a work which must prosper; and I only wish again that you were to be of the party to accomplish it.'[6] Unsuited to such a dangerously delicate mission, Conolly was to be brutally murdered at the court of the ruler of Kokand.

Kandahar was formerly the capital of Afghanistan, before Dost Mohammed had made Kabul the capital in 1826. Rawlinson lived inside the citadel and would soon be isolated from the army garrison, as cantonments were being constructed outside the city defences, with barracks that 'were built of mud and brick like the houses generally, wood being scarce for such a purpose'.[7] Separated from the city by an extensive plain, the cantonments were 'badly planned, and difficult, if not incapable, of defence'.[8]

Macnaghten was relying on Rawlinson's diplomatic skills and kept in close contact, saying in one worried letter in July: 'It is very consolatory to me to think that I have you at Candahar. Had Leech been in office at the present crisis, I should have been in a state of extreme disquietude.'[9]

A strong rapport also developed between Rawlinson and General William Nott, the military commander for the region. Their means of communication was also by frequent exchange of letters, and their assessment of the situation in the country was far more realistic than that of Macnaghten. An imposing figure like Rawlinson, and twenty-seven years his senior, Nott was 'an old Sepoy officer of good repute; a man of some talents, but blunt address – an honest, plain-spoken soldier, not always right, but always believing himself to be right – hearty, genuine, and sincere. His faults were chiefly those of temper.'[10]

Just before Nott had set off for Afghanistan nearly two years earlier, his beloved wife of thirty-three years had died suddenly at Delhi. He had sent his three unmarried daughters to their brother Charles, a barrister in Calcutta, and constantly wrote to them all, often revealing his harsh criticism of the government's policies and the officers of the Queen's Army. He was an East India Company army man and had a higher regard for his sepoy troops and the Afghan tribesmen than did most of his fellow-officers. In one letter he wrote: 'I like the people, in spite of all that has been said of them. True, the poorest man you can meet places himself perfectly on a par with you; but though free and bold in their remarks, there is no want of respect; so different from the mean, cringing people of Bengal. I go into their villages and their gardens for ten miles around, and I always find the people very civil . . . They are a warm and passionate people; but then they are so thoroughly *good-tempered*, and always cheerful. I must say that I like them.'[11]

In September Nott moved with part of his army from Kandahar to Quetta in order to safeguard the supply route from India by recapturing the fortress of Khelat, capital of Beluchistan, that had been taken a few weeks earlier by disaffected Beluchis. He found the expedition highly unsatisfactory, as he had insufficient troops, and at the end of the month wrote to his daughters, complaining bitterly, 'Had I been allowed to have acted on my own judgment when Khelat fell into the hands of the rebels, the fortress would now have been in my possession ... the authorities are never right, even by chance, and although most of them are stupid in the extreme, they fancy themselves great men, and even possessed of abilities and talents ... Thus it is to employ men selected by intrigue and patronage! The conduct of the *one thousand* and *one* Politicals has ruined our cause, and bared the throat of every European in this country to the sword and knife of the revengeful Affghan and bloody Belooch, and unless several regiments be quickly sent, not a man will be left to note the fall of his comrades.'[12]

Rawlinson was not included in this harsh criticism of political agents, since Nott had adopted a good impression of him, even though 'not always disposed to judge favourably by first appearances'.[13] Over the next two years Nott 'had never, upon a single occasion, the slightest reason to complain of either the presumption, the unfitness, or the interference of his political colleague. In one respect the two men were alike. They held opinions at variance with those of the Government they served. They saw the country was in a state of rebellion; they knew that the Shah (Soojah) was exceedingly disliked; and they firmly believed, that the country could only be held by the greatest caution, the most determined bravery, and the most decided distrust of the Affghans and the Beloochees.'[14]

At the beginning of December 1840, Rawlinson welcomed the arrival from Herat of Edward Mitford, the former travelling companion of Layard, the man who in five years' time would be sharing with Rawlinson the results of his incredible excavations in Assyria. After a journey of many months together, Mitford and Layard had travelled to Kermanshah and Bisitun, but they separated at Hamadan. Mitford carried on through Persia and crossed into Afghanistan, stopping first at Herat before moving on to Kandahar.

When Nott was first posted to Kandahar, he described the city in a letter to his children: 'This is a large and very filthy city, containing about 80,000 inhabitants. There is one street, quite through the city, which is some fifty or sixty feet broad; all others are narrow. The crowd is so great, that a man has difficulty in making his way.'[15] Mitford, arriving some months later, was a little less harsh: 'The city of Kandahar . . . presented much the same long line of mud wall with bastions as Herat, but [was] not elevated above the level of the plain . . .; here I found our troops, and redcoats mounting guard at the gates. I rode through the wide streets crowded with traders, Hindostanee soldiers, Afghans, etc., in every variety of costume; and made my way to the citadel, which is an inner enclosure on the north side of the town. The British Residency [where Rawlinson lived], as well as the Governor's palace, is within the citadel . . . Kandahar is nearly a mile square, protected by a moat, and surrounded on three sides by gardens and cultivation: on the north side are the cemeteries containing some elegant Moorish tombs on colonnades, railed round and planted with trees: and the white head stones indicating the graves of our own people are not wanting. Cantonments are being built outside the town on the west; in the meantime the troops are quartered in lines within the citadel . . . The town is divided by two broad streets which intersect each other in the centre and over the crossing is a large dome; the population is very dense, the town being crowded with the country people; the turban is here exchanged for a padded and embroidered chintz skull cap.'[16]

Rawlinson obviously met with Mitford's approval: 'I experienced a most friendly and kind reception from Major Rawlinson, the Political Agent, who cordially greeted me, but hearing my name, said, "Well, I never expected to see you alive." He had heard of my journey, and received various reports from natives about a wandering Englishman, but had given me up for lost.'[17] Mitford had been travelling with concealed silver and gold coins, cashing notes with the various consuls, as Constantinople had been the last city with a bank, and 'at Kandahar Sir H. Rawlinson, with open-hearted generosity, took pleasure in supplying the needs of a fellow-countryman'.[18]

In the few days that Mitford spent at Kandahar, he visited the ruins of Old Kandahar, a city that had probably been originally founded in 330 BC as Alexandria Arachosia by Alexander the Great as he swept across Persia, Afghanistan, the Hindu Kush and India. Limited excavations have since shown the city to have been built on an even earlier fortress that belonged to the Persian King Darius the Great who had also conquered this region, known then as Arachosia. His conquest of Arachosia and other regions of Afghanistan were actually recorded in the huge cuneiform inscription at Bisitun that Rawlinson had until recently been trying to understand. Cuneiform barely penetrated Afghanistan, the only evidence being less than half-a-dozen inscriptions, in Elamite and Old Persian, from Kandahar, Kabul, Bust and Herat. The Persians also introduced Aramaic, and a handful of inscriptions in this script are known, but when Alexander the Great conquered the region, Greek became the main writing system.

Although Alexander the Great's city was extremely close to Rawlinson at Kandahar, he found very little time for antiquarian research. A few months after Mitford's visit, he wrote to the Royal Geographical Society in London: 'Really and truly I cannot contrive to steal a single hour from my official duties to devote to my books or even to the arrangement of the multitudinous notes which I collected in Persia. When relieved from the official drudgery which the presence of an army entails on me at this place, you will again find me a zealous contributor to your Journal, but in the mean time you must be content to receive such occasional scraps of information as I may be able to pick up from time to time, relative to the countries in which my lot is now cast.'[19] The scraps he gave to the society on this occasion were his identification of several ruined sites he had already observed, such as Begram, to the north of Kabul, being Alexandria ad Caucasum, yet another city founded by Alexander the Great. The possibilities for research were obviously enticing, for he added: 'The valley of the Helmand . . . presents a noble field for comparative geography, and I hope to make some interesting discoveries of ancient sites ... I have not pushed my inquiries much as yet beyond the Hindú Kush, or to the westward between Afghanistan and Persia, but to the southward I have a tolerable list of identifications.'[20] Unfortunately, even if he had been allowed the time, the countryside was too dangerous to embark on expeditions such as he had undertaken in Persia.

While Mitford was still in Kandahar, Nott returned from recapturing Khelat to find that Rawlinson was even more worried by the threat posed by Yar Mohammed at Herat, who seemed to be colluding with Aktur Khan, a leader of the Durrani tribe in an area to the north-west of Kandahar. In the end, Rawlinson and Nott agreed that military action was necessary, and on 3 January 1841 a detachment of troops and artillery defeated and dispersed a force of some 1,500 Durrani cavalrymen.

Two months earlier, Dost Mohammed, the deposed ruler of Afghanistan, had unexpectedly surrendered to Macnaghten in Kabul, leading to the retirement of Sir Willoughby Cotton, who believed that his work in Afghanistan was over. Nott was the favourite to replace him as commander-in-chief, but he himself knew that he would be passed over, as his plain speaking was not appreciated. He was not surprised when the post was given to an officer of the Queen's Army, not the East India Company army. Major-General William Elphinstone, who arrived in Kabul in April 1841, was a disastrous choice, as he was already ill and had last seen active service at the Battle of Waterloo a quarter of a century previously, when Rawlinson was only five years old. At fifty-nine years of age, Elphinstone was also considered too elderly for the post, yet the energetic Nott was exactly the same age.

Added to the problems in Herat and with the Durranis, the Ghilzye tribes in the region between Kandahar, Ghazni and Kabul were becoming more violent. To Rawlinson it was obvious why British policies were failing and why the tribes were disaffected, and, along with political agents in other areas, he frequently issued warnings to Macnaghten, who was determined to discount them and became increasingly reproachful. In one letter to Rawlinson written from Kabul in mid-June, he complained, 'I don't like reverting to unpleasant discussions, but you know well that I have been frank with you from the beginning, and that I have invariably told you of what I thought I had reason to complain. This may be confined to one topic – your taking an unwarrantably gloomy view of our position, and entertaining and disseminating rumours favourable to that view. We have enough of difficulties and enough of croakers without adding to the number needlessly. I have just seen a letter from Mr Dallas to Captain Johnson, in which he says the state of the country is becoming worse and worse every day. These idle statements may cause much mischief, and, often repeated as they are, they neutralise my protestations to the contrary. I know them to be utterly false as regards this part of the country, and I have no reason to believe them to be true as regards your portion of the kingdom . . . We will take such precautions as shall prevent the Ghilzyes from annoying us; and this is all that is requisite for the present. We may safely leave the rest to time.'[21]

Rawlinson nevertheless continued to send warnings, and in early August Macnaghten again wrote to him with typical arrogance: 'You say, "The state of the country causes me many an anxious thought – we may thresh the Douranees over and over again, but this rather aggravates than obviates the difficulty of overcoming the national feeling against us – in fact, our tenure is positively that of military possession, and the French in Algiers, and the Russians in Circassia, afford us an example on a small scale of the difficulty of our position." Now upon what do you find your assertion that there is a national feeling against us . . . ? wherever we Europeans go we are received with respect, and attention, and welcome . . . You say, "The infatuated towns-people are even beginning now to show their teeth; there have been three cases today of stones thrown from the tops of the houses on Sepoys' heads walking along the streets." Certainly our troops can be no great favourite in a town where they have turned out half the inhabitants for their own accommodation; but I will venture to say there is not a county town in England where

soldiers are quartered in which similar excesses have not happened
... But these people are perfect children, and should be treated
as such. If we put one naughty boy in the corner, the rest will be
terrified.'[22]

By early October 1841, much of the resistance around Kandahar had been suppressed, and many of the Durrani tribal chiefs
had surrendered. The main threat was from their leader Akrum
Khan, but when his whereabouts was betrayed, General Nott
brought him back to Kandahar, where 'he was executed, being
blown from a gun'.[23] In this form of punishment adopted by
the British from the Mughals, the prisoner was secured to the
front of a field gun, which was then fired. The same punishment was also meted out to a ghazi (a religious warrior against
infidels, often a mercenary) who had attempted to assassinate
Rawlinson. Much of Rawlinson's day was spent in the Court House
hearing cases, but at sunset he would walk into the adjacent
square to mount his horse, held in readiness by a groom, and ride
out into the open countryside beyond the walls. On one occasion
business had been too pressing for three days to maintain his
routine, and this urgent work saved his life, because a prisoner
was brought in amid much commotion, having just stabbed and
killed Rawlinson's secretary. The prisoner exclaimed, 'I am a
Ghazee, and one of a band of forty, who met together three days
ago, and swore upon the Koran to take the life of the British
Resident [Rawlinson]. We were to draw lots, and he on whom
the lot should fall was to solemnly pledge himself neither to eat
nor drink until he had stabbed the Great Feringhee [foreigner]. I
was the man on whom the lot fell. Three mornings ago I entered
the town, disguised as you see, and with a dagger inside my vest.
I waited in the square all day for the Resident to come out. His
horse was there, but he never came. I returned the next day, and
waited, but again to no purpose; he did not come, and the horse
was taken away by the groom. This morning I came again – I
was nearly mad with thirst – I felt I could endure no longer, so I
resolved that, if for the third time the Great Feringhee did not
come out to take his ride before sunset, I would kill the biggest

Feringhee that I could see anywhere, and take the consequences.'[24] Justice was immediate: he was blown from a gun in
the great square within half an hour.

Believing that the unrest throughout the country was contained, Macnaghten was planning to leave Afghanistan with his
wife for good towards the end of October, as he had been given
the coveted post of Governor of Bombay. Meanwhile he was imple-
menting urgent orders from Lord Auckland in India to reduce
expenditure. Subsidies to tribes were cut or withdrawn, including
that traditionally paid to the eastern Ghilzyes who controlled the
most direct route to India from Kabul, through Jalalabad and the
Khyber Pass. Macnaghten took the disastrous decision to halve
their annual payment that had up to now guaranteed a safe
passage. Another economy was to reduce the number of troops,
and so one brigade was preparing to return to India under General
Robert Sale. The Ghilzyes, though, blocked the passes from Kabul
and started to attack and plunder all traffic taking that route.
When Sale's troops left Kabul in early October, they came under
attack and suffered heavy losses, but eventually reached Jalalabad,
intending to wait there for Macnaghten and Elphinstone to catch
up.

In his ignorance, Macnaghten brushed aside these attacks as
isolated incidents, and maintained his rosy view of the situation.
On Trafalgar Day, 21 October, he wrote to Rawlinson expressing
his gratitude as he prepared to leave for Bombay: 'We have had
a very trying time of it since we were first officially associated;
and it was no wonder that you, occupying as you did the post of
danger, should have occasionally yielded to despondency, especially when under the influence of severe illness [possibly malaria].
But in all other respects you have given me entire satisfaction,
and I feel that we are mainly indebted to your temper, judgement,
and energy for overcoming the numerous difficulties by which we
have been surrounded. Wherever I go, I shall carry with me a
pleasing recollection of your friendship, and of the laborious and
successful operations which have fallen to our joint lot.'[25]

While failing to trust Rawlinson's intuitive grasp of the overall situation, Macnaghten also did not appreciate the grave danger now confronting the British forces. Less than a week later a terrible uprising enveloped Kabul. Alexander Burnes, the Political Agent in Kabul, was eagerly anticipating nomination as Macnaghten's successor and had convinced himself that all was quiet. While the troops lived in the cantonments outside the city and Macnaghten close by, Burnes and his staff lived in a large courtyarded mansion in Kabul. Next door lived Paymaster Johnson of Shah Shuja's army, who for convenience kept the entire army treasury at home. Burnes failed to listen to warnings that he was in mortal danger as a conspiracy was unfolding and that he should move straightaway to the cantonments 2 miles away. At dawn on 2 November a mob surrounded the Residency, and Burnes was hacked to pieces while trying to escape. The Residency and the Paymaster's house were ransacked, and everyone inside slaughtered, with the rioters moving into the city, murdering, looting and burning.

Major-General Elphinstone failed to take the immediate, decisive military action that might have saved the situation, and within a few hours thousands of tribesmen were pouring into Kabul. By the next day they controlled the city, and the cantonments were attacked. The poorly defended army supply depot was looted, creating a shortage of food and a state of siege. That same day orders were sent for General Sale to march back from Jalalabad to relieve the city, while Macnaghten was forced to write to Rawlinson about the situation and advise him that troops should be sent from Kandahar: 'We have a very serious insurrection in the city just now, and, from the elements of which it is composed, I apprehend much disturbance in the surrounding country for some time to come. It would be only prudent, therefore, that the 16th, 42nd, and 43rd, with a troop of horse artillery and some cavalry, should come here immediately. General Nott will be written to officially in this respect . . . Unless you send up this reinforcement there will be a probability of our supplies being cut off.'[26]

Nott ordered three regiments to march to Kabul, but undoubtedly believed that the incompetent leadership in Kabul would endanger his troops. Before they left on 17 November, he addressed his officers: 'Remember, the despatch of this brigade to Cabul is not my doing. I am compelled to defer to superior authority; but, in my own private opinion, I am sending you all to destruction.'[27] It was normal for the road between Kandahar and Kabul to be closed for a few months each winter, so after the brigade had marched for two days, a light fall of snow and the death of baggage animals provided sufficient excuse to return to a sympathetic commander in Kandahar. Sale had also been unwilling to return to Kabul, even though his wife remained there.

The garrison at Kabul suffered further defeats, and without any effective leadership it became utterly paralysed. With very little food left, Macnaghten felt he had no other choice but to negotiate with the enemy, although he rejected Afghan demands that they should leave the country, that they should surrender all their weapons, ammunition, treasury and stores, and should leave behind hostages to ensure the safe return of the deposed ruler Dost Mohammed. By now Akbar Khan, the favourite son of Dost Mohammed, had returned from exile in Turkestan, accompanied by thousands of fighting men. Inside the besieged cantonments at Kabul, the animals were starving, while the troops were on short rations, reduced to eating the carcasses of dead camels and ponies. Bitterly cold conditions and snow were adding to the misery, particularly as Elphinstone would not allow fires to be lit. Driven to despair, Macnaghten rode out of the cantonments on 11 December to meet several Afghan chiefs, including Akbar Khan, and agreed that all the garrisons – at Kabul, Jalalabad, Kandahar and Ghazni – would leave the country in three days' time and that the Afghans should provide provisions for the journey.

With deep distrust on both sides, this agreement did not stop Macnaghten seeking a way for the British to remain in the country. It was secretly proposed to him that they could stay for a few more months and Shah Shuja remain on the throne, if Akbar Khan became the Vizier and all other Afghan leaders were excluded. On the morning of 23 December Macnaghten, accompanied by Captains Mackenzie, Lawrence and Trevor, went to a meeting with Akbar Khan that had been set up on a carpet in the deep snow just a few hundred yards from the cantonments, unaware of impending treachery. Two regiments should have been on hand, but they were not ready and instead looked on helplessly as the four men were seized and taken away. Lawrence and Mackenzie were held captive, and Macnaghten and Trevor were stabbed to death. Macnaghten's body was dismembered, his head and limbs being paraded triumphantly through the streets of Kabul, while his trunk and the corpse of Trevor were hung from meat hooks in the bazaar.

No punitive action was taken, but instead Elphinstone continued to negotiate the draft treaty as if nothing untoward had occurred. The humiliating conditions that Macnaghten had rejected in November were now accepted, and on 6 January 1842 some 4,500 British and Indian troops, 12,000 camp followers, wives and families, and 2,000 camels and ponies evacuated Kabul and began a retreat through deep snow towards Jalalabad and the Khyber Pass, ill-prepared and with virtually no provisions and tents. Three days later Akbar Khan appeared, promising to supply provisions and suggesting that all the British (but not the Indian) women, along with their husbands and children, should be handed over to him as prisoners for protection. With little choice, fewer than one hundred hostages were led off, including Lady Sale and the widowed Lady Macnaghten and Mrs Trevor.

The army continued its journey, but by 12 January all but a few hundred of the 16,500 troops and camp followers were dead, killed by the freezing conditions and by hunger or else slaughtered by Ghilzye tribesmen. As they approached the Jugdulluk Pass, still only 35 miles from Kabul, the survivors became trapped in the narrow defile. About sixty-five soldiers made it through, but they continued to suffer constant attacks. Only a few prisoners were taken by the Afghans, including Captain Souter, who was thought to be a person of importance having wrapped the regimental colours round his waist. On 13 January Surgeon Brydon, the only European member of the army to evade capture or death, made it safely to Jalalabad, to be greeted joyously by Sale's garrison at the fortress, although his wounded pony died. A few days later a handful of camp followers and sepoys also reached Jalalabad, but there were no more survivors.

Virtually cut off from communication with Kabul and India, Nott and Rawlinson in Kandahar were left to make their own decisions. The situation in and around Kandahar had become very tense, and one adjutant noted that 'the most distressing and desponding accounts from Cabul continued to reach us ... at length communication on every side was cut off, and we were placed in a complete state of blockade, and could not even walk through the city without being well armed. An insurrection being expected in the city, we were, during the greater part of the month of December [1841], obliged to furnish a company of Europeans to keep guard over all the guns, all of which had been brought thither.'[28] Rawlinson's policy was to try to turn individual tribes away from the rebel cause and against each other, with some success. He even received hostages from them as a sign of good faith, but more rebels moved in to threaten the city, more attacks took place, and by early January 1842 a force of several thousand Afghans was camped about 5 miles away. Despite all his efforts, conflict was inevitable.

The ensuing battle on 12 January was described by Nott in an official despatch, with him commenting that 'Major Rawlinson, political agent, with his accustomed zeal, was in the field, and gallantly led a small body of Persians and Affghan horse to the charge'.[29] Many years later, Rawlinson gave a simplified yet vivid description of the battle to his two young children in a style so different from that of his formal writing and political journals: 'Though I was there [in Kandahar] really in a political capacity, I had plenty to do in the way of fighting, for the Afghans were constantly trying to kill us, and we were obliged to keep always on the watch, our horses ready for use, pistols under our pillows and everything in order, so that in a few minutes we could be under arms. One day, we rather suspected they were thinking of attacking us, so I went up early in the morning to the top of a high tower which adjoined my house ... There was a long range of hills about 4 or 5 miles off, and on these I could see the Afghans swarming like bees – there they were coming down the hills towards us, with spears, horses and guns evidently going to attack us. So, say I, Mr Afghans! two can play at *that* game – away I went to General Nott – and told him the Afghans are coming down upon us – let us all go out and drive them away. And thus came to pass the battle of Candahar. The general gives the orders – the bugle sounds the Alarm . . . and in one hour or less we are all mounted and out of the gates of the town, a Regt. of European Infantry, Native Cavalry, 2 or 3 Regt. of Native Infantry and 6 guns. "Now" says Genl. Nott, "Rawlinson you like a skirmish. Take the Cavalry and do as you think best." Well we attacked the Afghans, knocked them about, with the guns, killed some, wounded others, and sent them flying here and there in disorder. But there still remained 2,000 horsemen on the heights. So says Genl. Nott – "Rawlinson, go after them and I will support you with the Horse Artillery". Now, I say to my men, Don't move till I hold up my sword, and when I point it so, Charge. I held up my sword, they fired, 6 guns, 12 Shots. This knocked over a good many horsemen and threw them into confusion. Then, I said, Charge, and away I went on my black Arab Shaitan and they followed at a tremendous pace – one poor fellow was killed by my side.'[30]

Rawlinson next explained how he himself was nearly killed: 'We routed them and I pursued the Chief . . . up the hills till we came to the pass – any Afghans I met I cut down with my sword – but the Chief got away. When in the pass I looked round and found myself alone, far ahead of my men. I shouted to them to come on and proceeded alone – there was a great big rock in the way and just as I was close upon it, going to pass round it, to my great astonishment, up got a grey bearded man with felt cap and an enormous blunderbuss in his hand. So close was he, that I seemed to look down the muzzle, as he held it up, intent upon firing it at me. He thought he was sure of me, pulled the trigger and – it missed fire! You shan't do that again Sir, thought I – dropped my sword, seized one of those very pistols you have seen in my room and bang it went, one bullet in the forehead and one in the head! And down he dropped – dead. The other pistol I reserved in case a second man might be concealed, but there was none – all the rest ran away when they saw this man killed. At last I reached the head of the pass ... The Chief I missed, but many others were killed and when I turned round, to my horror I found my Afghan servant had brought me the heads of three of my victims. "Be off Sir, I said, I don't want heads". For this I considered a savage and wanton cruelty and I never would permit *that*, though killing my enemies in self defence and in fair and open fight I considered only the necessary accompaniment of war.'[31]

The battle had the effect of creating relative peace in the area for a few weeks, even though the cantonments suffered constant harassment at night. Afghan leaders attempted to prevent the inhabitants of surrounding villages from selling supplies in Kandahar, and the army's cattle were starving through lack of fodder. Medicines and ammunition were running low, and 'the only flour we could obtain for making bread, was at least one-third honest desert-sand to two-thirds of flour'.[32] Fuel was desperately short, and when heavy snow fell in February, many men suffered from pneumonia and a few from cholera. On top of all this, the pay of the soldiers was months in arrears.

At the end of January news of Macnaghten's murder reached Kandahar, followed by orders that the army should immediately withdraw to India. Suspecting the orders to have been written under coercion, or were even forged, Rawlinson and Nott decided to wait for instructions from India. Two days later the Durrani chiefs sent Rawlinson a letter demanding his immediate withdrawal from the country – a demand he refused. News had reached him that relieving forces had been sent from India, and rather than retreat from Kandahar, Nott was determined to engage the rebel forces, although bad weather initially delayed these plans. On 17 February Rawlinson noted: 'A rumor is rife in the town today that our troops evacuated the Cabool cantonments and marched for Jellalabad, 3 days after the Envoy's murder.'[33] He therefore decided the time had come to expel the Afghans from the city, a harsh move, but he feared that they would rise in insurrection if disturbances occurred outside. On 3 March about 6,000 inhabitants were ejected – only those who were unlikely to cause a problem were allowed to stay. Nevertheless, the streets remained dangerous, with several European soldiers being attacked, 'and no one could safely move even a few paces from barracks, much less through the city, without being well armed'.[34] Steps were taken to strengthen the city's 27-foot-high defensive wall, and all but one of the six huge gateways were blocked up for easier defence. On 7 March, Nott led the majority of the troops out of this one open gate to try to engage the Afghans in battle. For the city's defence he left a few hundred men, too small a force for the events that followed.

While feigning to form up for battle, the Afghans just as quickly melted away again. Their objective was to lure Nott's force until it was a day's march from Kandahar and then attack the city itself. On the morning of 10 March sentries in Kandahar reported that tribesmen had come down from the hills under cover of darkness and could be seen nearby. Rawlinson immediately realized their intention and despatched three separate messengers to inform Nott. All day long the rebels flocked down out of the hills, until at dusk the city was surrounded by some 9,000 tribesmen. The fanatical ghazis, 'intoxicated with bang',[35] came close to the walls and set fire to the main gate. In his journal for 10 March, Rawlinson recorded the scene: 'The attack was made with extreme desperation, and was received with steadiness. Three rounds of grape were discharged from the gun upon the bastion; a shell was thrown in upon the mass of people at the gate; and the guard kept up a heavy fire of musketry from the ramparts. The enemy's success, however, in firing the gate seemed to give them confidence, and they pressed on with great resolution. We now brought the gun down from the bastion, and placed it in the gateway, supported this by another gun from the citadel, strengthened the point attacked with some 300 infantry . . . and formed a strong and high barricade of grain bags above those which had been heaped up before in rear of the burning gate. About nine o'clock the gate fell outwards, and then a number of the Ghazees climbed over the bags and endeavoured to force their way in.'[36] The battle raged for three more hours until past midnight, when suddenly the ghazis gave up and withdrew in despair, having lost around six hundred men.

General Nott returned two days later, but by now the successful repulse of the attack on the city was causing arguments among the besieging tribesmen, some of whom began to return to their villages. Others prepared themselves for further attacks on the British, encouraged by the news that the city and fortress of Ghazni had fallen to the Afghans, after being besieged for many weeks during severe winter weather, and that the isolated and bleak fortress of Kalat-i-Ghilzye was also being besieged, although it had not yet fallen.

In the midst of the crisis, Rawlinson took an opportunity to assess his career and character, something he had last done while setting out for Kermanshah: 'After a lapse of 5 years I make another entry on my birthday, upon this the 11th of April 1842 – at Candahar. Since I last wrote I have been flattered with honors and I have tasted power. Since my appointment to Afghanistan, the laborious duties of an official life, while strengthening my character and improving my knowledge of natives, have left me little leisure to cultivate literature or to study my own mind. I believe that I possess some powers of mind, but I do not think they are sufficient to lead to any brilliant results. Since the commencement of the Afghan conflict, I have been placed in very difficult circumstances, and up to the present time I see no reason to be dissatisfied with my own conduct ... My tastes incline to literature rather than to politics, and I look for fame solely in the former faith.'[37] Optimistically, he added: 'I hope to make my 1843 entry in England.'[38]

As the situation deteriorated, news arrived that General England's relief force had been stopped at the narrow Kojuk Pass and had retreated to Quetta. Nott was furious and sent urgent messages to England that supplies and reinforcements were desperately needed. He urged England to force his way through and promised that troops from Kandahar would make a simultaneous attack on the enemy from their side of the pass. This strategy proved effective, and the relieving force entered Kandahar on 10 May 1842. Thus supplied and strengthened, Kandahar now seemed too strong to be attacked, and many more tribesmen abandoned the rebellion in this area, leading to a period of comparative tranquillity.

News next reached Kandahar that General Pollock with troops from India had forced his way through the Khyber Pass and relieved Jalalabad and also that General Sale's garrison there had inflicted a crushing defeat on Akbar Khan, even though the fortress defences had been recently destroyed in a severe earthquake. With the weather improving and the army much more confident, Pollock and Nott were both eager to march to Kabul and so now awaited orders from the new Governor-General of India, Lord Ellenborough, who had replaced Lord Auckland at the end of February. Negotiations began with Akbar Khan over the release of the prisoners, although at the end of April one notable prisoner – Major-General Elphinstone – died of dysentery and his body was sent to Jalalabad for burial. Shah Shuja, the nominal king in Kabul, had been murdered at the beginning of April and after weeks of civil war was replaced by his second son, Futteh Khan.

It looked as if the British could soon regain control of Afghanistan, but in mid-May utterly unexpected orders came from India to evacuate the country without even regaining control of Kabul or releasing the prisoners. Rawlinson wrote straightaway to Major James Outram, the Political Agent at Quetta: 'The peremptory order to retire has come upon us like a thunder-clap. No one at Candahar is aware of such an order having been received, except the General and myself, and we must preserve a profound secrecy as long as possible. The withdrawal of the garrison from Kelat-i-Ghilzye and the destruction of the fortifications at that place must ... however, expose our policy, and our situation will then be one of considerable embarrassment ... It must be our object to collect carriage, on the pretext of an advance on Caubul; but how long the secret can be kept, it is impossible to say. When our intended retirement is once known, we must expect to have the whole country up in arms.'[39]

Towards the end of May Nott sent a brigade to Kalat-i-Ghilzye, to rescue the beleaguered garrison, and the fortress was abandoned and dismantled. While he was making plans for a withdrawal to Quetta from Kandahar, further orders arrived from Lord Ellenborough on 22 July, insisting that he withdraw immediately, but leaving him free to decide the route. It was what Nott had wanted, and he divided the troops between General England, who would take the southern route to Quetta and Sukkur, and himself, who would take the northern route via Ghazni and Kabul. Rawlinson's post as Political Agent at Kandahar ceased to exist, but he chose to accompany Nott to Kabul as an aide-de-camp.

The withdrawal from Kandahar to Kabul took place on 7 August 'in the most regular and orderly manner conceivable',[40] though with periodic attacks from the Afghans and further fatalities and injuries suffered on the way. In early September they arrived at the fortress of Ghazni, which the Afghans had retaken a few months earlier. The Afghan garrison soon fled under cover of darkness, deserting the town and citadel that in the eleventh century had become a splendid capital of the Islamic world under the powerful ruler Sultan Mahmud of Ghazni. The fortifications were destroyed by explosives, and the fortress was left to burn. Two miles from Ghazni was the village of Roza, with the tomb of Mahmud. Lord Ellenborough had written to Nott instructing him to 'bring away from the tomb of Mahmoud of Ghuznee, his club, which hangs over it, and you will bring away the gates of his tomb, which are the gates of the Temple of Somnauth'.[41] In this way, he was obviously intent on avenging the fall of Ghazni to the Afghans a few months earlier. Possibly built in the first century AD, the Hindu temple at Somnath on the western coast of Gujarat was the richest in India by the sixth century. Over 50,000 people were reputed to have been slaughtered at this pilgrimage centre by Mahmud, and huge quantities of gold, silver and gems were taken back to Ghazni, along with the temple doors.

Rawlinson examined in detail the tomb and recorded a Cufic

inscription: He established that the finely carved wooden gates, 12 feet high, were most certainly not originally from Somnath. They were nevertheless dismantled, as he recorded in his journal: 'The work was performed by Europeans, and all possible delicacy was observed in not desecrating the shrine further than was absolutely necessary. The guardians of the tomb, when they perceived our object, retired to one corner of the court and wept bitterly.'[42] Today the gates are recognized as of a Muslim design and could never have been removed from a Hindu temple.

The march to Kabul resumed on 10 September, and four days later the Afghans put up a determined opposition to the British force, but collapsed on receiving news that Pollock had decisively defeated their leader Akbar Khan. By the time Nott reached the outskirts of Kabul on 17 September, Pollock was already in possession of the city. Rawlinson agreed to travel in disguise to Pollock's camp 10 miles away in order to make contact: 'As it appeared desirable that a direct communication should be established between the camps as soon as possible, I proposed to the General [Nott] . . . that I should ride in and see General Pollock. My offer was accepted, and I immediately put on an Afghan dress, and escorted by the Parsewans who had come out to the camp, rode in through the town to the race-course, where I found the Jellalabad force encamped. I experienced no sort of difficulty or inconvenience on the road, being generally taken for an Afghan.'[43]

Nott became irritated because Pollock, the senior general, proposed that Nott should rescue Lady Sale and the other prisoners who were being held at Bamian in the mountains to the northwest, 'a city cut out of a rock, whose cavern abodes are scattered over a surface of eight miles. It contains some remarkable temples with colossal idols.'[44] Rawlinson recorded in his journal that Nott 'would not, however, listen to this proposal, declaring that he had only one object in view, that of marching his force to India via Caubul, without turning to the right or left; and that he considered, from the tenor of all Lord Ellenborough's despatches, the recovery of the prisoners to be a matter of indifference to government.'[45] Nott himself wrote at length to Pollock explaining that his men had just completed a difficult march of 300 miles, that many of them were sick, that he was running short of supplies and needed to move on rapidly, and that 'if the system of sending out detachments should be adopted, disaster and ruin will follow'.[46] In the end, General Sale took a brigade but met the prisoners (including his wife) being escorted back to Kabul, having already been released by Pollock's military secretary who had gone on ahead with a cavalry force.

Pollock was determined to punish Kabul in some way, and the chief engineer received instructions to destroy the great roofed bazaar where Macnaghten's mutilated body had been displayed. The buildings were so extensive that they had to be blown up with gunpowder, after which the soldiers and camp followers poured into the city. Rawlinson grimly recorded the atrocities: 'On the 9th our engineers set to work to blow up and destroy the *Char Chutta*. The cry went forth that Caubul was given up to plunder. Both camps rushed into the city, and the consequence has been the almost total destruction of all parts of the town ... Numbers of people (about 4000 or 5000) had returned to Caubul, relying on our promises of protection ... They had many of them reopened their shops. These people have been now reduced to utter ruin. Their goods have been plundered, and their houses burnt over their heads.'[47]

On 12 October, the combined British force began to march from Kabul, with the Somnath gates in the charge of a native regiment. All along the route were hideous half-mummified reminders of the atrocities of nine months earlier, with the passes 'literally strewed with the horrid remains of men – skeletons they could not be called, for in many the features were so hideously perfect, that little difficulty was experienced in recognising in this sad and changed state, those who had been known in life. Mingling with the corpses of our comrades, were those of camels, horses, &c ... All around was horror.'[48]

Even now the soldiers came under attack from the Afghans and also suffered from various diseases, including smallpox. They arrived at Jalalabad two weeks later, where earth tremors were felt, staying here a few days before heading for the Khyber Pass into India in early November. Rawlinson then rode on ahead, reaching Ferozepore on the Sutlej River on 1 December 1842 with the news of the army's progress. General Sale and his troops arrived there on 17 December, General Pollock two days later, and General Nott with the Somnath gates on 23 December. Lord Ellenborough welcomed the returning heroes in a triumphal reception, and the Somnath gates were taken in a procession to Agra, a city famous for the Taj Mahal, where they were deposited in the fort.

Rawlinson had been in Afghanistan for nearly three years and was one of the few officers who returned from the campaign with any credit. He had been unable to carry on his pursuit of cuneiform during this time, nor had he been able to communicate with scholars in Europe who had continued to work on the problem of decipherment. After the constant pressure of his diplomatic and military duties for such a prolonged period, he was hoping for some time to resume his studies, but was instead met with incredible news. During the withdrawal from Kandahar, to maintain the highest fighting efficiency on the way to Kabul, Nott had ordered that all non-essential baggage would return to India with General England via the southern route. He had made no exceptions, and all Rawlinson's private and official paperwork had been sent in this way. While being transported to Ferozepore on the Sutlej River, the boat loaded with all his account books, receipts and other papers caught fire and was destroyed. Nothing remained 'but a mass of blackened scraps and half-burnt fragments'.[49] As Political Agent, Rawlinson was personally responsible for the expenditure he had authorized, which was over a million pounds sterling, but without his accounts he would be obliged to reimburse the British government. Having survived the Afghan War, he now wrote home that he was an utterly ruined man.

Nine: Back to Baghdad

A debt of one million pounds left Rawlinson no choice but to attempt to reconstruct his accounts from scratch. In March 1843 he moved to Agra, rented a house and, using his prodigious memory and the scorched debris, wrote to everyone at Kandahar (mainly the Hindu merchants), asking for duplicate receipts. Such was the goodwill towards him that nobody refused, but even so the work took three months, during which time he was struck down by 'a severe attack of brain fever'.[1] This may have been meningitis, but it could equally have been an illness brought on by the immense anxiety. Once recovered, he submitted the accounts 'to the complete satisfaction of the financial Authorities – this was considered a wonderful feat of patience and memory'.[2]

Rawlinson was now thirty-three years old and had been away from England for nearly sixteen years – he was looking forward to returning home at long last for a period of leave. He travelled to Lucknow, capital of the independent kingdom of Oudh (today part of Uttar Pradesh), where he met Nott, who was now Resident to the court. Aggrieved that he alone had received no recognition for his services in Afghanistan, Rawlinson brought up the subject with Nott, who wrote to him on 18 July: 'Dear Rawlinson, I cannot allow you to leave for England without expressing to you the disappointment I felt on finding that your name was not included in the list of officers who received marks of her Majesty's favour for services in Affghanistan. I certainly expected that you would have been a C.B.'[3] Nott assured Rawlinson that he had been honourably mentioned in his despatches after several battles. 'I was always pleased with your zeal and gallantry,' he added, 'and as I have said, I deeply regret that you were not equally honoured and rewarded with those who had done less in the service of their country. However, as you are now going to Old England, I trust you will yet succeed. I shall always be ready to certify to your deserving reward. Wishing you every happiness.'[4]

Armed with this kind gesture, Rawlinson made his way to Allahabad and embarked on a steamer for the 500-mile trip eastwards, down the River Ganges to Calcutta, where he hoped to find a ship for England. By chance, Lord Ellenborough was a fellow-passenger on the steamer, and they spent many days together discussing a wide range of political issues. Rawlinson made such a favourable impression that Lord Ellenborough offered to give him any job that was vacant once they arrived in Calcutta.

What Rawlinson desired most was to resume his archaeological and cuneiform investigations, something that gave him the greatest pleasure and satisfaction above all else, and he now sacrificed his own career for this obsession. The most prestigious and highly paid appointment on offer was the Residency of Nepal, but the lesser post of Political Agent in Turkish Arabia, based at Baghdad, was also about to become vacant. In preference, Rawlinson accepted this position, in order, as he explained, 'to work at my old friends the Cuneiforms, although the appointment was of inferior rank and pay – and involved complete Isolation'.[5] His choice of appointment met with surprise, as he explained: 'I was offered, as a reward for my services, the highest political employment and an assured career in India; but I had not forgotten Behistun. It had become the ambition of my life to carry on my cuneiform researches . . . accordingly, to the astonishment of my friends, I deliberately declined the brilliant prospect opened out to me in India, and elected to what was called "exile" at Baghdad . . . doing penance in order to attain a great literary object.'[6]

Rawlinson would not find himself as isolated from other Europeans in Baghdad as he had been in Persia, because his friend John Ross was still the Residency's surgeon. An East India Company steamer was often based there, and a handful of merchants operated in the city, but very few visitors, and even fewer women, were seen. Although Baghdad had disadvantages, Rawlinson knew he would have light political duties, ample prestige and generous leisure time, as well as being relatively close to the inscriptions in Kurdistan, including Bisitun. He had enjoyed ten months of uninterrupted study in the city just before going to Afghanistan, so it seemed an attractive prospect. On receipt of formal notification of his appointment, Rawlinson was obliged to drop his plans for a trip to England. He therefore contacted Lord Ellenborough's military secretary, forwarding him Nott's letter, in the hopes of highlighting the unfair treatment he had received. In a few months' time his efforts would yield success when he was rewarded with the Companionship of the Bath, a coveted distinction for service to the Crown whose name was derived from a bathing ceremony that once took place as an act of purification. The honour allowed Rawlinson to place the letters CB after his name, but did not carry a title.

The journey from India to Baghdad began on 26 October, yet another departure on what he considered his 'fateful day'. First he travelled over 1,000 miles by a relay of horses from Calcutta to Bombay, and from here he set out by steamer for Basra at the head of the Persian Gulf. At Basra he journeyed up the River Tigris to Baghdad on board the East India Company's armed paddle steamer *Nitocris*, which was commanded by Lieutenant James Felix Jones. 'These steamers are made of iron, separated into three compartments; they carry six swivels and two large guns fore and aft'[7] commented Mitford, who had visited Baghdad several months before meeting Rawlinson in Kandahar. Explaining that they were brought out to Basra from England in pieces and assembled there, Mitford noted that 'these steamers, in descending the river, add the rate of the current to their speed, and make from twelve to fifteen miles an hour; but, in steaming up the river, subtract the current of about six miles an hour from their rate of progression, by which they only ascend from two to three miles an hour.'[8] At this leisurely pace, Rawlinson ascended the Tigris and reached Baghdad on 6 December 1843, where he 'landed under a salute of thirteen guns from the steamer, which was returned by the Pasha'.[9]

Baghdad had been founded over a thousand years before in AD 762 by al-Mansur, the second caliph (ruler) of the newly established Abbasid dynasty that was descended from al-Abbas, an uncle of the Prophet Muhammed. Al-Mansur decided to move his capital from Damascus in Syria to Baghdad, making it the latest in a succession of capital cities in that area of Mesopotamia, following on from Babylon, Seleucia and Ctesiphon. The ancient city of Babylon, 55 miles south of Baghdad, was on the Euphrates River and had been the capital of Babylonia. Conquered by Alexander the Great in 330 BC, it would have become his capital, but he died there seven years later, and his empire split up. One of his generals, Seleucus, took over Babylonia and founded a new capital at Seleucia on the Tigris, 37 miles north-west of Babylon. Seleucia was captured by the Parthians in 141 BC, and a new capital was eventually established at Ctesiphon on the other side of the river. The Sasanians defeated the Parthians in AD 224, and Ctesiphon became their capital until the Arab conquest in AD 637. Over a century later the capital of the Islamic Arab Empire was moved from Damascus to Baghdad, at the intersection of many trade routes.

The official name given to Baghdad by al-Mansur was Madinat al-Salam, the City of Peace, and it was located on the Tigris River at the junction of a canal leading to the Euphrates. The city expanded over both sides of the river and was noted for its huge numbers of mosques, markets and baths, but it also suffered disasters, mainly floods, fire and civil strife, and in 1258 much of Baghdad was destroyed when the city fell to the Mongols under Hulagu, grandson of Genghis Khan. After nearly four centuries of unrest, Shah Abbas I of Persia captured Baghdad in 1623, but it was taken fifteen years later by Murad IV. He was sultan of the Islamic Turkish Ottoman Empire that had originated around 1299 from the tiny kingdom in Anatolia of the minor Turkish ruler Othman I. At its height in the sixteenth century it had extended from Hungary to Iran, Egypt and North Africa and had its capital at Constantinople, but by Rawlinson's time it was very much in decline.

Baghdad was itself the capital of the Pashalic of Baghdad (also known as Arabian Iraq or Turkish Arabia), a province of the Ottoman Empire covering 100,000 square miles and whose governor bore the title Pasha. In the surrounding area were many different Arab tribes, as well as Bedouin, while the city itself had a very mixed population described by Felix Jones as comprising 15,000 families – 'Turks, or of Turkish descent, families, four thousand; Persians, or of Persian descent, families, two thousand five hundred; Jewish families, two thousand five hundred; Christian families, one thousand; Kurdish families, one thousand; Arab families, two thousand; nomade Arabs and strangers, temporarily located, two thousand.'[10]

Twelve years before the arrival of Rawlinson, plague had halved the population of the city and wiped out many of the inhabitants of the surrounding villages, and Baghdad was in a ruinous state. Subsequent neglect of the banks of the Tigris and Euphrates and of the irrigation canals had turned much productive agricultural land into desert and marsh, causing yet more disease and flooding. The corrupt government squeezed as much money as possible out of its people, who turned increasingly to robbing travellers. The only safe way to journey across the country was in a large well-armed group or by an armed East India Company steamer on the river.

The traveller Mitford had climbed an abandoned minaret, but all that could be seen of Baghdad was the winding course of the Tigris and an ocean of date palms virtually obscuring all the buildings. The river itself was crossed by a ferry or by a bridge of boats 6-feet wide that could be dismantled in times of flood. The city walls were reckoned by Jones to enclose an area of 737 acres. 'The bazars', he thought, 'offer nothing beyond the ordinary assemblage of men and goods pertaining to most eastern bazars . . . The streets are of the same narrow and confined form as other Asiatic cities; and a wander through them, if we except a few of the mosques and shrines, affords a view only of blank brick walls, with abutting balconies, closed or partially screened from a too prying curiosity. The interior of many of the older houses will, however, repay a visit, for they are handsomely ornamented with glass, and the walls are often embellished with arabesque scrolls and verses from the Koran, or with couplets from favourite poets in both Persian and Arabic characters. They are, too, comfortably fitted up within during winter time, while the summer vaults, or Sirdabs, under ground, are unique residences, as necessary to the climate as they are curious to the stranger in these parts.'[11]

Mitford's travelling companion Layard gave a more vivid description of the city: 'We came in sight of the city rising majestically on its banks – with its innumerable painted domes and minarets, its lofty walls and towers, its palaces and painted kiosks. It seemed to be all that I had pictured to myself of the city of the Caliphs . . . I was, however, doomed to disappointment, for we had scarcely landed . . . when I found that, instead of the magnificent capital whose distant view had enchanted me, I was in the midst of mean, mud-built dwellings and a heap of ruins . . . More than one quarter was nothing but a heap of ruins without inhabitants . . . In fact, with the exception of the tomb of Zobeide, the favourite wife of Haroun al Reshid, with its conical dome in the shape of a pine-apple, there appeared to be no legend or tradition attaching to the remains of edifices which recalled the memory of those illustrious princes who had raised Baghdad to the height of glory and renown, and had rendered it the most splendid and cultivated city of the Eastern world. The 'City of the Caliphs' had become a desolation and a waste.'[12]

Although the countryside around Baghdad was neglected and insecure and the city was in a ruined state, it was a joy for Rawlinson to be there, and his own accommodation was well appointed. He lived in a vast building that had been the East India Company's Residency since 1818, located on the left bank of the Tigris and facing south, with mooring for the Company's paddle steamers. It was the one of the most spacious and comfortable buildings in Baghdad and comprised two large courtyards (one used as a riding ground) surrounded by numerous galleries and rooms, as well as offices, stables and kitchens. The Residency had once belonged to an Egyptian Mameluke family and 'had been fitted up in the most luxurious and elegant fashion, with baths and fountains, nearly every room being painted with exquisite Eastern designs in rich but harmonious colours'.[13] Visitors 'passed through a vaulted entrance, at which was a sepoy sentinel, belonging to a guard of native Indian troops attached to the Residency, and a number of *cawasses* [guards] and attendants in every variety of attire. This entrance opened into a spacious courtyard, round which were balconies or terraces, and the doors of a number of rooms. This was the *Divan Khaneh*, or part of the house in which the Resident received visitors and transacted his official business.'[14] The reception rooms overlooked the Tigris 'whose rapid stream, sweeping beneath, cooled and refreshed the air'.[15] The *Divan Khaneh* was divided by a high wall from a second courtyard, surrounded by the apartments of the Resident, where Rawlinson's predecessor Colonel Taylor had lived with his wife and two daughters and where Rawlinson lived on his own, but with numerous servants.

Rawlinson's brother George described how the grand scale of the Residency necessitated 'an enormous staff of servants, cooks, grooms, stable-boys, attendants of all kinds, coffee-grinders, pipe-fillers, &c., &c. Considerable state had to be kept up, numerous entertainments given, a multitude of visits paid, and a guard of honour turned out to accompany the Resident whenever he went beyond the walls.'[16] One visitor described this guard of honour: 'Major Rawlinson . . . has a sepoy guard commanded by a native Indian officer, when he goes out drums are beaten and arms presented as to a general.'[17]

Added to his duties as the East India Company Political Agent, Rawlinson was appointed Consul at Baghdad from April 1844, so he was now the representative of the government as well, with 'frequent despatches to be written, both to Sir Stratford Canning, the British Ambassador at Constantinople, and to the Indian Government. The Pasha, moreover, required to be continually interviewed, since all persons under British protection, who had any complaint to make against either the authorities or Turkish subjects, preferred complaining through the "Resident".'[18]

For the first few months of 1844, Rawlinson established a routine of public and private business, able at long last to return to his cuneiform research after being away from his studies for over four years: 'The interest in the inscriptions with which my original researches had inspired me, had never flagged; it was sharpened perhaps by the accidents that had so long operated to delay its gratification; and I thus hastened with eager satisfaction to profit by the first interval of relaxation that I had enjoyed for many years to resume the thread of the inquiry.'[19]

Five years had passed since Rawlinson had last worked on cuneiform during his stay of several months at Baghdad following the withdrawal of the British detachment from Persia after diplomatic relations had been broken with the Shah. In Persia, he had been the first person to reach the Bisitun trilingual cuneiform inscription and to carry out the dangerous task of copying around two hundred lines of the Old Persian version. By studying the Bisitun and Elwand inscriptions, he had worked out the values of most of the Old Persian signs and translated all that he had copied. He was on the point of sending his final report to the Royal Asiatic Society in London, when his work had been brought abruptly to a halt by the First Afghan War. 'Those who have experienced a difficulty of combining a sustained application to literary matters with the ordinary distractions of business,' Rawlinson explained, 'will I believe admit that in the emergent condition of the public service in Afghanistan, calling for undivided attention and untiring care, I had no alternative but the abandonment of antiquarian research. To have continued my labours on the inscriptions during the few hours of leisure that I could legitimately command would have produced no result; to have devoted any considerable portion of my time to the inquiry, would have been incompatible with my duty to the Government.'[20]

He was now anxious to find out how far cuneiform studies had advanced since his involvement, but after all this time progress had been limited, and it was a relief to find he had not been left behind. The previous year, though, Niels Ludvig Westergaard, Professor of Indian and Oriental Philology at Copenhagen University and five years younger than Rawlinson, had been travelling in Persia, mainly collecting and recording Pahlavi and Parsi manuscripts and antiquities, but he also had an interest in earlier history, including cuneiform inscriptions. In reply to a letter that Rawlinson had long since sent him, Westergaard wrote from Shiraz, near Persepolis, at the beginning of April 1843: 'I cannot say how much obliged I feel for your so very kind and interesting letter, which I had the great pleasure to receive on my return hereto from Persepolis, and I think, shall we, whether we meet or not here in Persia, we will at least keep up a constant correspondence? I am sorry that I did delay so long writing [to] you and so commencing our correspondence. I can only say to my excuse, that my arrival in India just took place at the time when Affghanistan rose in arms and the winter had closed the road to Kandahar, and I did not like to risk a *first* letter.'[21]

Westergaard explained that his reason for being in Persia was to record manuscripts and antiquities that were later than cuneiform, adding, 'You will easily see we take similar though not exactly the same courses in our scientific pursuits and though we often will cross each others paths (e.g. the Sassanian inscriptions), still I hope and trust we may labour in the same field hand in hand without any petty jealousy, that so often disfigures the labours of learned men in the same line, but which I am glad to say is no more a fault of mine as it is of yours. As your department principally is the cuneiform inscriptions ... I offer you quite unceremoniously, the little I have or may yet find before we meet, and as I have no time or opportunity to ask for your acceptance, I take the liberty to enclose partly copies, partly collations of the different inscriptions at Takhi i Jamshed [Persepolis]; it may save you some time and your eyes some weakness.'[22]

He ended his letter by referring to Lassen's publication of 1836 that had pre-empted Rawlinson's Old Persian report, and described the reaction of Grotefend, who had been the first person to make sense of Old Persian cuneiform back in 1802: 'Grotefend unfortunately took it into his head to be angry at Lassen's discoveries, and not content with the great honour of being the first discoverer of this mystery, and the way into it, he laid claims to infallibility in a publication of 38 or 39, wherein he would not give way to Lassen in a single point.'[23]

Rawlinson had never managed to copy the trilingual inscriptions at Persepolis and had been obliged to rely on the drawings of travellers from the previous century. While more accurate versions sent by Westergaard were valuable, what he found even more exciting was an Old Persian inscription that nobody had ever copied: 'the gem of his [Westergaard's] collection, the most important record in fact of the class which exists in Persia, with the exception of the tablets of Behistun, I found to be the long inscription of Nakhsh-i-Rustam engraved on the rock-hewn sepulchre of Darius. This inscription was no less remarkable for its extent and interest than for the correctness of its delineation. I could not but observe indeed that Mr Westergaard's copy, defective as it necessarily was, both from the abrasion of the rock and from the difficulty of tracing letters through a telescope at so great an elevation, still indicated ... the immense advantage which a transcriber acquainted with the character and language enjoys over one who can only depend for the fidelity of his copy on the imitative accuracy of an artist.'[24]

Trilingual cuneiform inscriptions, written in three types of cuneiform and in three languages, like a string of Rosetta Stones, had now been found at Bisitun, Elwand, Persepolis and Naqsh-i Rustam, all in Persia, although Bisitun remained the most extensive. Naqsh-i Rustam was a sheer cliff located only 4 miles north of Persepolis, along which had been carved several reliefs, inscriptions and rock-cut tombs over a period of 2,000 years. The most notable was the tomb of Darius the Great himself, the Persian king who had founded Persepolis and ordered the Bisitun inscription to be carved. He died in 486 BC, to be succeeded by his son Xerxes, and his tomb had an elaborate façade and relief sculptures similar to those of Bisitun, accompanied by a trilingual inscription, a copy of which Rawlinson now had in his hands. He had visited Persepolis only once, when the British detachment was newly arrived in Persia, but given the opportunity to travel further in that area, he may well have managed to climb up and record the Naqsh-i Rustam inscriptions.

In mid-August 1844, the season when Baghdad was unbearably hot, Rawlinson set out on an expedition to the Persian frontier. The principal aims were political, because the frontier between Persia and Turkey was a constant source of conflict, with war between the two nations a real threat. A Commission had been established to take evidence from the individual tribes, with Russia and Britain as the mediators, and Rawlinson was required to go to the Kermanshah area to collect information and try to prevent localized clashes between tribes that could endanger the Commission's success. Felix Jones, captain of the *Nitocris*, was asked by Rawlinson to accompany the expedition while the steamer was undergoing its annual refit. Jones was very adept at surveying and map-making and had a genuine interest in history and geography. Rawlinson needed his assistance in collecting geographical information, because the area was little known and poorly mapped. 'As this request was made solely with a view to the acquirement of a better geographical knowledge of this little-frequented but highly interesting portion of Kurdistan (which is deplorably incorrect on our present maps),' Jones explained, 'it was willingly acceded to, particularly as Major Rawlinson's political labours would not allow him sufficient time to enter fully also into the duties of the surveyor.'[25]

The journey took nearly two months, during which time Jones reported that 'many interesting sites were visited, and their true positions astronomically obtained. On our return, a map constructed from the results of the observations, was executed by Major Rawlinson and myself, and forwarded by that officer to H.M.'s Ambassador [Sir Stratford Canning] at Constantinople, expressly to assist the Commissioners at Erzroum in their inquiry.'[26] Alexander Hector, a British merchant who had been in Baghdad for nearly a decade and who had not been on speaking terms with Rawlinson's predecessor Taylor, also accompanied the expedition as he was planning to exploit the produce of the Kurdish mountains in exchange for British manufactured goods. 'Gums, galls, and other drugs, abound in this vicinity', remarked Jones, 'and I believe only want an enterprising individual and an honest agent . . . to make them a source of considerable profit.'[27]

The party set off from Baghdad on 19 August 1844, heading north-eastwards across the desert towards the Zagros mountains, taking scientific observations as they went. Once over the border into Persia, they had to be very discreet for fear of arousing suspicion about their motives, but they continued to map their route, including measuring altitude by a comparison of air temperature and the temperature at which water boiled. Once they began to climb through the passes of the Zagros mountains, 'the oppressive heats of the plains were exchanged for the bracing air of the mountains, and the wearied spirits of the party rose in the same proportion: even the very mules, notwithstanding the labour they had undergone in the ascent, seemed to gain renewed vigour, and now trudged lightly along with their heavy loads at a quickened pace'.[28]

Two days were spent with the Kurds at Kirrind, a village with 'an extremely pretty appearance, being situated in a deep gorge'.[29] Here the party split into three, with the baggage being taken along the lower mountain passes and Hector following a route to search for what turned out to be an ancient Greek inscription. Rawlinson and Jones rode on horseback over a difficult, but direct route, where from the summit of the mountains they had a magnificent view – 'thousands of feet below us, extending as far as the eye can compass, are the fertile and long-coveted districts of Babylonia and Assyria'.[30] Arriving at Gahwarah, a small town that was the capital of the Guran Kurds, they were met with enthusiasm, and Jones noted that the 'presence of their old Colonel among them was hailed with universal delight by these wild mountaineers, and was testified by wild shouts, sham encounters, and firing of their matchlocks'.[31]

The next day they descended into the plain and made their

way to the nearby town of Kermanshah, where they were welcomed with great ceremony by the governor, and a house was
put at their disposal for the length of their stay. Being obliged to
stay in the area until instructions were received from the British
Envoy at Tehran, Rawlinson engaged himself in official duties for
the first three days, while Jones continued his surveying, but soon
they were free to visit the one place Rawlinson was longing to
see again – Bisitun. He had wide wooden ladders made for the
ascent of the rock, and the party set off towards the monument
on 4 September, following the same route that Rawlinson had
last taken nearly seven years before, when he was hurriedly
recording what he could, having been recalled to Tehran.

Jones recorded that 'we left Kirmanshah at 5.5 A.M., on a
delightfully cool morning. Proceeded due east, or 90°, until 6.5,
when the Kara-Su was crossed by a substantial bridge called Puli
Shah. Continued in the same direction over a fine plain, having
the Parrow range of hills at a distance of four miles to the left of
the road. Passed by several villages of cultivators, and exchanged
greetings with some caravans of pilgrims *en route* from the capital
to Baghdad and Kerbela. At 9 A.M. the road inclined a little more
northerly towards the hills over the site of some ancient buildings
whose alignments can now scarcely be traced; but the numerous
fragments of columns, cut stones, pedestals, and capitals, of a
Sassanian design, attest it as a ruin of that age. From 9.45 to
10.15, the road turned to the north in a gradual curve as we
rounded the termination of the Parrow range, known by the appel-
lation of the Rock of Behistan ... The arid and bare range of
Parrow, bounding the Kirmanshah plain to the north, terminates
abruptly at Behistan, about twenty-two miles east of that city. To
the east is the extensive and fertile plain of Chambatan ... Out
of this plain the rock of Behistan rises precipitously to an apparent
height of 2,000 feet, exhibiting a bold outline of naked crags,
unrelieved by a single trace of vegetation.'[32] After a five-hour
journey, they had reached their destination.

Rawlinson's party stayed a quarter of a mile to the south of
the rock, at the New Caravanserai (or Khan) of Bisitun, built in

the late seventeenth century, whose 'murky vaults, redolent of every effluvium, smoke-begrimed and covered with pendent bats, afford a striking contrast to the marble hall and fountained apartment of our abode of yesterday,' Jones observed, 'and yet, after all, this is the life that charms. The real traveller, indeed, knows neither inconvenience nor discomfort; he sits down to his scanty fare of an onion, cheese, and pure water, with more zest than awaits the epicure at a sumptuous repast. So long as he keeps his health, – which is certain unless in a very noxious climate, – he suffers neither indigestion nor *ennui*, and enjoys that quiet sleep which is only experienced after a day of active exercise both of the mind and body.'[33]

Without wasting time, they began the work of recording the cuneiform inscriptions and sculptures. Rawlinson had previously copied about two hundred lines of Old Persian, but the remainder of this text needed attention, as well as the Elamite and Babylonian texts and the relief sculptures. Jones described how they started their work: 'The afternoon of this day was devoted to cleaning the sculptures and inscriptions preparatory to Major Rawlinson revising his former labours. The ladders had been carefully fixed, and the requisite ropes for assisting the ascent up the steep face of the lower portion of the scarp properly adjusted, beforehand. In about a quarter of an hour, not without sundry scratches and bruises, the platform at the base of the tablet was gained, and operations commenced accordingly.'[34]

Jones reckoned that 'without the aid of ropes and ladders it would be a matter of serious difficulty to reach the spot, and even with these aids no weak-headed or nervous person should attempt the ascent'.[35] Yet that was exactly how Rawlinson had previously made the ascent, on many occasions – now at the age of thirty-four he felt less agile. He himself explained that it was more convenient 'to ascend and descend by the help of ropes where the track lies up a precipitate cleft, and to throw a plank over those chasms where a false step in leaping across would probably be fatal. On reaching the recess which contains the Persian text of the record, ladders are indispensable in order to examine the upper portion of the tablet; and even with ladders there is considerable risk, for the foot-ledge is so narrow, about eighteen inches or at most two feet in breadth, that with a ladder long enough to reach the sculptures, sufficient slope cannot be given to enable a person to ascend, and, if the ladder be shortened in order to increase the slope, the upper inscriptions can only be copied by standing on the topmost step of the ladder, with no other support than steadying the body against the rock with the left arm, while the left hand holds the note-book, and the right hand is employed with the pencil. In this position I copied all the upper inscriptions, and the interest of the occupation entirely did away with any sense of danger.'[36]

The work was not only dangerous but also physically demanding: 'The Major constantly and indefatigably employed himself, from daylight to dark, revising, restoring, and adding to his former materials. This was a work of great irksomeness and labour in the confined space he was compelled to stand in, with his body in close proximity to the heated rock and under a broiling September sun.'[37] Faced with these difficulties, Rawlinson nonetheless managed to copy every line of the five columns of the Old Persian inscription that were engraved beneath the relief sculptures – even copying afresh everything that he had done before.

The next task was to copy the 260 lines of the second Elamite inscription that had been carved in three columns to the left of the Old Persian inscription, when the space taken up by the original Elamite inscription was needed by Darius the Great to extend the relief sculptures. This was an even riskier exercise, as there was hardly any ledge to stand on, as Rawlinson described: 'To reach the recess which contains the Scythic [Elamite] translation of the record of Darius is a matter of far greater difficulty. On the left-hand side of the recess alone is there any foot-ledge whatever; on the right hand, where the recess, which is thrown a few feet further back, joins the Persian tablet, the face of the rock presents a sheer precipice, and it is necessary therefore to bridge this intervening space between the left-hand of the Persian tablet and the foot-ledge on the left-hand of the recess. With ladders of sufficient length, a bridge of this sort can be constructed without difficulty; but my first attempt to cross the chasm was unfortunate, and might have been fatal, for, having previously shortened my only ladder in order to obtain a slope for copying the Persian upper legends, I found, when I came to lay it across to the recess in order to get at the Scythic translation, that it was not sufficiently long to lie flat on the foot-ledge beyond.'[38]

The edges of the ledge were uneven, and Rawlinson's shortened ladder did not bridge the gap securely. His solution was to turn the ladder on its side, but this nearly met with disaster, as he explained: 'One side of the ladder would alone reach the nearest point of the ledge, and, as it would of course have tilted over if a person had attempted to cross in that position, I changed it from a horizontal to a vertical direction, the upper side resting firmly on the rock at its two ends, and the lower hanging over the precipice, and I prepared to cross, walking on the lower side, and holding to the upper side with my hands. If the ladder had been a compact article, this mode of crossing, although far from comfortable, would have been at any rate practicable; but the Persians merely fit in the bars of their ladders without pretending to clench them outside, and I had hardly accordingly began to cross over when the vertical pressure forced the bars out of their sockets, and the lower and unsupported side of the ladder thus parted company from the upper, and went crashing down the precipice. Hanging on to the upper side, which still remained firm in its place, and assisted by my friends, who were anxiously watching the trial, I regained the Persian recess, and did not again attempt to cross until I had made a bridge of comparative stability.'[39]

In the end, Rawlinson managed to record the Elamite inscriptions by making paper casts (more normally called squeezes), which he did 'by laying one long ladder, in the first instance, horizontally across the chasm, and by then placing another ladder, which rested on the bridge, perpendicularly against the rock.'[40] He explained how the casts were prepared: 'The method of forming these paper casts is exceedingly simple, nothing more being required than to take a number of sheets of paper without size [glue], spread them on the rock, moisten them, and then beat them into the crevices with a stout brush, adding as many layers of paper as it may be wished to give consistency to the cast. The paper is left there to dry, and on being taken off it exhibits a perfect reversed impression of the writing.'[41]

He also managed to copy the few separate panels of Babylonian inscription that were high up above the Old Persian inscription, alongside the relief sculptures. The main Babylonian inscription had been carved on a projecting rock to the left of the relief sculptures, above the later Elamite inscription, but proved impossible to reach and seemed to be badly eroded. He did not attempt to copy the original Elamite inscription, not understanding what it was, and believing it unreadable. Jones thought it was 'so much destroyed, either by time or the action of water, that it is even difficult to distinguish the nature of the character'.[42] During his close examination of the rock face, Rawlinson worked out how it had been prepared by the craftsmen of Darius the Great: 'The mere preparation of the surface of the rock must have occupied many months, and on examining the tablets minutely, I observed an elaborateness of workmanship which is not to be found in other places. Wherever, in fact, from the unsoundness of the stone, it was difficult to give the necessary polish to the surface, other fragments were inlaid, embedded in molten lead, and the fittings were so nicely managed, that a very careful scrutiny is required at present to detect the artifice. Holes or fissures which perforated the rock, were filled up also with the same material, and the polish which was bestowed on the entire sculpture, could only have been accomplished by mechanical means.'[43]

The engraving of the inscriptions was remarkable, Rawlinson considered, because only iron tools, not steel, could have been used. Several engravers are known to have worked on the inscriptions, because variations in the way the inscriptions were carved are discernible, and Jones was most impressed by the quality of the work: 'The natural rock, indeed, is not difficult to cut, but the prepared portion resisted a steel chisel that we brought with us, with which we could only succeed in chipping the surface. The great depth and well-defined outline of the letters exhibit considerable skill on the part of the engraver. They are one and a quarter inch in length.'[44] What amazed Rawlinson was that the entire inscription had been covered with a varnish (although Jones thought the prepared surface was varnished before the engraving): 'I cannot avoid noticing a very extraordinary device which has been employed apparently to give a finish and durability to the writing. It was evident to myself, and to those who, in company with myself, scrutinized the execution of the work, that after the engraving of the rock had been accomplished, a coating of siliceous varnish had been laid on to give a clearness of outline to each individual letter, and to protect the surface against the action of the elements. The varnish is of infinitely greater hardness than the limestone rock beneath it. It has been washed down in several places by the trickling of water for three-and twenty centuries, and it lies in flakes upon the foot-ledge like thin layers of lava.'[45]

The varnish they observed was not a deliberate coating, but was caused by the action of the weather over the centuries. The inscription was generally well preserved, not just because it was carved high up the cliff, with all access subsequently quarried away, but by the position of the cliff, as Jones noted: 'a shoulder of the mountain here projects to the eastward, forming nearly a right angle with the scarp on which the work is inscribed. This projecting crag shelters the design, in some measure, from the violent NE. winds and rain that are said to prevail from that quarter; to this, to its elevated site, and to its being left in shade after 2 P.M., I attribute its excellent preservation.'[46] Although protected from vandalism and the worst of the wind and rain, the inscription has suffered considerably from water seepage and erosion from springs higher up the mountain, which have left a calcareous tufa deposit over the inscription or simply worn it away, at times making the surface look as if it had been varnished, which might well explain Rawlinson's theory. There is also gunshot damage, something alluded to by Mitford when passing the

monument on his way to Kandahar: 'The mountain-wall of
Besitton looked very commanding in the moonlight, and the dis-
charges from the guns and pistols of some of the party re-echoed
from its surface in thundering reverberations.'[47]

While Rawlinson was copying various parts of the inscription
and Hector was helping out in any way he could, Jones took on
the dangerous task of copying the relief sculptures above the Old
Persian inscription that portrayed Darius the Great and the conquered rebel leaders, watched over by the god Ahuramazda, on
a panel 18 feet wide and nearly 10 feet high. Because the rock
surface for the sculptures had been prepared in a similar way to
that for the inscription, Jones was tempted to look for coins
behind the lead that filled the fissures, knowing that Darius had
been the first Persian king to mint gold and silver coins, copying
the designs of ancient Greek coins. 'A peculiar care has been
evidently exercised in the performance of the whole work, for
where the rock has exhibited fissures or decay, a piece has been
ingeniously substituted, he recounted. 'In the figure of the king,
one of these pieces is observed as morticed into the right shoulder;
and in the body of the last of his attendants a similar piece has
been abstracted, leaving the lead wherewith it was clamped still
attached to the bottom and sides of the vacuity. A sacrilegious
desire to ascertain if any coins existed in the person of the monarch
induced me to attempt the removal of the piece inserted in the
shoulder. I had reached the summit of the two ladders, which
were lashed together, and planted nearly perpendicular against
the face of the rock, and was busily employed with the hammer
and chisel on my desecrating task. Both hands were thus occupied.
An unfair blow, delivered in my awkward position, caused the
chisel to slip, and another instant would have consigned me to
the depths below had I not fortunately grasped the full bushy wig
of the injured king: even as it was, a sickness assailed me that left
but little strength to descend to the platform. The thoughts of my
narrow escape prevented for some time a return to equanimity; I
then vowed, however, to refrain in future from such iconoclastic
tendencies.'[48]

As well as recording the Bisitun inscription, 'a series of astronomical observations were daily made in the forenoons, and the afternoons were devoted to sketching the various objects of interest in the locality, and in taking the dimensions of the magnificent rock before us'.[49] After a week they had done all that was possible in the time available, and so, as Jones graphically recorded, 'the ladders were cast headlong from the rock into the plain below, to prevent mutilation of the tablets. They were shivered into a thousand pieces, and caused a shudder at the thought of a false footstep consigning one to the same fate.'[50]

Ten: Introduction to Layard

The air was raw and cold when Rawlinson, Jones and Hector rose very early the next morning, 11 September 1844, and set off on a five-hour journey by horseback from Bisitun to the Sasanian rock reliefs of Taq-i Bustan. These reliefs had been carved over nine centuries later than those at Bisitun, and Rawlinson had first seen them nine years previously. Depicting kings, gods and the royal hunt, the sculptures were considered by Jones to be 'the finest in this part of the country'.[1] He noted that they were being defaced by travellers through the 'barbarous mania of name-cutting'[2]: all three had just engraved their own names at Bisitun.

The party finally reached Kermanshah just before sunset, and two days later they left the city and travelled along mountain paths that were often narrow and treacherous towards the town of Zohab, achieving 'about a mile and three quarters per hour'.[3] As they approached the town, they were sorry to be leaving the deliciously cool mountains 'for the pestilential atmosphere of the neighbouring plains',[4] and Zohab itself was found to be even poorer than when Rawlinson was last there. Jones complained that their stay 'was very unpleasant, and the heat oppressive in the extreme. Towards evening all felt languid, and the very cattle partook of the general depression. The evening set in dull and cloudy, without a breath of wind to aid the circulation; and the swarms of mosquitoes and sandflies that infested the dwelling prevented the obtainment of sleep.'[5] The tremendous physical effort and mental stress of recording the Bisitun monument from the precarious ledge on the cliff had taken its toll, and Jones recorded: 'Major Rawlinson is seized with fever, and worn out and restless.'[6]

Very early the following morning they left Zohab, 'preferring the excitement of the march to the stagnant air of the village'.[7] Over nine hours later, at noon, they spotted the hamlet and tents of Abdullah Beg, robber chief of the feared Sharaf Byenes tribe. The group was concerned about its safety, 'for Major Rawlinson, when in the service of Persia, was employed against this very individual, and should he recognise, even after so many years, the leader of the troops who occasioned the loss of some of his tribe, he may retaliate in a way peculiar to these people'.[8] Jones recounted that 'the robber chief was seated alone on the platform, surrounded by a band of as sinister a set of cut-throats as could well be looked upon ... Talking of his wrongs, he said he had been hunted like a wild beast, and alluded to the time when the Gurans, under Major Rawlinson, drove him into Sulimaniyeh territory, and sacrificed many of his people. This was touching on the dreaded point, and we immediately perceived that he had recognised the leader of the adverse party in the person of his present guest.'[9] Fortunately, they had kept their guns with them and came to no harm: 'We finished the day in partaking of his evening meal in company with him, and scarcely ever enjoyed one so much ... but a thought would now and then cross the mind, that the bony fingers dipping in the same dish with you had often performed other services for their owner, and might even exert their strength by a tenacious grasp on one's own throat.'[10]

A few hours into the next morning's journey, they had to halt for a while to allow Rawlinson to rest, as he was 'again prostrated with the fever caught at Zohab'.[11] Early in the afternoon of 22 September, they crossed back into Turkish Kurdistan. At this point Jones became too ill to continue, attributing his condition to the 'pernicious quality of the water ... I am now rendered so weak that I must leave Kurdistan. My poor Arab, whose gentle and quiet paces induced me to bring him into this mountainous tract ... is a sufferer as well as myself, and for the last twenty days has been straggling after the party without either halter or rider.'[12] Jones arrived at Baghdad at the beginning of October, where the 'wholesome waters of the Tigris soon restored my condition, but my Arab horse died of debility the day after his arrival'.[13] Rawlinson and Hector, meanwhile, stayed in the area of Sulimaniyeh for several days and then returned 'by a route previously unexplored along the Diala River'[14] taking a fortnight longer than Jones to reach Baghdad.

Rawlinson embarked on a routine of work at Baghdad once again, spending a few hours each day studying the Old Persian material he had recently acquired at Bisitun and continuing his official duties. His favoured place of study within the Residency was a summer-house at the end of the garden. It was built out over the Tigris, and a waterwheel constantly poured water over the roof to reduce the extreme heat. His companions were various wild animals that he dared to tame, including a mongoose (useful for destroying snakes and vermin), lion and leopard, of which he became very fond.

Over two decades later, he entertained his children with tales of his wild companions: 'I had a young Leopard called Fahed, which I kept for several years – he used to lie under the verandah, or was occasionally chained to one of the pillars – he certainly did now and then alarm the children who came into the courtyard by sniffing at them, and licking his lips, but his education and sense of right and wrong overcame his wilder and more savage propensities – and he was perfectly obedient to my orders. On one occasion particularly I saw him roll a child over, sniffing him with great gusto slowly up from his little feet to the back of his neck!! Just in time I called him, Fahed, Fahed, in a displeased voice. He instantly obeyed me – came crouching up very much ashamed and lay down to beg my pardon. He slept in my room or rather on my house top! For in the hot weather I slept on the flat roof of, or terrace of, the house under an awning – now towards dawn it got rather chilly sometimes – so one night, Fahed was lying on the floor by my bedside, and feeling cold, and seeing a comfortable cashmere covering over me, he thought he should like it himself, and began drawing if off me – now to this I could not submit, and I scolded and laid hold of my counterpane, to drag it away. Fahed objected so strongly to this interference with his comfort, that he shewed fight, and growled and would not give it up. Now with all my affection for Fahed, I could not allow this, so every time he growled and clutched at me, I hit him over the head, till he thought better of it and yielded his prize – and became quite gentle and submissive again, begging my pardon as it were for his impertinence.'[15]

When not in his study writing despatches and working on cuneiform, Rawlinson was often out hunting, especially for boar, but before Christmas he fell and broke his collar-bone. Falls from horses were an ever-present hazard, as the 'ground is full of holes made by the buffaloes trampling over the ground in the wet season, and if a horse puts his foot into one while going hard he is sure to fall'.[16] That did not prevent him from filling the Residency with guests at Christmas, including the twenty-four-year-old Henry James Ross (no relation of the surgeon John Ross), who had travelled from Mosul where he was trying to carve out a career. This was his first visit to Baghdad, and he was enjoying himself in hunting, hawking and 'a round of dinners and fun'.[17]

One evening Ross dined at the Residency, enjoying Rawlinson's hospitality but seeing little of him owing to his injury: 'Major Rawlinson had a Bombay Portuguese cook – very good he was – and everything was done according to Indian fashion; cheese and ale was served after sweets and then came in the major-domo and said *Sahib, thcai hadr* (Master, tea is ready), and we left for the tea-room, where we were served with tea and "kalians" (Persian water-pipes). Half-an-hour later we were summoned again into the dining-room and Rawlinson said, "gentlemen you'll excuse me as I am still on the sick list, I depute Capt. Felix Jones (of the *Nitocris*) to take my place." We found the table cleared of fruit and wine and in their place a tureen full of smoking punch; scattered about the table were devilled herrings and turkey's legs. Capt. Jones filled up the glasses with punch and sent them round, observing that the contents were to be drunk off and the glasses reversed. This was repeated time after time.'[18]

At two in the morning, Henry Ross was one of only a few who were still capable of going in to Rawlinson to say good-night, as he wrote in a letter to his sister: 'I hope I have made a friend of Major Rawlinson, for in spite of his broken collar bone he got up and escorted me to the door of his room when I left, and invited me to return to Baghdad, saying he wished he had seen more of me but his unfortunate accident had prevented it, and added, "I hope, Mr Ross, whenever you have anything to say you will write to me yourself." This is a good deal from him, for I should say he is rather haughty and keeps all round him at a certain distance. He is excessively clever and bears a high reputation amongst the diplomatists both at home and in India.'[19]

In the new year Rawlinson began to rewrite his original report on Old Persian. He had once hoped for its publication by the Royal Asiatic Society back in 1840, and although he would not be able to claim his revised publication as a breakthrough in the decipherment of Old Persian, he would still be the first to publish so extensively on the subject. He had returned from Bisitun with masses of rough drawings and paper casts of the inscriptions and relief sculptures, and the first task was to draw up good copies, so that he could study and publish them. He needed to examine each cuneiform sign so that he could work out a transliteration of the Old Persian text and then a translation. The work was laborious, as Rawlinson could not entrust it to anyone else, for fear of errors from an inexperienced hand, but all the while he was copying the inscriptions, he was learning from them and realized that he himself had made copying errors. Of column 4, line 55, for example, he admitted in his report: 'In taking a copy of this inscription, I unfortunately omitted this line, and did not discover the oversight until it was too late to remedy it.'[20] In February 1845, Rawlinson renewed his contact with the Royal Asiatic Society and sent a translation of the entire Old Persian text to London: 'I took the precaution of forwarding to the Royal Asiatic Society, a literal translation of every portion of the Persian writing at Behistun, and of thus placing beyond the power of dispute the claim of the Society at that date to the results.'[21] He was anxious to stake his claim to being the first translator of such an extensive cuneiform inscription.

Up to now, Persia had been the focus of attention for the study of cuneiform, as its trilingual inscriptions were visible to travellers on rock faces and the ruins of buildings, as at Bisitun and Persepolis. What Rawlinson and other scholars did not appreciate was that these instances of cuneiform represented only a fraction of surviving texts, as the bulk remained invisible within the featureless mounds of ancient cities in Mesopotamia. Although Rawlinson had moved to Baghdad to be relatively close to the inscriptions of Kurdistan, he was actually at the very centre of Mesopotamia where cuneiform had been used as a writing system for two thousand years before the reign of Darius the Great. By now Rawlinson was not just concentrating on Old Persian, but was beginning to study Babylonian and Elamite cuneiform. However, he needed to obtain more inscriptions, especially trilingual ones, so as to have as much comparative material as possible. He was fascinated to read accounts that were being published by Austen Henry Layard in the *Malta Times* of amazing discoveries at Khorsabad, in northern Mesopotamia, which included cuneiform inscriptions. Layard was obviously receiving first-hand reports of these discoveries, and Rawlinson was extremely keen to make his acquaintance.

Seven years younger than Rawlinson, Layard (pronounced 'Laird') was born in Paris on 5 March 1817. His parents returned to England for three years, but his father suffered from chronic asthma, and so the family moved to Florence, where Layard reckoned that, 'I learnt little at my school except the alphabet'.[22] He much preferred roaming round the countryside and was also very fond of birds, 'but I remember that my mother did not like me to keep them, as our Italian man-servant put their eyes out in order to make them sing – a cruel and barbarous practice still prevailing in Italy'.[23] His mother's relatives persuaded the family to return to England so that Layard could receive an education. Of his school in Putney, he wrote: 'I there learnt, I suppose, what was taught at that time in institutions of this nature, which was not much.'[24] His father's health was again so poor that when Layard was eight years old, the family moved to central France. At school, he was the only English boy and soon learned the French language, 'but at the cost of no little suffering. The feeling of hatred and contempt which the long wars of Napoleon had engendered between the English and the French had not yet been removed by the peace.'[25]

Layard was far happier when the family next moved to Switzerland, but his father remained constantly ill, and so they returned to Florence. Although Layard adored the city, he still much preferred wandering the countryside than attending school: 'I was never tired, stretched under the shade of an olive tree, of contemplating the glorious view of Florence beneath, with the majestic cupola of Brunelleschi and the graceful Campanile of Giotto rising above the city.'[26] He learned little at school except Italian, but benefited greatly from the constant flow of visitors, as his father kept open house. He also developed a love of fine art from his father and read many books with him, as well as having his own favourites, including *The Arabian Nights*. Decades later he wrote: 'My admiration for the "Arabian Nights" has never left me ... They have had no little influence upon my life and career; for to them I attribute that love of travel and adventure which took me to the East, and led me to the discovery of the ruins of Nineveh.'[27] This life of travel and adventure had to wait a few years, as his godfather and uncle, Benjamin Austen, thought Layard's education so far was not suitable for the career his family wanted for him – to be an articled clerk in London. When Layard was twelve years old, therefore, he came to England (twenty months after Rawlinson had left as a cadet for India) and was placed in a school at Richmond. Because he knew French and Italian, Layard found himself the target of bullying, explaining that: 'This contempt for foreign languages arose from the prejudice against Frenchmen which survived long after the close of the wars of Napoleon ... both in public and private schools.'[28]

Ancient Greek and Latin were on Layard's curriculum, but not being destined for university, he was given little encouragement: 'Had I been properly taught, and had I received a university train- ing, I might have become a fair scholar, as I was extremely fond of such works of the great writers of antiquity as I was able to master, and I had some aptitude for acquiring languages.'[29] His own opinion of himself at that time was that he had a talent for learning and sport, when he chose to apply himself: 'I was not altogether an idle nor a bad boy, although high-spirited and some- what disposed to get into mischief and rows, and to resist legiti- mate discipline . . . But I was naturally quick, and able to do more than most of my school-fellows with less labour, and could work very hard when I liked. So that I not only held my place amongst them, but generally obtained the prizes, and was at the top of my class, when I chose to take trouble to go there. Nor was I behind my companions in the usual athletic exercises of an English school . . . But I had no passionate fondness for any of these pursuits.'[30] The principal of the school was 'a sound Tory'[31] who, Layard believed, 'strongly objected to my political opinions, which were even then very radical and democratic. I was even accused of preaching sedition and revolution.'[32] He was punished for his views, leaving him 'very indignant at what I considered an undue and tyrannical interference with my political opinions'.[33]

In late January 1834, at the age of sixteen, Layard was articled as a clerk to his uncle, Benjamin Austen, who asked him to reverse the order of his first names, so that having been Henry Austen Layard, he became known as Austen Henry Layard. As his aunt and uncle had no children, his father believed that Layard would be his uncle's heir and successor to his business. After a cosmopoli- tan upbringing, and his love of living on the Continent, life in London was claustrophobic and boring: 'Nothing could have been less calculated to prepare me for the dry and monotonous work of an attorney's office and its drudgery than the education . . . that I had hitherto received.'[34] While Rawlinson spent the next few years in Persia, Layard was studying law, but, he explained, 'It soon became evident to me that I should never master the science of law, or take any pleasure in its pursuit. Its study became, indeed, repugnant to me.'[35] He was also very lonely, as he lived in lodgings and had very little money and few friends in London. The monotony was broken on Sundays when he dined with his aunt and uncle, together with many guests who were artists and authors. Otherwise, he spent a good deal of time in the nearby British Museum.

Layard's father died in October 1834, and the following summer Layard realized that his own health was suffering from being confined in an office, so he spent the long vacation in the Alps. The next summer was passed walking in France and the following year in northern Italy. In 1838 he went first to Denmark, then Sweden, Finland and Russia, relating that, in Copenhagen, 'I was especially interested in the collections of Scandinavian and prehistoric remains, which had then been recently formed ... I thus took at Copenhagen my first lesson in northern and prehistoric antiquities.'[36] On his return he was placed by his uncle as a pupil in a conveyancing firm to gain additional legal experience, and although he had considered abandoning his career, he managed to pass his law examinations in June 1839. An uncle from Ceylon thought that he should go there to practise as a barrister, and Benjamin Austen acquiesced, which was a relief to Layard, because he knew that his uncle would never include him in his business, as they disagreed violently over matters of politics and religion.

As Layard's mother was able to advance him £300 for his journey, he decided to travel overland through Europe, central Asia and India with Edward Ledwich Mitford who was going to Ceylon as a coffee planter. This plan, Layard said, 'coincided entirely with my love of travel and adventure, and, if carried out, would enable me to visit many of the most interesting parts of the East, and to realise the dreams that had haunted me from my childhood, when I had spent so many happy hours over the "Arabian Nights".'[37] They decided to travel wherever possible in areas previously unexplored or rarely visited, and so contacted the Royal Geographical Society for advice on the best route. Layard equipped himself for the journey, including a double-barrelled gun and a pair of double-barrelled pistols. As he was hoping to do surveys, he took lessons in the use of the sextant and trigonometry. Added to the luggage were 'one or two pamphlets referring to the countries which we intended to visit – especially . . . Rawlinson's account of his journey to Susiana, from the journal of the Geographical Society – and such treatises as had then been published, and they were very few, on the cuneiform and Pehlevi writing, as inscriptions were believed to exist in both those characters in the border mountains of Persia'.[38] This was Layard's first contact with cuneiform inscriptions and with Rawlinson, whose report on his 1836 expedition from Zohab to Susa had just been published in the society's journal. At the age of twenty-two, Layard left London on 10 July 1839, 'experiencing a happy sensation of relief at leaving England and abandoning a pursuit which was odious to me . . . I had nothing to regret except the separation from my mother.'[39]

Travelling together on horseback across Europe, Layard and Mitford reached Constantinople after two months. Fever, undoubtedly malaria, badly affected Layard. The normal cure for such fever was copious bleeding and application of leeches, and he wrote to his mother: 'The good doctor also taught me to bleed myself, recommending me to have recourse to this somewhat heroic measure whenever I had reason to apprehend a return of the fever, and was beyond the reach of medical aid.'[40] It was over two weeks before Layard had the strength to continue the journey, and he and Mitford travelled through Asia Minor in native dress, taking routes 'untraversed by Europeans'[41] over mountains and through forests, looking for ancient Greek and Roman ruins, making notes and mapping their route, as at that time maps of the area were almost blank. Layard found the number of ruins overwhelming, as 'neither my companion nor myself had sufficiently prepared ourselves for exploring regions so rich in classic and historic associations, and so full of objects probably new to science. I had turned my attention but little to archaeology, and I had but a mere smattering of scientific knowledge of any kind.'[42]

They next travelled through Syria, formerly under Turkish

control, but since June under the control of Egypt following its conquest by Ibrahim Pasha. Many more ancient ruins were encountered, as well as those of the Crusades. In Lebanon, Layard travelled alone to see the cedars: 'I cut my name on one of the trees – no doubt a foolish custom – but one which may perhaps be justified in this particular instance; at any rate, those who had done so before me had left pleasing and interesting records of their visits to the celebrated spot ... No monument of ancient art was disfigured and the place was then beyond the reach of the vulgar tourist who wrote his name wherever he went.'[43]

New Year's Day 1840 was spent at Tyre in the company of Horace Vernet, the French artist who had painted battle scenes of Napoleon and who was in Syria preparing to paint a representation of the Egyptian victory over the Turks. Layard said that they 'struck up a friendship, and many years after, when passing through Paris, I always received a warm welcome in his studio'.[44] In one of history's strange coincidences, a previous studio of Vernet's in Paris (an attic in an unremarkable house in the rue Mazarine) was where Jean-François Champollion had made the crucial breakthrough in deciphering Egyptian hieroglyphs. At Jerusalem in mid-January, Layard set out alone for Petra, on an expedition that was regarded as foolhardy and dangerous, and during which he constantly faced threats and was robbed of his possessions. Even so, the ruins of Petra filled him with awe, as 'the silence and solitude, scarcely disturbed by the wild Arab lurking among the fragments of pediments, fallen cornices, and architraves which encumber the narrow valley, render the ruins of Petra unlike those of any other ancient city in the world'.[45]

Layard rejoined Mitford at Aleppo, which they left in mid-March 1840, not long after Rawlinson had arrived in Afghanistan. In early April they reached Mosul, a town over 200 miles to the north of Baghdad and also on the Tigris: 'The town, with its walls and minarets and gardens, stretching along the right bank of the Tigris, has the appearance of a considerable city. It was only when we entered it that we realised the condition of ruin and decay to which it had been reduced by long misgovernment and neglect

... Whole quarters were in actual ruins and almost without inhabitants, and a great part of the population dwelt in mere hovels.'[46] To Mitford it looked even worse: 'an ill-constructed mud-built town, rising above the banks of the Tigris, and backed by low hills; in the centre is a tall brown ugly minaret, very much out of the perpendicular ... the ground between the walls and the town is occupied by stagnant pools, ruins and dead bodies of camels and cattle, which is enough to breed a pestilence; the bazaars are mean and dirty.'[47]

There were thought to be 40,000 to 50,000 inhabitants in Mosul, and Layard noted that they comprised 'Mussulmans, Christians of various denominations, and Jews. The Christians were chiefly Chaldeans, as the converts from the ancient Nestorian faith to Roman Catholicism are termed, Jacobites and Syrian Catholics, or Jacobites who had gone over to Rome. There were in addition a few Jewish families in the town.'[48] He also noted that the busy and noisy bazaars added to the mix of people, 'as the inhabitants of the surrounding villages, the sedentary Arabs who pitch their tents on the borders of the Tigris and its confluents, the Bedouins of the desert and the wild Kurds from the mountains, were dependent upon Mosul for their supplies of all kinds, and for a market for the produce of their respective districts'.[49]

Although Mosul failed to impress the two travellers, Layard was especially inspired by his first sight of Nineveh on the other side of the Tigris: 'In front of us were the vast mounds that marked the site of ancient Nineveh, and covered the ruins which it was my destiny at a future period to discover. I was deeply moved and impressed by their desolate and solitary grandeur.'[50] A week was spent in Mosul, and Layard recorded: 'I was daily amongst the ruins of Nineveh, taking measurements and searching for fragments of marble and bricks with cuneiform inscriptions, which were then occasionally found amongst the ruins. The site was covered with grass and flowers, and the inclosure, formed by the long line of mounds which marked the ancient walls of the city, afforded pasture to the flocks of a few poor Arabs who had pitched their black tents within it. There was at that time nothing to indicate the existence of the splendid remains of Assyrian palaces which were covered by the heaps of earth and rubbish.'[51] Layard continued: 'It was believed that the great edifices and famous and magnificent cities of the ancient world had perished with her people, and like them had left no wreck behind. But even then, as I wandered over and amongst these vast mounds, I was convinced that they must cover some vestiges of the great capital, and I felt an intense longing to dig into them.'[52]

While at Mosul, the French architect and artist Charles Texier arrived and showed Layard all the drawings he had made at Persepolis: 'They excited my imagination, and added to the ardour I felt, after seeing for the first time the great mounds of Nineveh, to discover the remains of those great nations which had spread civilisation through the East, and whose traces, I felt convinced, were yet to be found beneath these vast and shapeless masses of earth.'[53] Layard's intuition that the mounds could reveal information about past civilizations through archaeological excavation was remarkable. He also made an excursion from Mosul to Hatra, an ancient Parthian city in the midst of the desert. John Ross, the surgeon at Baghdad, had tried to record the ruins of this city a few years earlier, but his party had been robbed. At their first night's camp site near the ancient city of Nimrud, Layard described his reaction: 'I saw for the first time the great conical mound of Nimroud rising against the clear evening sky. It was on the opposite side of the river [Tigris] and not very distant, and the impression that it made upon me was one never to be forgotten. After my visit to Kouyunjik and Nebbi Yunus [Nineveh], opposite Mosul, and the distant view of Nimroud, my thoughts ran constantly upon the possibility of thoroughly exploring with the spade those great ruins.'[54]

His party lost the route they were trying to take to Hatra, but in doing so they came across Qalah Shergat, the ancient city of Ashur, as Layard described: 'a huge mound in the distance, which, from its rising in a cone at one of its corners, we at once recognised as marking the extensive Assyrian ruins of Kalah Shirghat, which has been described by Dr Ross . . . We reached them in a couple of hours, and spent the rest of the day amongst them, taking plans and measurements. Amongst the fragments of stone, bricks, and pottery which cover them in all parts, we discovered a few traces of cuneiform inscriptions, and in the ravines formed by the winter rains, and where the river had washed away the soil, we found walls of sun-dried bricks and the foundations of buildings of the same materials. These remains, with a wall of hewn stones carefully joined together without cement . . . were all that was then to be found above ground at Kalah Shirghat.'[55]

At the end of April, still intending to reach Ceylon, Layard and Mitford moved to Baghdad, travelling down the Tigris by kellek, a raft made from inflated goatskins. These rafts, a common form of river transport, were broken up at their destination as they could not return against the current. The journey prompted Layard to say that 'I know of no more enchanting and enjoyable mode of travelling than that of floating leisurely down the Tigris on a raft, landing ever and anon to examine some ruin of the Assyrian or early Arabian time, to shoot game, which abounds in endless variety on its banks, or to cook our daily food.'[56] He added: 'I thought that I had never seen anything so truly beautiful, and all my "Arabian Nights" dreams were almost more than realised.'[57]

At Baghdad they were the guests of Rawlinson's predecessor, Colonel Taylor, and there they met other members of the European community, including Alexander Hector and Felix Jones. They spent a few weeks here learning Persian in readiness for the next part of the trip, as their Arabic would be of little use in Persia and Afghanistan. They also made an excursion to Babylon, and Layard was again seized with a desire for further exploration: 'I shall never forget the effect produced upon me by the long lines and vast masses of mounds, which mark the site of ancient Babylon, as they appeared in the distance one morning as the day broke behind them. The desolation, the solitude, those shapeless heaps, all that remain of a great and renowned city, are well calculated to impress and excite the imagination. As when I first beheld the mounds of Nineveh, a longing came over me to learn what was hidden within them.'[58]

The more he saw of these featureless mounds, the more Layard was convinced that the few clues they yielded on the surface were nothing to what remained concealed: 'At Babylon, I visited all the principal ruins, including the Birs Nimroud, believed by the old travellers to be the ruins of the Tower of Babel itself, and the vast mound which they had identified with the palace and hanging gardens of Semiramis. At that time no remains of antiquity were to be found above ground, except a rude sculpture in black basalt representing a lion standing over a prostrate man.'[59] He found that the inhabitants of Hillah, a small town that had grown up near the ancient city, regularly dug into the mounds to retrieve mud bricks for their own houses. These bricks often had cuneiform inscriptions, as did the cylinder seals that were also discovered. Sometimes these seals were brought by pedlars to Baghdad, where Taylor and Ross especially were keen to buy them. On the ride back from Babylon to Baghdad, Layard noted: 'what I think struck me most and gave me the most convincing proofs of the greatness, scientific knowledge, and civilisation of the ancient Babylonian Empire, were the innumerable lines of lofty and solid mounds, which traversed the plain in every direction; the remains of the great canals, now dry, which once formed a marvellous system of irrigation, converting this part of Mesopotamia into one great garden.'[60] So innumerable were these mounds of former ancient cities that, 'in the dusk of morning and evening, and in the gloom of the night, they looked like ranges of natural hill'.[61]

Layard and Mitford discussed cuneiform with Taylor, who only the previous year had been host for several months to Rawlinson after he had left Persia, before setting off to India and Afghanistan. Taylor must have held discussions with Rawlinson while he studied cuneiform, but was evidently unconvinced by the research, as Mitford reported: 'Colonel Taylor, the Resident at Bagdad, who is one of the first of our Oriental scholars, put no faith in the pretended translations that had been made public, and was sceptical as to the inscriptions being ever elucidated. It is true that an expert in cypher can work out the alphabet of any language he is acquainted with; but with Oriental languages, not only are there letters which have no equivalents in Western languages, but there is no division of words, no punctuation, and a variety of signs or points added to the letters; but admitting that the alphabet is discovered, and admitting that the words are disentangled, the next question is, What is the language? Assuming that it is a cognate language to the Arabic and Hebrew, the interpreters have had recourse to the Arabic Lexicon, Arabic being the oldest Oriental language that we are acquainted with.'[62] Mitford added sceptically: 'There is one thing in their favour, that they can trade on the ignorance of the public, for whatever translation they may put forth, no one is capable of proving a negative, and boldness of assertion usually insures belief, especially when the majority have a laudable desire to accept any and everything that appears like an illustration or corroboration of Biblical history.'[63]

The next stage of the journey was to cross Persia to Isfahan and then proceed to Kandahar in Afghanistan, but as diplomatic ties had recently been cut between Britain and Persia, they were unsure how far it would be possible to travel. As it was unsafe to travel on their own, they set off from Baghdad in mid-June 1840 with a caravan of mules and horses, travelling at night. Layard became extremely weary of the insulting way they were treated as non-believers: 'The women were made to pull down their veils whenever we approached them, and even the children were taught to run away from us as if we were infected with the plague.'[64] Quarrels with their fellow-travellers frequently drove Layard 'into threatening acts of violence with the butt-end of my gun, or with a stout stick with which I had armed myself for the purpose ... On one occasion I was struck by a fanatic whose religious feelings were offended by something that I had unwittingly done. Had it not been for the intervention of the mûnshi [their language teacher] I should have broken his head.'[65]

Layard perceived a bad feeling towards Europeans in Persia at that time, and to be English was probably dangerous, because 'although England was not actually at war with Persia, she had suspended her diplomatic relations with the Court of Tehran, had withdrawn her ambassador, Sir John MacNeill; and had occupied the island of Karak in the Persian Gulf, belonging to Persia. It was expected that actual hostilities would soon break out between the two nations, and the air was full of rumours of war.'[66] On 1 July they reached Kermanshah, from where Rawlinson had been recalled to Tehran nearly three years previously. The following day they rode to the Sasanian sculptures and inscriptions of Taq-i Bustan, where they spent the entire day with the French artist Flandin and the architect Coste, who were then in Persia drawing monuments. Mitford recorded that 'he [Flandin] had already succeeded in copying the whole of the Cuneiform inscriptions at Besitoon',[67] something that he had emphatically failed to do, in spite of a courageous attempt.

Back at Kermanshah, Layard and Mitford were told that to cross Persia they needed permission from the Shah himself, who was encamped with his army near Hamadan. They left the town at sunset on 6 July, travelling by night along the road that passed Bisitun. Mitford described that they 'had a moonlight ride of five farsaks, winding through picturesque mountains, which, under the pallid light, had an ever-changing and beautiful effect; we stopped at the caravansera at Besitoon, in a valley at the foot of a stupendous perpendicular cliff springing up to the height of 1000 feet, and seeming to impend over us in majestic grandeur.'[68] The next day they spent several hours exploring the ruins, which Layard noted 'were at so great a height from the ground, and so completely inaccessible, that it was impossible to make copies of them'.[69] In fact, Rawlinson had already repeatedly climbed up and down to the inscriptions without the aid of ladders, when he was based at Kermanshah.

It was now one year since their departure from England, and while waiting at Hamadan for permission to cross Persia, they went to see some inscriptions near the village of Abbasabad: 'From the foot of the hills we wound up a thickly-wooded gorge, the bed of a mountain torrent; about half a mile above the village we found two large tablets of Cuneiform inscriptions . . . they were deeply cut on the steep rocky face of a ravine on the right of the road, where the stream comes tumbling through the rocks in three or four broken cascades.'[70] Layard noted: 'It took me three hours to make as careful a copy of the inscriptions as my then limited acquaintance with the character, the difficulty of access to one of the tablets, and the condition of their surface, which in many places had been worn by the effects of the weather, allowed me to obtain.'[71] This was Mount Elwand, where Rawlinson had copied the same trilingual cuneiform inscriptions some five years earlier.

After many entreaties with the Shah's ministers, Mitford and Layard obtained permission to continue their journey in early August, but not along their intended route, so they decided to part company, with Mitford heading for northern Persia and into Afghanistan, first of all to Herat and then to Kandahar, where he met Rawlinson in December. Layard wrote to his mother: 'I have also obtained permission to proceed to Isfahan through Luristan, instead of taking the high road . . . Major Rawlinson is, I believe, the only European who has seen much of Luristan.'[72]

At Isfahan, Layard met the governor Manuchar Khan, with whom Rawlinson had experienced difficulties in Kermanshah, and then headed into Luristan, where he spent many eventful and perilous months in the mountains, living with one of the feared Bakhtiari tribes. He occupied himself by examining ancient ruins, assessing trade possibilities and supporting the tribe in its struggle against the Shah. In Shuster he again met Manuchar Khan, who complained that Englishmen were always interfering in the affairs of other countries, but informed Layard that in Afghanistan they had all been put to death, with nobody escaping – and he described how Macnaghten's corpse had been treated in Kabul. It was now August 1841, four months before these events occurred, which later led Layard to realize that Manuchar Khan had been privy to a plot to massacre the British. A month later Layard returned to Baghdad, but shortly after he went back to Bakhtiari territory. He was again in Baghdad in the middle of May 1842 and prepared to return to England, having given up the idea of Ceylon.

Because of Layard's first-hand knowledge of the border disputes between the Persian and Ottoman Empires, Colonel Taylor entrusted him with taking despatches to the British Ambassador Sir Stratford Canning in Constantinople. On his journey northwards, a three-day wait at Mosul allowed Layard to become acquainted with the newly installed French Consul. It was the description by Claudius James Rich of the ancient sites in Mesopotamia, rather than a desire to facilitate commerce, that had inspired the French government to send Paul Emile Botta as its consul to Mosul, with instructions to investigate the ancient mounds. Rich had been the East India Company's first Resident in Baghdad, from 1808 until his early death from cholera in 1821, and his interest in Mesopotamia had been aroused by the accounts of early travellers, who had collected stamped bricks, cylinder seals and other small objects, especially from Babylon. He travelled to many of the mounds of Mesopotamia, making observations and taking measurements, notably at Nineveh and Nimrud, and at Babylon he employed workmen to undertake the first excavations. Because only Rich had ever attempted excavation, nobody knew what to expect or how to undertake the work of investigating the mounds. Inspired by Rich's reports, Rawlinson had recently proposed setting up a joint-stock company to excavate the mound of Nimrud, but gained no support in England. Botta decided to begin digging at Nineveh, the huge mound just across the Tigris River from Mosul, but found little to interest him.

With his Continental upbringing and ability to speak French, Layard must have been a welcome companion to Botta: 'We visited together the great mounds opposite Mosul,' Layard related, 'which were believed to occupy the site of ancient Nineveh ... He had opened one or two trenches in the largest of these mounds, known as Kouyunjik, but had only discovered a few kiln-burnt bricks and fragments of alabaster inscribed with cuneiform characters ... The conviction that remains of great interest and importance were concealed within these shapeless accumulations of earth and rubbish, induced me to encourage M. Botta in his experiments.'[73] Layard thought highly of Botta, but considered harmful his habit of opium smoking: 'M. Botta was a delightful companion . . . He was liberal in his views, large-minded, willing to impart what he knew, and ready to acknowledge the merit of others. His scientific attainments, especially as a botanist, were considerable. He had been employed in the Consular service in China, where, unfortunately, he had acquired the fatal habit of opium-smoking, which ruined his health and rendered him liable to occasional fits of melancholy and despondency of the most painful nature.'[74]

From Mosul, Layard resumed his journey to Constantinople, reaching the city in July 1842, exactly three years after leaving England. He spent many months working for Canning on secret missions and as an unpaid private secretary, short of money and uncertain of his position, but with the promise of an official appointment in due course. Meanwhile, Botta turned his attention to Khorsabad, a mound 12 miles north-east of Mosul, having heard hints of finds there. His discoveries were momentous: colossal statues of bulls, relief sculptures of gods, kings, battles and sieges, all with cuneiform inscriptions, and numerous rooms of a palace belonging to the new capital city that had been founded in 713 BC by Sargon II, King of Assyria, then moved to Nineveh on his death eight years later. Botta kept Layard constantly informed of his results: 'My friend M. Botta had continued his excavations amongst the Assyrian ruins, and had commenced those great discoveries at Khorsabad . . . With a generosity and liberality rare amongst discoverers, he had allowed me to see his letters to his official superiors in France, describing the remains that he had uncovered, and accompanied by copies of cuneiform inscriptions and by drawings of the bas-reliefs found in the buried Palace of Sargon. These letters were sent to the care of M. de Cadalvène, a highly accomplished French gentleman who was then at the head of the French Post-Office at Constantinople, and who, after allowing me to see them, forwarded them to their destination in France. I was, at the same time, in constant correspondence with M. Botta, who kept me fully informed of his discoveries.'[75]

Layard was thrilled by Botta's discoveries, and while he waited

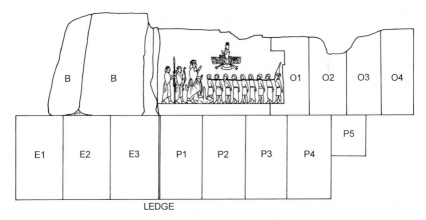

The Bisitun monument, with its trilingual cuneiform inscription and relief sculptures above the narrow ledge. O1–O4 are the original columns of Elamite cuneiform that were replaced by columns E1–E3 when the relief sculptures were extended. P1–P5 are the columns of Old Persian cuneiform, and B is the Babylonian cuneiform on the projecting rock face.

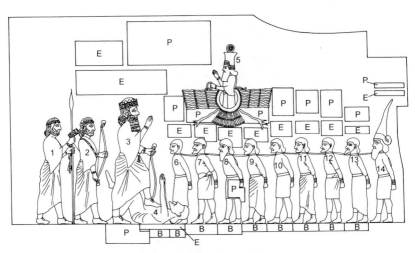

Bisitun monument relief sculptures with detached panels of E Elamite cuneiform, P Old Persian cuneiform and B Babylonian cuneiform. 1 and 2 attendants of Darius the Great; 3 King Darius the Great; 4 Gaumata; 5 the god Ahuramazda; 6–14 defeated rebel leaders.

ABOVE Henry Rawlinson at
the age of fifty-five: drawing
by George Frederic Watts.

LEFT Henry Rawlinson at the
age of forty: an oil painting
by Henry Wyndham Phillips,
engraved by Samuel Cousins.

ABOVE Austen Henry Layard
at the age of thirty: drawing
by George Frederic Watts.

LEFT Henry Rawlinson at
the age of seventy-five: oil
painting by Frank Holl.

Tomb of Austen Henry Layard in the churchyard at Canford Magna in Dorset, adjacent to the home of his cousin Lady Charlotte Guest.

ABOVE Georg Friedrich Grotefend.

LEFT Sir William Nott: engraving taken from a full-length portrait by Thomas Brigstocke painted after Nott's death.

The Bisitun mountain and the surrounding plain, with the caravanserai bottom left. The trilingual inscription is slightly right of centre.

The approach to the Bisitun monument, which can be seen at the top of the picture.

Bisitun monument showing the Babylonian inscription, relief sculptures and, below, the Elamite inscription and part of the Old Persian. The inscriptions to the right are out of sight.

Engraving of the entire Bisitun monument to accompany Rawlinson's published lecture to the Society of Antiquaries of London in 1850.

Standing on the ledge of the Bisitun monument, with the Old Persian cuneiform columns on the right.

in vain for a job at the British Embassy, he prepared for his own excavations in Mesopotamia: 'The success of M. Botta encouraged me to persevere in the design that I had formed of returning some day to Mosul, and of exploring the great mounds on the left bank of the Tigris, supposed to occupy the site of Nineveh . . . I determined, therefore, to prepare myself, as well as I was able, to undertake the work, and to turn such discoveries as I might make, if the plans I had formed were eventually carried out, to the best account in my power. I accordingly set myself to the study of the Semitic languages – one of which, I was convinced, was represented in the cuneiform inscriptions existing in the Assyrian ruins. I obtained from England such dictionaries and elementary works as my limited means allowed me to purchase, to enable me to acquire some knowledge of Hebrew, Chaldee, and Syriac. I worked industriously many hours a day at the study of these languages which, I hoped, might assist me in the decipherment of the inscriptions that I might hereafter discover in Assyria.'[76]

Being the first to hear of Botta's discoveries, even before the news reached Paris, Layard was well placed to report on these discoveries: 'I was thus enabled to be amongst the first to announce them to the public and to give a full account of them. This I did in a series of letters to the *Malta Times*, which were republished in *Galignani's Journal* and in many European newspapers. I endeavoured in these letters to fix the period of the wonderful monuments which my friend had unearthed, and to connect it with the great Empire which, before the fall of Nineveh, had flourished in the vast plains of Mesopotamia.'[77] The *Malta Times* was, as Layard recorded, 'a newspaper published in that island and conducted with some ability, and which was then widely circulated in the Levant'.[78]

By the time Rawlinson returned to Baghdad from his expedition to Bisitun with Jones and Hector in mid-October 1844, Botta's excavations at Khorsabad were drawing to a close. The artist Flandin, who had previously recorded monuments in Persia, was an assistant there from May, and excavations continued to the end of October. Botta's final task was transporting the finds to

Paris, and for this he had to cut up the colossal bulls to make them more manageable for the long trip down the Tigris to Basra, and then by ship to Europe.

Layard's reports were read by Rawlinson, who mentioned to Hector that he would like to make contact. When Hector was writing to Layard in mid-February 1845, he added: 'Major Rawlinson has told me to tell you that he would like very much to see any inscriptions you have got . . . *write to the Major by all means – he told me he would be glad to hear from you.*'[79] Rawlinson heard nothing, but Hector advised him that Layard intended to write, which was very pleasing news. On 2 April, though, Rawlinson decided to make the first move and wrote to Layard: 'Have long wished to commence a correspondence with you, but a preoccupation of my time on the one hand and ignorance of your whereabouts on the other have hitherto thwarted me. Have been encouraged at length . . . to break ground by hearing from Mr Hector that you entertain a similar design [of writing], and our letters may thus perchance cross each other on the road.'[80] He added: 'The subject which at present engrosses all my leisure and on which I am therefore most anxious to communicate with you refers to the Cuneiform Inscriptions.'[81]

So began a lengthy and sometimes difficult association between two men of very different backgrounds. This association between a soldier-turned-decipherer and a traveller-turned-archaeologist was to be the greatest contributing factor to the next phase of cuneiform decipherment.

Eleven: Old Persian Published

At Baghdad on 11 April 1845, Rawlinson again assessed his life, this time on his thirty-fifth birthday. He saw 'no reason to modify the brief mental analysis'[1] that he had recorded eight years previously at Kermanshah, believing himself then to be 'unsteady, indolent but ambitious'.[2] Having been in Baghdad as Political Agent for over a year, he confessed that his Afghanistan experience had affected him greatly: 'The ordeal . . . was passed successfully, but not without a severe trial which shook all my energies, physical and mental, terribly and from which I have not yet fully recovered . . . The constitution of my mind is the same – it was somewhat overworked at Candahar and has not yet regained its elasticity – but in essentials I am the very identical character who commenced this journal in 1831.'[3] It was a shock, though, to learn that after all they had achieved together in Afghanistan, Nott had died at the beginning of the year.

Regarding his studies, Rawlinson noted: 'I am now again striving for literary fame, but not with quite the same zest as formerly – a respectable niche in the temple of fame will suffice me.'[4] Over the following months, he therefore worked hard at the report – what he called his 'Memoir' – on Old Persian cuneiform, with the inscription at Bisitun being its centrepiece. He discussed various ideas with Layard in Constantinople, declaring in the first letter to him of 2 April that he now understood the Old Persian script and language: 'The Persian writing you are aware is closely allied to the Sanscrit and is intelligible throughout. In the Memoir I am now rewriting to illustrate the historical record of Bisitun, I give a copious vocabulary and grammar of the language – it will probably be ready for publication in the autumn, unless public business should intervene and causes me to turn my thoughts in another direction.'[5]

Rawlinson knew that mastering related ancient languages, particularly Avestan and Sanskrit, was indispensable if he was to work out the grammar and meaning of words in Old Persian. On the point of leaving Calcutta to take up his Baghdad post eighteen months earlier, he had met a Sanskrit student, Robert Cust, and many years later Cust recalled that Rawlinson had asked 'several intricate questions on Sanskrit Grammar, explaining that he was going to try to interpret some Old Persian Inscriptions at Behistún. So entirely was he in advance of his Epoch, that neither I, nor any of the company, understood what he was after.'[6]

Although the report concerned Old Persian, Rawlinson had also been working on Babylonian and Elamite cuneiform over the last few months, as he admitted to Layard: 'Hitherto I have not taken up the Babylonian writing in earnest, being anxious in the first place to exhaust the Persian tranch of the enquiry and to proceed from that to the Median [Elamite], but I have still, thanks to the Bisitun key, identified the phonetic powers of some 30 of the Babylonian characters, and I hope in time to complete the alphabet.'[7] By assuming that in trilingual inscriptions the Babylonian version would have similar wording to the Old Persian, Rawlinson was able to look in the Babylonian for the same proper names and formulaic phrases – always a useful starting point in decipherment, although he incorrectly believed at this stage that Babylonian signs were an 'alphabet'. He did know enough now to take issue with Layard's pronouncements in the *Malta Times* on cuneiform discoveries at Khorsabad, especially as he had seen some of Botta's finds when they were being shipped southwards through Baghdad to Basra for embarkation to France. He rightly recognized the similarity between the Assyrian cuneiform from Khorsabad and what he had so far seen of Babylonian inscriptions and dismissed the suggestion that the Khorsabad cuneiform might be Elamite: 'Have lately perused with much interest your letters in the Malta Times on Monsieur Botta's discoveries – but I am altogether at issue with you on the classification of Cuneiform writing. I have examined a number of the sculptured slabs which are now lying at Baghdad and I have also been in frequent correspondence with Botta on the subject, and the result to which I have come is that the Assyrian writing is Babylonian and not Median. There is but one character at Khorsabad and not two as you suppose. The tablets look different it must be allowed, but the varieties are merely those of alphabetic modification and dialectic change. My idea is that one general Semitic alphabet prevailed from Ararat to the Persian Gulf.'[8]

Rawlinson could make out the Elamite cuneiform script, but he admitted to Layard that he was puzzled by the language: 'In the Median [Elamite] alphabet I have identified about 90 out of the 100 letters of which it is composed and I can thus read the inscriptions with tolerable fluency, but the language is a mystery which I have hitherto failed to penetrate. It is unquestionably a Scythic dialect but with what living tongue it may be best compared I know not, and I doubt if the point will ever be elaborated.'[9] With Layard living at Constantinople, Rawlinson had found somebody with whom he could share his latest theories fairly quickly, even though many would turn out to be wrong. He was not prepared to submit his developing ideas to publication without extensive research. In a letter to Layard two months later, he proposed: 'The Median [Elamite] writing, that of the centre columns at Hamadan, Persepolis and Bisitun is, as far as my experience goes, confined to the trilingual tablets. I can confidently affirm that it has no connection whatever with the character employed at Van and Khorsabad – and I have never seen it employed singly except on a solitary tablet at Besitun. I can read it with tolerably [sic] fluency and find that it embodies a Scythic dialect.'[10] Many clay tablets with Elamite inscriptions have since been found in archaeological excavations, but Rawlinson was right to be puzzled by the language as it has no known connection with other languages and is still not fully understood today.

In his next letter on 11 June, Rawlinson announced to Layard that one major stage of his report was nearing completion: 'I hope by the next post to send to Constantinople for transmission to England the Bisitun Inscriptions with translations &c complete, and I will request Mr Hawkins to open the case for you if you have any curiosity to inspect them.'[11] He also said that the rest of the report was progressing well, but his proposed publication date had slipped a few months: 'The Memoir I am busily employed in writing out will follow in a few months and the whole thing will be before the public early in the spring [of 1846].'[12] The Royal Asiatic Society had been disappointed by the delay in the greatly anticipated Bisitun report, but now expressed delight in soon being able to publish it, agreeing with Rawlinson that the inscriptions 'should be presented entire to the public, with the facsimiles, and the critical, historical, and grammatical notices which he has made ready to accompany and illustrate them'.[13]

Even though Rawlinson needed to complete this Old Persian report, he could not resist the excitement of trying to decipher Babylonian: 'I daily find new words and names in the Babylonian Inscriptions, which confirmed previous conjectures, and I do not by any means despair before long of forming a complete alphabet.'[14] All his studies, though, were further delayed by official duties and a bout of ill-health, and it seemed likely that French scholars with their access to Botta's finds would surge ahead. Towards the end of August he remarked to Layard that he was 'fully alive to the importance of anticipating the French in the matter of Cuneiform discovery, but still I have a great antipathy to imperfect publication – what with indifferent health indeed, the excessive heat of the season and the necessity of the most careful scrutiny both of text and translation before the final despatch of my papers from Baghdad, I have again allowed this day's post to leave without the packet for Hawkins. The delay is provoking, but I really cannot make up my mind to consign the papers to the irrevocable press, while any passage remains imperfectly understood.'[15] He went on to say that Hector would have trouble selling a load of muskets imported from England, as he had contravened regulations, and regretted that Hector had not consulted him earlier, adding: 'I have tried every possible means of getting him out of the scrape but I have not succeeded.'[16]

Just as Rawlinson was about to send the first batch of Bisitun material to London, his father Abram died, on 1 September 1845, at the age of sixty-eight. Only two years earlier, Rawlinson's uncle Richard Smith at Bristol had died. Rawlinson had seen neither of them since leaving England eighteen years before, but in that time Abram had continued to run the Chadlington estate and train racehorses. Four years previously, while Rawlinson was in Afghanistan, a horse owned and trained by his father, by the name of Coronation, had won the Epsom Derby – a remarkable victory that his father attributed to his stud-groom being deaf and unable to read and write, and so could not be bribed. At the same event, the Epsom Oaks was won by Ghuznee, appropriately named after the capture of the fortress Ghazni in Afghanistan. In all the time Rawlinson had been away, his father only ever wrote once – to give the news about his Derby win. Equally inexplicably, his mother was little better as a correspondent, writing to him only about twice a year.

On 2 September, Rawlinson was ready to 'send by this post to Constantinople a roll of preliminary papers on the Persian cuneiform inscriptions of Bisitun'.[17] His package contained drawings, transliterations, translations and notes relating to the four complete columns of Old Persian, the short fifth column and the detached examples within the relief sculpture panel. Layard was welcome to view the material as long as its journey by steamer to England was not delayed: 'If you or any of the English party at the Embassy would like to cast an eye over the M.S.S. you are at liberty to open the case. It is very desirable at the same time that the papers should reach England with as little delay as possible, for the process of publishing the text, whether type be employed, or copper plate or lithography, will certainly be tedious.'[18]

He described in detail what he was sending: 'The contents of the roll are as follows. 1. General view of the sculptures. 2. Cuneiform text of the 4 Persian columns with restorations in outline.

3 & 4. Copy of the same with the Roman characters with an interlineary of literal Latin translations. 5. Fragments of the 5th half column with partial restorations, and transliteration. 6. My sketch of the detached inscriptions. 7. Text and translations of the Persian detached tablets. Copious notes on the outline text, explanatory of the restorations, doubtful points of orthography.'[19]

Apart from this basic record, Rawlinson revealed that the rest of his report would contain eight chapters: '1. All Cuneiform writing in General. 2. Persian Alphabet. 3. Analysis of the Persian Bisitun inscriptions. 4. Restored copies and translations of all the other Persian inscriptions at present known. 5. General vocabulary. 6. Grammar of the ancient Persian. 7. Historical illustrations. 8. Geographical illustrations. Most of these papers are in a good state of preparation and will be sent home singly as they may be completed.'[20] In the end, Rawlinson was to write six chapters, not the projected eight.

In October, only a month after sending off the drawings and notes, Rawlinson completed the first two chapters, which he despatched to Layard: 'I send by this post under a separate cover to your address the opening Chapters of my Memoir on the Cuneiform Inscriptions – which after perusal pray be kind enough to place under another cover and direct to Professor Horace Hayman Wilson LLD, Director of the Royal Asiat. Soc, Royal Asiatic Society's Rooms N° 14 Grafton S¹ Bond Street London . . . You will find an attempt in the 2nd Chapter to classifying all Cuneiform writing and even to explain the principles of the Median and Babylonian writing.'[21]

The Royal Asiatic Society decided this material was too important to be held back. Without waiting for the remaining chapters, they went ahead with the publication of the Bisitun drawings, transliterations, translations, notes and these first two chapters. Because of its complex and extensive nature, it took a year for the report to be published, but for the first time the Bisitun inscription was available to scholars in the society's journal. The drawings were printed as foldouts because they were so large and detailed. There were eight drawings in all, comprising one of the entire Bisitun monument, one of the relief sculptures, the five columns (over 400 lines) of Old Persian cuneiform inscription below the relief sculptures, and the individual Old Persian inscriptions within the relief sculpture panel. In May 1846, Rawlinson heard that for a while part of his manuscript was believed lost, but in the end it was located in Constantinople. He only found this out once the material had arrived safely in England and was being prepared for publication.

Edwin Norris at the Royal Asiatic Society was responsible for editing Rawlinson's Memoir for publication. Born at Taunton in Somerset in 1795, Norris had become a clerk in the East India Company's offices in London, but his flair for learning languages led him to resign the post in 1837 to become the society's Assistant Secretary. While Rawlinson's drawings were prepared by lithography, Norris worked out how to print the cuneiform signs. Text was at that time typeset by assembling by hand the required letters, numerals and punctuation signs that were individually cast on reusable pieces of metal (moveable type) in countless different sizes and fonts. Nobody had ever before dealt with cuneiform signs in this way, only as lithographed drawings, and no moveable type was available to represent cuneiform.

Norris designed the Old Persian cuneiform types, which were specially cut by Harrison & Co. of St Martin's Lane in London. Each sign needed a separate type. When Layard published a popular book on his Nimrud excavations, the same printers were used, but as the Assyrian cuneiform signs were different, they needed their own set of types, as he explained: 'The cuneiform type used in this text has been cut by Mr Harrison . . . they are remarkable instances of the ingenuity, and I may add taste, of a British printer . . . That the inscriptions of Assyria should be perpetuated, and be made accessible to all through the medium of moveable types, after the loss of the character for nearly 2500 years, is . . . one of the . . . many wonderful achievements of printing.'[22] As editor, Norris read Rawlinson's work thoroughly. He rapidly grasped the subject and was soon correcting errors in the transliteration and restoring missing parts of the cuneiform text. In correspondence with Rawlinson, he pointed out where he was doubtful about the signs that had been copied, suggesting that Rawlinson should check them if he ever visited Bisitun again.

In the society's journal, what Rawlinson called notes were published as seventy-one printed pages, beginning with a transliteration of the entire Old Persian inscription, in which the cuneiform signs were converted into Roman characters. In column 5, for example, he converted the opening words to 'Thátiya. Dár(a)yawush. k'hsháyathiya. ima. tya. adam. akhunawam', and for one of the detached inscriptions by the relief sculptures he converted the initial signs to: 'Iyam. Gumáta. hya. Maghush. adhur'ujiya'. Below these transliterations, he added a translation from Old Persian into Latin, once the common language of European scholars, though by 1845 it was going out of fashion. For these two sentences his translations were: 'Dicit Darius rex: hoc(est) quod ego feci' and 'Hic Gomatus, qui Magus, mendacium dixit'. Rawlinson's expertise in Latin had not faded, and this section did not include his later English translations of 'Says Darius the King: this is what I have done' and 'This Gomates, the Magian, was an imposter', as his readers were considered sufficiently well versed in Latin.

The second part of the notes amounted to a series of footnotes on the difficulties Rawlinson had experienced copying the Bisitun inscription, along with his suggested restoration of missing or dubious signs, and queries over the original spelling of words. He was able to restore missing signs by comparison with similarly worded lines elsewhere in the inscription, particularly where formulaic wording was repeated, such as 'King Darius states', a phrase that started virtually every paragraph in order to emphasize that these were the very words of Darius.

One of the detached Old Persian inscriptions proved very useful in restoring damaged or missing text, as Rawlinson explained for column 1: 'The detached inscription marked A in the key sketch, being a copy of the first ten lines of the great tablet, furnishes a very valuable means of restoration. From this source I have supplied all that portion of the writing which is lost in the fissure on the right hand of the 1st column as far as the 11th line.'[23] In his visit to

Bisitun with Jones and Hector, Rawlinson had also copied the
Elamite inscription, which he began to use as a key to understanding the Old Persian, such as line 94 of column 2, where 'the name
of *Vispáwushtisa*, which is only partially legible, is completed after
the Median orthography',[24] and line 2 of column 3, where the
'third letter from the right hand is doubtful on the rock, but I
have no hesitation whatever in restoring ⟨⟩ to complete the name
of *Ragá*, which is found in the Median copy'.[25]

Rawlinson highlighted the problems in copying the Old Persian
inscription, such as column 3, about which he wrote: 'There
appear to have been only 92 lines in this column, instead of the
96 which we find in the preceding two tablets; but so lamentably
defaced is the lower portion of the rock, that this point even cannot
be positively ascertained. I must observe also, that the number of
lines in columns 3 and 4, whether ninety-two or ninety-three,
occupy the same space as the ninety-six lines of columns 1 and
2, and that the blank surfaces therefore below the lines, which
appear in my copy of the text, are incorrect.'[26] In fact, column 1
has ninety-six lines and columns 3 and 4 ninety-two lines each,
but column 2 actually has ninety-eight lines.

Moving to column 4, Rawlinson opened his discussion by saying: 'The fourth is at once the most mutilated and the least intelligible of all the columns. A fissure, similar to that in the 2nd
column, transects the tablet longitudinally, and throughout the
lower half of the column, the surface of the rock is more or less
broken by the trickling of water from above.'[27] The short column
5 worried Rawlinson the most: 'This tablet, which is supplementary to the preceding columns, is in a state of such deplorable
mutilation, that it would be a waste both of time and ingenuity
to undertake an analysis of the text, or to attempt anything like
a connected and intelligible translation. A few lines, at the same
time, may be restored in the opening paragraph with some plaus-
ability; for the names are fortunately preserved, and the narrative
evidently follows the same construction with which we are already
familiar.'[28]

The ledge below the inscription in column 5 was far too narrow to rest a ladder, and unlike the gap in the ledge beneath the Elamite, he was unable to rig up a bridge here. Consequently, Rawlinson felt his results were flawed: 'I cannot depend on the accuracy of this copy with nearly the same confidence as on that of preceding columns; for, in the first place, the writing is exceedingly difficult of access, owing to the abrupt falling off of the ledge of rock on which the foot of the ladder requires to rest; in the second place, the fragments on the left hand, in the centre, and on the right hand of the tablet, will not admit of being copied in continuous lines, but can only be taken in separate columns, the chances of erroneous collocation being thereby greatly multiplied; and in the third place, with very little time at my disposal, and in despair of obtaining any satisfactory information from the tablet, I neglected to verify the copy after it was taken by comparison, line for line, with the writing on the rock; a precaution which I adopted, for the most part, in the preceding columns, and which I consider to be indispensable to a perfect confidence in the fidelity of the transcript.'[29] He was being scientifically rigorous in admitting possible errors in order to establish the level of reliability of each part of his transcription.

Two chapters concluded this stage of Rawlinson's publication. The first one was an eighteen-page history of the study of cuneiform, starting with the discoveries of Grotefend. Much of this was his original report written in 1839 that had been interrupted by the Afghan War, but was now updated with notes and additional paragraphs to show what had been subsequently achieved by scholars, in particular by Westergaard and by Lassen. In 1844 Lassen published a lengthy report on Old Persian inscriptions, correcting some of his earlier work and giving translations of all Old Persian inscriptions known to him – excluding the most important, Bisitun, as Rawlinson was the only person to possess that inscription apart from what he had sent to Burnouf. Although a copy of Lassen's work was posted to Rawlinson the previous summer, he received it only as he was finishing off chapters one and two, in August 1845, 'owing to the difficulty of communicating between Bonn and Baghdad'.[30]

At the end of his first chapter, Rawlinson commented on Lassen's publication: 'This is I believe the last [latest] work that has appeared upon the subject, and as might have been expected, it anticipates in some degree the novelty of the present Memoir. I have received a copy of the pamphlet whilst I have been writing the following pages, and I have found it of the greatest convenience, as a manual of reference. The marginal notes, indeed, that I have added to the present text, will show the care with which I have consulted it; but at the same time, I am bound to say that my translations, already completed when the book arrived, were, if not independent of assistance, at any rate beyond the reach of alteration, and I have further to regret that an ignorance of German has deprived me of that aid on questionable points of grammar, which, if I had been able to follow the Professor's arguments, I could not have failed to derive from the matured opinions of so eminent and correct a scholar.'[31]

It was now Rawlinson's opinion that the study of Old Persian cuneiform was drawing to a close, 'for the materials available for analysis or verification, are now, I believe, entirely exhausted; and unless excavations should be undertaken on a great scale either at Susa, Persepolis, or Pasargadae, we must rest content with the sorrowful conviction that we have here, comprised in a few pages, all that remains of the ancient Persian language, and all that contemporary native evidence records of the glories of the Achaemenides.'[32]

In chapter two, Rawlinson discussed in thirty-four pages his own views on cuneiform writing, which he thought 'was a very early, if not the earliest, method employed by man for embodying language in an artificial form'.[33] He reckoned that Babylonian was the most ancient of 'the three great classes of Cuneiform writing'[34] (Babylonian, Elamite and Old Persian), a justifiable opinion because no examples of the earlier Sumerian writing had then been encountered. Although his entire report was devoted to Old Persian, Rawlinson included in chapter two a discussion of Babylonian and Elamite (what he was calling Median), although he originally planned to include more detail, as he told Layard: 'I had an idea at one time of adding the alphabets of these two systems [Babylonian and Elamite], but I thought it hazardous to give the key before I was prepared to push the enquiry further.'[35] Even though he knew the French were a threat, he preferred to hold back until Botta had published a compilation of the different cuneiform signs from the Assyrian inscriptions at Khorsabad.

While Botta had been studying an extensive number of inscriptions, Rawlinson explained that he himself had only examined a few Babylonian inscriptions dating to the time of the kings of Persia: 'My own labours have been restricted to the Achaemenian Babylonians, as I have found it at Persepolis, Hamadan, and Behistun, and I have attempted nothing further at present than the determination of the phonetic powers of the characters.'[36] He had worked out a fairly extensive Babylonian alphabet from twenty-seven proper names in the inscriptions, but, he said, 'I have left the grammar and construction of the language hitherto untouched'.[37] Of the other cuneiform script, Elamite, Rawlinson suggested: 'the time is rapidly approaching in which we shall be enabled to examine the subject in a more critical and elaborate manner. The tablets of Persepolis and Behistun have furnished above ninety proper names of which we have the equivalents in the Persian character, and the repetition of these names in many places, with variations of orthography, has contributed a further help to the classification of the signs. With such facilities, then, for alphabetical identification, and with the extensive field of grammatical comparison afforded by the Behistun translations, it must be evident that under patient investigation, the language must be recognised, if it have a living representative; or if entirely extinct, that it may be in a measure resuscitated. That investigation I have not yet completed.'[38]

While Rawlinson and Layard had been exchanging ideas on cuneiform, Layard himself had continued to work unpaid for Canning at Constantinople, forced to endure a frustrating wait for a chance of a paid position or an opportunity to fulfil his great desire to investigate the mounds of Nimrud and Nineveh near Mosul. His former travelling companion Mitford had now reached

Ceylon and, unaware of Layard's involvement, wrote to him in March 1845: 'I saw in the papers an account of a Frenchman Mr Botta having excavated at Nineveh [Khorsabad was often called the 'French Nineveh'] and made great discoveries ... If you find any account of this in any of the papers or periodicals I wish you would send it to me.'[39] He then added a note about Rawlinson, having met him in Kandahar: 'Rawlinson made a good move from Candahar to Bagdad, he was one of the very few efficient men in Affganistan. The whole of the business in that country from beginning to end was scandalous and disgraceful.'[40] In a letter written at Mosul in April, Alexander Hector also fuelled Layard's longing to excavate: 'I should like to have a dig in some of the Mounds here, for Antiquities ... Mr Sterling [his associate in England] is trying to get some money subscribed in England for excavating in these parts – but our rich people at home seem to be wrap't up in their Capital that it is difficult to get them to open their hearts in a matter of this kind; if I had money I would do it at once.'[41]

It looked as if Canning was about to go on leave to England, which would leave Layard in a precarious situation, so in the summer of 1845 he persuaded the Ambassador to allow him to embark on his expedition: 'I, therefore, suggested to him that I might proceed to Mosul and continue the excavations in the Assyrian ruins, which M. Botta had now abandoned ... Sir Stratford not only agreed to my proposal, but offered to share in the expenses which would be incurred in making tentative excavations in the mounds I had indicated. I was able to contribute a small sum from my own resources, which, added to the sixty pounds he was ready to advance, would, if employed with the strictest economy, meet the expenses of my journey to Mosul, and of experimental researches amongst the ruins. I was persuaded that, if the results proved such as I expected them to be, funds for carrying on the explorations on an adequate scale would be forthcoming in England, where M. Botta's discoveries had already created considerable interest.'[42]

At Constantinople, Layard took lessons in surveying and

mapping in readiness for leaving for Mosul, arriving there in the cooler weather at the end of October. Botta had left three months earlier, but Layard was welcomed by Christian Rassam, the British Vice-Consul, who introduced him to the Pasha, a native of Crete (also part of the Ottoman Empire) and greatly feared by Mosul's inhabitants. Layard did not let the Pasha know the true object of his visit: 'There were many reasons which rendered it necessary that my plans should be concealed, until I was ready to put them into execution. Although I had always experienced from M. Botta the most friendly assistance, there were others who did not share his sentiments; from the authorities and the people of the town I could only expect the most decided opposition. On the 8th of November, having secretly procured a few tools, and engaged a mason at the moment of my departure, and carrying with me a variety of guns, spears, and other formidable weapons, I declared that I was going to hunt wild boars in a neighbouring village, and floated down the Tigris on a small raft constructed for my journey. I was accompanied by Mr Ross, a British merchant of Mosul, my Cawass, and a servant.'[43]

Although Henry Ross had already met Rawlinson at a Christmas gathering at Baghdad, this was his first encounter with Layard, and they got on well, with Ross writing to his sister: 'Layard is such a nice fellow – very clever and very amusing.'[44] Rather than a boar-hunting expedition, their goal was in fact the mound of the ancient city of Nimrud, and it took them five hours to descend the Tigris to Naifa, a village near Nimrud that had been ruined through the depredations of the Pasha. Layard slept little that night: 'The hovel in which we had taken shelter, and its inmates, did not invite slumber; but such scenes and companions were not new to me: they could have been forgotten, had my brain been less excited. Hopes, long cherished, were now to be realised, or were to end in disappointment.'[45] To his aunt in London a few days later, Layard wrote, 'You will probably not before have heard of the miserable village from which I am writing to you, which still bears the name of the 'mighty hunter,' and which stands near the ruins of what tradition declares to be his

[Nimrod's] peculiar city. Whatever the old may have been, the new Nimroud is a very wretched place ... I must tell you that I came down here five days ago, and immediately began excavating in the great mound which forms the nucleus of the ruins ... The ruins called Nimroud are situated near the Tigris, about 18 miles from Mosul. They consist entirely of artificial mounds, and are very extensive. The great mound into which I am digging is about 1800 feet in length, 900 in breadth, and 60 or 70 in height.'[46]

Rawlinson heard of Layard's arrival in Mosul, but was pessimistic about the possibility of Nimrud possessing sculptured stone slabs like those Botta had found at Khorsabad, because of Nimrud's distance from a source of stone. He wrote to Layard on 12 November: 'I was equally surprised and delighted at hearing of your arrival at Mosul and of the object which you are commissioned to execute. I almost fear Nimrood is too far from the mountains to possess marble palaces like those of Khorsabad, but you can hardly fail to find inscriptions and other relics that will repay your labor.'[47] Instead, he felt that Nebbi Yunus, one of the Nineveh mounds next to Mosul, would be far more productive. As for cuneiform, Rawlinson thought that it would soon be possible to read any inscriptions that Layard might find: 'I feel quite certain that with Botta's table of variants and my Bisitun key, we can make out the Assyrian alphabet, but I cannot be seduced into the enquiry until I have finished the Persian branch at which I am now working'[48] – he still had several chapters of his Old Persian Memoir to complete and send to the Royal Asiatic Society.

On his very first day Layard proved Rawlinson wrong about the presence of stone slabs. From Naifa it took Layard twenty minutes to walk to the site, where it was easy to examine the surface of the mound because there was no vegetation: 'Broken pottery and fragments of bricks, both inscribed with the cuneiform character, were strewed on all sides. The Arabs watched my motions as I wandered to and fro, and observed with surprise the objects I had collected. They joined, however, in the search, and brought me handfuls of rubbish, amongst which I found with joy the fragment of a bas-relief. The material on which it was carved had been exposed to fire, and resembled, in every respect, the burnt gypsum of Khorsabad. Convinced from this discovery that sculptured remains must still exist in some part of the mound, I sought for a place where excavations might be commenced with a prospect of success.'[49]

The place chosen was where a large piece of stone protruded above the surface and could not be removed: 'I ordered all the men to work around it, and they shortly uncovered a second slab to which it had been united. Continuing in the same line, we came upon a third; and, in the course of the morning, laid bare ten more, the whole forming a square, with one stone missing at the N.W. corner. It was evident that the top of a chamber had been discovered, and that the gap was its entrance. I now dug down the face of the stones, and an inscription in the cuneiform character was soon exposed to view. Similar inscriptions occupied the centre of all the slabs, which were in the best preservation; but plain, with the exception of the writing.'[50]

Next Layard moved half his workmen to the south-west corner of the mound: 'I dug at once into the side of the mound, which was here very steep, and thus avoided the necessity of removing much earth. We came almost immediately to a wall, bearing inscriptions in the same character . . . but the slabs had evidently been exposed to intense heat, were cracked in every part, and, reduced to lime, threatened to fall to pieces as soon as uncovered. Night interrupted our labours. I returned to the village well satisfied with their result.'[51] Everything, it seemed, was covered with cuneiform, and similar discoveries were made over the next few days, with more inscriptions but no sculptures, as he described to his aunt on 10 November: 'I have been hitherto sufficiently fortunate to find several chambers of white marble covered with cuneiform inscriptions; as yet no figures; but, from fragments discovered in the rubbish, I have no doubt they will come; at any rate, I shall have a very rich collection of inscriptions.'[52]

Layard now decided to return to Mosul to see the Pasha. He found the people in the town terrified, as the Pasha had just feigned his death, in order to punish those who participated in the widespread rejoicing. Although the Pasha and others now attempted to place obstacles in his path, Layard nevertheless hired agents to begin digging into other mounds nearby and also rode out to see some sculptured figures that had just been discovered elsewhere, but they turned out to be nothing: 'Such disappointments were daily occurring; and I wearied myself in scouring the country to see remains which had been most minutely described to me as groups of sculptures, and slabs covered with writing, and which generally proved to be the ruin of some modern building, or an early tombstone inscribed with Arabic characters.'[53]

On 19 November Layard returned to Nimrud, where work had continued in his absence, and a week later the first sculptured slabs were unearthed, depicting scenes of warfare and all bearing cuneiform inscriptions. He recorded that 'the Arabs were no less excited than myself by the discovery; and notwithstanding a violent shower of rain, working until dark, they completely exposed to view two slabs'.[54] He wrote to his mother at the end of the month: 'Since I last wrote to you I have been employed like the veriest mole in grubbing up the earth, and with such success that, after having discovered several chambers built of slabs of white marble, I yesterday alighted upon sculptures resembling in character those of M. Botta's monument at Khorsabad. I have now no doubt that the whole mound of Nimroud, vast as it is, contains the ruins of one great palace ... The slabs I have uncovered, forming the side of a chamber, are pretty well preserved. One represents warriors fighting in chariots; another, the siege of a city; others, men on horseback; all executed with much spirit. The inscriptions already discovered are exceedingly numerous, amounting fully to one hundred, and I have been, as you may suppose, fully occupied in copying these extraordinary specimens of penmanship. I need scarcely say that they are all in the cuneiform character, very long and very complicated.'[55]

Just when incredible discoveries looked imminent, on 30 November the Pasha ordered Layard to cease excavating, having learned, he said, that 'the mound in which you are digging had been used as a burying-ground by Mussulmans, and was covered with their graves; now you are aware that by the law it is forbidden to disturb a tomb, and the Cadi [Muslim judge] and Mufti [Muslim legal adviser] have already made representations to me on the subject . . . I cannot allow you to proceed; you are my dearest and most intimate friend: if anything happens to you, what grief should I not suffer! your life is more valuable than old stones.'[56] Layard knew there were no such graves, but decided to return to Nimrud the next day to draw the sculptures and copy the inscriptions so far uncovered. He left in a great hurry, explaining to his mother: 'I am again resuming my excavation, and my horse is at the door waiting for me to start for Nimroud. I have just heard that my old friend, Mr Hector of Baghdad, has run up to pay me a visit, and that he is waiting for me at the mounds. His stay with me will be very agreeable, as it is somewhat dull to be all alone.'[57] He added: 'I hope soon to set to work in good earnest digging and removing sculpture, and that some day you will have the pleasure of seeing some of the fruits of my labour in the British Museum or some other public place in England.'[58]

Alexander Hector had brought with him a letter from Rawlinson, written when he thought Layard had only found stone slabs with inscriptions, not relief sculptures as well: 'I cannot tell you how exceedingly gratified I was to hear of your successful excavation of Nimrud – for my own part I regard Inscriptions as of infinitely greater value than sculptures – the latter may please virtuosi – they have no doubt a certain degree of intrinsic interest, but the tablets are bona fide histories, and very shortly I feel perfectly certain they will be completely intelligible. The building at Nimrood will hardly be worth a transport en masse to London, but your copies of the Inscriptions will be of the very highest interest.'[59] He went on to say that he had just completed the third chapter of his Old Persian cuneiform report: 'Have today sent off [to the Royal Asiatic Society in London] my Chapter on the Cuneiform alphabet . . . 130 closely written pages of the most abstruse enquiry possible.'[60]

Rawlinson's 130 pages would be reduced to 122 printed pages by the Royal Asiatic Society, when published with chapters four and five in eighteen months time. He warned the society that the chapter was 'extremely elaborate and will I fear be hardly intelligible to those who are not conversant with the subject. It will also require a very careful supervision of the press.'[61] In the chapter, Rawlinson drew extensively on his knowledge of Avestan, Sanskrit, Persian and ancient Greek in order to present his discussion of the values and use of individual signs. At the start of the chapter a foldout table of thirty-nine signs compared the interpretations of different scholars, such as Grotefend, Saint-Martin, Burnouf and Lassen, along with his own extremely accurate ideas. For example, for the sign 𐎭 he showed that it was universally agreed that this was the letter *d* (though it is now thought to be *da*), whereas for the sign 𐎰 he showed that it was considered to be *i* by Grotefend, *h* by Saint-Martin, *y* by Burnouf, and *t'h* by Lassen. He himself was in agreement with Lassen, interpreting it as *th*, while today it is believed to be *tha*. Towards the end of the chapter, Rawlinson presented the signs used to express numbers, and ended with a discussion on how one sign was used as a word divider.

Now that he had finished chapter three, Rawlinson said to Layard in his letter: 'Have now, however, plain sailing before me and feel quite relieved with having got rid of the preliminary assignment.'[62] He also invited Layard to Baghdad: 'I sincerely hope to see you here at Christmas and the longer you can stop with me, the better I shall be pleased.'[63] For the moment, though, Layard was back at Nimrud, even though the Pasha had asked him to cease his excavations. He employed a few men to guard the sculptures, but after two days he had these same men digging new trenches. Shortly afterwards they found new sculptured slabs, including representations of winged bulls and lions.

Convinced of the great potential of Nimrud, Layard contacted Canning to ask for a firman (official permission) to continue excavating, and returned to Mosul on 18 December 1845. On hearing of his new discoveries, Rawlinson became enthusiastic about the idea of sculptures: 'I need hardly say how much I was gratified to hear that you have found sculptured slabs at Nimrud. I see every prospect now if the Ambassador will hasten himself and obtain you a Strong Firman of our being in the field before the French. If you could have a chamber or two cleaned out by the beginning of March, and the rafts ready, I would send up the Steamer at that time with tackles &c &c and the whole of the marbles might be down in Baghdad in a fortnight. The Nitocris [steamer] could then tow the river boats freighted with the marbles to Bussorah [Basra] in April. They might reach Bombay before the monsoon and be in England in the Autumn ... The priority of European exhibition [over the French] would I think be a great triumph for us.'[64]

After the completion of his excavations at Khorsabad, Botta had spent the winter of 1844–45 occupied in transporting some of the finest objects by raft down the Tigris, but at the end of 1845 they were still at Basra awaiting shipment to France. The race was on with the French to get the sculptures from Nimrud on display at the British Museum before the French could do the same at the Louvre with the finds from Khorsabad. Rawlinson advised Layard that he had written to Canning about using the *Nitocris* steamer, 'pointing out the political advantages of having our flag on the upper Tigris, as well as the physical assistance we may give you at Nimrud – and I have no expectation that he will disapprove of the arrangements'.[65]

At this stage nobody had any real idea of the date of the discoveries at Nimrud, or those of Botta at Khorsabad, nor was it possible to find out the original names of these places. Prehistoric sites can be dated in archaeological excavations by stratigraphic analysis, by comparison with similar sites and finds, and nowadays by various scientific means. Layard had the advantage at Nimrud of excavating a historical site containing written records – but in Assyrian cuneiform that nobody could yet read. Nimrud, the modern name for the site, had originated from the local legend that supposed it to have been built by Ashur, the son of Nimrod, who was the great-grandson of Noah and the founder of the first cities after the Flood. The Bible relates: 'Cush [a grandson of Noah] was the father of Nimrod, who became a mighty warrior on the earth. He was a mighty hunter before the LORD: And the beginning of his kingdom was Babel, Erech, and Accad, and Calneh, in the land of Shinar [Babylonia]. Out of that land went forth Asshur, and builded Nineveh, and the city Rehoboth, and Calah, and Resen between Nineveh and Calah: the same *is* a great city'.[66] Layard explained to his aunt what he thought the site of Nimrud was: 'I believe the city to be Resen, mentioned in Genesis X. 12, as between Nineveh and Calah, a great city, built by Ashur. And it is curious that tradition still assigns to it this origin; the Arabs around calling the great mound the palace of Asur or Athur. This city was probably afterwards known as Larissa, and under that name mentioned by Xenophon.'[67] Nowadays, it is no longer accepted that Ashur was a person's name, but the region Assyria, changing the reading of the Biblical passage to: 'Out of that land he [Nimrod] went to Assyria, where he built Nineveh, Rehoboth, Calah and Resen'.[68]

Rawlinson had another idea. 'I have lately examined with some attention the Geographical and historical questions connected with Nimrud,' he told Layard, 'and I can come to no other con- clusion that it is the original Nineveh which was destroyed under Sardanapalus, the ruins at Nebi Joonus being those of the Second Nineveh ... We shall no doubt find out all these matters before long, for I hold [that] with extensive tables of variants and the Bisitun key, the Inscriptions must yield to enquiry and give up their mysterious contents.'[69] Rawlinson later found that this identification was wrong, but at the time it was good enough for Layard, who went on to publish his findings at Nimrud as the remains of the legendary Nineveh. Nimrud is now known to be the city called Calah in the Bible, while the two mounds of Koyun- jik and Nebbi Yunus, opposite Mosul, are the actual remains of Nineveh. Resen has not been located, and there may never have been a city by that name.

Once again, Rawlinson invited Layard for Christmas: 'Whether you are permitted to resume your labors or not, I should think at Christmas you might well allow yourself a few days relaxation at Baghdad ... I shall accordingly expect you with Mr Hector by the next post and promise myself the greatest pleasure in making your personal acquaintance.'[70] Back in Mosul on 18 December 1845, Layard found that the population was in a state of joy, as a new Pasha had been appointed and the former Pasha and his followers instantly reduced to poverty: 'During these events the state of the country rendered the continuation of my researches at Nimroud almost impossible. I determined, therefore, to proceed to Baghdad, to make arrangements for the removal of the sculptures at a future period, and to consult generally with Major Rawlinson, from whose experience and knowledge I could derive the most valuable assistance. A raft having been constructed, I started with Mr Hector . . . and reached that city on the 24th of December'[71] – after nine months of constantly exchanging information and ideas by letter, this was to be the first meeting between Layard and Rawlinson.

Twelve: Nimrud, Niffer
and Nineveh

The first meeting between Rawlinson and Layard seemed to go
well, with Layard writing to his mother from Baghdad two days
after Christmas: 'I could not resist the temptation of running down
to spend Christmas and New Year Days with old friends and with
Major Rawlinson, from whom I had received the most kind and
pleasing invitation – you know in these countries a distance of
three or four hundred miles only, makes near neighbours ... I
had long wished to make the formal acquaintance of Major Rawlinson, with whom I had long kept up a constant and regular
correspondence, and I received no disappointment on meeting
him. You may suppose that we are already deep in discussing
researches on Assyrian, Persian and Babylonian antiquities, languages & geography etc etc – for on these subjects, you know,
the Major is perhaps the first living authority. The results of our
deliberations lead me to hope that before two or three years have
expired we shall be able to get at the mysterious contents of the
Assyrian cuneiform inscriptions and then Nimroud will furnish
us a rich historical collection.'[1]

He related that Rawlinson had a good library and was 'finishing
his translation of a memoir of the Persian cuneiform portion of
the great inscription of Bisitun and he then intends to take the
Assyrian seriously in hand. For myself, for the present, I must

content myself with my manual labor.'[2] Layard returned to Mosul at the beginning of January 1846, but it was a fortnight before he rode out to Nimrud. Constant rain had transformed the appearance of the countryside: 'The mound was no longer an arid and barren heap; its surface and its sides were equally covered with verdure.'[3] With the countryside more settled under the new Pasha, Arab tribes were moving back into the surrounding plain from the mountains, and Layard now felt it was safe enough to transfer his lodgings to the village of Nimrud. Hormuzd Rassam, the brother of the British Vice-Consul Christian Rassam, was employed to oversee and pay the workmen.

Almost immediately attempts were made to stop the work. 'I had scarcely resumed my labours,' Layard remarked, 'when I received information that the Cadi of Mosul was endeavouring to stir up the people against me, chiefly on the plea that I was carrying away treasure; and, what was worse, finding inscriptions which proved that the Franks [foreigners] once held the country, and upon the evidence of which they intended immediately to resume possession of it, exterminating all true believers. These stories, however absurd they may appear, rapidly gained ground in the town.'[4] The decipherment of the Assyrian inscriptions from Nimrud had actually hardly begun, and Rawlinson's first letter to Layard after their Christmas meeting shows that he was still trying to work out the values of Akkadian (Assyrian and Babylonian) cuneiform signs. A major problem was the paucity of trilingual inscriptions, because he had not been able to copy the main Babylonian inscription at Bisitun. Over two years previously he had received from Westergaard the Old Persian version of the trilingual inscription at Naqsh-i Rustam, but now decided to wait for the Babylonian version to be sent to him. 'I expect it will go far to complete the Babylonian alphabet,' he told Layard in late January. 'The next point will be to identify the Babylonian characters with their Assyrian correspondents ... Interpretation however is quite a difficult affair – that will I think only yield to the most laborious analysis, for we have little or nothing to guide us in reconstructing the lost language.'[5] He thought he should be able to work out the

Assyrian and Babylonian signs, but would be no farther forward in working out the language.

In mid-February, Layard resumed excavations at Nimrud with just a few men digging in the south-west palace area. Up to now, the sculptured slabs that were discovered had evidently been reused from another building and had been subsequently damaged by fire, with none good enough to transport to England. His new discoveries were little better, as they were very decayed, though not burnt. Layard therefore moved his men further north on the mound, where sculptured slabs lining the walls of another palace began to appear, in excellent condition, and some still painted in different colours. One morning as he approached the mound, he was met by two Arabs riding urgently towards him. '"Hasten, O Bey," exclaimed one of them – "hasten to the diggers, for they have found Nimrod himself. Wallah, it is wonderful, but it is true! we have seen him with our eyes. There is no God but God".'[6] At the mound, Layard climbed down into the new trench, and the Arab workmen removed a makeshift screen to reveal an enormous human head that he realized from Botta's discoveries at Khorsabad could only belong to a colossal winged bull.

The Arabs had been amazed and terrified at their discovery: 'One of the workmen on catching the first glimpse of the monster, had thrown down his basket and run off towards Mosul as fast as his legs could carry him. I learnt this with regret,' Layard commented, 'as I anticipated the consequences.'[7] Soon after, a sheikh with half his tribe rode up to the edge of the trench and exclaimed: 'This is not the work of men's hands, but of those infidel giants of whom the Prophet, peace be with him! has said, that they were higher than the tallest date tree; this is one of the idols which Noah, peace be with him! cursed before the flood.'[8] Layard's workmen were persuaded to continue, and before nightfall had discovered that this head belonged to a colossal winged human-headed lion, not a bull, about 12 feet high and covered with cuneiform inscriptions. It formed one of a pair of lions guarding the western entrance of a room, not as freestanding sculptures, but placed against the side of a wall. Layard realized why they had five legs: 'The head and fore-part, facing the chamber, were in full; but only one side of the rest of the slab was sculptured, the back being placed against the wall of sun-dried bricks. That the spectator might have both a perfect front and side view of the figures, they were furnished with five legs; two were carved on the end of the slab to face the chamber, and three on the side.'[9]

In order to demonstrate that the discovery was worthy of cele-bration, Layard ordered a sheep to be slaughtered and engaged some wandering musicians. Dancing was maintained all night, but in Mosul the terrified Arab had broadcast to everyone he met that Nimrod had appeared. The outcome was much as Layard had expected, with the intervention of the Cadi forcing him to halt his excavations. He dismissed all but two of his workers and carried on digging at a leisurely pace. Writing to his mother, he described his progress: 'I am sure you will be glad to hear that my excavations are proving as successful as I could possibly have anticipated. Every day brings fresh discoveries, and I am now anxiously waiting for instructions to begin on a large scale ... I am exceedingly busy with drawing and copying inscriptions. There will be an immense number; but a very small part of the mound is yet explored.'[10]

In early March, Rawlinson let Layard know that for the past few days he had been travelling in the desert with Hector, tracing the old beds of the Tigris and Euphrates. One visit was to Niffer, over 100 miles south-east of Baghdad, with a huge and intriguing mound of the former city of Nippur towering 65 feet high above the surrounding desert. Nothing whatsoever was then known about the city, but it is now believed to date back seven thousand years and was a major religious centre dedicated to Enlil, a god of the storm winds and responsible for devastating floods. Nippur was in the northernmost part of Sumer, and tens of thousands of Sumerian cuneiform tablets have since been discovered in exca-vations. Rawlinson described his pioneering expedition many years later to his two young sons: 'I determined to go on an expedition to the Ruins of Niffer – for some distance we steamed down the River Tigris to the place where we were to meet the horses and escort, ready for our 3 or 4 [mile] ride to Niffer. The Steamer [*Nitocris*] was desired to meet me on its return up the river from Bussorah [Basra] at a certain point on a certain day. We start off with our tents, hunting, shooting and surveying for 3 days – then I sent my tent to the point near the river where the Steamer is to meet me, and go myself with a small party of horsemen at daylight to the Ruins of Niffer. These ruins are supposed to be the place where Nimrod fell and to be now the abode of Hobgoblins, and Devils ... so that I had great difficulty in enducing any body to accompany me to such a haunted spot.'[11]

Once there, Rawlinson became engrossed in his work: 'We were a long time digging and examining the mounds – as I was the first European who had visited them. The largest is called the Bint el Ameer or the chief's daughter – stated in the Inscriptions to be the great Temple of Jupiter, of which the top reached to the Heavens, and the foundations (roots) were in the centre of the earth ... Being much interested in my work I forgot how fast the time was passing, and that I had a ride of some hours to accomplish before dark – if we did not wish to be lost in the desert. I lingered until at last my companions dragged me away. We mounted our steeds and cantered on for many miles, but still our tents were far distant – darker and darker it grew. We wandered first one way then another, looking in vain for the fires which Redzib was to keep burning as a guide for us in case we were late.'[12]

In the end Rawlinson refused to go any farther and laid down on the sand to sleep, with his pistols as a pillow, but he suddenly jumped up on hearing his dog Tiger barking. The dog, having left the tents and found the party, now led them back to the river, where they discovered that Rawlinson's servant had extinguished the fires, fearing they were all robbers. 'We then had some excellent dinner,' Rawlinson continued, 'and I did not forget to give a large share to Tiger. Next day I went down to meet the Steamer, but saw no sign of her. We remained for a couple of hours shooting Francolin and hares to Tiger's great amusement, but still no

steamer came. Then we held a council of war to decide what to
do. Should I wait or start to ride back 6 or 7 days to Baghdad?
The Arabs thought the Steamer had passed – but while they
debated, I sauntered up to the top of a mound, and looking to the
South I saw a small thin line of smoke in the far distance! Then
I came down and said I think I see the Steamer coming! but they
laughed me to scorn, and declared it was burning reeds in the
marshes. Then I went down to the edge of the river and putting
my ear close to the water listened intently for some seconds – and
sure enough I heard distinctly Pit Pat, Pit Pat, Pit Pat, of the
Paddles. The sound is conveyed along the surface of the water,
much quicker and farther than it can be by land . . . The Arabs
were still incredulous, till after waiting an hour we saw the noble
vessel rounding a point in the distance.'[13]

Even in this remote location, the accustomed ceremonies in
Rawlinson's honour were carried out, as he described: 'Presently
we heard the Captain call out at the top of his voice Ease her –
Stop her – Let go the Anchor, hrrrr . . . and as the chain runs
out, the vessel comes proudly up against the bank of the river to
receive us – a plank is thrown out as a bridge – I pass over. The
marines present arms, the Resident flag is run up to the mast
head. Tiger rushes on board to pay his respect to Dr Hyslop [assis-
tant surgeon] who is his special friend, when suddenly Bang goes
the first gun as they proceed to fire a salute for the Resident. Tiger
who can't bear a gun takes the alarm and jumps clean overboard
on the outer side.'[14] At this point mayhem ensued as the dog
landed on a boar that was swimming away with several others,
having been disturbed by the steamer. Everyone snatched up their
rifles, and 'we finished with a famous haul of 2 fine large boars
and 3 smaller ones, which supplied the crew with fresh pork for
over 2 or 3 days steam to Baghdad, and so ended our trip to
Niffer'.[15]

Only briefly mentioning this expedition in his letter to Layard,
Rawlinson then explained the latest situation with the steamer.
Not aware of Layard's magnificent discoveries in Nimrod's north-
west palace, Rawlinson thought that his work was not sufficiently

advanced to make good use of the steamer yet. He had originally promised the steamer to Layard at the beginning of March, but Rawlinson now needed it for a trip to Basra. Instead, he hoped it would leave for Nimrud at the end of the month or the beginning of April. As the French finds from the rival site at Khorsabad were still at Basra, there was no sense of urgency.

Two weeks later Rawlinson gloomily advised Layard that there was no hope of ever reading the newly discovered inscriptions until they had worked out the meaning of all the cuneiform signs. Even then they would need to use trilingual inscriptions to try to understand the language: 'You must remember however that until we identify the Babylonian and Assyrian characters, we have made no progress whatever – and that even when the alphabet is complete we shall not be able to understand the inscriptions, unless our attentive analysis of the trilingual tablets obtain for us some insight into the languages. I have no doubt but that the difficulty will ultimately yield to research, but it will take, depend on it, many years of intense labor, before we arrive at satisfactory results.'[16]

It was now the middle of March, which, Layard noted, 'in Mesopotamia is the brightest epoch of spring. A new change had come over the face of the plain of Nimroud . . . Flowers of every hue enamelled the meadows; not thinly scattered over the grass as in northern climes, but in such thick and gathering clusters that the whole plain seemed a patchwork of many colours. The dogs, as they returned from hunting, issued from the grass dyed red, yellow or blue, according to the flowers through which they had last forced their way.'[17] Towards the end of the month another pair of colossal winged human-headed lions were discovered, guarding the northern entrance of the same room, while sculptures in another room beyond were also uncovered. When the cuneiform was eventually deciphered, inscriptions would reveal this building to be the earliest known Assyrian palace, built by King Ashurnasirpal II in the ninth century BC, about a century before the mythical foundation of Rome in 753 BC.

Layard was particularly struck by the lions: 'I used to contemplate for hours these mysterious emblems, and muse over their intent and history ... These winged human-headed lions were not idle creations, the off-spring of mere fancy; their meaning was written upon them. They had awed and instructed races which flourished 3000 years ago. Through the portals which they guarded, kings, priests, and warriors, had borne sacrifices to their altars, long before the wisdom of the East had penetrated to Greece, and had furnished its mythology with symbols long recognised by the Assyrian votaries. They may have been buried, and their existence may have been unknown, before the foundation of the eternal city [Rome]. For twenty-five centuries they had been hidden from the eye of man, and they now stood forth once more in their ancient majesty. But how changed was the scene around them! The luxury and civilisation of a mighty nation had given place to the wretchedness and ignorance of a few half-barbarous tribes. The wealth of temples, and the riches of great cities, had been succeeded by ruins and shapeless heaps of earth.'[18]

Even though Layard had made incredible discoveries, he was still waiting for official permission from Canning at Constantinople to excavate, and, more importantly, further funding. In exasperation, Layard wrote to his aunt: 'Botta has just informed me that he gets 60,000 francs from his Government for his Khorsabad discovery, I have vague apparitions of 3000 gold pieces fleeting before my eyes, and for the first time in my life have become intent on the prospect of accumulating riches. But these happy visions are backed by the hideous skeleton of Government generosity, and not much improved by the retrospection of time, health and labour thrown away upon empty pockets ... I am still in ignorance of the intentions of the Government with regard to Nimroud, whether the excavations are to be carried on, or whether the field will be abandoned to the French. The discovery is so full of interest that it would be really a disgrace not to make the most of it.'[19]

Rawlinson was also exasperated about the apparent lack of interest in funding Layard's work, but had to be diplomatic: 'The Money business fairly puzzles me. I would myself willingly place a sum at your disposal for excavation if I were to get a share of the marbles – but Sir Stratford would certainly think this an improper interference – he writes to me – "I am working on my own account, though with a view to national benefit and Govt support in due season" – and if I were therefore to come forward he would evidently think me an interloper.'[20] Nevertheless, Rawlinson did offer Layard funding: 'Consider this and if you care in fairness to Sir Stratford admit me to a participation in the spoils, draw on me at Mosul for 5000 Tomans as a commencement – it is a very delicate business and I confess I do not understand it.'[21]

In fact Canning was trying to secure government funding, but not with the haste that Layard required. Just after Christmas he had written to his wife in England: 'Layard is making very important discoveries in Mesopotamia . . . all of great antiquity and superior in workmanship to anything discovered by M. Botta. The French are jealous to an extreme, and the wicked Pasha of Mosil under their influence is trying to counteract us. But I have a scheme, which I think will defeat them and secure us all we want for ourselves, and much more for the benefit of the world at large. Major Rawlinson writes me from Baghdad in high admiration and offers to send up a steamer in the spring to secure whatever Layard may have succeeded in getting out. I am quite proud of my public spirit in the cause of antiquity and fine art. But I must not ruin either you or the children; and I propose to call in the aid of the Government – whether Whig or Tory – to accomplish what may easily prove beyond my reach . . . perhaps you think me crazy for caring so much about such trifles, but they are trifles for which colleges, universities and nations would take each other by the ears, and as Major Rawlinson tells me, the inscriptions are likely to throw much light upon Scripture history.'[22] It would be many more months before government money was forthcoming.

Lack of money was a constant problem for Layard during his excavations, and in later years he was bitter that credit was given to Canning for funding all the work, denying that this was the case: 'He contributed . . . £60 towards them, when I left Constantinople on my expedition, and he may subsequently have advanced small sums (all of which were repaid to him out of the grant). I received, moreover, £100 a year out of public funds at his disposal as a remuneration for my services in the Embassy. But the greater part of those expenses were met from my slender means, and by borrowing from my mother, who most generously advanced to me out of her very small income the little she could spare, in order to enable me to continue my work. I subsequently discharged my debt to her. I received no remuneration for my labours. The sum that was allowed me for personal expenses was entirely spent in carrying on the excavations.'[23]

Unable to do much with little money and no formal permission, Layard left his two workmen at Nimrud at the end of March and went on an expedition into the desert with Christian Rassam, Rassam's wife and Henry Ross. Their aim was to visit the chief of a large tribe of Arabs and to see once again the ruins of Hatra. On his return, Layard received a letter from Rawlinson that had been written at the beginning of April with the latest news: 'I have been laid up almost the whole of the last fortnight, and can hardly say what has been the matter with me . . . however I am now at work again . . . The Steamer leaves tomorrow morning – and will be at Nimrud I hope by the 12th [April].'[24] Just after the steamer left, Rawlinson advised Layard about his own plans to visit the site: 'I shall if possible ride up and look at your work and return in the Steamer, trying to get Jones to ship a few slabs on board. I have no time to say anything about inscriptions except that I am making progress, real good progress.'[25]

Rawlinson did not make the trip, because the *Nitocris* unexpectedly failed to reach Nimrud, as Layard explained: 'Major Rawlinson had obligingly proposed that . . . the small steamer navigating the lower part of the Tigris should be sent up to Nimroud, and I expected the most valuable assistance, both in removing the slabs and in plans for future excavations, from her able commander, Lieutenant Jones. The Euphrates, one of the two vessels originally launched on the rivers of Mesopotamia, had some years previously succeeded in reaching the tomb of Sultan Abdallah, a few miles below Nimroud . . . It was found, however, that the machinery of the Nitocris was either too much out of repair, or not sufficiently powerful to impel the vessel over the rapids, which occur in some parts of the river. After ascending some miles above Tekrit the attempt was given up, and she returned to her station.'[26]

In London, the first part of Rawlinson's Bisitun report was being prepared for publication by the Royal Asiatic Society, and earlier in the year he had sent off chapter four. At the end of March he wrote to the Royal Asiatic Society saying that he had hoped to have finished chapter five, 'but I have been again unfortunately suffering so severely from Rheumatism in the right side as to have been unable to hold a pen for many days together'.[27] Instead, he sent several amendments for chapter four and reckoned he would soon be back in England. No longer able to visit Nimrud, he put the finishing touches to chapter five, completing it on 20 April 1846. It was posted straightaway to the society, but more than twelve months would elapse before chapters three, four and five were published.

Chapter four's eighty-two pages of printed text was entitled 'Analysis of the Persian Inscriptions of Behistun'. It formed the heart of Rawlinson's work on the Old Persian inscription at Bisitun and is arguably his most remarkable achievement. The initial eight pages are a discussion of the origin of the name of the rock of Bisitun and the historical events in the first part of the reign of King Darius the Great that had led to the carving of the inscription. Some of these events were mentioned by the ancient Greek historian Herodotus, who wrote about the conflicts between the Persians and Greeks only a few decades after Darius came to the throne. Rawlinson complained that Herodotus had largely ignored the events recounted in the Bisitun inscription, preferring to concentrate on wars that took place further west in Asia Minor and Greece, 'with the pardonable predilections of a Greek'.[28]

Classical scholars took a different viewpoint, believing that Bisitun was unique proof that Herodotus was a reliable historian. At a meeting of the Royal Asiatic Society in June, Rawlinson was applauded for his work by one such scholar, Reverend Dr Francis Hessey: 'The members of those venerable establishments [universities] were already highly interested in the discoveries of Major Rawlinson, who had succeeded in so ably combining in his investigations the results of much previous study on the part of Professor Lassen and other Orientalists in Germany, France, and England. Those discoveries, independently of their own interest, were valuable to the learned, as confirming the truth of the great historical writers of Greece, whom sciolists [superficial scholars] in Oriental Literature had for some time looked upon as mere imaginative or boastful triflers, who had perverted the little which they knew of Eastern history, in order to aggrandize the greatness of their own petty conquests. This reproach could be no more uttered; the term 'Graecia mendax' [lying Greece] must for ever be forgotten; and Herodotus must be restored to his rank as the father of history as well as the most candid and persevering of investigators.'[29]

Chapter four made Rawlinson's earlier transliteration, Latin translation and notes on the Bisitun Old Persian inscription largely redundant, even before the Royal Asiatic Society had published it all. The major part of the chapter was a revised transliteration, along with a new translation, this time into English not Latin, as well as a commentary on the etymology, grammar and spelling. The inscription was dealt with paragraph by paragraph, and each line of cuneiform was individually numbered, a system still used today. Of his commentary, Rawlinson remarked: 'In a document of this sort, in which the language is as little known as the contents are deeply interesting, explanatory notes and illustrations are of course suggested by every passage; but as all such digression tends to divert attention from the immediate subject-matter of the inscription, and to interrupt the historical continuity of the record, I shall introduce it as sparingly as possible.'[30] His longest discussion was of column 1, paragraph 14, which he found especially troubling: 'This is probably the most difficult paragraph which occurs in the Behistun Inscriptions. Of several of the most important words the orthography is doubtful; of others the etymology is almost impenetrable, and the construction, moreover, in some parts renders the division into sentences, a matter of serious embarrassment. I am compelled, therefore, to adopt a more elaborate commentary than usual.'[31]

Rawlinson revised much of his earlier transliteration, such as the beginning of the difficult column 5, which he had written as 'Thátiya. Dár(a)yawush. k'hsháyathiya. ima. tya. adam. akhunawam', but he now modified it to 'Thátiya Dár(a)yavush khsháyathiya imatya adam akunavam'. His original Latin translation, 'Dicit Darius rex: hoc (est) quod ego feci', was now expressed in English as 'Says Darius the King: – This is what I have done'.[32] For the beginning of one of the detached Old Persian inscriptions, Rawlinson's original transliteration had been 'Iyam. Gumáta. hya. Maghush. adhur'ujiya', which he now modified to 'Iyam Gaumáta hya Magush adurujiya'.[33] His translation into Latin of 'Hic Gomatus, qui Magus, mendacium dixit' was put in English as 'This Gomates, the Magian, was an imposter'.[34]

On the relief sculpture, the captured prisoners are standing, hands tied behind their backs and chained together at their necks, but Gaumata (Rawlinson's Gomates) – a priest or magus – was prostrate, being trampled by Darius, and this, said Rawlinson, 'proves beyond question, that the sculpture refers to the arch imposter from whom the Persian throne was recovered. I conceive also an attitude of extreme abjectness to have been assigned to this figure, while the other captives are erect, in order to mark the difference of character between the Magian usurpation and temporary disorders of the provinces.'[35] The sculptures were not intended to show a specific event where the prisoners were all brought together, as the inscription related that Gaumata was assassinated and that many of the rebellious leaders were executed when they were captured – it was a symbolic sculpture, just as Rawlinson interpreted it.

The most impressive aspect of chapter four was the accurate fluency with which Rawlinson was able to translate this extensive inscription, such as the first paragraph of column 3: 'Says Darius the King:- Then I sent from Rhages a Persian army to Hystaspes. When that army reached Hystaspes, he marched forth with those troops. The city of Parthia, named Patigapana, there he fought with the rebels. Ormazd brought help to me. By the grace of Ormazd, Hystaspes entirely defeated that rebel army. On the 1st day of the month of Garmapada, then it was the battle was thus fought by them'[36] – virtually identical to a modern translation, though the god is today translated as Ahuramazda not Ormazd.

Underlying the scholarship that led to this translation was the fact that Rawlinson – like his contemporaries – had experienced an education where he had been thoroughly acquainted with the grammatical structure of language, especially when studying Latin and Greek. His comments on dative, genitive and accusative forms, masculine plurals, the subjunctive imperfect and the like would have been far more widely understood a century and a half ago. Scholars would not have found impenetrable a sentence such as: 'In the sixth clause, *hagamata* is the nom. plur. of the past participle for *hamgamatá*, and *paraitá* is the 3rd pers. plur. of the middle imperf.; the particle *par*, "again," being prefixed to the verb, which of course requires the temporal augment.'[37] The difficulties of writing for a varied readership were appreciated by Rawlinson: 'To the general reader the comments will appear unnecessarily prolix; by the philologer they will be regarded as superficial. I would recommend the one accordingly to attend exclusively to the translations, and I would claim from the other a suspension of his judgment until he shall have attentively consulted the succeeding chapters, which comprise the vocabulary and a brief examination of the grammatical structure of the language.'[38]

His next chapter was not, as he suggested, on vocabulary and grammar. Instead, chapter five brought together in eighty-one printed pages all the known Old Persian cuneiform inscriptions. Before Bisitun, these had been the only inscriptions available to European scholars working on decipherment. Many had been copied and published by early travellers such as Niebuhr, with more recent translations by scholars such as Lassen. Rawlinson now offered amended transliterations, translations and commentaries, particularly of Lassen's work, but admitted that these shorter, largely formulaic inscriptions were not as interesting as

Bisitun: 'In the place of varied and historical recital, we must be content for the most part to peruse a certain formula of invocation to Ormazd [the god Ahuramazda], and a certain empty parade of royal titles, recurring with a most wearisome and disappointing uniformity.'[39] The invocation to Ahuramazda reminded Rawlinson of how he had observed buildings being constructed in Persia: 'The evidence which these legends afford, that it was customary with the early Persian kings to invoke the protection of Ormazd and the other gods, for the edifices of their construction, is illustrated by the practice which prevails in Persia to the present day, of chaunting a prayer over every brick as it is laid in the walls of a building; at present, the chaunt of the bricklayers is supposed to render the edifice secure against "the evil eye".'[40]

Chapter five ended with Rawlinson inviting other scholars to correct his work: 'I have now exhausted the Persian Cuneiform records . . . With regard to the general interpretation that I have adopted in these two chapters, I shall not fear the test of any such augmentation of materials; but there are many particular parts of the translation of which I should see the verification with pleasure, and the refutation without surprise. Remembering that St Martin, a short time before his decease, declared his readings to be "à l'abri de la critique;" [beyond criticism] and that Grotefend is still inclined to champion the antiquated notions of the last century, I am provided with a useful lesson against overconfidence. When Professor Lassen shall have perused my translations and vocabulary which I shall give with full etymological explanations in the succeeding chapter, I shall be quite prepared to bow to his superior Oriental knowledge in all cases of disagreement between our respective readings.'[41]

Rawlinson's next task was to complete chapter six, his Old Persian vocabulary, but that would take many more months. To some extent he had probably lost interest in Old Persian, as there were more exciting challenges ahead, particularly with all the inscriptions found by Layard at Nimrud. At the end of April, Rawlinson wrote to Layard: 'Since I sent off Chapter 5 of my Cuneiform Memoir I have been working in earnest at the Baby-

lonian Inscriptions and I can now read these with tolerable fluency
– but as I always foresaw, the language is quite impenetrable.
Semitic analogies are very rare indeed. The language is apparently
Semitic.'[42] He felt he understood many of the signs and now knew
the Babylonian language was Semitic, but he could not translate
it.

In early May, Layard's situation improved a little. A new Pasha
had been appointed at Mosul, who immediately allowed him to
continue his disrupted excavations. As he still had little financial
support, he returned to Nimrud in the exhausting heat of the
summer with just a few workmen: 'The change to summer had
been as rapid as that which ushered in the spring. The verdure
of the plain had perished almost in a day. Hot winds, coming from
the desert, had burnt up and carried away the shrubs; flights
of locusts, darkening the air, had destroyed the few patches of
cultivation . . . the plain presented the same naked and desolate
aspect that it wore in the month of November. The heat, however,
was now almost intolerable. Violent whirlwinds occasionally
swept over the face of the country. They could be seen as they
advanced from the desert, carrying along with them clouds of
sand and dust. Almost utter darkness prevailed during their passage, which lasted generally about an hour, and nothing could
resist their fury.'[43]

At Nimrud, amid the heat and dust, further sculptured reliefs
were uncovered in the palace, which depicted remarkable scenes
such as winged protective spirits, a besieged city under attack
from a battering ram, lion and bull hunts, and a colossal winged
human-headed bull. Layard was particularly excited by the hunting scene: 'The most remarkable of the sculptures hitherto discovered was the lion hunt; which, from the knowledge of art
displayed in the treatment and composition, the correct and effective delineation of the men and animals, the spirit of the grouping,
and its extraordinary preservation, is probably the finest specimen
of Assyrian art in existence.'[44]

Early one morning, Layard was woken by an Arab bringing
letters from Mosul, and so he 'read by the light of a small camel-

dung fire, the document which secured to the British nation the records of Nineveh, and a collection of the earliest monuments of Assyrian art'[45] – he had at long last received from Constantinople a permit from the Grand Vizier to excavate wherever he pleased and to remove any objects discovered. No further funds were mentioned, but Layard did not delay in opening trenches in the great mound across the river from Mosul, the original site of Nineveh. 'I had not previously done so,' he explained, 'as the vicinity of the ruins to Mosul would have enabled the inhabitants of the town to watch my movements, and to cause me continual interruptions before the sanction of the authorities could be obtained to my proceedings.'[46]

Even now, everything did not go smoothly, because the new French Consul tried to claim the site as French property and began to dig in the mound at the same time as Layard. Still worse was an incident that threatened serious consequences. Having worked late one evening, Layard hired the last boat to ferry him and some workmen back across the Tigris to Mosul. Noticing a group of men hurrying to the river, he ordered the boatmen to return to the river bank. These men turned out to be the Cadi and his attendants, who accepted Layard's invitation to share his boat. Layard stood on the narrow prow with the steersman. 'The Cadi stood just beneath me,' he related. 'We were making the best of our way over the river, which was then fully half a mile broad, and in parts running with dangerous velocity, when he said in a loud voice, alluding to me, "Shall the dogs occupy the high places, whilst the true believers have to stand below?" and then mumbled some curses on Christians in general. This gratuitous insult, and the ill return that the Cadi thus made for my civility to him, provoked me so much that I lost my temper, and dealt him a blow on his head with a short hooked stick ... As he wore a thick turban, I did not believe that the blow would have had much effect, and I was surprised to see the blood streaming down his face.'[47]

His attendants were about to use their pistols and swords, but Layard jumped down from the prow and seized the Cadi, threatening to throw him in the river if they attacked, and held him in this position until they landed. Layard described what next occured: 'The Cadi, with the blood still on his face, proceeded at once to the town, which was a short distance from the landing-place, and rushed through the bazaars and streets, exclaiming that he had been assaulted and beaten by a *Giauor* – an Infidel – and that the Prophet and his faith had been insulted, in the person of the head of the Mussulman religion and law. His bloody face and his appeals to the Mohammedans caused great commotion; and an outbreak on their part, in which the Christians might have been ill-treated, and even massacred, was apprehended.'[48]

Layard went straight away to see the Pasha, who was sympathetic as he himself had a feud with the Cadi, but advised Layard to stay put until the excitement had died down. Refusing to comply, Layard defiantly rode to the residence of Christian Rassam to inform him of the events. Rawlinson in Baghdad was very afraid of the consequences: 'The affair with the Mufti is I think unfortunate,' he informed Layard on 10 May 1846, 'and I fear we have not seen the end of it. His insult was certainly gross, but no provocation justifies violence ... I hope my judgment may be wrong. We are all fallible ... As the thing stands you must of course fight it out and if unsupported at Stamboul [by Canning] you must quit Moosul. It has created quite a sensation amongst the Priesthood here.'[49]

Rawlinson then offered Layard a place of refuge: 'It is most annoying that this fracas should have occurred just as you were beginning to reap the fruits of your probationary residence in Assyria. Nimrud must now be second at all risks, and if you should find it necessary to absent yourself for a time from Moosul you had better come down and live with me at Baghdad, while you get Rassam's brother [Hormuzd] to carry on the excavations for you in the interim.'[50] Even though his life was in danger, Layard decided to carry on as normal, and Canning in Constantinople took no action, although, as Layard noted, he privately advised that 'although he considered that the Cadi had deserved the punishment I had inflicted upon him for insulting me and my faith, he hoped that I would be more cautious in future in not exposing myself to the fanaticism of the Mohammedans amongst whom I was living'.[51]

Thirteen: An Irish Intruder

A whole month of digging at Nineveh produced only a few fragments of sculpture and cuneiform inscriptions, and so Layard decided to return to Nimrud, employing thirty men to dig in the north-west palace, though with no further finance. More sculptured reliefs were uncovered, as well as colossal bulls and lions, some broken into pieces. 'As I advance further into the mound', he informed his aunt, 'the sculptures become more perfect in preservation, and superior in execution to those in the chambers on the edge of the building . . . God knows when the ramification of rooms and passages will stop. The discovery is already beginning to make a noise in Europe, and every post brings me letters from people wanting information and offering (scientific) assistance. I only hope that as much interest will be excited in England as on the Continent, and that the Government will not be able to back out of the matter.'[1] Rawlinson confessed to Layard: 'Sir Stratford's parsimony is to me quite inexplicable. What was the like of a Firman [permit] without funds? If I were you I would ask his Excellency's leave to send home a prospectus in order to obtain voluntary contributions from the Societies and patrons of art in England . . . I believe you might get a couple of thousand Pounds subscribed in England at any rate.'[2]

By now the assault on the Cadi had been forgotten, and writing to Layard on 24 June 1846, Rawlinson expressed his pleasure that the 'business has taken so satisfactory a turn. I drew my inferences from the sensation created here – nothing else was

talked about at Baghdad for a week after the news arrived.'[3]
Rawlinson himself, struggling to understand Elamite and Babylonian cuneiform, continued his letter by telling Layard that he
had no idea how they would ever work out the Babylonian language: 'No doubt the Median and Babylonian alphabets are very
nearly allied and the phonetic structure of the two languages is
almost identical. I can *read* pretty well to my satisfaction all the
Inscriptions Median as well as Babylonian given by Westergaard
– but this does not enable me by any means to *understand* a [single]
Babylonian Inscription, of which I have not [achieved] a [single]
translation. The language as I have often told you has to be
reconstructed "ab origine". It is in my opinion *utterly unknown* –
correspondents do not exist in any available speech, Semitic, Arian
or Scythic – so how we are ever to interpret it with anything like
certainty I am at a loss to divine.'[4]

Almost nineteen years had passed since Rawlinson had left
England, with service in India, Persia, Afghanistan and now Baghdad. He very much hoped to return home on leave, and it seems
incredible that it was disallowed, as he told Layard in early July:
'I regret to say that my leave has after all been refused. The
Court of Directors [of the East India Company] say the thing is
an absolute impossibility unless I vacate the Residency which I
cannot afford to do at present.'[5] His health continued to suffer,
and two weeks later he was only able to write briefly to Layard:
'You must excuse a short letter, as I am quite knocked up with
the hot weather. I have felt the heat indeed so much this year
that I fear I shall be obliged to take shelter within the mountains
before it is over.'[6]

At Nimrud, Layard was also feeling the heat, as he wrote to his
aunt: 'The weather is so hot I must give up hard work ... The
Arabs can hardly stand the digging, though accustomed to the
climate, and I am compelled to release them for three hours during
the middle of the day. It is no joke, I can assure you, to draw
with the thermometer at 115, and even 117, in the shade.'[7] He
was anxious that some of the finds should be transported to England, but was on his own after Jones had failed to reach Nimrud

with the steamer. Deciding it would be impossible to transport the colossal figures, Layard instead prepared the relief sculptures by sawing off the reverse of the slabs to reduce their thickness and by removing many of the inscriptions: 'The inscriptions being mere repetitions, I did not consider it necessary to preserve them, as they added to the weight.'[8] The prepared reliefs were removed from the trenches, packed in felt and matting, placed in wooden cases and taken to the Tigris on carts, ready to be loaded on a raft for the journey to Baghdad. Layard then left Nimrud to spend a few days at Mosul, explaining: 'The heat had now become so intense that my health began to suffer from continual exposure to the sun, and from the labour of superintending the excavations, drawing the sculptures, and copying the inscriptions. In the trenches, where I daily passed many hours, the thermometer generally ranged from 112° to 115° in the shade, and on one or two occasions even reached 117°.'[9]

At Mosul, Layard wrote to his aunt that not only had he been drawing the sculptures and inscriptions, but he had started to make moulds from which plaster casts could be taken, following advice from Hiram Powers, the American Neo-classical sculptor: 'I am happy to say that I have just packed up and embarked for Busrah, on their way to England, twelve cases of antiquities from Nimroud . . . Mr Powers, the sculptor, has been kind enough to send me the fullest instructions for taking moulds and then casting. He did this very kindly without any application from me. I find my *papier mâché* moulds so good that I shall adopt them as soon as I get to work. I have not yet seen any of the plaster casts taken from them, but Rawlinson, to whom I sent one or two of the moulds to make the experiment, writes me that they succeed admirably.'[10]

At Baghdad in early August, Layard's relief sculptures were shifted from the raft to a boat for their journey to Basra and Bombay, where they would be transferred to a ship for the journey to England. Rawlinson had been ill again, but managed to look at them before they continued their journey, and described his impressions to Layard: 'I have been ailing so much all this last

fortnight that I have had serious thoughts of taking shelter some-
where in the mountains . . . Your cases arrived all right and we
have been regaling our antiquarian appetites on the contents ever
since. The dying Lion and the two Gods (winged and Eagle headed)
are my favorites. The battle pieces, Seiges &c are curious, but I
do not think they rank highly as works of art. [Dr John] Ross is
altogether disappointed with the specimens and I must confess I
think the general style crude and cramped, but still the curiosity
of the thing is a very great, if not a full compensation.'[11]

After all his hard work and enthusiasm, Layard was dismayed
by this reaction, especially as he considered the style of art accomplished. Rawlinson, though, was wedded to the notion that Classical art was supreme and could see little artistic merit in the
sculptures. Two weeks later Rawlinson tried to explain his position: 'I am sorry you have taken such desperate alarms at my
criticisms. I never pretended to depreciate the *value* of the marbles.
I merely objected to their style & execution, which in my opinion
have nothing whatever to do with value. You ask by what standard I compare them. Why of course, in any abstract matter we
adopt the highest standard available – and I say therefore the
Elgin marbles . . . I look upon the Nimrud slabs as *invaluable* and
my opinion of them would be the same were they ten times inferior
to what they are. Their value consists in unfolding to us the
history, theology, language, arts, manners, military skill, political
relations to one of the most illustrious nations of antiquity, and
in this filling up an enormous blank in our knowledge of the early
history of the world . . . Why quarrel with the Assyrians because
they were not as far advanced in the arts of design and execution
as the Greeks in the time of Pericles? We have them as they were
and that is what we want . . . Heaven forefend that I should do
anything to impede the excavations. I look upon the sculptures
as of more value than Pompeii or Herculaneum and view every
new inscription as equal to gaining one of the lost decades of
Livy.'[12]

Since completing his fifth chapter back in April, Rawlinson had
concentrated on Assyrian and Babylonian rather than on the sixth

chapter on Old Persian vocabulary. Old Persian cuneiform was still very much in his thoughts, though, because in trilingual inscriptions it revealed what was written in Babylonian. In his third chapter Rawlinson had already presented an 'alphabet' of thirty-nine Old Persian signs, but he now changed his mind about the way these signs operated, mainly in response to an English translation he had received of Lassen's publication, which was very close to the solution.

After being unwell in the heat of Baghdad for two or three weeks, in August Rawlinson managed to complete a report on his latest discovery – that the Old Persian cuneiform signs were not after all simple alphabetical-type letters, such as *k, d, dh* and *r*, as he had suggested in chapter three. Instead, apart from the signs for *a, i* and *u*, they were all syllables containing a consonant followed by a vowel. Different signs were used for the same-sounding consonant, depending on its vowel, and three systems operated, depending on the type of consonant. Sonants (voiced consonants, such as the letter *d*) had different cuneiform signs according to the vowel that followed, such as in *da, di* and *du*, so that Rawlinson no longer thought 𐎠 was *d*, but *da*, and 𐎭 was no longer *dh*, but *du*. Surds (half-complete consonants, like the letter *t*) had some signs that were the same, so that *t* was the same sign 𐎫 if followed by *a* or *i*, but not by *u*, when it was 𐎬. Previously, Rawlinson thought these signs were *t* and *t'h*. The signs for aspirates (such as *th* – 𐎰) all remained the same, whatever vowel followed.

The additional essay on this breakthrough for Old Persian was posted to the Royal Asiatic Society in London on 25 August 1846 and was received by them forty-four days later, on 8 October. The initial part of Rawlinson's report had already been printed, so no changes could be made. The third chapter on the Old Persian alphabet was also printed, but before publication this new supplementary work was placed at the end, twelve printed pages in all. Changes were subsequently made to chapters four and five before they were printed. It was a relief to Rawlinson to discover how Old Persian cuneiform signs really worked: 'it will be seen that I have modified in several essential points', he wrote, 'the opinions announced in the preceding chapter, and that the system which I have now adopted for expressing the old Persian in English, and which I shall continue to use through the succeeding portions of the Memoir, is far more simple than that originally proposed.'[13] He ended the supplementary note with a list of the new values he attributed to each sign, a system that is still in use today with hardly any corrections.

By now Layard was back at Nimrud, where he found yet more sculptured slabs, but his health was too weak to continue, and at the end of August he set off on an expedition into the mountains where three years earlier thousands of Nestorian Christians had been massacred by Kurds and many more enslaved. On his way a visit was paid to the now rather sad ruins of Khorsabad: 'Since M. Botta's departure the sides of the trenches had fallen in, and had filled up the greater part of the chambers; the sculptures were rapidly perishing; and, shortly, little will remain of this remarkable monument.'[14] Rawlinson had still not visited Nimrud, and a few days later wrote to Layard: 'I shall certainly run up to Mosul as soon as you return . . . and commence work again, for I am most anxious to see the wonders of Nimrod "in situ". '[15] However, a terrible cholera epidemic – which was to sweep across Europe and reach Britain in 1848 – put paid to these plans, forcing him and his staff to abandon Baghdad and set up camp in the desert at the ancient capital of Ctesiphon, 30 miles south-east of Baghdad. Nobody then knew that the disease was transmitted through infected water and not by breathing. Rawlinson described the situation to Layard at the end of September: 'During the last ten days the disease has been very general throughout the town, but it is not by any means of a virulent character. At least two-thirds, very possible three fourths of those attacked have recovered.'[16]

Layard had been suffering badly from malaria, and Rawlinson expressed concerned about him: 'I am very sorry to hear these bad accounts of your health . . . you fret yourself too much at the difficulties that are thrown in your way. I should recommend you to come down and pass a quiet winter with me and to make a fresh start in the Spring.'[17] Layard had to forgo this invitation, because he received the long-awaited news from Canning that extra funds were available. He was relieved, but not impressed: 'The grant was small, and scarcely adequate to the objects in view. There were many difficulties to contend with, and I was doubtful whether, with the means at my disposal, I should be able to fulfil the expectations which appeared to have been formed, as to the results of the undertaking ... I determined, however, to accept the charge of superintending the excavations, to make every exertion.'[18] What concerned Layard especially was not having an artist to copy all the sculptures and inscriptions that could not be removed: 'I had neither knowledge nor experience as a draughtsman; and this I felt to be a great drawback, indeed a disqualification, which I could scarcely hope to overcome. Many of the sculptures, and monuments discovered, were in too dilapidated a condition to be removed, and others threatened to fall to pieces as soon as uncovered. It was only by drawings that the record of them could be preserved ... and I made up my mind to do the best I could; to copy as carefully and accurately as possible, that which I saw before me. I had therefore to superintend the excavations; to draw all the bas-reliefs discovered; to copy and compare the innumerable inscriptions; to take casts of them (Casts of the inscriptions and some of the sculptures were taken with brown paper, simply damped and impressed on the slab with a hard brush); and to preside over the moving and packing of the sculptures. As there was no one whom I could trust to overlook the diggers, I was obliged to be continually present.'[19]

While in isolation at Ctesiphon, Rawlinson's studies were limited, as he had no books with him, but he managed to examine inscriptions on mud bricks found at Babylon written in Babylonian cuneiform. In his letter to Layard at the end of September, he described what he had found: 'I have at length made out pretty well to my satisfaction the legend on all the bricks which are found at Babylon and in the vicinity. It was this "Nebuchadnezzar, the great king, the ruler of the land of the Chaldees, the son of

Nabuhassar the great king".'[20] Usually known today as Nebuchadnezzar II, this king was the son of Nabopolassar and reigned from 605 to 562 BC. He was famous for the rebuilding of Babylon, in which thousands of bricks stamped with his name were used. Rawlinson was unaware that another scholar had already identified Nebuchadnezzar. Thirteen weeks earlier in the *Literary Gazette* in London, a letter had been published that began: 'It was, I understand, mentioned at the last meeting of the Royal Society of Literature, that I had been fortunate enough to ascertain the import of the inscription on the Babylonian bricks which have so long puzzled the learned, and have given rise to so many conjectures. The first and third lines . . . are, "The god Nebuchadnezzar, king of Babylon – son of the god Nebuchadnezzar, king of Babylon".'[21]

The author was Edward Hincks, and he continued with an explanation of how he had deciphered the name – the kind of information that Rawlinson rarely made public throughout his years of decipherment work. Hincks had come to the notice of the Royal Asiatic Society only the month before, when the President reported that he had received 'an elaborate, though short paper, on the Median [Elamite] Cuneiform Inscription . . . from a learned Clergyman in a remote part of Ireland'.[22] Although Hincks was not a member of the society and was unknown to Rawlinson, he was already his most serious rival.

Born in Cork on 19 August 1792, Hincks studied at Trinity College Dublin from the age of fifteen, gaining a degree three years later and winning many prizes. He was elected a junior fellow in 1813, but unaccountably left after six years. He married Jane Dorothea Boyd in 1823, and they had four daughters. In 1825 he became pastor at Killyleagh, a village on the shores of Strangford Lough 20 miles south of Belfast, where he spent the rest of his life. At Trinity College he had studied Hebrew and probably Syriac, and was also proficient in Arabic and mathematics. In 1832 he published a Hebrew grammar and the following year began to publish a series of articles on the ancient Egyptian language. With a family to support, money was a constant worry for Hincks, who found it difficult to maintain his research. Even so, while he continued to contribute to Egyptian research, he turned to the decipherment of cuneiform, thinking it might throw light on hieroglyphs. Although having access to only a limited range of material, he grasped the concepts so completely that on 9 June 1846 he presented his first paper on Old Persian and Elamite cuneiform to the Royal Irish Academy, which was published two years later. His section on Old Persian contained ideas similar to those in Rawlinson's supplementary note written two months later, but his achievement was the more remarkable because he did not have a copy of Rawlinson's Bisitun inscription, the first part of which was only just about to be published.

Having written to the Royal Asiatic Society in May 1846, Hincks forwarded a further summary of his ideas in two letters in June, asking to be informed of progress by others on Elamite and Babylonian. He also began to correspond with Edwin Norris and other scholars, but not with Rawlinson. On 17 July, in his first reply to Hincks, Norris provided information about Rawlinson's achievements: 'Major Rawlinson has given us the most complete detail, glossarial, etc. – respecting the Persian inscription of Behistun, but nothing respecting the Median [Elamite] and Babylonian; he promises much also on the Median, and occasionally reads a doubtful passage by its aid, but has sent no transcripts whatsoever. Of the third sort [Babylonian], you will be as sorry to learn as I was that the translation is wholly destroyed; the rock on which it was engraved is in a very exposed part, and Major R. reached it at much personal risk; when close to the surface he found to his great disappointment that the surface was all peeled off, and that barely enough was left to shew that the character was Babylonian. Very luckily the small inscriptions over the heads of the captive kings are perfect in all three writings, and the Major has them all copied; but he has not sent us any of those of the last two sorts. It is fortunate that these little inscriptions are full of names, and that we shall be able to do much by their aid . . . I am delighted to learn you are reading phonetically the great Babylonian inscription. I am working at the same, but with so

little leisure that I have no hopes of success. I have ascertained
the meaning of several of the words from their resemblance with
the 3rd Persian, and I flatter myself I have a glimmering of the
language, but I have not time to put my ideas on paper yet.'[23]

By 'the great Babylonian inscription,' Norris meant an inscription carved on both sides of a stone slab nearly 2 feet high that
would later become known as Nebuchadnezzar's East India House
inscription. It was a building inscription of Nebuchadnezzar II that
had been found at Babylon at the beginning of the century and
had been sent to East India House in London. Although it was
then the longest Babylonian inscription – 621 lines – to have been
published, without accompanying parallel inscriptions in other
languages, the signs were of limited use to decipherers. On 25 July
Hincks had another letter published in the *Literary Gazette*, in
which he identified the name Nebuchadnezzar in the East India
House inscription, saying: 'The name and titles of this king form
the introduction to this inscription. The bricks contain the same
name, with the titles in a shorter form. The legend upon them
was not a form of prayer, as Grotefend imagined, but a *stamp*;
indicating either that the bricks were made for the king's use, that
they were manufactured by his workmen, or that a duty imposed
on the manufacture was paid.'[24]

Norris was impressed: 'I congratulate you on the progress
detailed in the *Literary Gazette* of Saturday, and think you must
read the whole soon.'[25] A week later he wrote again to Hincks: 'I
wish you were in town, for I am quite sure that you are on the
right road, though perhaps not in all cases; and I think also that
all the labourers in the same vineyard, whose results I have seen,
are wrong; of course my own vanity makes me except myself.'[26]
On 20 August Hincks replied to Norris and informed him of his
latest discoveries on vowels and consonants in Old Persian, just
as Rawlinson in Baghdad was finishing off his supplementary
note along the same lines. That same day Norris sent Rawlinson
lithographs of his Bisitun drawings and a letter alerting him to
Hincks and what he was achieving with cuneiform. Rawlinson
only received that letter in early October, the same time that

the Royal Asiatic Society in London received from Rawlinson his supplementary paper on the Old Persian signs.

While Layard prepared to return to Nimrud, the cholera epidemic was subsiding at Baghdad, and in mid-October Rawlinson decided to leave Ctesiphon, telling Layard: 'I believe we have at length got pretty well quit of the Cholera and I break up my Camp accordingly tomorrow. At the lowest computation I should say 5000 souls had perished in Baghdad and the vicinity, but on the whole we may consider it a light visitation.'[27] Since his last letter to Layard, he had received the lithographs from Norris and news about other scholars, as he informed Layard: 'Cuneiforms are at present in great favor at home and a certain Dr Hinckes [sic], an Irishman, has got much farther than I, and pretend[s] to have succeeded. A German also, Lowenstern, tells of reading the Khorsabad writing with fluency – he pretends to have found in it an account of the campaign of Esachaddad, but on referring to Botta's plates for his discoveries I am convinced the whole thing is a humbug.'[28]

Isidore Löwenstern, a traveller and linguist, had published in Paris a paper on Assyrian cuneiform the year before. It was based on Botta's discoveries, but Löwenstern had made very little further progress. The real threat lay with Hincks, and Rawlinson was right to add: 'Dr Hinckes is certainly on the right track and a long way before me.'[29] After his years of work on cuneiform, including personal sacrifice and physical danger, Rawlinson could not have welcomed this intruder, although the intense distrust and rivalry that developed between the two would be fuelled by mutual correspondents sharing information without permission and even disclosing personal comments that had been written.

Rawlinson's supplementary paper was received by Norris on 8 October, but Norris delayed writing to Hincks until late November and first asked about his publications: 'I have just received a letter from Major Rawlinson, in which he says he is very anxiously looking for something from you respecting the Babylonian inscriptions; he is looking with much interest at the abstracts which appear in the literary journals, but he wishes me to procure and send him anything you may have published, in extenso. Will you have the kindness to tell me what you have published and where it may be obtained, for I am as ignorant here as Major Rawlinson in Baghdad.'[30] In fact, Hincks had published nothing on cuneiform, except for letters in the *Literary Gazette* – then, as now, the publishing process took a long time, and indeed the first part of Rawlinson's Old Persian memoir had only just been published by the Royal Asiatic Society.

Norris went on to say: 'You may be gratified to learn that he [Rawlinson] says "Dr Hincks is in the right track, and I look with much interest at anything from him" . . . You will perhaps be pleased to learn that we have received a supplementary paper from him in rectification of his alphabet, and that he has fallen upon the same theory of primaries and secondaries of which you communicated to me a hint in August last. Major Rawlinson's paper is dated at Baghdad on the 27th of August, your discoveries are consequently quite independent, and therefore the more satisfactory.'[31] Seven years previously, Rawlinson had been beaten by Lassen as the first person to have worked out the Old Persian alphabet, and now he was pre-empted by Hincks in the major modification to the system. His own supplementary paper, though, was published in the first half of 1847 and Hincks's paper the following year, so Rawlinson was able to claim priority of discovery.

At a meeting of the Royal Asiatic Society in early December Norris read out extracts from Rawlinson's supplementary paper and announced: 'about four months ago [August], Dr Hincks had written to him, announcing and giving some details of his mode of reading the cuneiform characters; and these he [Norris] communicated to Major Rawlinson, in a letter which left England on the 20th of August; and that on the 27th day of the same month, Major Rawlinson despatched from Baghdad the paper now before the Society'[32] – in other words, he confirmed that Rawlinson had written his paper independently of Hincks. This did not prevent controversy, including a charge of plagiarism, and nearly forty years later, just a few months before Rawlinson's death, a bad-tempered exchange of views on this point took place between him and Professor Friedrich Max Müller in the pages of *The Athenaeum*.

Born in Germany in 1823, Müller was a philologist, specializing in Sanskrit and other eastern languages as well as religion, and became a professor at Oxford University. Rawlinson took exception to Müller's accusations, who replied: 'As to the decipherment of the cuneiform inscriptions, I believe I am one of the few men left who know the history of that glorious siege as eye-witnesses. I know, from having seen many of Sir Henry Rawlinson's letters to Edwin Norris, the learned secretary of the Royal Asiatic Society in London, how perfectly true it is that, if his letters had been published at the time, he might have claimed priority in determining directly or indirectly the final value of several of the letters of the Persian alphabet. But Sir Henry Rawlinson knows as well as I do that, according to a rule universally recognized by scholars as well as by men of science, priority of publication constitutes priority of discovery. I know myself that this rule seems sometimes very hard, but everybody submits to it, because without it a door would be opened to endless and most disagreeable controversies. Besides, there is a great difference between communicating a discovery to our friends, or even committing it to writing in a letter, and really publishing it. Until a paper is published we can modify it, or even withdraw it altogether. The full responsibility begins with publication only.'[33]

Müller went on to describe who had been first to work out particular letters of the Old Persian alphabet, adding: 'I now come to the discovery of the inherent vowels. I know, of course, that Sir Henry Rawlinson's 'Supplementary Note' is dated Baghdad, August 25th, 1846, and that it was received in London October 8th, 1846. But I also know that Oppert's 'Das Lautsystem des Altpersischen' was published in 1847, and before the volume of the *Journal* of the Royal Asiatic Society which contained the 'Supplementary Note' was issued. I well remember the joy with which I read Oppert's paper, because it removed some very serious misgivings which every scholar had felt up to that time as to the grammatical structure of the language of the cuneiform inscriptions. A language in which the genitive bases in *u* is the same as the nominative was felt to be an impossibility. By means of the inherent vowels that reproach was removed, and the genitive of *Dáryavush* became *Dáryavaush*, &c. I have little doubt that this discovery was made independently, and probably contemporaneously, by Rawlinson, Hincks, and Oppert, but who can tell the exact day on which each of these scholars saw the light dawning? No one can for one moment suppose that there could be a suspicion of dishonesty or unfair anticipation among such scholars as Rawlinson, Hincks, and Oppert. What, then, is the historian to do? He must follow the old rule, and assign the discovery to him who was the first to publish it – that is, in this case, I believe, to Oppert.'[34]

Not only had Rawlinson and Hincks discovered how the Old Persian alphabet really worked with its inherent vowels, but Julius Oppert had done the same. This German scholar had been born in Hamburg in 1825 and had studied under Lassen. Rawlinson retorted that Müller was wrong, because Oppert's paper on consonants and vowels was dated June 1847, after the publication of his own work: 'On referring to M. Oppert's paper quoted by Prof. Müller, I find that it is dated Hamburg, June, 1847, nearly a year after my Baghdad note of August, 1846. The exact date of the issue of part ii. of the tenth volume of the *Journal* of the Royal Asiatic Society, in which my "Supplementary Note" was first printed, I cannot ascertain; but it certainly preceded by several months the issue of M. Oppert's paper at Berlin.'[35] Oppert's fifty-eight-page book was actually published in Berlin after July 1847, but only lagged behind Rawlinson's publication date by several weeks, not months as he remembered it.

As soon as Rawlinson was back at work in Baghdad in mid-October 1846, he informed Norris at the Royal Asiatic Society that he was working steadily on Old Persian vocabulary, but that he planned to drop or postpone other proposed parts of his report: 'It will doubtless be a disappointment to many that the Median and Babylonian transcript at Behistun are not published simultaneously with the Persian originals, but you will I think acknowledge when so many competitors are in the field, that I could hardly in justice to myself publish the key, without taking care at the same time to appropriate some of the results.'[36] Rawlinson was bothered by the increasing numbers of rivals, most notably Hincks, saying to Norris: 'Dr Hinckes [sic] is evidently on the right track but he is going I think a little *too fast*. His reading of Nebuchudressar at any rate on the bricks is certain ... and I watch his progress accordingly with great interest.'[37] At the same time he admitted to Layard that Hincks was ahead of him in Babylonian, and at the end of October he wrote to George Cecil Renouard, the rector at Swanscombe in Kent and a member of the Oriental Translation Committee of the Royal Asiatic Society: 'How Dr Hinkes [sic] succeeded in sinking his first shaft, I hardly understand – but sunk it he certainly has, and unless I look about me, he will anticipate all I have to say on the subject.'[38]

At the end of October, Layard was back at Nimrud with a large workforce, the first task being to build himself a house in the village and one for his Nestorian workers on the mound, while numerous tents housed the Arabs and their families. 'Mr Hormuzd Rassam', Layard explained, 'lived with me; and to him I confided the payment of the wages, and the accounts, and the general management of the workmen.'[39] On 1 November large-scale excavations began right across the mound and unearthed numerous sculptured reliefs, as well as further pairs of human-headed lions, sphinxes, pottery, alabaster and glass vases, scale armour and helmets. His paltry funds dictated the manner of excavation: 'The smallness of the sum placed at my disposal, compelled me to follow the same plan in the excavations that I had hitherto adopted. I dug along the walls of the chambers, and exposed the whole of the slabs with which they were panelled, without removing the earth which filled up the rest of the room. Thus, few chambers were fully explored ... As I was directed in the instructions from the Trustees of the British Museum to re-bury the buildings with earth after they had been examined, I filled up the trenches, to avoid unnecessary expense, with the rubbish taken from those subsequently opened, having first copied the inscriptions, and drawn the sculptures.'[40]

Layard realized that the sculptured stone slabs originally lined walls made of mud bricks, but could not read the inscriptions to discover the king who built the palace: 'I had not yet had sufficient experience in the Assyrian character, to draw any inference from the inscriptions occurring on the bricks, found amongst the ruins in this part of the mound, so as to connect the name of the King upon them, with that of the founder of any known building.'[41] Having to go to Mosul on business, Layard decided that on his return he would abandon a particularly unprofitable trench, but he was immediately called back as a remarkable obelisk-shaped stone monument had been uncovered there. 'We raised it from its recumbent position', Layard recorded, 'and, with the aid of ropes, speedily dragged it out of the ruins. Although its shape was that of an obelisk, yet it was flat at the top and cut into three gradines. It was sculptured on the four sides; there were in all twenty small bas-reliefs, and above, below, and between them was carved an inscription 210 lines in length. The whole was in the best preservation; scarcely a character of the inscription was wanting . . . I lost no time in copying the inscriptions, and drawing the bas-reliefs, upon this precious relic. It was then carefully packed, to be transported at once to Baghdad.'[42]

Too much of Layard's time was spent copying the inscriptions and reliefs, as he was still unable to employ an artist. He described a typical day: 'I rose at day-break, and, after a hasty breakfast, rode to the mound. Until night I was engaged in drawing the sculptures, copying and taking casts of the inscriptions, and superintending the excavations, and the removal and packing of the bas-reliefs. On my return to the village, I was occupied till past midnight in comparing the inscriptions I had copied with the paper impressions, in finishing drawings, and in preparing for the work of the following day.'[43]

By early December 1846, Layard had enough reliefs to send a second load by raft to Baghdad and from there to England, and while he was gathering together packaging materials – mats, felts and ropes – he had a visit from a small party of English travellers, the only Europeans apart from Henry Ross in Mosul ever to see the excavated palace. Even Rawlinson failed to make a visit, although he was still intending to do so, as is clear from a letter Dr John Ross wrote to Layard from Baghdad three weeks earlier, obviously unwell: 'I received your note yesterday – so you have got the cholera amongst you, thank God we have got rid of the d—d thing ... Many thanks for your kind invitation to go up with Rawlinson, I cannot do it, in the hot weather I might be able to screw along at a snail's pace, in this cold weather I dare not try.'[44] By mid-December Layard had the second cargo of finds ready, and so using the buffalo carts of the Pasha, they were moved to the Tigris and embarked on a raft: 'On Christmas-day I had the satisfaction of seeing a raft, bearing twenty-three cases, in one of which was the black obelisk, floating down the river. I watched them until they were out of sight, and then galloped into Mosul to celebrate the festivities of the season, with the few Europeans whom duty or business had collected together in this remote corner of the globe.'[45] The Black Obelisk of Shalmaneser III is today a key exhibit in the British Museum and was a glorification of the achievements of this king who ruled Assyria in the ninth century BC. It contains the only surviving picture of an Israelite, showing King Jehu bringing tribute to Shalmaneser.

Fourteen: Battling with Babylonian

At Baghdad the raft with Layard's Black Obelisk arrived, and on 6 January 1847 Rawlinson, suffering from a very bad cold, wrote to say that 'yesterday morning the cases were hauled up to the high open space in front of our Naval depot – they cannot be taken inside – but they are out of reach of a rise of the water, and I will have a tent pitched over them from the rain. I took a squint at the black obelisk last night and liked its appearance vastly.'[1] Once the case was opened, he was amazed by it, admitting that 'I have during the last fortnight thrown aside all other Cuneiforms and set to work tooth and nail at the Assyrian ... I have copied the obelisk Inscription, but not yet attacked it in form – indeed, I wish to work out the elements satisfactorily before I go into details. The monument itself is, I conceive, the most noble trophy in the world and would alone have been well worth the whole expense of excavating Nimrud. I have now pretty well made up my mind to run up to Mosul during next month or at the latest in March – and we would there arrange all details about publication.'[2] He felt that this exciting discovery, once fully deciphered, 'will, I suspect, cast Egyptology entirely into the shade'.[3]

The decipherment of Akkadian (Assyrian and Babylonian) cuneiform had not reached anywhere near the point where this well-preserved inscription could be read, but in Ireland, whenever his duties as a clergyman allowed, Hincks continued to work hard on decipherment. A few months earlier John Lee, a scientist and collector of antiquities living near Aylesbury, had advised him to contact Reverend George Renouard of the Royal Asiatic Society who had access to Rawlinson's Bisitun manuscript and could therefore supply Hincks with more recent information. In mid-December 1846, Renouard received the letter Rawlinson had sent him six weeks earlier and immediately divulged some of it to Hincks, including Rawlinson's fear of being beaten by Hincks in Babylonian cuneiform. He also quoted from Rawlinson's letter: 'I am indebted to him [Hincks] indeed for a most notable discovery, one in fact which has proved of more use to me even than my Behistun key.'[4]

What proved significant to Rawlinson was that Hincks had mentioned in a letter to the *Literary Gazette* back in July that a fragmentary clay cylinder, published over twenty years previously by the traveller Ker Porter, had a cursive version of the East India House Babylonian inscription, both of which had been discovered at Babylon. The scripts appeared different, because one was inscribed with reeds on damp clay (a 'cursive cuneiform') and the other was engraved in stone (a 'lapidary cuneiform'). Rawlinson therefore realized that the clearly defined inscriptions on the stone relief sculptures being excavated by Layard at Nimrud were the same script and language as the more indistinct inscriptions on clay objects.

By now Hincks had received the first part of Rawlinson's Memoir published by the Royal Asiatic Society, which contained the detailed drawings of the Bisitun relief sculptures and the Old Persian inscription, as well as the copious notes, transliteration, translation into Latin, the first chapter on the history of the study of cuneiform and the second chapter on the nature of Babylonian, Elamite and Old Persian cuneiform. At the end of November 1846, Hincks gave a paper to the Royal Irish Academy, with a follow-up paper two weeks later, in which he corrected several of Rawlinson's readings – unaware that Rawlinson himself had already made many corrections in his subsequent work. Hincks's sixteen-page paper was not published by the Academy until 1848, although a separate version was issued with very limited distribution.

Hincks not only considered Rawlinson's Old Persian readings, but also gave further thoughts on Elamite and his latest ideas on Babylonian, rightly comparing it with one of the scripts seen at Persepolis: 'To the third kind of Persepolitan writing the name of Babylonian may be given with perfect confidence, from the identity in form of its characters, and those of the cursive writing on the clay cylinders, barrels, &c., found at Babylon. Since the date of my last paper I have made considerable progress in deciphering both this cursive character, and the lapidary characters used on the Babylonian bricks, and in the great inscription of the East India Company. Although much remains to be done, I have thought it right to take the earliest possible opportunity of communicating to the Academy the progress which I have already made.'[5]

The fact that Hincks was willing to make public his results at an early stage was a major difference between him and Rawlinson; while Hincks presented his ever-evolving ideas in successive papers and letters, Rawlinson preferred to wait until he was confident of his facts. He also combined fieldwork on the ground with his scholarship, while Hincks only used the results of other people's fieldwork, as he would never have an opportunity to travel further afield than London. Hincks objected to Rawlinson withholding information, while Rawlinson was exasperated by Hincks publishing too often and too soon, so that the public became confused about which theories were redundant. While Hincks revealed his half-formed theories, he convinced himself that Rawlinson was using them to further his own research. An irrational feeling of distrust between the two men developed, fuelled by the mischief-making of onlookers such as Renouard.

In his paper to the Academy in December, Hincks presented the first ever list of Babylonian cuneiform signs, seventy-six in all, with their values in English. As a basis for his study, he explained that he had used the already published trilingual inscriptions from Persepolis and elsewhere (but not Bisitun), the first step being to compare the already deciphered Old Persian names with their

Babylonian counterparts, and, where available, parallel Hebrew and Greek versions: 'This deciphering of proper names determined the value of many characters; more were determined by comparing different modes of writing the same words in the inscriptions which commence with the same formula, and in phrases of common occurrence found elsewhere. I also observed some Median [Elamite] words transcribed in one of the inscriptions, and a few other words that, though altered, appeared to be of Persian or Median origin. When the equivalence of the two sets of characters, lapidary and cursive, was ascertained, more values were determined by comparing the proper names in the great inscription [the East India House one], in their various forms, with their representatives in other languages, and by comparing the different forms in which words of the great inscription which occur in formulas that are frequently met with, are written.'[6] Many of his signs were incorrect, or only partially correct, but nevertheless this was a major advance.

Hincks sent the list of his Babylonian signs to Renouard in London, who received it the day after writing to Hincks about Rawlinson. Renouard therefore wrote to Hincks again: 'My eagerness to try your Alphabets has caused me to lose a Post; however, it gives me more time for extracts from Rawlinson.'[7] He informed Hincks what Rawlinson had told him about his supplementary note on Old Persian and the use of vowels with consonants: 'He laments that his interlinear version was not corrected according to his own emendations . . . He insists, however, principally on the "new phonetic system" proposed by him in a supplementary note sent to England in August, which discards all the aspirated sonants (medials) from the Alphabet and shews all the secondary forms of the characters to belong to the vowels i and u without any changes whatever of phonetic power. "Under this reformed system", he adds, "I can shew the *guna* to be intended in the oblique case of nouns, in the root of verbs, in the special tenses and in the medial terminations precisely as it is in Sanscrit, and the language is thus, I think, for the first time exhibited under its true appearance."'[8]

Renouard went on to accuse Rawlinson of plagiarizing Hincks's Old Persian ideas: 'It is evident that Major R. caught the idea of simplifying his alphabet and the use of the guna from you. Your hint in L.G. [*Literary Gazette*] 25 July would have escaped most readers, but . . . he availed himself of a clue which scarcely anyone else could have followed. Your remark (p.7) that "*a* must be interposed as a guna to the vowel" is almost identical with his; and the coincidence, as you will readily suppose, was very striking.'[9] No such words were published in this letter by Hincks, although he used the phrase in the paper on Old Persian that was read in June before the Royal Irish Academy and published two years later. Rawlinson was not yet aware of this paper and was only alerted to what Hincks was doing with Old Persian in a letter he received in October, long after he had sent off his 'plagiarizing' note to the Royal Asiatic Society.

Suddenly Hincks was alarmed that Renouard had posted his Babylonian sign list to Rawlinson, who would adopt all his readings and claim the glory, when Hincks himself intended to publish a paper with the Royal Asiatic Society – a paper that was never written. He contacted Renouard, but too late. Renouard sent Rawlinson the list on 21 December, and just after Christmas he advised Hincks to submit his paper very soon: 'I am very much rejoiced to hear that you mean to send a paper on the Babylonian Inscriptions to the R.A.S. and think you will do well to send it without further delay. You may justly claim priority of anything like a well grounded (I should say *rational*) interpretation of those monuments, and it is very desirable that your labours should not be anticipated. Had Major R. given any clue to the method by which he came at his results, or sent any copy of his Alphabet when he first sent a translation of the Behistun Inscriptions, he would have been hailed throughout Europe as the solver of a problem which had remained unattempted for 20 centuries. As it is, his tardiness will rob him of half the meed [reward] due to him.'[10]

Renouard went on to sow further seeds of distrust: 'My notion is this: that you have laid a solid foundation, and that future repairs of parts to the superstructure, or even the removal of some

fundamental stones themselves will in no degree authorise anyone
to dispute the skill and science of the master builder: but if from
the hints you have already thrown out others catch a glimpse of
those facts which have hitherto escaped their notice, they may,
as I once before remarked, play the same prank to you, as Leibnitz
did to Newton.'[11]

It was also just after Christmas that Layard returned to Nimrud
from Mosul and concentrated on the north-west palace before
turning to Qalah Shergat, an impressive mound that he had first
seen seven years earlier and had long wished to excavate. Accompanied by Hormuzd Rassam and several well-armed men, he took
two days to ride to this site, about 68 miles south of Mosul, on
the west bank of the Tigris. Passing pits of bitumen, Layard
observed that it 'is extensively used for building purposes, for lining
the boats on the river, and particularly for smearing camels, when
suffering from certain diseases of the skin to which they are liable.
Before leaving the pits, the Arabs, as is their habit, set fire to the
bitumen, which sent forth a dense smoke, obscuring the sky, and
being visible for many miles.'[12]

Camped at the foot of the ancient city, Layard described the
isolation of the place: 'The great mound could be distinguished
through the gloom, rising like a distant mountain against the
dark sky. From all sides came the melancholy wail of the jackals –
thousands of these animals having issued from their subterranean
dwellings in the ruins as soon as the last gleam of twilight was
fading in the western horizon. The owl, perched on the old
masonry, occasionally sent forth its mournful note. The shrill
laugh of the Arabs would sometimes rise above the cry of the jackal
. . . It was desolation such as those alone who have witnessed such
scenes, can know.'[13] The only major discovery here was the first
statue of a person, a life-size figure of King Shalmaneser III sitting
on a throne covered in cuneiform inscriptions. Little else to interest
Layard was found, and he was unable to identify the original
name of the site. For years he remained sceptical of Rawlinson's
identification of the ancient city as Ashur, yet Rawlinson was
right.

While Layard was working at Ashur, Rawlinson had been intently studying the Black Obelisk, and in mid-February 1847 he wrote to Layard about his progress on Assyrian cuneiform: 'I have been studying the whole series of complicated Cuneiform inscriptions deeply during the past fortnight and I must confess I am fairly bothered with the anomalies of the Assyrian character . . . It would be useless to give a paper on the Nimrud names alone. I must show a general alphabet with proofs from a dozen different sources, before the reading of the names would be entitled to my attention, and I confess that notwithstanding all your assistance I am far from being able to do this at present.'[14]

Rawlinson had just received Hincks's list of Babylonian signs with their values, eight weeks after Renouard had sent it, and was sufficiently confident to recognize that many values were incorrect: 'I was afraid, as you know, of Dr Hinckes, but having received a private tracing of his alphabet by this post, in which he professes to give the value of 76 Babylonian characters, I am much relieved for he has not above a dozen correct identifications.'[15] He added: 'I think I must run up to Nimrud before the middle of March and satisfy myself on several points which are at present perfect enigmas to me . . . I have numerous letters about Cuneiforms from England . . . the best thing is that the French and Germans are therefore cleared out of the field.'[16]

By now Rawlinson had decided that he must return to Bisitun to try to copy the main Babylonian inscription in order to help his Assyrian and Babylonian decipherment. He mentioned this to Norris who, in mid-February, revealed the plans to Hincks: 'I am waiting anxiously for Major Rawlinson's communications; I hear from him every month, but always on the first class of writing [Old Persian]. You will be glad however to hear that he intends shortly to go to Behistun again with scaffolding and long ladders, when he will devote himself solely to the remains of the Babylonian there; and he hopes that by his exclusive attention to that part of the inscription, aided by his increased knowledge of the character, he may recover parts which before he considered lost.'[17]

Norris had recently received from Hincks a new list of ninety-five Babylonian cuneiform signs, that updated the seventy-six signs just received by Rawlinson. He agreed to Hincks's proposal that he should forward the list to Baghdad without their corresponding values – so that Rawlinson was denied the key. These signs, along with those for numerals, were presented by Hincks in a paper to the Royal Irish Academy on 11 January, in which he discussed their individual values and how he had reached his conclusions. He began with his reasons for his 'rectifications':[18] 'When I laid before the Academy, at its last sitting [14 December 1846], my alphabet of the third Persepolitan writing, with the corresponding lapidary characters, I by no means expected that it would prove perfectly correct. No first attempt at the alphabet of an unknown language has been so. I considered it, however, an approximation, and, probably, as near a one as could be attained by means of the data in my possession; and I looked forward to its being amended by those who had the command of more numerous inscriptions.'[19] To this eight-page paper, published the following year, Hincks added a comment on the Old Persian alphabet: 'There is now, then, I believe, an almost perfect agreement between the Major and me as to the first Persepolitan alphabet. That used in his transcription of the Bisitun inscription differed from that given in my first paper (read on the 9th June last), as to fifteen characters. As to three of these, I have adopted his values; as to nine others, he has adopted mine, though, as I understand, without any knowledge of my having given them; and as to two more, we have both altered our values, so as to be now in agreement. We now differ, I believe, as to only one character, No. 12; and it is of little consequence whether this is *properly* represented z or zh, as it was the only character that could be used to express both these sounds.'[20] This sign ⟩↔⟨ was thought to be zh by Hincks and z by Rawlinson, although in his supplementary note Rawlinson listed it as z followed by a and possibly by u. Today it is known to be za.

In mid-February, at the same time that Rawlinson informed Layard that he was no longer afraid of Hincks being a threat,

Rawlinson also wrote to Renouard. In mid-May Renouard repeated to Hincks the disparaging comments contained in that letter: 'He [Rawlinson] begins by saying that mine of the 21st of last December relieved him of his apprehension that Dr Hincks had appropriated to himself the field of Babylonian discovery. "Dr Hincks", he adds, "has no doubt done a good deal, considering the very few and the defective names from which he has had to cull his alphabet, but he certainly cannot employ that alphabet in its present state as a key to the Inscriptions with any prospect of success; – for fully one half of the powers he has assigned, I can prove to be wrong from the orthography of the names at Behistun; and many of the others which he has taken from the Persepolitan names, he has so tied up by his introduction of a system and a precision unknown to the alphabet, that they are hardly recognizable. His observations in support of his readings must be curious, for if he will only analyse the Persepolitan materials which are at his disposal, he will find many contradictions that it would almost puzzle an Oedipus to solve, and if he had the more extended data which I am fortunately able to command, he would discover evidence of fluctuating phonetic powers (between the nasal and dental, for instance, and the nasal and the guttural) that would, I think, fairly stagger him." '[21]

Renouard divulged what Rawlinson had planned for Babylonian cuneiform: 'As he [Hincks] has however braved all difficulties, and taken the field, I must needs follow his example. By this post, I have sent a skeleton alphabet to Mr Norris, and I am now writing out a condensed explanatory chapter which will I hope be ready next month. The day however is still, I think, far distant in which we shall be able to read and understand independent Babylonian and Assyrian Inscriptions, for we want the grand desideratum of language: and unless it may lurk in the old Egyptian or Aethiopic, I am sure I know not where to look for it.'[22]

Norris himself wrote to Hincks on 10 May about this 'skeleton alphabet': 'I have compared Major Rawlinson's alphabet (which I have held in my possession since the beginning of April) with yours, and find that the disagreement is far less frequent than the agreement,'[23] which did little to allay Hincks's fears of his own alphabet being stolen. A few days later, Renouard sent Hincks further extracts from Rawlinson's letter, including details of his plans to return to Bisitun and Persepolis in the summer, noting: 'the Major will be much pleased to find, on looking at your papers, how nearly many of your *solutions* (for I cannot help considering you as working out a difficult problem) approached his'.[24]

While intermediaries continued to encourage the rivalry between Rawlinson and Hincks, Layard had returned from Qalah Shergat to Nimrud. He decided to send a colossal bull and a similar lion to England, choosing two smaller examples from the thirteen pairs and several fragments that had by now been discovered. He had a sturdy cart made, obtaining a pair of iron axles that had been used by Botta at Khorsabad, and in order to diminish the weight of each sculpture, Layard decided to cut away as much as possible from the side that stood against the wall, which was never intended to be seen, rather than saw them into pieces, as Botta had done. By mid-March the bull was ready to move, but all did not go to plan while it was being lowered, because the ropes broke and the bull crashed to the ground. Luckily, it did not break, and an Arab sheikh who was watching expressed his joy, but said he could not understand why all these carved stones were being removed and how their existence was known in the first place. Layard himself admitted that he was constantly assailed by such thoughts at each new discovery: 'A stranger laying open monuments buried for more than twenty centuries, and thus proving to those who dwelt around them, that much of the civilisation and knowledge of which we now boast, existed amongst their forefathers when our "ancestors were yet unborn," was, in a manner, an acknowledgement of the debt which the West owes to the East.'[25]

From the mound, the bull was dragged over a mile to the river, a journey that presented more problems, especially when the cart's wheels sank into disused storage pits. The bull was left on a specially constructed platform by the riverside to await the arrival of the lion, and on 22 March Layard wrote to his mother that the 'worst part of this business is consequently over, and I rejoice that I have succeeded in my attempt with the small means at my disposal, while the French bull is still sticking half-way between the river and Khorsabad . . . The only difficulty is the embarkation on a vessel, but I think that can be accomplished with proper care. Altogether, I shall be able to send between 70 and 80 bas-reliefs to England. I shall have above 200, perhaps 250, finished drawings, and a large collection of inscriptions.'[26]

Rawlinson had been forced to give up the idea of visiting Nimrud, as he had to visit Basra to help suppress the ongoing slave trade. In early March he was also 'laid up with a nasty bilious attack brought on by the sudden change from winter to summer, and although not exactly on my beam ends, am quite incapacitated from any work'.[27] Two weeks later he was still no better: 'I have been ailing on and off, and have tried everything, diet, medicines and change of air, without much benefit.'[28] He told Layard that he was planning to stay outside Baghdad for a month in tents, as he had done during the cholera epidemic, and then he hoped to obtain some leave and go to the Kurdistan mountains for the summer to restore his health, 'otherwise I fear I must go home, for 20 years in the East with the knocking about I have had is no joke – and although I should be loth to forfeit the Baghdad post, I should be still more loth seriously to endanger my health'.[29] By the end of March he was much better, having moved out of Baghdad as planned, and admitted that, 'in fact I have never had anything I believe really the matter with me, only what you may call bedevilled . . . I find the country air delightful after being shut up in the town so long'.[30] Rawlinson explained to Layard why it was impossible for him to return home: 'The question of leave to England is one of the standard regulations of the Indian Army and has I believe never been overruled in a single case. Officers and Civilians may go on sick leave to the Cape, Syria or Egypt without any permanent sacrifice, but to set foot in England vacates an appointment . . . so that there is no real grounds for complaint . . . The Directors it is said would consent, but the Board of Control is opposed. I have no particular wish however to remain here more than another year.'[31]

An anonymous and substantial review of Rawlinson's Old Persian Memoir had appeared in the January issue of the *Dublin University Magazine*, a publication with limited circulation that was devoted to literary topics. Rawlinson had just received a copy and, knowing it was written by Hincks, forwarded it to Layard: 'Dr Hincks is, as I deduce you knew, the best Egyptian scholar living, but he is I suspect going a little too fast in Cuneiforms, if I may judge by his Median and Babylonian alphabets. Let me have the number when you have done with.'[32] The review was generally favourable towards Rawlinson, apart from criticizing his Elamite copy of the Bisitun inscription that 'had not yet been communicated to the public, nor even to the Royal Asiatic Society'.[33]

Hincks ended the review with a history of what individual scholars had done, as he felt that Rawlinson's achievements were beginning to eclipse all others, including his own in Ireland, commenting: 'Many persons think that in deciphering, the first step is everything; but the fact is, that, though one false step will often interpose an insuperable bar to the making further discoveries, it by no means follows that one right step will lead to their being made. In deciphering unknown languages, there are many steps to be taken, and the honor of taking them must be divided among many discoverers. To claim the whole merit for the person who takes the first right step, is an injustice which has sometimes been committed through national prejudice.'[34] Similar research had been published by Lassen and Burnouf, and Hincks was especially critical of Lassen, saying that: 'With these publications is connected an unpleasant piece of literary scandal.'[35] He accused him of using the ideas of Burnouf, commenting that, as a translator, Lassen was 'completely destitute of the peculiar talent of the decipherer; and his attempts at translation were consequently as bad as could be made by one who had been put upon the right way'.[36] Hincks even suggested that Rawlinson's translation of Bisitun was still probably far better before it was revised than anything

Lassen had ever produced, though he injected a note of doubt: 'Between the translation he [Rawlinson] has now given and those of Lassen there is really no comparison to be made. We by no means affirm that it is immaculate. There are several passages in it which we cannot help regarding with suspicion, and even more than suspicion; but the faults in it, if faults they be, are of a totally different character from those in the German translations.'[37]

Apart from sending Layard this review, Rawlinson also reported that he had heard the clergy in England felt threatened by what was being discovered in Mesopotamia, fearing that the Old Testament might be contradicted: 'They write to me from England that Assyrian antiquities were exciting great interest and that the Clergy had got perfectly alarmed at the idea of there being contemporary annals whereby to test the credibility of Jewish history. A brother indeed of mine [George], a Fellow of Exeter College and joint Editor of the "Oxford Magazine", protests most vehemently against the further prosecutions of the enquiry. Did you ever hear such downright *rot*?'[38] His brother George, who was later to write a biography of Rawlinson, had entered the Church and was destined to become Canon of Canterbury cathedral.

Rawlinson was now thirty-seven years old and, on 11 April 1847, made a lengthy entry in his birthday journal, in order, he explained, 'to gauge my feelings, character and power of mind. Doubtless ambition is the mainspring of my life and yet in many moods I feel its emptiness. I am now bent on becoming H.E. Her Majesty's Envoy to the Court of Persia.'[39] Ambition, he believed, 'must not be sought in politics, but in letters – and in that line also I am accordingly still at work. I have published my first Memoir on Persian Antiquities and ... shall thus at any rate be handed down to posterity as having contributed a new chapter to the History of the Earth. I hope however to do much more than this.'[40] Rawlinson felt that curiosity was necessary: 'In my own case it is so certainly, I have now a certain pleasure in discovery for its own sake only. My mind is still tolerably vigorous, but is yielding I think to an infirmed constitution.'[41]

Religion again proved to be a matter of concern, with Rawlinson thinking that 'it seems there is proof in nothing but mathematics and the exact sciences – in everything else it is merely a preponderance of probability only. In this view it would be worth my while I think to go again carefully over the evidence of Christianity. On natural religion I have never had a doubt – revelation is what has staggered me, but if I were to sift the matter merely as I would a difficult question in politics or a doubtful point in antiquities, I might perchance still end in becoming a Christian. As far as . . . conduct is concerned, I am neither too good or too bad . . . As an English gentleman I spurn anything dishonourable – pleasant vices I tolerate . . . In fact I am a man of the world like three-fourths of my educated countrymen.'[42]

By mid-April, Layard was ready to move the lion. Although he had successfully moved the colossal bull from Nimrud to the Tigris, Rawlinson was worried about how these monuments would reach Basra. 'With regard to the future transit of the marbles, I shall be very happy to do everything I can to assist in their export – but I am no great hand at mechanics,' he told Layard, 'and in the absence of the Steamer I shall almost doubt if I could manage the Bull and Lion. It might be possible to get them landed here as you suggest, but how are they to get on board the river boats to be taken to Bussorah?'[43] Layard had already decided that they should be shipped from Nimrud to Basra on two specially constructed rafts, without being transferred to river boats at Baghdad as was customary. Nobody could be found in Mosul to undertake this task, with everyone declaring it impossible, but Alexander Hector in Baghdad hired a raft builder there who 'was indebted in a considerable sum of money, and being the owner of a large number of skins, now lying useless, he preferred a desperate undertaking to the prospect of a debtor's prison'.[44]

Moving the lion was a more precarious operation than moving the bull, because it was cracked in several places, but after two days it reached the river, where both sculptures were transferred to the rafts. They set sail on 20 April, and Layard commented: 'As I watched the rafts, until they disappeared . . . I could not forbear musing upon the strange destiny of their burdens; which, after adorning the palaces of the Assyrian kings, the objects of the wonder, and may be the worship of millions, had been buried unknown for nearly twenty-five centuries beneath a soil trodden by Persians under Cyrus, by Greeks under Alexander, and by Arabs under the first successors of their Prophet. They were now to visit India, to cross the most distant seas of the southern hemisphere, and to be finally placed in a British Museum. Who can venture to foretell how their strange career will end?'[45]

Work continued at Nimrud, and by the end of April, twenty-eight individual rooms of the north-west palace had been traced, all with relief sculptures lining the walls, and several trenches had been opened in other parts of the mound. 'Much, of course, remained to be explored in the mound; but with the limited means at my disposal,' Layard complained, 'I was unable to pursue my researches to the extent that I could have wished. If, after carrying a trench to a reasonable depth and distance, no remains of sculpture or inscription were discovered, I abandoned it and renewed the experiment elsewhere.'[46] In drought conditions, the countryside became increasingly dangerous from the incursions of Arabs from the desert, and when the inhabitants of a nearby village were murdered, Layard decided to cover any exposed ruins with earth to protect them and leave Nimrud. By mid-May his house was dismantled and everything was carried to Mosul. It was now too late for Rawlinson to visit.

With only a small amount of his grant left, Layard turned to the immense mound of Nineveh just across the Tigris from Mosul, riding out from the town and crossing the river to the excavation each morning. The French Consul had been excavating there for some time, but Layard was critical of his methods: 'He was satisfied with digging pits or wells, a few feet deep, and then renouncing the attempt, when no sculptures or inscriptions were uncovered. By excavating in this desultory manner, if any remains of building existed under ground, their discovery would be a mere chance.'[47] The accumulation of rubbish and earth over the former buildings was so considerable that trenches 20 to 30 feet deep were needed.

After careful consideration of the landscape, Layard decided to begin digging in the south-west corner of the mound, and after a few days without finds, a palace that had been destroyed by fire was encountered, once again with walls of mud bricks lined with sculptured slabs. Colossal winged human-headed bulls similar to those of Khorsabad were also found, some with four legs, others with five. Henry Ross wrote to his sister from Mosul: 'Layard is excavating in a new mound called Kouyunjik, just opposite the town on the other bank of the river, and has found the remains of another Assyrian Palace; so far, the sculptures are much defaced and broken by the action of fire, but I dare say that he will at last meet with something in better preservation. This new discovery will probably detain him here some months longer. I shall be very sorry when he leaves for I like him exceedingly, and it is a great thing for me to see another Englishman occasionally.'[48]

'Inscriptions', reported Layard, 'were not numerous. They occurred between the legs of winged bulls, and above the head of the king, and on bas-reliefs representing the siege or sack of a city, in the form of short epigraphs, and on the backs of slabs; but they were all more or less injured.'[49] One notable discovery was a relief sculpture depicting two scribes, who were 'writing down on rolls of leather or some other flexible material, the number of the heads of the slaughtered enemy laid at their feet by the Assyrian warriors'.[50] Layard had not yet recognized any finds of clay tablets and so was unaware that this picture represented one scribe writing down details in Aramaic on a leather or papyrus scroll with a pen and ink, while the other scribe was writing in cuneiform on a clay tablet with a reed stylus. Describing some of the smaller objects encountered on the floors of the rooms, Layard observed 'several small oblong tablets of dark unbaked clay, having a cuneiform inscription over the sides'[51] – the first tantalizing hint of Nineveh's huge libraries of clay tablets.

By the middle of June, Layard had done all he could in Assyria and, with little money left, he prepared to leave for England, rightly commenting: 'Scarcely a year before, with the exception of the ruins of Khorsabad, not one Assyrian monument was known.'[52]

On 24 June, he left Mosul for Constantinople, accompanied by Hormuzd Rassam, who was going to Oxford to study. That same month Hincks was also heading for Oxford, which he reached on the 25th to attend a meeting of the British Association for the Advancement of Science. From here he wrote letters to his daughters about all he saw and heard, revealing himself as an affectionate father. At the British Museum, where Layard's first case of sculptured reliefs from Nimrud had just arrived, the Trustees requested that Ross should continue the excavations at Nineveh in Layard's absence.

Also in June Rawlinson set out on a three-month excursion to the mountains of Kurdistan, 'to combine a search for health with pickings of every sort and description available'.[53] His main intention was to copy the Babylonian inscription at Bisitun, though he had to drop plans of visiting Persepolis because Persia was too unsettled. 'I had assembled a decent working retinue, something different from the suite that would be selected for "le grand tour", but almost indispensable to travelling with comfort in this part of the East . . . In travelling in these countries the object is to combine comfort with lightness and despatch.'[54] In all, he had sixteen servants, including grooms, a cook and tent pitchers. They left Baghdad on the 29th, 'my good friends Jones on one side and young Hector on the other, these two having resolved to accompany me to my night's stage'.[55]

Despite his preparations, comfort could not be guaranteed, as Rawlinson found on the first night: 'I was half eaten with fleas. Baghdad fleas by the bye are not like the solitary tenants of your English feather beds – they come in swarms like the Egyptian plague. I saw this spring one of the prettiest girls in Baghdad with her neck and shoulders perfectly tattoed . . . but found afterwards it was nothing but innumerable flea bites.'[56] On his journey to Kermanshah, the heat was intolerable, as were the flies, but on 11 July he came in sight of the city, welcomed 'by all the officers of the troops and many of the local chiefs . . . ordered by the Amir in my honor, but against my express request, as I have repeatedly declared I am on this trip a mere private traveller and not a public officer'.[57] Not paid for out of public funds, his trips to record Bisitun on this and the previous occasion with Jones and Hector cost Rawlinson over £1,000 – a massive commitment on its own, without the considerable risks he took to recover a copy of the inscriptions.

At Kermanshah, Rawlinson was the guest of the governor and learned from him that Muhammed Shah had obviously been following his researches, since he had given orders 'to engrave at Bisitun a Persian translation of the annals of Darius – M^d Shah wishing to emulate the petroglyphic fame of his remote ancestor on the throne of Persia, or at any rate to render the antique annals of the empire intelligible to the multitude – the task is I suspect beyond the powers of the present age'.[58]

Rawlinson set out for Bisitun on the morning of 17 July and recorded his routine over the next few days: 'I am the greater part of the day up the rock, verifying and correcting my old copies, filling up lacunae, taking paper casts and recovering such fragments of the Median [Elamite] tablet as are in any way like made out.'[59] On 20 July he wrote a long letter to Norris in London, initially about Hincks, having discovered what he had written about Old Persian – that Rawlinson had supposedly borrowed some of his values, and vice-versa. Rawlinson dismissed the idea: 'as if we really had been thus mutually indebted to each other. His however, I fancy, is what they call Irish reciprocity. I do not think the D^r a very liberal critic and it is on that account I let him flounder with his Median and Babylonian and keep back the Bisitun material until I can perfect my own scholarly systems.'[60] He recounted his own progress to Norris: 'Having furnished myself with scaffolding and the longest ladders that can be made in this country, I have been able to examine nearly every portion of the great sculpture. I have been very poorly repaid for all my trouble and expense. The Tablets 6, 7, 8 & 9 of the published plate which must I thought yield me some information, when closely examined prove to be entirely illegible – there are probably not more than half a dozen letters in all this immense surface or rock which can be made out.'[61] Rawlinson was trying to copy the inscription that had been carved to the right of the relief sculpture, not realizing it was the original Elamite version that had been later obliterated when Darius the Great extended the sculpture panel and, incredibly, had ordered the inscription to be copied out word for word below.

In his letter to Norris, Rawlinson drew other incorrect conclusions from this obliterated inscription: 'From the enormous extent of the writing however in these tablets, it is quite evident to me they must have contained supplementary records, that is a continuation of the history given in the lower columns. Perhaps it might have been an account of the Grecian and Thracian expeditions that was added in these upper columns – whatever it was it must have been of interest.'[62] More accurately, he observed: 'I think moreover the entire writing is Median [Elamite] without any Persian or Babylonian adjuncts, for the few characters I have been able to recognize in different parts of the 4 columns are all of that alphabet.'[63] Discussing his latest ideas about Elamite cuneiform and language, he advised Norris not 'however to mention this to Dr Hincks as he would probably claim it before the Savans [scholars] of Dublin as his new discovery. I do not admit his principles of Babylonian reading at all.'[64]

Rawlinson recorded that up to now, 'I have been chiefly at work comparing, correcting and filling up lacunae, and I shall have to furnish you with a pretty copious list of Errata . . . I have taken casts of all the separate Persian, Median and Babylonian tablets, which I intend for your Museum. The doubtful characters in several of the Babylonian names I have determined.'[65] But the main Babylonian inscription remained a problem: 'The Babylonian translation contained in tablets 10 & 11 is very difficult to be reached. I think I shall be able to make out a few names of the genealogy, for the right hand corner of N° 10 still preserves the flint varnish, but throughout the others the surface is so abraded and honeycombed, that . . . I doubt my ability to detect or copy a single name.'[66] He ended: 'I must now go to my perch on the rock.'[67]

The work at Bisitun proved excessively difficult, because 'the weather is . . . so atrociously hot that I cannot risk exposure to the sun'.[68] For a few hours around midday, he was confined to his tent or the stifling caravanserai, either place being 'perfect purgatory'.[69] The intense heat began to make all members of the party ill, and Rawlinson was about to postpone the work until September, when he suffered 'a pretty sharp attack of bilious fever brought on by exposure on the Bisotun rock. For one entire week I was on my back incapacitated from all exertion . . . I entertained serious thoughts of returning straight to Baghdad. At last however the disagreement gave way to medicines.'[70] Although still weak, he left Bisitun for a change of air in a nearby village, from where he could still see the Bisitun mountain. He spent the daytime in a nearby garden: 'the sloping garden itself and the milky plain beyond were something quite delightful in my present exhausted state, and I thus lay all day in a sort of half dreamy enjoyment listening to the babbling of the waters, gazing on the really beautiful scene before me.'[71] He hoped that he would regain strength by inhaling the 'breath of the mountains – what is life alas without health?'[72]

Over the next few weeks Rawlinson travelled about the countryside, visiting Hamadan and making new copies of the inscriptions of Elwand, but by 8 September he was back at Bisitun, ready to tackle the monument, with 'renovated health and spirits'.[73] This time he was determined to copy the Babylonian inscription, carved on a mass of rock jutting out over the Elamite inscription below and separated from the relief sculptures by a deep fissure. 'The mass of rock in question is scarped,' Rawlinson wrote, 'and it projects some feet over the Scythic [Elamite] recess, so that it cannot be approached by any of the ordinary means of climbing.'[74] The sculptors of Darius the Great had found the rock surface too unstable to cut it level with the surrounding rock face, and Rawlinson thought he was just in time to copy the inscription, because 'the mass of rock on which the inscription is engraved bore every appearance . . . of being doomed to a speedy destruction, water trickling from above having almost separated the overhanging mass from the rest of the rock, and its own enormous

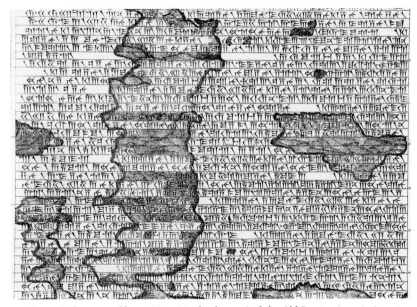

Rawlinson's drawing of lines 50 to 83 of column 4 of the Old Persian inscription at Bisitun as published by the Royal Asiatic Society.

Ruins of the palace of Darius the Great at Persepolis.

LEFT Walled city of Kandahar in Afghanistan.

BELOW LEFT Interior courtyard of the British Residency at Baghdad.

BELOW Discovery of the first colossal winged human-headed lion in Layard's excavations at Nimrud in 1846.

ABOVE Moving the colossal winged human-headed bull at Nimrud in 1847 at the start of its journey to the British Museum.

LEFT Layard drawing relief sculptures inside one of the rooms at Nineveh that had been filled with clay tablets.

Inside one of Layard's excavation tunnels at Nineveh.

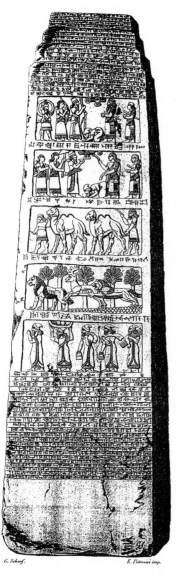

Engraving of the Black Obelisk from Nimrud that accompanied the publication of Rawlinson's lectures to the Royal Asiatic Society in 1850.

Black Obelisk from Nimrud, now in the British Museum.

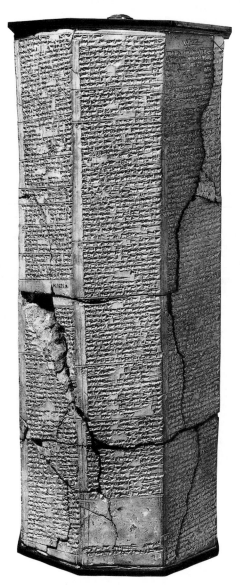

Clay prism of Tiglath-Pileser I found at Ashur that was used in the cuneiform competition held by the Royal Asiatic Society.

Clay tablet fragment found at Nineveh recognized by George Smith as the flood story from the Epic of Gilgamesh.

weight thus threatening very shortly to bring it thundering down into the plain, dashed into a thousand fragments.'[75]

Rawlinson found that it was impossible either to gain a foothold or to prop a ladder on the ledge against the projecting inscription: 'The Babylonian transcript at Behistun is still more difficult to reach than either the Scythic or the Persian tablets. The writing can be copied by the aid of a good telescope from below, but I long despaired of obtaining a cast of the inscription; for I found it quite beyond my powers of climbing to reach the spot where it was engraved, and the craigsmen of the place, who were accustomed to track the mountain goats over the entire face of the mountain, declared the particular block inscribed with the Babylonian legend to be unapproachable.'[76] By examining the rock with his telescope, he realized that the inscription was not so badly damaged as he previously thought, so he decided to try something different: 'Having first satisfied myself that a considerable portion of the tablet was legible, I got hoisted up on the opposite precipice and from a little nook in the scarp set to work with my big telescope – the letters are only distinguishable for a couple of hours during the day, that is from ten to twelve, and even then a novice would I suspect make a sad hack of the writing.'[77] He went through this process twice, so that he had two completely separate copies of the inscription.

More than that, Rawlinson also obtained 'a decent paper impression',[78] because he managed to find two Kurdish boys who were brave enough to climb to the inscription. Rawlinson expressed his delight to Layard about his achievements: 'The results have exceeded my most sanguine expectations – for I have actually recovered about one half of the entire Inscription. I have taken two independent copies to guard against the chance of error, and for the sake of reference I have also bribed two Kurds (the only two individuals in that country who could or would venture on the scarp) to take a paper impression.'[79]

Although he told Layard that two Kurds climbed up and took casts, in a later report he spoke of just one Kurdish boy: 'At length, however, a wild Kurdish boy, who had come from a distance,

volunteered to make the attempt, and I promised him a considerable reward if he succeeded . . . The boy's first move was to squeeze
himself up a cleft in the rock a short distance to the left of the
projecting mass. When he had ascended some distance above it,
he drove a wooden peg firmly into the cleft, fastened a rope to
this, and then endeavoured to swing himself across to another
cleft at some distance on the other side; but in this he failed, owing
to the projection of the rock. It then only remained for him to
cross over to the cleft by hanging on with his toes and fingers to
the slight inequalities on the bare face of the precipice, and in this
he succeeded, passing over a distance of twenty feet of almost
smooth perpendicular rock in a manner which to a looker-on
appeared quite miraculous. When he had reached the second cleft
the real difficulties were over. He had brought a rope with him
attached to the first peg, and now, driving in a second, he was
enabled to swing himself right over the projecting mass of rock.
Here with a short ladder he formed a swinging seat, like a painter's
cradle, and, fixed upon this seat, he took under my direction the
paper cast of the Babylonian translation of the records of Darius.'[80]

Rawlinson informed Layard that he was finding the new inscription very important for the decipherment of Babylonian: 'The
results of course are invaluable – my old alphabet is, as far as it
went, I find to be almost entirely correct, but I have been able of
course greatly to extend it, and I have moreover new vocabulary
of between two and three hundred words . . . I have not yet had
time to apply my discoveries to the Assyrian Inscriptions – but I
have recognized, as I have been copying, scores of the Nimrud
words with the forms of which I was already familiar, and I am
quietly sure that the two languages are so nearly allied, the same
key will answer for both . . . Immediately I get to Baghdad I shall
rewrite my Babylonian chapter and get it honed I hope for publication before the end of the year.'[81]

That same day at Bisitun, he wrote a similar letter to Norris,
saying that he had not studied what he had copied methodically,
but already he had 'a list of above 60 Babylonian names and a
very tolerable vocabulary'.[82] He did add one note of caution about

the inscription: 'Unfortunately I know nowhere an entire paragraph, for it is merely the right hand portion of the tablet on which the characters have been preserved. On the left hand the writing has been entirely destroyed.'[83] He was now very confident of success, and admitted to Norris: 'I was before a good deal alarmed at Dr Hincks progress – in fact I thought he was going to appropriate the field – but am now quite easy [relaxed]. On these points I have as little jealousy as most people, but I certainly do admire the Cavalier way in which he disposes of my pretensions to Assyrian discovery.'[84]

Just to ensure that Hincks would not gain an advantage while he himself was far away in Persia, he asked a favour of Layard: 'All I beg of you is not to supply Dr Hincks with materials before I can also have access to them – otherwise I fear he might give me the go bye.'[85] He finished his letter by saying: 'Persia is in a terrible state . . . I shall have enough to do during the winter in writing up the produce of this tour. I had hoped the new Indian Furlough Regulations would have been out in time to admit of my getting home in the spring – but there seems little chance of that now – immediately I can get home with the option of returning to my appointment, I shall not delay a single day at Baghdad.'[86] After ten days at Bisitun, Rawlinson returned to Baghdad at the beginning of October 1847 – 'by easy stages (227 miles) . . . This is the last time I ever cast eyes on Behistun'[87] – but it was to be two more years before he could leave for England.

Fifteen: A Brief Encounter

Once he was back in Baghdad, Rawlinson embarked on studying his newly acquired Babylonian inscription from Bisitun, so that he could prepare a paper for publication in the journal of the Royal Asiatic Society. In Ireland, Hincks also wanted to write a paper for the society and so had contacted Norris, who replied discouragingly in mid-October 1847: 'I have been thinking over the hint at the close of your letter, but can make no official reply, as we have no meetings until November. The Society is not bound to Major Rawlinson . . . and there should be no rivals, but helpers, in such a field. Still, until one memoir is completed it would hardly be practicable to print another; notes perhaps by another writer might be brought in, by way of criticism.'[1] Three weeks later Norris gave Hincks the society's official answer: 'However much the Council prize the labours of Major R. and appreciate the zeal and talent which he had displayed, there is no feeling in his favour to that degree which could prevent their giving publicity to any temperate criticism on his memoir. I should rather say the Council is favourably inclined to receive any papers on the subject from you, though the general opinion is that they would be better delayed until the Major's work is completed.'[2]

It cannot have been welcome news for Hincks to learn that he was effectively blocked from publishing anything substantial on Babylonian cuneiform with the society, as Rawlinson had priority. As a further blow, he was unsuccessful in his attempt to obtain a position as rector in Edgware, then a village 8 miles outside

London, which would have meant no longer relying on the good-will of other scholars to send him publications. Rather than submit an article on Babylonian, Hincks instead offered one on what was later known as Urartian cuneiform. A few years earlier, the *Journal Asiatique* in Paris had published plates of the rock-cut cuneiform inscriptions that Schulz had copied just before he was murdered. They were from the Lake Van area of south-east Turkey, some 150 miles north of Mosul and 60 miles south-west of Mount Ararat. The Urartian tribe of this region had adapted the cunei-form script of their Assyrian neighbours for their own unrelated language around the thirteenth century BC. Hincks studied these Van inscriptions and was the first person to attempt the de-cipherment of Urartian, examining both the cuneiform script and the language. His paper was read out at the Royal Asiatic Society's meeting in London on 4 December and accepted for immediate printing. He received printed copies of the thirty-five-page article in January 1848, which he distributed to scholars at home and abroad, including Lassen, Grotefend and Layard.

After eight years abroad, Layard was back in England, after a favourable welcome in Paris, which he described to his aunt: 'My short residence here has been very agreeable. I discovered Botta immediately; he received me with more kindness than I could have expected . . . The consequence was an invitation to attend the sitting of the "Académie des Inscriptions et Belles Lettres," on the following Friday.'[3] Layard's talk was a huge success, and the following day he was informed that they would elect him as a Corresponding Member. He arrived in London on 22 December and then travelled to Cheltenham to stay with his mother, where, although suffering repeated attacks of malaria, he began to write an account of his excavations for the publisher John Murray, as well as a volume on the inscriptions for the British Museum.

Henry Ross wrote sympathetically from Mosul: 'I was indeed sorry to see by your letter of the 10th December [1847] that you have suffered so much from illness and fever. I used to wonder when you exposed yourself day after day, and month after month at Nimrood, how you stood it.'[4] Ross was keeping an eye on the few workmen at Nineveh, but to minimize the amount of digging with his limited funds, he excavated mainly by tunnels lit by vertical shafts. 'I have just come from Kouyunjik,' he told Layard, 'where the excavations are regular catacombs, and in spite of the perforated skylights, I had to examine some of the slabs by candle light.'[5]

Having received a copy of the Van paper, Layard wrote back to Hincks straightaway to explain what he was doing with the inscriptions and offering to share information – it was far easier to forge a working relationship with Hincks in Ireland than try to obtain information on cuneiform from Rawlinson in Baghdad. Hincks responded instantly on 22 January, taking the opportunity to send copies of other papers he had written and explaining that his first paper on Babylonian with its seventy-six signs was to a large extent incorrect, while the second one was greatly improved, although inferior to what he could now achieve. On 26 January Layard replied: 'I have been confined some days by an attack of periodic fever and have not had time to read the papers you were kind eno' to send me with the attention they deserve . . . I am now preparing for publication a very detailed comparative table of the standard inscription of Nimroud, which will, I think, be very useful, as giving every word in the inscription and a large number of variants, and of words substituted in place of others.'[6]

That same day Grotefend, now working at Hanover in Germany, wrote to Hincks: 'Your two earlier articles . . . led me at once to conjecture that your energy and talent would succeed in deciphering all the cuneiform writings that are yet unknown. I have been still more convinced on that point since I have understood from your articles on the Lake Van inscriptions that you are proceeding on the same lines as I did when I laid the foundations of cuneiform deciphering. Of course I still have some doubts, as your results do not altogether accord with my own, and unfortunately I have not been able properly to test your discoveries. Last summer all my papers and books which were not in daily use were packed up in a trunk because His Majesty suddenly saw fit to have my house knocked down, in order to have a clear view from his castle.'[7]

From Baghdad, Rawlinson also contacted Layard to say that he had been in Basra all month, where he had seen Layard's relief sculptures and the Black Obelisk loaded on a ship. It had been managed very well, especially as the navy usually complained about filling their vessels 'with what they call rubbish'.[8] He had travelled to Basra with their old friend Dr John Ross, who was now on his way to India. 'Poor Ross is fairly off,' commented Rawlinson, 'he was in a most dangerous state when he left, having all the premonitory symptoms of deleriens tremens, but I trust the change of scenery may break him of his fatal fondness for the bottle and that the sea air may also help to set him on his legs again – he is now on his way to Bombay . . . and will go home on sick certification by the first opportunity.'[9] When he wrote, Rawlinson had not long returned to Baghdad from Basra: 'I am now hard and steadily at work again. I have now pretty well determined all the Alphabet, so that I can read any Inscriptions, Armenian, Assyrian, Babylonian or Elymaean, but the languages puzzle me most confoundedly.'[10]

Illness intervened, and Rawlinson was unable to make much progress on his Babylonian paper, to the disappointment of the Royal Asiatic Society, who announced at a meeting: 'The health of Major Rawlinson has prevented his completing a paper on this branch of the investigation; and in his last letter, which was dated on the 25th February, he complained of fever and inability to study; at the same time he spoke of his hopes of sending a chapter on the Babylonian language within a post or two.'[11] It was of equal disappointment to hear that the Babylonian inscription at Bisitun was not proving as valuable as anticipated, especially as 'no complete sentence has been found: one corner only of the rock is legible; and the half, at least, of every line discovered is irrevocably lost. The names too, in many instances, are not transcriptions of those we find in the Persian; but either translations, or else denominations quite unconnected.'[12]

Further disappointment was expressed by the society concern-

ing the anticipated Elamite report: 'the superior interest excited
by the Babylonian and Assyrian remains has induced Major
Rawlinson to abandon for a time his labours upon the valuable
copies he has made of the great Behistún inscription in that language [Elamite], which afford such large materials for study. This
delay is the more to be regretted, as the Major has made very
complete transcripts; and his memoir on the reading and language
is understood to have been near completion.'[13]

Probably after hearing about Hincks's Van paper, Rawlinson
wrote in exasperation to Layard in mid-March: 'As for old Hincks,
I am sick of him – he gives a new alphabet every month and
ultimately perhaps by dint of guessing may arrive at something
– as all his theories are propounded in the same tone of dogmatic
confidence, people will be puzzled at last to know which to
believe.'[14] Rawlinson admitted that he now desperately wanted to
go home as he was weary of Baghdad, and he knew that Ross
would soon be applying for leave to England: 'By the last account
he was improving in health, having given up the Brandy bottle.'[15]
In May, greatly concerned, Rawlinson wrote to Layard: 'Ross has
returned to Baghdad quite unexpectedly – he looks tolerably well,
but really keeps himself alive I fancy by strong stimulants – he is
however just the same excellent fellow.'[16]

In France the monarchy of Louis Philippe had been overthrown
in the revolution of 23 February 1848, setting off a series of
revolutions across Europe, though not in Britain. In March, Layard
went to Canford in Dorset, where he worked on his publications
at the home of his cousin Lady Charlotte Guest, from where he
wrote to Henry Ross: 'You have, of course, heard of all the wonderful occurrences in France . . . I was quite prepared for the Revolution which has taken place, by what I heard when in Paris, and
announced it in England, but no one would believe me . . . I am
now with Lady Charlotte Guest, at Canford, a fine old mansion in
Dorsetshire. These comfortable places, and the pleasure of English
country life, spoil one for the adventures and privations of the
East. I find a great improvement in the upper classes; much more
information, liberality of opinion, and kindness towards those

beneath them.'[17] Layard requested Ross to send sculptures from Nimrud to Canford, and over the next few years several of these, along with a colossal bull and lion, were shipped to England and on their arrival at Canford were housed in a specially constructed annexe called the Nineveh Porch.

In May, Hincks's Van paper was published in the journal of the Royal Asiatic Society. It was an expanded version from the one he had previously circulated and included an 'additional memoir' on numerals, which was printed as a twenty-six-page supplement. Having been advised that the society would rather not publish anything by him on Babylonian, this supplement was supposedly on numerals from Van inscriptions, but dealt as well with Assyrian and Babylonian inscriptions, updating the talk he gave to the Royal Irish Academy over a year ago. Hincks added footnote amendments right up to the last minute, because he continued to receive new material, including an article in which Botta had published one of Rawlinson's Bisitun Babylonian inscriptions. From this, Hincks realized that he had made an error in working out the value of one Babylonian sign, but added that although tiny corrections like this might be needed, 'the values of the great majority of the characters are, however, in my judgment, *already settled beyond the reach of criticism*'.[18]

In August 1848 Henry Ross wrote to Layard from Malta to announce that he had left Mosul for good, travelling first to Constantinople. 'Sir Stratford Canning ... was evidently much preoccupied, and moreover had forgotten me so entirely that he thought I was dead! He said: "I was sorry to hear that the young gentleman who went to Mosul some years ago and dined with me here had died there." I was puzzled as you may suppose, and said I was not aware that any young Englishman had died anywhere near Mosul, but H.E. insisted that he had talked to him and liked him, and knew he had died. It then flashed across me that it was myself, and I told him that I had been near dying but had stopped short of actual death.'[19] Ross was also amused to read an incorrect account of the excavations: 'If you have not seen the *Bombay Monthly Times* for May get it, and you will find that at the Bombay branch of the Royal Asiatic Society they have made the wonderful discovery that the remains found by *Major Rawlinson* at Nimrood, are of the time of Darius Hystaspes! and that the figures on the black marble obelisk were probably copied from the Egyptian!! So much for learned societies.'[20]

Rawlinson himself was finding the summer weather a trial, as he wearily wrote to Layard: 'The dog days at Baghdad after 21 years residence in a Tropical climate try one sorely – no contrivance in the world will keep one decently cool, and it is really as much as I can do to sit up and write at all.'[21] Although he applied for leave again in August, the next month Muhammed Shah of Persia died, leading to an upsurge in tension between the tribes on the border of Persia, as well as intrigues to gain the throne. As Political Agent, Rawlinson immediately became immersed in the crisis, and abandoned all prospect of going home.

In a letter to Layard in early November, Rawlinson mentioned that Botta had sent him a copy of his published inscriptions from Khorsabad, though they were 'on such fine paper I am almost afraid to touch them',[22] while the French Consul at Mosul had recently offered to sell Rawlinson a pair of colossal bulls that Botta had excavated there. Hector, meanwhile, was at Bushire loading his ship with wheat, Jones was at Basra with the steamer, and Ross was 'in statu quo'.[23] News of their way of life had reached Constantinople, because Rawlinson related: 'Sir Stratford read me a bit of a lecture lately on the immorality of our society at Baghdad, and I rather suspect that my defense must have made the matter worse – this comes of Jones and Hector keeping *pieces* [women] – for my own part I must marry or be gelt.'[24] Rawlinson was now too prominent a public figure to be able to live with a local woman as he had done in Kermanshah, and marriage was the only politically acceptable solution to his sexual needs, short of more drastic measures.

By November, Layard's manuscript for his two-volume *Nineveh and Its Remains* was with his publisher and his volume on inscriptions from Nimrud was with the British Museum. Layard had already left England for Constantinople to work yet again as an unpaid attaché at the embassy, after turning down a post with the Turco-Persian Frontier Commission that had been established to settle the border dispute between Persia and the Turkish Ottoman Empire. Just before leaving, several crates of finds from Nimrud arrived at the British Museum, but the contents were in complete disarray, with many smaller objects missing, the crates having been opened and looted at Bombay and later almost lost at sea in a storm.

On 20 December 1848 Rawlinson sent Layard a hasty message: 'A bad cold renders me unfit for despatch writing or anything like work, but perhaps I may be able to manage a short note to welcome you again to the East.'[25] He added that he had purchased from the French Consul the two bulls found at Khorsabad, and Hormuzd Rassam was cutting them into pieces to load them on a raft. Shortly afterwards, when Layard received news that he himself had been criticized for removing parts of the sculptured reliefs and sawing them in half to lessen the load, Rawlinson was sympathetic: 'I certainly do think you have been treated shamefully – it makes one almost blush for ones country – how different would it have been if you [had] been either a Frenchman or an American!'[26]

Yet again Rawlinson applied for leave, this time from April 1849, provided that his Baghdad post remained open – otherwise he intended going to India for three or four months to work on cuneiform in seclusion: 'Unless I can get to England I despair of doing anything . . . people seem to think that a public officer at Baghdad enjoys all the same facilities for study and knowledge as a German professor or Parisian Savant.'[27] A few months previously, he had recorded how he 'inched pretty steadily at Cuneiforms and found the later Assyrian language to be nearer to the Babylonian than I had first suspected',[28] but by mid-January 1849 he was thoroughly despondent after studying Botta's inscriptions, which threw into doubt everything he had worked out. He revealed his despair to Norris: 'I am really quite ashamed to write to you month after month, merely to excuse myself . . . the real fact is however that I am perfectly cowed with the extraordinary difficulties of the Babylonian and Assyrian Inscriptions. I have been going through all Botta's voluminous papers and many of the results which I thought best established have been shivered to atoms. I . . . have no heart to bear up against such repeated disappointments. I now consider Egyptology a mere joke compared with the Cuneiform puzzle, and I have been tempted a hundred times to throw the whole of my papers into the fire.'[29] To Layard, two days later, he admitted that 'Patience and perseverance I suppose will in the end lead to something, but really I am almost disheartened.'[30] He added that John Ross had gone with the steamer to Basra for a change of air: 'He is in a very ticklish state – and will not give up the brandy bottle, [despite] all that we can say to him.'[31] A month later he reported to Layard that Hector had left for Tehran to try to sell his muskets, Jones and the steamer were still at Basra, 'and we are here as at a Methodist meeting house. Such little scandal as there is, I must leave for Ross to tell you.'[32]

Layard's prospects had improved because he had just become a paid member of staff at the Constantinople Embassy, following several deaths during another cholera outbreak. His anger over the previous criticism was wiped away by his delight at the huge success of his book as soon as it was published early in the new year. In the end he had followed Rawlinson's and not Hincks's translations and ideas on dating, although Hincks would have been a safer bet at that stage, as some of Rawlinson's identifications were seriously wrong, such as Ninus being the builder of the palace at Nimrud, whereas Hincks thought the king's name began with 'Assur', a correct reading as the king was Ashurbanipal. Even the book's title reflected Rawlinson's original erroneous identification of Nimrud with Nineveh – most of Layard's book actually concerned Nimrud.

Hincks took exception to what he felt were his own discoveries being attributed to Rawlinson, and a lengthy eighteen-page review of the book was published anonymously in the April issue of the *Dublin University Magazine*. Renouard wrote to Hincks that the review 'was pointed out to me as yours; but I immediately saw that it could not be yours, as it expressed opinions which, I feel certain, you do not entertain; and you had already told me that you had not seen Layard's book'.[33] The review was certainly written by an Irish scholar of wide learning, who was a supporter of Hincks, if not Hincks himself. It criticized the lack of Layard's learning, although 'Our London contemporaries, however, seem very well satisfied with it; but small learning goes a great way with most of them . . . There is also a vast deal of what is popularly called book-making in Mr Layard's volumes. Gossip of the most trivial character is mixed up with the account of his discoveries . . . But we do not blame Mr Layard for not producing a book of ripe scholarship. He is a discoverer whose business ought to be to tell what he has found, leaving the inferences to be drawn by those who have had the leisure for books while he was in the trenches.'[34] This view was destined to irritate Layard and Rawlinson, both of whom had been self-educated and combined scholarship with practical fieldwork and discovery, risking their lives and health in the process.

On 11 April 1849 Rawlinson reviewed his ambitions for the last time in a journal entry on his birthday: 'Behold me at my desk again on this my 39th birthday – I should be grateful that I have been spared so long in this world, but really that is a reflexion that very early intrudes itself on my mind.'[35] His prime aim was to be posted to Persia: 'I am still at Baghdad and still hoping to get transferred to Persia, but not with that intensity which I felt 2 years back. Years, a tropical climate and hard study have done their work on me, and I am either incapable, or at any rate I have no wish for any extraordinary mental exercise . . . Lately however wrote a political article on Persia for publication in India, which may attract attention and thus indirectly further my views.'[36] As for cuneiform, he declared: 'this informal puzzle has aged me before my time and yet I am still at it . . . The world still expects great things of me, and the world I take it will be disappointed. If I were to go home . . . I might yet go down to posterity as one of the great names of the age – but as long as I remain here at Baghdad I shall do nothing'[37] – Rawlinson had expected his request for leave of absence from April to have been granted, but had heard nothing.

Now that Henry Ross had left Mosul, new discoveries at Nineveh and Nimrud were very few, with Christian Rassam watching over small-scale excavations to maintain a presence for the British Museum. In late March 1849, on his way to the Persian Gulf to begin work for the Turco-Persian Frontier Commission, Colonel Fenwick Williams stopped at Nineveh to undertake his own excavations and a detailed survey. In early May, Williams, joined by the rest of his party, including the geologist William Kennett Loftus, travelled by raft to Baghdad. Loftus described that 'the whole population of Bághdád was in a state of the utmost alarm and apprehension . . . In consequence of the rapid melting of the snows on the Kúrdish mountains . . . the spring-rise of the Tigris had attained the unprecedented rise of 22½ feet. This was about five feet above its ordinary level during the highest season . . . Nedjib Pasha had, a few days previously to our arrival, summoned the population *en masse* to provide against the general danger by raising a strong high mound completely round the walls. Mats of reeds were placed outside to bind the earth compactly together.'[38] On the riverside, the houses, including the British Residency, acted as a barrier. 'If the dam or any of the foundations had failed,' Loftus noted, 'Bághdád must have been bodily washed away. Fortunately . . . the inundation gradually subsided. The country on all sides for miles was under water . . . it was a full month before the inhabitants could ride beyond the walls.'[39]

Worse was to come: 'As the summer advanced, the malaria arising from the evaporation of the stagnant water, produced such an amount of fever that 12,000 died from a population of about 70,000. The mortality at one time in the city reached 120 per day . . . The streets presented a shocking spectacle of misery and suffering.'[40] In these trying circumstances, the commissioners could not proceed with their work, but Rawlinson made them all very welcome, noting that they were 'snugly domesticated in the Residency',[41] while Loftus recorded that 'much of our leisure was passed in the agreeable society of the English residents at Bághdád;

and our sojourn there must ever be a subject of pleasing reminiscence to the members of the commission. Nothing could exceed the attention and hospitality lavished upon us by the consul-general, Colonel Rawlinson, Captain Felix Jones, and that small party of Englishmen whose lot it was to make the city of the khálífs their temporary home.'[42]

In Ireland, Hincks had become despondent about his research, as well as lack of money, declaring to Renouard in late March 1849 that he needed to give up his studies and look for something more remunerative. In reply, Renouard urged him 'not to allow considerations formed in a desponding moment, to induce you to abandon what you have so ably begun and what you, perhaps, are the only man in Europe likely to accomplish'.[43] In May, Hincks wrote an embittered letter to the *Literary Gazette* about Layard's book, implying he had only recently seen it. The letter was not published until August, and his complaint began: 'It is only within the last few days that I was aware of the *injustice* with which I have been treated in this work.'[44] He asserted, but did not explain why, that Layard was not to blame. In fact, Hincks thought he had been snubbed because he was from Ireland, whereas Rawlinson's Irish origins had been forgotten. Rawlinson's family roots were in Lancashire and Gloucestershire, but a few months earlier Renouard had misled Hincks by writing: 'You, of course, are aware that he is a native of Erin [Ireland].'[45] This caused Hincks to pour out his resentment in this letter to the *Literary Gazette*: 'It was not likely that an author [Layard] who sought popularity at the present time in England, should, without necessity, have introduced the name of a native of unhappy Ireland; – one who had not, like Major Rawlinson, the good fortune to be so long transplanted from it, that his connexion with it by birth might be forgotten.'[46]

The letter went on to complain that Layard had attributed his own discoveries to Rawlinson: 'Dr Layard speaks of it as unquestionable fact, that the Babylonian bricks contain the name of Nebuchadnezzar, King of Babylon; but he attributes the discovery that they do so to Major Rawlinson, who, however, learned it from a letter of mine in the *Literary Gazette* of 27th June 1846'[47] – a letter that Rawlinson did not see until October 1846, a month after writing to Layard about his own discovery of this name when camped at Ctesiphon to avoid Baghdad's cholera epidemic. Hincks's letter ended with him declaring that the decipherment of Assyrio-Babylonian inscriptions 'is now a *fait accompli*',[48] although he hoped the *Literary Gazette* would report further discoveries. In fact, the very next page contained an account of a meeting in London in late May 1849 of the Royal Society of Literature, where a paper written by Hincks on Assyrio-Babylonian and Van inscriptions was read out. Far from giving up decipherment, he had surged ahead of anything that Rawlinson had published.

A greatly extended paper by Hincks, 'On the Khorsabad Inscriptions', was read to the Royal Irish Academy in Dublin a month later and was published with several amendments the following year. It concentrated on Akkadian (Assyrian and Babylonian) cuneiform, but included a wider discussion of Elamite and Urartian (Lake Van) inscriptions. As with his Royal Society of Literature talk, Hincks's research was based largely on Botta's published inscriptions from Khorsabad, as he had little access to those of Nineveh, Nimrud and Bisitun. He rightly concluded that the Khorsabad inscriptions were similar to those from Nimrud, as well as to the 'third script' of the Persian trilingual inscriptions and to Babylonian inscriptions, using his term Assyrio-Babylonian to cover them all – nowadays the term Akkadian is preferred.

Although Old Persian inscriptions could be translated with reasonable fluency, progress on Babylonian and Assyrian was still at an early stage; working out the values of individual cuneiform signs was still far from complete, while the language had barely been tackled. 'The first step towards the decipherment of these inscriptions', Hincks noted, 'is to determine what are distinct characters, and what are different forms of the same character',[49] which he illustrated with the letter *a* printed with different fonts and in upper-case and lower-case, yet it remained the same letter. He explained that many signs, now termed polyphones, possessed more than one value or reading, so that some could represent one or more syllables to spell out a word (phonetic signs) or else could represent a whole word (logogram or ideogram). Some of this complexity is because Akkadian had its roots in Sumerian, a discovery towards which Hincks was edging. He intuitively guessed that 'the word from which the phonetic value is derived may be one belonging to a different language'[50] and he gave examples of how this had occurred in the Irish language through the copying of earlier Latin manuscripts. His paper also included a discussion of the dating of dynasties, for which he is regarded as the founder of the science of Assyriology.

Rawlinson in Baghdad had heard that Hincks was writing his papers on Assyrio-Babylonian, and wrote to Layard: 'I shall be interested to see Hincks paper, for he is a very shrewd guesser – in fact notwithstanding his entire ignorance of the alphabet and language he has made some extraordinarily clever links in the Van paper as to signification and probable application'[51] – a grudging admission of Hincks's progress. Layard was unhappy about the harsh review of his book in the *Dublin University Magazine*, believing Hincks to be its author, and Rawlinson was equally mystified: 'Why he should be ill-natured against you I cannot understand – you have not in any way molested him that I can see – but on the contrary have given him credit in many instances.'[52] Despite his earlier despondency, Rawlinson had made immense progress on Babylonian cuneiform and was now much more confident. He was hoping to finish his Babylonian paper during the summer, 'but I have a horror of imperfect and rash conclusions'.[53]

On 5 June Rawlinson received the wretched news that he should have been in England by now. The letter agreeing to his leave was written the previous December, but had been held up for months at Bombay waiting for a ship. 'The Indian Govt behaved most handsomely about my leave,' he told Layard, 'permitting me to go home when I pleased . . . and writing so strongly in my favor to the Court of Directors that there could be no question about my optional resumption of the appointment after a year's absence in England.'[54] Unfortunately, he could not now ask the Vice-Consul from Basra, Arnold Burrowes Kemball, to take over as his temporary replacement, because the very hot season was due. Instead, he planned to leave Baghdad in early October. There was also bad news about Ross: 'I am very sorry to tell you that poor Ross is rapidly breaking up . . . he is thoroughly paralytic and cannot I think last another month. It was perfect fatuity his risking another hot weather here – we all advised him against it, but he would not listen to reason.'[55]

Just two weeks later, Rawlinson wrote again: 'My dear Layard – We have buried poor John Ross this morning . . . Poor Ross had been gradually sinking for the last fortnight, his constitution being entirely gone and life being only kept in him by the strongest stimulants. He was as cool as a cucumber to the last moment, examining himself in a glass and saying he could not last many minutes longer, then comparing his watch with the Steamer time which had just struck 8 bells, so as to be sure of the precise minute of extinction . . . There could not have been a more edifying death bed scene . . . Although we all knew the poor fellow could not last long, his death seems to leave a sad blank among us.'[56] Layard was greatly saddened by his death as well, writing: 'In him Arab as well as European, rich as well as poor, Mohammedan as well as Christian, had lost a generous and faithful friend.' Ross died only two days after his forty-fourth birthday.[57]

By July, Rawlinson thought he was on the point of being able to translate the Assyrian inscription on the Black Obelisk, as he told Layard: 'I can give now very nearly as *literal* and as *certain* a translation of the obelisk Inscription, as I did of the Persian record at Behistun, but I still say I *know* nothing of the age of the record and am very loth to set about guessing.'[58] He was becoming convinced that many of the ancient Greek names he had been trying to find in the inscriptions were incorrect, and he began instead to consider names that occurred in the Old Testament. The Black Obelisk itself had arrived at the British Museum in November 1848. Casts were made, and one was given to the Royal Asiatic Society. At a meeting of the society the following May, it was reported that the inscription on the obelisk was imperfectly understood, but 'More positive results . . . we doubt not, are now in the possession of Major Rawlinson, which will, in all probability, be communicated to the Society in the course of the year; for we derive a cheering prospect from the recent letters of this indefatigable archaeologist, who has laboured with such marvellous success in the other languages expressed in the characters formed of the same arrow-headed elements: after some fluctuations of hope and disappointment, he states that he now trusts to be able to read the inscriptions almost as satisfactorily as he read the Persian text at Behistun.'[59]

Later that year the society published what they had of Rawlinson's long-awaited chapter on Old Persian vocabulary. He had sent the first half of the chapter from Baghdad at the end of 1846, but after delaying its publication for so long because it was incomplete, the society decided to proceed, intending to publish the rest later. This first ever dictionary of Old Persian amounted to 192 printed pages, with the words arranged alphabetically, written first in cuneiform signs, followed by a transliteration, examples of inscriptions where the words were present, their meaning (given in Latin, not English), and copious notes. The last page ended in mid-sentence ('and I observe, moreover, that although the characters composing this particular word are sufficiently dis-'),[60] with Rawlinson's remaining words or sentences no doubt supposed to be printed with the second half of his chapter. Rawlinson never finished it, probably because he became too involved with Akkadian cuneiform. Years later Wallis Budge, an Egyptologist and Orientalist working in the British Museum, reported that from the many conversations he had had with Rawlinson, it was clear that he ceased publishing Old Persian because he became weary of disputes over priority of discovery.

In Constantinople, Layard heard that he had been given further funding to undertake excavations for the British Museum, but was shocked to learn of the inadequate sum that was meant to pay for the services of a doctor, Humphry Sandwith, an artist, Frederick Charles Cooper, and Hormuzd Rassam, who was not pleased to be recalled from Oxford. Layard left Constantinople for Mesopotamia at the end of August, travelling first to Lake Van to see the rock-cut inscriptions whose decipherment Hincks had pioneered. Arriving at Mosul after an absence of two years, Layard first visited Nineveh and found sculptures visible in deep underground tunnels: 'After the departure of Mr [Henry] Ross, the accumulation of earth above the ruins had become so considerable, frequently exceeding thirty feet, that the workmen, to avoid the labor of clearing it away, began to tunnel along the walls, sinking shafts at intervals to admit light and air . . . The subterraneous passages were narrow, and were propped up when necessary either by leaving columns of earth, as in mines, or by wooden beams. These long galleries, dimly lighted, lined with the remains of ancient art, broken urns projecting from the crumbling sides . . . were singularly picturesque.'[61]

Layard recorded: 'The accumulation of soil above the ruins was so great that I determined to continue the tunnelling, removing only as much earth as was necessary to show the sculptured walls.'[62] Soon afterwards he was off on a short excursion, having been invited to the annual festival of the Yezidis, or devil-worshippers, and took the opportunity to see the rock-cut Assyrian sculptures at Bavian with Christian Rassam and the artist Cooper. By 12 October 1849 he was back at Nineveh, where about one hundred workmen were now employed. Six days later Hormuzd and Layard rode out to inspect Nimrud, and Layard described the scene: 'The mound had undergone no change. There it rose from the plain, the same sun-burnt yellow heap that it had stood for twenty centuries. The earth and rubbish, which had been heaped over the excavated chambers and sculptured slabs, had settled, and had left uncovered . . . the upper part of several bas-reliefs. A few colossal heads of winged figures rose calmly above the level of the soil.'[63]

The next day Layard gathered together workmen and resumed excavations at Nimrud, including a tunnel dug into a high conical feature in one corner of the mound – a ziggurat, like the Tower of Babel. On the 20th, Layard wrote: 'As I ascended the mound next morning I perceived a group of travellers on its summit, their horses picketted in the stubble. Ere I could learn what strangers had thus wandered to this remote region, my hand was seized by the faithful Bairakdar. Beneath, in an excavated chamber, wrapped in his travelling cloak, was Rawlinson deep in sleep, wearied by a long and harassing night's ride. For the first time we met in the Assyrian ruins, and besides the greetings of old friendship there was much to be seen together, and much to be talked over. The fatigues of the journey had, however, brought on fever, and we were soon compelled, after visiting the principal excavations, to take refuge from the heat of the sun in the mud huts of the village. The attack increasing in the evening, it was deemed prudent to ride into Mosul at once, and we mounted our horses in the middle of the night.'[64]

This chance encounter in the ruins of Nimrud and the dramatic midnight ride to Mosul that was recorded by Layard in a book he published four years later does not tally precisely with his own and Rawlinson's journal accounts. Rawlinson had set out from Baghdad for England five days earlier, leaving Kemball in charge. Accompanied by a single Greek servant, George, and his leopard Fahed, he travelled first by the Company's steamer up the Tigris as far as the village of Moadhem, just a few miles to the north. At Arbil, on the 19th, he headed westwards to the River Zab, a tributary of the Tigris, as was recorded in his diary: 'Reached the Zab just as it was getting dark, was ferried across and found a party of horsemen from Mosul waiting my arrival – slept outside the village and in the morning Oct 20 found myself ailing, the extreme difference of temperature by day and by night (varying in a few hours from about 100 to 40) having brought on a bilious attack. Hoping the exercise would cure me started for Nimrud, sending the loads straight on to Mosul and neglected to take my medicine case with me – reached Nimrud at 8 oclock and was soon after joined by Layard. Looked over the ruins partly then and partly in the afternoon, but did not enjoy it much as I was suffering all day and Layard had no medicine to relieve me.'[65] Layard's own diary entry for the 20th merely noted: 'Major Rawlinson arrived in the morning. We rode over the ruins together and examined such inscriptions as are still exposed to view – much interesting talk on Assyrian matters. He had an attack of fever and had suffered much from his ride.'[66]

Even though he was ill, Rawlinson did record that he acquired new information about inscriptions concerning the genealogy of the rulers at Nimrud and observed: 'There must still be much to be discovered, as the mound has certainly not been half tried – and not a tenth part actually excavated.'[67] That evening, his journal entry recorded that he 'slept at the village in the plain below the mound and had a sharp attack of fever during the night – so that I had considerable difficulty riding into Mosul in the morning. Oct 21 – in the Doctor's hands all day and hope to get over the attack without any further consequences, as the constipation has yielded immediately to medicine, though I doubt as yet if the bite has been removed or even touched. Mr & Mrs Rassam very kind and attentive and Layard sat with me all day, discoursing, de rebus omnibus . . . Oct 22 Kept quiet all day and lounged and simmered by which means I avoided the fever in the evening.'[68]

Later the next day Rawlinson travelled with Layard across the river from Mosul for his first ever visit to Nineveh, but was unable to pay much attention to what he was shown, being too upset by a fatal incident earlier in the day: 'Visited Kojunijuk [one of Nineveh's mounds] in the evening . . . Looked carefully over all the sculptures but could scarcely enjoy them as Mrs Rassam's horse, which she insisted on my riding out, killed her pet Kavass [guard] at the door of her house, kicking the poor devil's testicles into a jelly. It was certainly no fault of mine, but the poor wretch's look of extreme agony as he rolled on the ground has haunted me ever since.'[69] This dreadful accident was not mentioned by Layard, who simply wrote in his journal: 'Rode with Rawlinson to the mound – and go over the ruins with him. He then leaves for Constantinople.'[70] The brevity of the entry probably reflected the extreme disappointment of Layard at Rawlinson's visit, which was marred by his sickness and the death of the servant. In his book Layard wrote: 'During two days Col. Rawlinson was too ill to visit the excavations at Kouyunjik. On the third we rode together to the mound. After a hasty survey of the ruins we parted, and he continued his journey to Constantinople and to England, to reap the laurels of a well-earned fame.'[71]

In London news quickly spread that Rawlinson was due back, and Renouard wrote to Hincks in late October to say: 'If you have not yet received the remainder of Rawlinson's papers, I will take care they shall be sent to you. Having missed Mr Norris at the R.A.S., when last there, I only know that R. is daily expected home and the papers talk of his discoveries at Nineveh, so he has perhaps stopped there by the way ... He was perhaps abroad when your letter reached him.'[72] Three weeks later Renouard frankly advised Hincks that he remained little known because he had largely published in obscure journals: 'I hope you will be able to get some more communications printed in the *Journal* of the R. Asiat. Soc. as your name and writings are not sufficiently known in this country, and still less on the Continent.'[73]

Although Hincks wanted a cast of the Black Obelisk, Renouard had to inform him that it was not possible: 'I suppose Mr Birch [of the British Museum] has told you that there were not many casts of the Obelisk made, and that they thought the size, weight, and carriage of so large a cast would be cogent objection to their sending one to Killyleagh. You have, however, now got a copy of part of the inscription on the Obelisk, so that you can form some idea of its age, and the information it gives.'[74] He added reassuringly: 'I do not think there is any disposition on the part of the Museum officials to withhold their treasures; but they are so much interrupted by crowds of visitors, to some of whom an assiduous attention must be paid, that it is wonderful they can find time for a more essential part of their duties.'[75] The enthusiasm of the public for ancient Mesopotamia, sparked by the British Museum exhibits and Layard's book, was now in full flood. On 22 November Renouard told Hincks that he had tried to obtain a copy of the obelisk at the British Museum, but it was too difficult: 'The crowd yesterday made it inconvenient to climb up to the top of the obelisk so I only collated the lower lines, but the cast at the Asiatic Society proved to be very accurate, and I went through the whole with it ... I sincerely hope my notes will not be obliterated in their progress through the P.O.'[76]

By early November Rawlinson had reached Constantinople and met Canning for the first time. He stayed for a few days at the Embassy, his discussions with Canning naturally including the discoveries in Mesopotamia, and he was surprised to find Canning jealous of Layard's success. From Constantinople, Rawlinson's journey took him 'to Trieste by the Austrian Lloyds Steamer – and on by Vienna and Berlin and Ostend home'.[77] A sketch in one of his journals shows a full-bearded man on horseback, about to spear a wild boar. This may have been a self-portrait, as Rawlinson next recorded: 'At Ostend [I] denuded myself of my beard and appeared in London (Dec 18, 1849) for the first time since 1827.'[78]

Sixteen: Celebrity

Rawlinson had not seen England or any of his family for over twenty-two years – a whole generation – during which time tremendous changes had occurred. He had sailed for India in the reign of King George IV, and returned in the Victorian age. In London he found that railway lines and stations had been built, the suburbs were spreading, new bridges crossed the Thames, major new cemeteries had been created at Highgate, Kensal Green and Norwood and new hospitals had been established. While he was away Nelson's Column in Trafalgar Square was finally finished, the Houses of Parliament had burned down, University College in Bloomsbury opened its doors (the first university not to be affiliated to the Church of England), followed quickly by its rival King's College, and in the world of books, subscription libraries had become popular, the London Library was founded, and at Euston, W.H. Smith opened its first station bookstall.

His own family had suffered changes, not least with the death of his father four years earlier that had led to the sale of the house and estate at Chadlington. Rawlinson now had several nieces and nephews, his older sister Georgiana had married a few months before his return, and only a few days after arriving in London his younger brother Richard died. Rawlinson rented rooms at 39 St James's Street, on the corner of Piccadilly, and joined the nearby Athenaeum Club in Waterloo Place (with its statue of Athena, Greek goddess of science and technology, over the entrance) that had been set up in 1824 to cater for scientists, writers and artists. Athenaeum was also the name used by the weekly scientific and literary magazine, established in 1828, as well as by several other literary establishments across Britain.

From this club on 23 December 1849, Rawlinson wrote a rapid note to Layard, who was still dividing his time between Nineveh and Nimrud. He reported that Norris from the Royal Asiatic Society had shown him round the British Museum, which he found less than impressive, especially the way the Assyrian monuments were displayed. Having barely set foot in England, he had already been invited to give a talk to the society on 19 January about Assyrian history in general and the Black Obelisk in particular.

Unlike Layard's previous low-key return to England, Rawlinson's arrival was one that caused ripples through London society, and straightaway he proved to be as popular at social gatherings in England and Scotland as he was formerly with his regiment in India: 'Invitations poured in upon him on all sides from friends,' his brother George wrote, 'and still more from strangers; all the leaders of fashion coveting the glory of exhibiting in their drawing-rooms the "lion" of the season. Her Majesty invited him to dinner in Buckingham Palace, to meet a select party, and kept him nearly the whole evening in conversation. The Prince Consort expressed the greatest interest in his researches, and volunteered to take the chair at the first lecture which he gave in the rooms of the Royal Asiatic Society. Publishers made overtures to him for books, and learned societies for papers to be read at their meetings.'[1]

Rawlinson travelled to see his mother who had moved to Westbury-on-Trym, not far from his widowed aunt in Bristol. George Rawlinson recorded: 'His first visits . . . were paid to members of his family. His mother was still living, and he hastened to gratify her natural longing to embrace a son from whom she had been separated for nearly a quarter of a century . . . I was staying in the house at the time, and witnessed the meeting, which was most touching. We were together for about a week; and, before my duties at Oxford called me away, at the earnest request of our mother, who was herself a good chess-player, we had an encounter in the noble game, which I think we, neither of us, ever forgot ... the result was, that after a contest which had lasted above three hours, the game was pronounced drawn. The prolonged struggle had exhausted both of us, and we neither of us seemed to desire, and we certainly never engaged in, another encounter.'[2] Chess was also a favourite occupation of Hincks, and at about the same time as the game watched over by Rawlinson's mother, Hincks's journal entry for 3 January 1850 recorded him playing chess by correspondence with another clergyman: 'We began two games 17th July last; he surrendered one of them on my 33rd move on Dec. 22nd. His 35th move in the other game arrived to-day, to which I replied.'[3]

While staying with his mother, Rawlinson went to Bristol to donate his leopard Fahed to the Clifton Zoological Gardens, as he could not keep him in London. Years later, he recounted to his two young children that, after another absence abroad, he did not visit his pet for four years: 'I found a gathering of people outside his den, so that he could not see me, but I had made the noise by which I had always been accustomed to call him, and I saw he remembered it; for he pricked up his ears and looked about as if seeking to know whence the sound came. I then went into his cage – he knew me at once – jumped upon my shoulders and licked me all over. I always went to see him when in England. He lived for 10 or 12 years, but the last time I was at Clifton in 1862 there were only 2 fine young Leopards, his children, to represent him.'[4]

Rawlinson gave his first public lecture to a London audience on Saturday 19 January at two in the afternoon at the Royal Asiatic Society's rooms in New Burlington Street. Although he had already submitted an extensive paper to the society on the Babylonian inscription at Bisitun that he had not long completed at Baghdad, this first talk was a discussion of Assyrian and Babylonian history as proved by cuneiform inscriptions, along with the first translation of the Black Obelisk. It proved an enormous success. The *Literary Gazette* published an extensive report, noting that in addition to the members of the society, 'the meeting was attended by a large number of distinguished visitors'.[5]

Four weeks later Rawlinson gave the second part of his paper, and having missed the first lecture, the Prince Consort took the chair at what was a packed meeting, as the *Literary Gazette* reported: 'His Royal Highness Prince Albert, Vice-Patron of the Society, presided; and a number of distinguished visitors, including the Chevalier Bunsen; Mr Hallam, the Dean of St Paul's; Sir R. Murchison; Mr Hamilton; Colonel Mure, &c.; surrounded the table. After the ordinary business had been dispatched, Major Rawlinson commenced the reading of his paper.'[6] This talk concentrated on the decipherment of Assyrian and Babylonian cuneiform, with a final look at historical questions. 'Paper casts of many Babylonian inscriptions, which had been brought home by Major Rawlinson, were suspended around the walls of the room; and among them was a cast of the Babylonian translation of the great Behistun inscription'[7] – a tangible illustration of the actual monument.

Everyone was highly impressed by the extent of Rawlinson's knowledge and his confident handling of the information, even though, he told his audience, 'I will frankly confess, indeed, that after having mastered every Babylonian letter, and every Babylonian word, to which any clue existed in the trilingual tablets, either by direct evidence or by induction, I have been tempted, on more occasions than one, in striving to apply the key thus obtained to the interpretation of the Assyrian Inscriptions, to abandon the study altogether in utter despair of arriving at any satisfactory result. It would be affectation to pretend that, because I can ascertain the general purport of an inscription, or, because I can read and approximately render a plain historical record like that upon the Nineveh Obelisk, I am really a complete master of the ancient Assyrian language. It would be disingenuous to slur over the broad fact, that the science of Assyrian decipherment is yet in its infancy.'[8]

Where Hincks tended to be optimistic, Rawlinson erred on the side of caution, and gave further warnings, drawing a reasonable comparison with the decipherment of Egyptian hieroglyphs: 'Let it be remembered, that although fifty years have elapsed since the Rosetta Stone was first discovered, and its value was recognized as a partial key to the hieroglyphs, during which period many of the most powerful intellects of modern Europe have devoted themselves to the study of Egyptian; nevertheless, that study, as a distinct branch of philology, has hardly yet passed through its first preliminary stage of cultivation. How, then, can it be expected, that in studying Assyrian, with an alphabet scarcely less difficult, and with a language far more difficult than Egyptian ... two or three individuals are to accomplish in a couple of years, more than all Europe has been able to effect in half a century?'[9]

Rawlinson explained how cuneiform decipherment was being tackled: 'As the Greek translation, then, on the Rosetta Stone first led the way to the decipherment of the hieroglyphic writing of Egypt so have the Persian texts of the trilingual Cuneiform tablets served as a stepping-stone to the intelligence of the Assyrian and Babylonian Inscriptions. The tablets of Behistun, of Nakhsh-i-Rustam, and Persepolis, have in the first place furnished a list of more than eighty proper names, of which the true pronunciation is fixed by their Persian orthography, and of which we have also the Babylonian equivalents. A careful comparison of these duplicate forms of writing the same name, and a due appreciation of the phonetic distinctions peculiar to the two languages, have then supplied the means of determining with more or less certainty, the value of about one hundred Babylonian characters, and a very excellent basis has been thus determined for a complete arrangement of the Alphabet.'[10]

He went on to summarize some of his decipherment methods – by comparing the same words (mainly the geographical names) from various inscriptions, he could see where different signs or spelling had been used, rather like '&' and 'and' or 'recognise' and 'recognize'. From this he could see that different cuneiform signs might express the same sound – homophones. He estimated that he had now worked out the values of 150 signs in what he and others persisted in calling an 'alphabet' and had tried to find a theory to explain why it appeared that signs sometimes represented a single letter, sometimes a syllable and sometimes an entire word. Like Hincks in his earlier talk at Dublin, Rawlinson realized that the signs might originate in another language, but had no idea of the existence of Sumerian, incorrectly suggesting Egyptian instead: 'the whole structure of the Assyrian graphic system evidently betrays an Egyptian origin'.[11]

Rawlinson was rapidly getting to grips with the script and language, and his translation of the Black Obelisk was a remarkable feat, even if it was not entirely accurate. Over 6 feet high, the four-sided stepped obelisk was erected at Nimrud around 825 BC as a freestanding monument by the Assyrian king Shalmaneser III in celebration of three decades of military victories across an area from the Persian Gulf to Asia Minor. Some two hundred lines of cuneiform writing describe his victories, and five rows of pictures round the upper four sides show tribute being brought to the Assyrian king from various states, each identified by a line of cuneiform. From the Bisitun monument Rawlinson had been able to discover in the Old Persian inscription forgotten events in history from the reign of Darius the Great. He now did the same with the inscription on the Black Obelisk (three centuries earlier in date), although he read Shalmaneser's name as Temenbar, because royal names were especially difficult to translate. He was well aware of this weakness, admitting to his audience that 'considerable difficulty still attaches to the pronunciation of the proper names'.[12] He went on to relate: 'The inscription on the Obelisk commences with an invocation to the gods of Assyria to protect the empire. I cannot follow the sense of the whole invocation, which takes up fourteen lines of writing, as well as from the obscurity of the titles appertaining to the gods, as from the lacunae in the text owing to the fracture of the corner edge.'[13]

After attempting a translation of this invocation, Rawlinson dealt with the main body of the text, which described year by year the events of Shalmaneser's reign. The second row of reliefs includes the figure of a man prostrate before the Assyrian king, but he was unable to translate its identifying caption properly: 'The second line of offerings are said to have been sent by Yahua, son of Hubiri, a prince of whom there is no mention in the annals, and of whose native country therefore I am ignorant.'[14] Rawlinson was almost right, but failed to make the crucial connection between the name Yahua and the Biblical king Jehu. Rather than 'Yahua, son of Hubiri', he should have transliterated this as 'ia-u-a mar hu-um-ri-i', which translates as 'Jehu, son of Omri'. Jehu was not in fact Omri's son, but a usurper to the throne, and the Assyrians meant 'house of Omri', which was their way of referring to ancient Israel. Jehu is mentioned in the Biblical Book of Kings, but not this particular event of him submitting to Shalmaneser. This was the first monument to be discovered that independently confirmed the existence of a person mentioned in the Old Testament. It also showed that the Old Testament and cuneiform texts could present differing versions of the same history.

At the end of the meeting, Rawlinson pointed out the immense potential of cuneiform inscriptions: 'Undoubtedly, through the partial intelligence which we have as yet acquired of their contents, a most important avenue has been opened to our knowledge of the ancient world. Nations whom we have hitherto viewed exclusively through the dim medium of myth, or of tradition, now take their definite place in history; but before we can affiliate these nations on any sure ethnological grounds – before we can trace their progress to civilization or their relapse into barbarism – before we can estimate the social phases through which they have passed – before we can fix their chronology, identify their monarchs, or even individualize each king's career, much patient labour must be encountered – much ingenuity must be exercised – much care must be bestowed on collateral, as well as intrinsic evidence, and above all, instead of the fragmentary materials which are at present alone open to our research, we must have consecutive monumental data.'[15]

After some amendments and footnotes, the two lectures were published together later that year as an eighty-three-page article in the society's journal, with an introductory explanation from

Rawlinson: 'When I drew up the following Notes upon the Inscriptions of Babylonia and Assyria, and read them at the Royal Asiatic Society's Meetings of January 19th, and February 16th, I had no intention of publishing them in their present form. I merely wished, as much interest had been excited by the exhibition of the Nineveh marbles, to satisfy public curiosity, by presenting at once, and in a popular shape, a general view of the results at which I had arrived in my labours on the Inscriptions; and I judged that this object would be more conveniently attained by oral communication than by publication in the pages of a Scientific Journal. At the same time, of course, I proposed to follow up the oral communication, by publishing with the least practicable delay, a full exposition of the machinery which I had employed both for deciphering and rendering intelligible the Inscriptions.'[16]

Rawlinson explained that he had been persuaded to publish his lectures to establish his priority of discovery, particularly because it would be a lengthy process before the Bisitun Babylonian report was published: 'Weeks, perhaps months, will be required to carry through the press the Memoir in its complete state, and with all its typographical illustrations.'[17] Meanwhile, he noted, other researchers could use the information he had given in his lectures, and so 'my claim to a priority of, or even to independent, discovery might be very seriously endangered; for many inquirers are known to be already in the field . . . Without wishing then to impute any spirit of unfairness to the parties with whom I am competing, with every disposition indeed to unite cordially with them in disentangling the very intricate questions upon which we are engaged, I now think it advisable, for the due authentication of my own researches, to place on record the various discoveries, philological, historical, and geographical.'[18]

His only true rival was Hincks, who a few months earlier in Dublin had presented his impressive paper on cuneiform to the Royal Irish Academy using the evidence of the Khorsabad inscriptions. Just a short summary had so far been published, and two days before Rawlinson gave his first talk in London, Hincks was

still writing amendments, as his journal entry showed: 'In bed
this morning I made an important rectification of my views on
the Sanscrit character of the Cuneatic syllabary; it caused me to
be late rising, and to begin re-writing my appendix.'[19] Already,
though, this scholarly clergyman was overshadowed by the highly
sociable, attractive and popular Rawlinson, a renowned racont-
eur, and a heroic explorer who could re-create, in anecdotes of
his personal experiences, as much as in dry academic papers, the
geography and ancient history of such mysterious lands.

Two days after the talk in front of Prince Albert, Rawlinson
was a guest of the Society of Antiquaries of London at their apartments in Somerset Place, where he exhibited small stone and clay
figurines he had collected from Niffer and elsewhere in the desert
south of Baghdad. After discussing in detail the worship of Babylonian and Assyrian gods, he exhibited pottery jars that he had
dug up at Babylon. Two weeks later, he gave a lecture to the
same society, adroitly describing Bisitun and the dangers and
difficulties encountered in copying the inscriptions. As with the
Royal Asiatic Society, he again displayed records of Bisitun: 'The
small paper Casts which are lying on the table are impressions of
the epigraphs that are attached to the line of captive figures sculptured on the great triumphal Tablet of Behistun; and the two large
sheets which are suspended against the side wall of the room are
from the same locality.'[20] In the next few weeks he remained much
in demand for talks to other learned institutions in London, Oxford
and Bath.

At the beginning of March, Samuel Birch of the British Museum
contacted Layard, having already forwarded him reports of
Rawlinson's lectures that had appeared in *The Athenaeum*, to
explain that full details would not be published by the Royal
Asiatic Society until later in the year, whereas Hincks's paper
would be published that month – 'so that the two are running
neck and neck'.[21] A real sense of rivalry was evident. He added:
'Rawlinson is fêtéd in all possible manners – indeed so much so
as to be a serious drawback to his studies: I have seen him several
times.'[22] For so long desperate to return to England to study in

peace and quiet, Rawlinson had never expected to be the focus of attention.

Layard also received a letter from Rawlinson with the latest news: 'I gave another lecture last Saturday at the Asiatic Soc with Prince Albert in the chair and went briefly through the entire subject. I can get you a copy ... I have had no communication with Hincks as yet and do not think there is much chance of our fighting, for we seem pretty well agreed on all points but the Chronology.'[23] Rawlinson, who was approaching his fortieth birthday, confided to Layard that he was likely to remain single: 'I don't think there is much chance of my marrying ... and besides I have seen very few girls indeed who come up to my ideal standard – hitherto I have been going out a good deal every night in fact to 2 or 3 places, but I am now going to shut myself up and work steadily'[24] – something he did not manage, because two months later he confessed to Layard that, 'I find the interruptions in London quite dreadful – what with visitors during the day, parties at night, and the calls that other Societies make on me, I have really very little time indeed to devote to mere Cuneiform study'.[25]

Before this latest round of lectures, Rawlinson had been working hard on publishing his results, and at the beginning of February his final contribution to Old Persian cuneiform was completed. When visiting Bisitun two years previously, he had been able to look at indistinct parts of that inscription 'under every possible variety of light'[26] and now published some revised readings, along with an inscription from the tomb of Darius at Naqsh-i Rustam that had been in a batch copied 'by Mr Tasker, a young man of great promise, who visited Persepolis in the year 1848, and who literally died a martyr to science, having sunk under a fever brought on by the toil and exposure he encountered in obtaining copies of these legends'[27] – only the constitutionally fit or the extremely lucky survived the perilous work of the archaeologist.

Rawlinson assured Layard: 'People talk of you more than I ever suspect, at any rate wherever I go. I hardly hear of anything else but Nineveh and Babylon ... I dined last night with your relations the Austens. Of course the whole conversation was about you.'[28] Since leaving England, Layard had become well known because of the enormous success of his book, *Nineveh and Its Remains*. Writing from Mosul in late March to his former travelling companion Mitford, Layard explained: 'I had very little idea of publishing when I returned to Europe after my Nineveh explorations, but my friends pressed the thing so much . . . that I *nolens volens* felt bound to rush into print. I can assure you that I did so tremblingly, and had very great doubts indeed as to my probable success. But the time was favourable, the subject interested all parties, and there were no books in the market owing to the state of political matters at the time – three very material elements in success . . . Of notoriety I have plenty, and the very liberal arrangement of my publishers has enabled me to realise a *very handsome* sum. Nearly 8000 copies were sold in the year – a new edition is in the press, and Murray anticipates a continual steady demand for the book, which will place it side by side with Mrs Rundell's Cookery.'[29]

He updated Mitford with news of his latest excavations: 'The British Museum, elated at the success of the first expedition and delighted at the crammed houses which the new entertainment brought them, determined upon producing something new; and, well imbued with the economical spirit of the times, determined to do the thing as cheaply as possible . . . The consequence is, that I am terribly crippled, and without my own resources could really do nothing at all. I left England in November of '48, remained a few months at my post in Constantinople . . . I have since been very busy excavating, have made some important discoveries, and have added as much as I could reasonably expect to our knowledge of the Ancient Assyrians. I am now starting on an exploratory expedition to the Desert.'[30] He added: 'In the meantime Rawlinson is in England, propounding theories, and delighting and astonishing numerous audiences with his versions of the inscriptions, and his novel views on the ancient world in general. The correctness of which time and further discoveries must test.'[31]

By now Hincks had received news of the favourable impression made by Rawlinson. In early February Renouard had written to Hincks: 'I am waiting with much impatience to see your forthcoming paper in the *Transactions* of the R.I.A. In the meantime I have seen Major Rawlinson and was pleased to find that his results and yours approximate very closely, except in names of Kings and Gods.'[32] A week later Birch also wrote to Hincks: 'To-day Major Rawlinson has read a second paper at the Asiatic Society on the inscriptions at Khorsabad, giving a very masterly précis of the results of his interpretations.'[33] The Khorsabad paper written by Hincks was published in late March in the *Transactions of the Royal Irish Academy*. Copies were sent to scholars, including Renouard, whose response was guarded: 'Your speculations have taken a wider range than I contemplated, and some of your positions I have not yet mastered. An investigation of the sounds given to their letters by the ancients is "periculosae plenum opus aleae" [a task filled with dangerous gambling]: and Porson once told me, when I was I boy, that "the attempt was fruitless, as language changes so much in the course of time, that *we* should be unintelligible to our ancestors".'[34] In spite of Renouard's caution, Hincks had made a considerable advance in the understanding of Akkadian cuneiform, and had published ahead of Rawlinson.

After harbouring suspicions of Rawlinson, Renouard could not help expressing his delighted reaction to Hincks: 'I have . . . seen Major Rawlinson, who fully appreciates your powers and whose reading will, I can scarcely doubt, approximate closely to yours, tho' he says that want of materials has often led you into error . . . R. has got impressions on paper of almost all the cuneatic inscriptions extant and has acquired, as might be expected, a surprising facility in reading off such words and phrases as he can interpret. You have probably seen a summary of his *lectures* to the Asiatic Society, which from the day of the week when that Society meets (Sat.) I could not attend, but I had the pleasure of hearing him read a large portion of the second, in which he very ably and candidly summed up the pros and cons of his chronological system. I cannot but think he goes too far back [in time] and other objections have occurred to me, but till his views are more developed it is too soon to criticise them . . . I had no opportunity of enquiring whether Major R. has looked at the Van inscriptions. There, I imagine, you stand alone.'[35]

Apart from the paper casts of inscriptions and the objects he had exhibited during his talks, Rawlinson had also brought back in his luggage other small objects such as cylinder seals that had been collected during his two decades away. He proposed selling this collection to the British Museum, a not uncommon practice with diplomats at that time. His brother George recorded: 'It had been his good fortune to acquire during the course of his Oriental travels a number of valuable antiquities – Babylonian, Sabaean, Sassanian – many of them quite unique, and all of extreme rarity. Having selected one specimen as a present to the Prince of Wales, Major Rawlinson offered the rest of his collection to the Trustees of the British Museum.'[36] The Prince of Wales was eight years old, the eldest son of Queen Victoria and Prince Albert, but he was not to keep his present for long. In April the Trustees accepted Rawlinson's price of £300, but they 'were not satisfied without the gem of the collection – the terra-cotta relic which Major Rawlinson had presented to the Prince of Wales. Accordingly, they made an application to the Prince . . . Of course, consent was given, and the terra-cotta relic was added to the National Collection.'[37] The gem of the collection was a small plaque from Birs Nimrud, near Babylon, that depicted a man leading a guard dog.

At the end of April 1850, Rawlinson complained to Layard about problems printing cuneiform: 'I hope to be able to send you by today's post a copy of my lectures – but am not sure, for the Printers are desperately slow with the Cuneiform type, and although you will see I use the characters but sparingly, they have actually taken more than a month to print off the notes, owing to their containing a few Assyrian and Babylonian examples.'[38] His major paper on the Bisitun Babylonian inscription was not yet with the printers, but he was fearful of the outcome: 'How they will ever manage with the other paper with all

Cuneiform I know not.'[39] Rawlinson may have been impatient with the printers, but the Royal Asiatic Society rapidly published his two lectures, which included the translation of the Black Obelisk, as was enthusiastically announced at their annual meeting in May: 'We are at length able to congratulate the Society upon its being the medium of communicating to the world the first fruits of Major Rawlinson's discoveries in the ancient history of Babylonia and Assyria . . . That interesting paper has now been printed. It forms part of the Journal on the table, and is likewise published, for more general circulation, as a separate pamphlet, entitled "A Commentary on the Cuneiform Inscriptions of Babylonia and Assyria; including Readings of the Inscription on the Nimrud Obelisk." The detailed events of a period when Rome had not yet risen; when Egypt was still governed by the Pharaohs, and the children of Israel were living under their early Kings, or more probably their Judges; and when the history of Greece is lost in fable – these events are placed before us with the minuteness of a chronicle; and although the monarchs by whom the deeds were done, and the towns and provinces where they were performed, are as yet in many cases unknown to us, there is every hope that further discoveries, and a more minute investigation of the stores which are being brought to light, will afford a clue by which we may see our way through the darkness which still envelopes these long-past events.'[40]

Towards the end of the meeting, a resolution was put forward that was carried unanimously: 'That the best thanks of the Royal Asiatic Society be offered to Major Rawlinson, for the warm interest he has manifested in the objects and reputation of the Society, by his important communications on the subject of Cuneiform Inscriptions, equally those with an Indo-Germanic base, as the more recent inscriptions from Nimrud and neighbourhood of a Semitic origin, the result of a course of patient and laborious investigations, characterized by ingenuity and comprehensiveness. The Society also tender their acknowledgements for his instructive personal Addresses to the Society at their late Meetings.'[41] The society was pleased to pay tribute to a loyal member, one of over four hundred members worldwide – Hincks had never applied for membership.

In his reply, Rawlinson explained what had led him to pursue the study of cuneiform: 'I certainly do feel, and ever have felt, the utmost gratitude to the Royal Asiatic Society for the assistance and encouragement it has afforded me in the prosecution of my Oriental studies. When I first took up these studies, it was rather to wile away the idle hours of an Eastern life, than as a serious occupation, or with any expectation, or even hope, that they would lead to results of general interest. It was not, indeed, until I entered into communication with the Secretary of the Royal Asiatic Society [Norris], that I recognized any higher object than desultory reading and individual amusement. Then, however, having explained the preliminary researches on which I had been engaged, I found that a large and influential body of my countrymen were deeply interested in the particular inquiry I had taken in hand; and I learnt that, by a steady and systematic course of study, I might possibly add a new chapter to the history of the world, and thus secure the approbation of all lovers of knowledge. Gentlemen, I will not affect to be insensible to such approbation. There is, I submit, a vast difference between a morbid craving for notoriety and the legitimate aspirations for fame, aspirations which I take to be at the bottom of all the great and good works that were ever done.'[42]

Not everyone was won over to Rawlinson. Hincks's recently published Khorsabad paper had been read by William Desborough Cooley, a London scholar who was especially interested in African geography. He wrote anonymously (as 'Suum cuique') to *The Athenaeum* in order to support Hincks, who he felt was not receiving due recognition for his discoveries. For Old Persian, Cooley wrote, Hincks and Rawlinson made their discoveries independently, 'unknown to each other and wide asunder, the one on the banks of the Euphrates [sic], the other on the shore of Lough Strangford'.[43] For Babylonian cuneiform, though, Cooley remarked that Hincks had been the first to discover ideograms (a cuneiform sign that represented an entire word), and this discovery had been widely adopted by Rawlinson. He added: 'It must not be supposed that these remarks are intended to detract from the well-merited reputation of Major Rawlinson; their object is merely to vindicate the merits of a comparatively recluse student who, with the great disadvantage of possessing but a small supply of texts to study, has nevertheless laboured with signal success – thanks to his extensive learning and great analytical powers – in solving some of the most difficult literary problems which have ever claimed the attention of the learned . . . Discoveries which are worth claiming ought at least to be fairly recorded. In the bye-ways of learning, injustice is easily and often done by mere suppression of the truth.'[44]

Hincks received a letter from Cooley towards the end of May: 'I hope you have received a copy of the last *Athenaeum* which I ordered to be sent to you. It contains the long promised paragraph in vindication of your rights as a discoverer . . . The letter in question will, I trust, attain the desired end, namely, of calling attention to your investigations.'[45] It was the continued difficulty of obtaining the Irish publications of Hincks that proved a setback to his recognition. Only a few days before, he had received a letter from James Whatman Bosanquet, a London banker and writer on aspects of Biblical archaeology, especially interested in the chronology of events. He was trying to find out how he could obtain Hincks's publications: 'I have just been reading with much interest Major Rawlinson's Commentary on the Cuneiform Inscriptions, which of course you have already seen. In it, I observe that he refers frequently to a publication of yours on the Inscriptions at Khorsabad. I have been unable to learn where your work is published, and I have taken the liberty, therefore, of writing to you to ask the name of your publisher.'[46]

Rawlinson continued to be greatly in demand, and the many honours awarded to him that year included an honorary degree from Oxford. Earlier in the year his portrait was painted by Henry Wyndham Phillips and was exhibited in the Royal Academy's summer exhibition, with the *Literary Gazette* stating that it was 'a capital resemblance of the celebrated Assyrian traveller and

explorer and expounder'.[47] The oil painting shows Rawlinson
seated at a desk with sheets of cuneiform drawings, a small leather-
bound notebook – possibly one that survives in the archives today
– and two original cylinder seals.

In early July, Rawlinson applied to the East India Company for
promotion, as he had remained a Major of 'local rank' since 1837,
as he explained to the Court of Directors: 'A custom has prevailed
for many years past of granting superior local rank to officers of
her Majesty's and of the Honourable Company's army, employed
in military or political duties in the Turkish and Persian Empires,
the object of such promotion being to enable the officers in question, by the increased consideration which local rank may give
them in the eyes of the natives of the country, more efficiently to
discharge their duties to their own Government. The rule which
has been adopted in the allotment of such rank has been to grant
two or more steps in advance.'[48]

He went on to explain his circumstances: 'In my own case,
the local rank of major was conferred on me by her Majesty's
Government in 1837, whilst serving as a lieutenant in Persia; but
although I have continued ever since to be employed out of India
in situations of great responsibility, and although during that
interval of thirteen years I have almost attained to a regimental
majority, I have up to the present time received no additional
local rank whatever ... I take the liberty of adding, that my
present post of Political Agent in Turkish Arabia, and her Majesty's
Consul at Baghdad, would seem to be one of all others in which
the grant of superior local rank might be expected to be attended
with advantage; for the civil administration of Baghdad has been
recently confided to an officer of high rank in the Ottoman army,
and the strictly military tone which has been introduced in consequence into all the proceedings of the Government, renders the
Political Agent dependent in a great measure upon the rank with
which he may be honoured by his own Sovereign for maintaining
among the Turkish officers the dignity and efficiency of his position. Upon these united grounds, then, I respectfully solicit of the
Honourable the Court of Directors that they will be pleased to

recommend to her Majesty's Government to grant me the local rank of lieutenant-colonel whilst serving in a double capacity, both under the Crown and under the Indian Government, in the dominions of his Majesty the Sultan.'[49]

Rawlinson duly became a Brevet Lieutenant-Colonel, and his brother George remarked: 'How military honours are dispensed and distributed is a mystery to all excepting the initiated; but perhaps an outsider may be allowed to express his surprise, that in this case an application should have been needed.'[50] In addition, Rawlinson obtained an extension to his leave, so that he did not have to return to Baghdad in the autumn as originally planned.

Over the last few months Layard had continued to work at Nimrud and Nineveh, but in March he went on the expedition into the desert that he had mentioned to Mitford, his party including Hormuzd Rassam, Dr Sandwith, the artist Cooper and various Bedouin in charge of the camels. He had moved two more colossal lions from Nimrud to the Tigris, but as the river was too low to send them to Baghdad, Christian Rassam agreed to supervise the operation when appropriate. Layard went back to Nimrud in May and learned that vicious storms and melting snow from Kurdistan the previous month had caused a devastating flood, covering the lions in silt and mud. They had been loaded on to rafts, but one lion broke in two, and on leaving Baghdad for Basra the raft with the broken lion was dragged through the river embankment by the floods and became stranded. 'Captain Jones, with his usual skill and intrepidity,' Layard recorded, 'took his steamer over the ruined embankment, and into the unexplored morass. After great exertion, under a burning sun in the midst of summer, he succeeded in placing the two parts of the sculpture on large boats, provided for the purpose, and conveying them to their destination.'[51]

Returning to Nineveh once again, Layard was forced to pitch his tents on the mound rather than make the daily journey to and from Mosul, because the Tigris was still too swollen to cross. He found that in his absence a mass of clay tablets had been discovered in two small rooms of the palace: 'To the height of a foot or more from the floor they were entirely filled with them; some entire, but the greater part broken into many fragments, probably by the falling in of the upper part of the building. They were of different sizes; the largest tablets were flat, and measured about 9 inches by 6½ inches; the smaller were slightly convex, and some were not more than an inch long, with but one or two lines of writing. The cuneiform characters on most of them were singularly sharp and well defined, but so minute in some instances as to be almost illegible without a magnifying glass . . . The adjoining chambers contained similar relics, but in far smaller numbers.'[52]

Now that both Layard and his excavations were much better known, he was receiving a steady stream of visitors, and one such party included the Honourable Frederick Walpole, third son of the Earl of Oxford and a Lieutenant in the Royal Navy. He was present when the library of clay tablets was being excavated and compared them with a popular perfumed brown-coloured soap: 'Tablets were found (they seemed, by their number, to have entered the record office of Nineveh); many of them resembled cakes of Windsor soap, except, instead of "Old Brown Windsor," they were covered with most delicately cut arrow-headed hieroglyphics.'[53]

Up to now, most cuneiform inscriptions had been found carved on rock faces, as at Bisitun, on stone buildings, as at Persepolis, or on stone slabs and monuments, as at Nineveh and Nimrud. Many inscriptions had also been encountered on smaller objects, such as clay cylinders, stone cylinder seals and the ubiquitous mud bricks. Very few clay tablets had been found, and none at all at Nimrud. Layard did not yet know it, but this astonishing discovery was a library belonging to the palace of King Sennacherib, who rebuilt Nineveh and moved the capital there from Khorsabad around 700 BC. When talking of Rawlinson's work at its annual meeting, the Royal Asiatic Society had only just declared: 'There is every hope that further discoveries . . . will afford a clue by which we may see our way through the darkness which still envelopes these long-past events.'[54] The discovery of such a library could hardly have been contemplated – the epic decipherment of cuneiform was about to begin a new chapter.

Seventeen: Rivals

Hincks was now fifty-seven years old, his income was greatly diminished and his financial difficulties were affecting his cuneiform and hieroglyphic studies. He therefore began to approach influential people to try to obtain an annual government grant or a pension. In June 1850 he contacted Henry Holland, a physician and traveller, who was well known in London society and was physician to Queen Victoria and Prince Albert. Holland replied that he did not feel confident in Hincks achieving his aims, but added: 'Should you deem it worth while to come to London, I hope to see you, to talk over any possible access to the object desired, but none of those you mention seem very feasible.'[1] His next comment was probably unwelcome: 'Have you had any communication with Major Rawlinson? He frequently comes to breakfast with me, and when next this happens I will speak to him on the subject. He is a man for whom I have high esteem.'[2]

The following month Hincks did make the journey to London and met Rawlinson for the first time on the 20th after an introduction by Norris. The journal entry of Hincks recorded: 'Called on Mr Norris, and then with a letter from him, on Major Rawlinson, with whom I had some talk.'[3] This was the first meeting between the two rivals, but it did not lead to the establishment of friendship or even a working relationship.

They next met again a fortnight later at Edinburgh in Scotland, at the conference of the British Association for the Advancement of Science, which lasted a week from Wednesday 31 July. Hincks recorded his first day as: 'Attended central meeting, and gave notice of my paper to Secretary of Section – complimented by many – saw Dr Lee, Col. Sykes, and many others.'[4] The next day he noted that he 'Attended Ethnological Section, of which I am V.P. Read the first part of my paper.'[5] Both Rawlinson and Hincks had been selected as two of the four vice-presidents of the Ethnological Section, and Hincks was to give a paper, 'On the Language and Mode of Writing of the Ancient Assyrians', the first part of which he read on Thursday 1 August. The next day was devoted to papers on Sicilian and Sardinian languages, New Zealand natives and their practices, and the Scottish Picts. Hincks noted: 'Heard a paper on Sardinian and Sicilian languages – had some talk in Committee room with Tattam and Rawlinson.'[6]

The following Monday he gave the rest of his paper, but the *Literary Gazette* was critical: 'It was impossible to follow Dr HINCKES [sic] in his learned disquisition, both in consequence of the matter and the manner of his delivery.'[7] Hincks was still trying to make sense of the complexity of Akkadian cuneiform, with its combined use of ideograms and syllables, stating that 'though the language of the Assyrians was Semitic, their mode of language was not so'.[8] Both Rawlinson and Hincks rightly perceived that the Assyrian writing system and language owed a debt to another language, but Sumerian was still unsuspected. Hincks suggested, incorrectly, that the writing system 'was adopted from some Indo-European nation who had probably conquered Assyria; and he thought it likely that this nation had intercourse with the Egyptians, and had, in part at least, derived their mode of writing from that most ancient people'[9] – Egypt had already been mooted by Rawlinson in his now published talk that he had given in front of Prince Albert.

A lengthy reply to Hincks's talk by Rawlinson was reported in full by the *Literary Gazette* and *The Athenaeum*. Rawlinson disagreed with Hincks, who had claimed that Rawlinson believed the signs were alphabetical letters, rather than syllables. Rawlinson said this was untrue, yet he obviously did think that many of the signs represented only one letter, whereas Akkadian signs actually represented single vowels, or one or more consonants with a vowel – such as *i*, *il* and *kal*. *The Athenaeum* reported that Rawlinson thought his own and Hincks's systems of interpretation 'might now be said to be nearly identical; so far, indeed, as he understood Dr Hincks's paper, there appeared to be only about half a dozen out of a hundred letters on the phonetic powers of which they were not agreed'.[10] Between them, Rawlinson and Hincks had worked out the value of about one hundred Akkadian signs, though this was some way short of the six hundred signs, many with more than one value, that are now known to have been used.

Rawlinson informed the conference that he felt the initial stages of decipherment were straightforward and gave a personal account of how he had originally worked out the Old Persian alphabet. He made no reference to other decipherers, such as Grotefend, whose publications he had not seen until he was some way into his work: 'Our first acquaintance with these Cuneatic writings was of modern date. Certain inscriptions were found in various parts of Persia, engraved in three different languages and alphabets, all of which were originally unknown. One of these three forms of writing was at length found out, and by the help of it, the others were eliminated. The first mode of writing was the more simple, and being applied to a language which very nearly resembled the Sanscrit, it was the first deciphered. The method of this decipherment might appear to people unacquainted with the subject somewhat marvellous; but, after all, the process was not so very difficult.'[11] Starting with two identical inscriptions from Mount Elwand, one of Xerxes and one of Darius, Rawlinson explained: 'The mode of the discovery of the letters was simply this . . . on comparing the one inscription with the other, the exact groups which represented these proper names could be determinately identified. The next step was to apply certain names to see if the letters answered, and the very first attempt was by a happy chance successful. That gave the decipherer a certain number of characters, which were then applied to vowels and names found in other tablets and inscriptions, and thus by degrees a complete alphabet was formed. It was accomplished with the less difficulty, because the language was of the Sanscrit family, which was very easy to read. By the help of this Persian key an attempt was then made to read the inscriptions in the other two languages.'[12]

The bulk of Rawlinson's argument was on the 'ethnological relations' of the three languages, looking at their origins and dating. He rightly refused to believe Hincks's idea of an Indo-European origin for Assyrian writing, but wrongly agreed with him that the writing system had its origins in Egypt, suggesting that 'civilisation first showed itself in Egypt after the immigration of the early tribes from Asia. He [Rawlinson] thought that the human intellect first germinated on the Nile, and that then there was, in a later age, a reflux of civilisation from the Nile back to Asia. He was quite satisfied that the system of writing in use on the Tigris and Euphrates was taken from the Nile; but he admitted that it was carried to a much higher state of perfection in Assyria than it had ever reached in Egypt.'[13]

At the end of the session a discussion ensued, and in reply to a question put to Hincks and Rawlinson on the probable origins of the alphabet, 'Major Rawlinson stated his view . . . that it was actual picture-writing, the same as Egyptian'[14] – very much a guess on his part, but Sumerian did indeed begin as picture writing, although Sumerian sites were only just beginning to be excavated. Rawlinson was able to reveal news of discoveries at such sites to the conference. 'In Lower Chaldea,' he announced, 'Mr Loftus, the geologist to the Commission appointed to fix the boundaries between Turkey and Persia, had visited cities which no European had ever reached before, and had everywhere found the most extraordinary remains . . . At Wurka, (or Ur of the Chaldees), whence Abraham came out, he had found innumerable inscriptions; they were of no great extent, but they were exceedingly interesting, giving many royal names previously unknown. Wurka (Ur or Orchoe) seemed to be a holy city, for the whole country, for miles upon miles, was nothing but a huge necropolis. In none of the excavations in Assyria had coffins ever been found, but in this city of Chaldea there were thousands upon thousands.'[15]

William Loftus and the other members of the Turco-Persian Frontier Commission had stayed on in Baghdad after Rawlinson's departure in October 1849. Early in the new year, Felix Jones transported most of them in the steamer *Nitocris* to the disputed boundary line in the south, but Loftus and a colleague rode overland from Baghdad to Basra with the servants and luggage, protected by cavalry troops, in order to examine the geology of the marshland and the principal ancient mounds. On learning of their observations, Colonel Williams, who had recently excavated at Nineveh, sent Loftus back to dig some trenches. In the flat alluvial plain and marshland in southern Mesopotamia, far from sources of stone, buildings did not possess the relief sculptures and colossal statues that were a hallmark of Layard's excavations further north. Archaeology was a new science, and while crude excavation techniques could trace walls lined with stone relief sculptures, the sophisticated techniques needed to make sense of mud-brick construction had not been developed. Loftus was only able to excavate for three weeks, as the surrounding marshland started to flood, but he focused on Warka, where his finds included a few clay tablets and 'piles on piles'[16] of coffins. Rawlinson reported to the Edinburgh conference that Warka must have been an early holy site, where pilgrims brought their dead for burial, as the Shi'ite Muslims still brought their dead from Persia to Kerbela, south of Baghdad.

In Mesopotamia, some graves and tombs have been discovered, but for much of the three thousand years when cuneiform was used, little is known about funeral practices – dead bodies may have been left out in the open for nature to deal with, or they may have been cremated and the ashes scattered. What Loftus had actually found was a temple and a huge cemetery with glazed clay coffins, dating to the Parthian period from around the second century AD, two centuries after cuneiform had ceased on this site. Neither Rawlinson nor Loftus realized that this was the first Sumerian city to be excavated, and that Warka was not Ur of the

Chaldees, but the Old Testament city of Erech. Earlier still it was known as Uruk, home of the legendary King Gilgamesh, where proto-cuneiform, the earliest form of Sumerian cuneiform, developed – probably the place where writing was invented.

Having recently heard from Layard, Rawlinson also gave his Edinburgh audience the exciting news that masses of clay tablets had been found at Nineveh: 'The palace at Nineveh . . . had evidently been destroyed by fire, but one portion of the building seemed to have escaped its influence, and Mr Layard, in excavating in this part of the palace . . . found a large room filled with what appeared to be the archives of the empire, ranged in successive tablets of terra cotta, the writings being as perfect as when the tablets were first stamped. They were piled in huge heaps from the floor to the ceiling . . . he had already filled five large cases for dispatch to England, but had only cleared out one corner of the apartment. From the progress already made in reading the inscriptions, he believed we would be able pretty well to understand the contents of these tablets – at all events, we should ascertain their general purport, and thus gain much valuable information . . . The chamber recently found might be presumed to be the house of records of the Assyrian kings, where copies of the royal edicts were duly deposited.'[17]

Hincks was very unhappy that Rawlinson had failed to acknowledge Grotefend and himself in the discussion at the conference, but rather than express his disagreement in public, he outlined his complaints to Dr Charles William Wall of Trinity College Dublin, while enclosing for him a copy of his Khorsabad paper. At the end of August Wall replied: 'I am glad to see you have also taken the recreation of a trip to Edinburgh, where you had the opportunity of meeting some of the more remarkable savants – Rawlinson in particular. I have read the paper to which you refer in the last *Athenaeum* and feel no little disgust at the egotism and unfairness he betrays in virtually ascribing to himself what really belongs to old Grotefend, the discovery of the alphabetic nature of the Persian species of Cuneiform writing: for the manner in which he describes the finding out of the alphabet employed in this writing applies not at all to Grotefend but only to himself.'[18]

Wall had never accepted that Egyptian hieroglyphs had been deciphered successfully, and now professed not to understand Hincks's Khorsabad paper: 'As for the paper you have inclosed to me, I must candidly confess to you, it appears to me no better than mere moonshine and I have very little doubt that, if as much Chinese were laid before you as you have samples of Assyrian cuneiform writing, and if you applied the same industry and ingenuity to the investigation, you could coin as plausible fragments of a language from one set of materials as from the other.'[19] Effectively dismissing Hincks's work, he added: 'Where I think your labours have been really useful is in ascertaining the use of the secondary set of consonants in the Persian cuneiform alphabet, for which I have taken care to shift the credit from the Major to you, in a work which will probably be overlooked and neglected as long as the present rage lasts for deciphering undecipherable records.'[20] Hincks at this time was ill and disillusioned, and for several months ceased cuneiform research.

While Wall was failing to placate Hincks, Rawlinson was trying to placate Layard: 'I have just run up to London for a day after visiting and grouse shooting in Scotland and have found your note of July 8 waiting for me at the Athenaeum. Many thanks for it. I shall be very curious to see your new Inscriptions . . . What I said in my lecture about "over confidence" referred to Hincks and not to yourself. I have, I believe, uniformly backed you and took occasion in my address at the United Service Institution to make just "eloge" in due form, though really you have no need of anything of the sort, and moreover in my simplicity I fancied you rather preferred being criticised to being puffed. I mention this, as I cannot help seeing from your note . . . that you are sore at something you supposed me to have said or done.'[21]

He also gave Layard his view of the meetings with Hincks: 'Dr Hincks and myself had to hold forth at the British Association at Edinburgh on Assyrian and Babylonian Antiquities – and I found that the Dr had pretty well adopted all my readings and was inclined to appropriate them. There is hardly any difference now in our systems of interpretation, though my alphabet is the more extensive.'[22] He went on: 'I am enjoying myself most amazingly, being quite overwhelmed by attention from all parties, that is from Princes and Dukes downwards – and really when one knows the value of these things, and there is thus no danger of having one's head turned, the whole thing is very enjoyable. I have got my Brevet Lt Col – and may hopefully accomplish a civil K.C.B. which is the only honor I have any ambition for – this however is doubtful.'[23]

Although he failed to be knighted on this occasion, he had been promoted and was enjoying his fame to the full, in a world so different to that of Hincks. Rawlinson's plans for the future were less clear: 'I am now going down into the country to remain with my own family and work steadily for a month; after which I shall take another months run amongst the English country houses, shooting, talking and flirting . . . I hardly think I shall return to Baghdad till October 1851 if indeed I go back at all which is by no means certain.'[24]

By now, Layard and most of his party had fallen ill in the exhausting summer heat. For the last few weeks every effort had been spent in packaging sculptures and clay tablets from Nineveh and Nimrud, and in mid-July 1850 one batch was sent by raft down the Tigris. Half-delirious with malaria, Layard along with Rassam set off for the mountains, where they joined Sandwith and Cooper, who became increasingly sick and returned to Europe. Layard and Rassam continued their journey through the Lake Van area, copying Urartian inscriptions, but after seven weeks they returned to the excavations at Nineveh. Most of the workforce from Nimrud had moved here, and in Layard's absence many more rooms in Sennacherib's palace had been discovered, with yet more doorways protected by colossal human-headed bulls. The relief sculptures lining the walls invariably depicted scenes of Assyrian warfare, with cities being captured, loot piled high, the fleeing enemy hunted down in marshland, some prisoners led into captivity, and others shown being tortured or with their heads cut off. By mid-October Layard had packed these often fragile sculptures into around one hundred cases, which were dragged to the river's edge for transport by raft to Basra.

With winter approaching and the heat abating, it was a good time to explore sites further south in Babylonia, and so leaving some workmen at Nineveh, Layard picked thirty of his most skilled Arabs to accompany him and Rassam. They left Mosul by raft, all well armed with guns to protect themselves and their cargo of sculptures, because Bedouin along the river banks were preying on travellers. They reached Baghdad without incident and, as Layard recorded, 'anchored beneath the spreading folds of the British flag, opposite a handsome building, not crumbling into ruins like its neighbours, but kept in repair with European neatness. A small iron steamer floats motionless before it. We have arrived at the dwelling of the English Consul-general and political agent of the East India Company at Baghdad.'[25]

Layard landed at the Residency's quay on 26 October, Rawlinson's lucky day, to be welcomed not by Rawlinson, but by his temporary replacement Kemball. In Layard's opinion, Baghdad had declined since his last visit over a decade ago: 'Tyranny, disease, and inundations have brought it very low. Nearly half the space inclosed within its walls is now covered by heaps of ruins, and the population is daily decreasing, without the hope of change. During my residence in Baghdad no one could go far beyond the gates without the risk of falling into the hands of wandering Arabs, who prowled unchecked over the plains, keeping the city itself in a continual state of siege.'[26] Other changes were also unsettling, and in November Layard wrote to Henry Ross to say that he missed Rawlinson and Dr Ross very much.

For over a month Layard was trapped inside Baghdad by malaria and the dangerous situation. One of the rafts with cases of sculptures was attacked as it continued its journey to Basra, resulting in his men killing twenty-five of the assailants and wounding many more. The problem became so bad that the Pasha was forced to attack the rebellious tribes, and finally in early

December Layard's party was able to leave Baghdad. They travelled southwards towards ancient Babylon and then on to the nearby town of Hillah, where they were to stay in a spacious house, belonging, as Layard noted, 'to one of the principal families of the place. It had once contained rich furniture, and handsomely decorated rooms in the Persian style, but was now fast falling into utter ruin. The cold wind whistled through the rotten wooden panels of the windows, for there was no glass, and the crumbling ceiling and floor threatened to give way together. In this frail dwelling we prepared to pass a part of our winter in Babylonia.'[27]

In contrasting surroundings, Rawlinson continued to enjoy himself in England and Scotland, including hunting at Chipping Norton, near his former home of Chadlington, when he was the guest of his older brother Abram, and he also paid further visits to his mother. Just before Christmas 1850 Rawlinson signed a contract with the publisher John Murray to work with his brother George on a new translation of the ancient Greek historian Herodotus. He and the Egyptologist Gardner Wilkinson were to supply the historical and geographical background to George's translation. This was a major undertaking, and the first of the four volumes was not published until 1858. For now, though, Rawlinson admitted to Layard that he still found it hard to settle to work: 'I am sorry to say that for my own part I have been very idle. I find society so appealing after having been for 23 years in the East, that I cannot persuade myself to stick to my closet & work.'[28] Proving his point, he added that he was just leaving to spend Christmas with Lord John Russell (the Prime Minister) at Woburn Abbey.

Having lived at St James's Street for over a year, at the beginning of 1851 Rawlinson moved his lodgings to 8 Cork Street, just a few minutes away. The following months were to prove similarly distracting. 'Continued my mingled course of dissipation and work in London'[29] was how he summed up his remaining time in England. With all his contacts, he had become involved in the Nineveh Fund that was officially launched in January to seek donations for Layard's excavations, and Rawlinson told Layard: 'I have got

Prince Albert to head the Nineveh Fund with 100£.'[30] Having been particularly encouraged by the reports of the excavations that Loftus had done at Warka, Rawlinson hoped that the funds would enable Layard to continue excavations in Babylonia, where since December he had been investigating Babylon and Nippur. Layard's own excavations, though, were proving to be far less productive than those of Loftus, and he accused Rawlinson of exaggerating the discoveries at Warka. The finds at Babylon, he thought, 'were far less numerous and important than I could have anticipated, nor did they tend to prove that there were remains beneath the heaps of earth and rubbish which would reward more extensive excavations'.[31] An attempt to move to Warka was thwarted, because the countryside was too unsettled, and eventually his party was forced to return to Baghdad for fear of being cut off by rebellious Arabs, even though Layard was very ill with 'pleurisy and fever'.[32]

At Baghdad it took Layard more than two weeks to recover his strength under the twenty-eight-year-old Dr James McAdam Hyslop, who had replaced Dr Ross, and on returning to Mosul in early March he found that the new artist, Thomas Bell, had just arrived, sent by the British Museum to replace Cooper. Layard thought him too young and inexperienced. In the wake of his illness, he became depressed by the low level of support from the British Museum and was unhappy about the concept of the Nineveh Fund, which he declined to accept. After sending off a raft of further sculptures, he left Mosul for good to return to England at the end of April 1851, leaving Bell in charge. A few days later, on an excursion to draw the rock-cut reliefs and sculptures at Bavian, Bell drowned in the dangerous river below the monument.

In London, Rawlinson continued to oversee the preparation for publication by the Royal Asiatic Society of his paper on the Babylonian version of the Bisitun inscription. Part of the paper was displayed at the society's meeting in May, but the members were advised not to expect too much: 'The Council are authorised by the learned decypherer himself, to warn the Society against entertaining an exaggerated idea of the direct value of this key

... He considers the two branches of Archaeology, represented by the Cuneiform inscriptions of Persia and Assyria, as hardly admitting of a comparison. The number of monuments of the Persian class is very limited ... whereas, in the other class, there exists a very large number of monuments, extending over a period exceeding a thousand years. These records are expressed in different dialects, with considerable variety of graphic forms, and are found not to be written with an alphabet, but with a very large admixture of phonetic syllables, and ideographic symbols; and they treat of times and dynasties of which we have no contemporary intelligence from ancient historians, and only a few incidental notices in the sacred writings.'[33] What had so far been printed for the members to see were all 112 lines of the Babylonian inscription that Rawlinson had copied. Beneath each line he gave the transliteration of the Babylonian words, and beneath that a translation in Latin, with missing parts reconstructed from the Old Persian version. When published, this formed the beginning of his paper, presented as seventeen foldouts to accommodate the great width of each line.

Also printed at this stage were the individual Babylonian inscriptions from around the relief sculptures, as well as those from Naqsh-i Rustam, followed by an eleven-page list of 246 cuneiform signs. Although much of the Babylonian report had been written in Baghdad, Rawlinson made amendments while it was being prepared for printing. At Edinburgh a few months earlier, he claimed to have worked out around one hundred signs, but in spite of constant diversions, he had made much progress since then. The list of 246 signs was divided into five columns: the first column was the number he gave to the sign; the second column was the cuneiform sign; the third column gave its phonetic value (a syllable, such as *gu* and *ku*, rather than an individual alphabetical letter) when known to him, although around one-third remained unknown or uncertain; the fourth column gave the ideographic value, such as a sign representing the word for 'fire' or 'father'; and the final column gave the phonetic value arising from the ideographic value. Although he made many errors, much was also correct – it was a good foundation for working out the values of all Akkadian signs.

In late August, Rawlinson made further significant discoveries, and he announced the details in *The Athenaeum*. It was not possible to present his findings at one of the scientific societies, which were closed for the summer, but he was anxious to stake his claim in case Hincks was studying the same material. Rawlinson had worked out the names of successive kings who had built the palaces that Layard and Botta had been excavating at Nimrud, Nineveh and Khorsabad, names such as Shalmaneser, Sargon and Sennacherib. More importantly, he recognized one inscription as containing the annals of the first seven years of the reign of Sennacherib, the king who had rebuilt Nineveh and campaigned against the fortified cities of Judah – events that were related in the Biblical Book of Kings. In July, Layard had brought back to England a copy of this inscription from a colossal bull guarding the main entrance of the palace of Sennacherib at Nineveh, and using this in combination with other inscriptions, Rawlinson had identified names that occurred in the Old Testament, such as Judah, Hezekiah, Jerusalem and Samaria.

This announcement created enormous interest, because it provided the first real link between the Assyrians and the Old Testament and the promise of constructing a true, well-dated history. In *The Athenaeum*, Rawlinson suggested that Sennacherib might have conducted two military campaigns against Judah. Two weeks later Hincks published a letter disagreeing with this idea, and it remains a disputed issue even today. Hincks also disagreed, wrongly, with Rawlinson's reading of Samaria, but generously finished his letter: 'While, however, I thus express my dissent from what Co. Rawlinson has stated ... I have no doubt at all of the correctness of what he has stated concerning the account of Sennacherib's war with Hezekiah; and I heartily congratulate him on his having made so important discovery.'[34] Decipherment of Akkadian was a gradual process, but this was its defining moment when inscriptions started to be read with fluency, and knowledge was rapidly accumulated about the values of signs, grammar and vocabulary. Both Hincks and Rawlinson continued to make errors, but they were about to pass beyond decipherment into the stage where the history of these ancient civilizations could be understood through their writing.

Hincks had been doing very little on cuneiform over the past year and was still trying to obtain a government pension for his work, although despondently believing he was 'to be quietly laid on the shelf'[35] and that it was 'useless to complain'.[36] He even approached Layard and Rawlinson for help, and Layard replied on 1 September 1851: 'I found your letter in London on my return from a visit in Wales. I lost no time in seeing Col. Rawlinson, who fortunately happened to be still in London, and in consulting with him on what we could do to further your views. At this time no one who would be of any use is in London ... Col. Rawlinson is leaving town and promised me that he would take every opportunity of bringing your case and your wishes before such persons as might have any influence and would be likely to assist. I need scarcely add that I will not fail to do the same thing, tho' I fear my interest is nothing, and my acquaintance amongst the great far more circumscribed than that of the Colonel. It would indeed give me great pleasure to learn that you are prosecuting research which you have so successfully commenced.'[37] Hincks was also being tipped for promotion within the church, but met with more disappointment.

Rawlinson could not afford to lose his position in Baghdad, and was preparing to return there after being in England for nearly two years. During this time his reputation had been greatly enhanced, and he was now known to scholars as far afield as the United States. In 1851 the American Oriental Society published in the first volume of its journal a lengthy analysis of Old Persian cuneiform, mentioning Rawlinson and other scholars, but not Hincks, whose publications were still overlooked. Rawlinson left England in October, travelling via Marseilles, Athens, Constantinople and Samsun, where he spent a few days with Victor Place who was on his way to take up the post of French Consul at Mosul, with the intention of resuming work at Khorsabad and

Nineveh. The pair came to an agreement over the division of Nineveh, because now that Layard had left, Rawlinson was taking over the responsibility of conducting excavations for the British Museum. He next rode on horseback to Mosul and spent a week examining the excavations that Christian Rassam had been continuing at Nineveh, after which he travelled by raft to Baghdad, relieving Kemball of his post at the Residency in December.

Following on from Rawlinson's identification of so many Biblical names, Hincks resumed his cuneiform studies, even though he was still unsuccessful in securing a government pension. In his journal just before Christmas, he made a note about the Black Obelisk: 'Thought of an identification . . . with Jehu, king of Israel, and satisfying myself on the point wrote a letter to the *Athenaeum* announcing it.'[38] His letter was printed on 27 December: '*Nimrud Obelisk*. – The following identification will, I dare say, interest many of your readers. The king who is represented in the second line of the sculptures on the obelisk is none other than Jehu, king of Israel. He is called *Ya. u a'* the son of *Kh'u.um.r'i.i*; that is . . . *Jehu*, the son of *Omri*.'[39] What gave Hincks the clue was that he now accepted what Rawlinson had written about the identification of Samaria: 'Samaria (called *Samarina* . . .) and the tribes of the country of *Beth Omri* (. . . 'Omri being the name of the founder of Samaria).'[40] Hincks finished his note for *The Athenaeum* by suggesting a date of about 875 BC for the obelisk – just half a century too early. The identification of Jehu was not only another link between the cuneiform texts and other historical records: the relief sculpture remains the earliest known picture of an Israelite king.

On 1 January 1852 Rawlinson's Bisitun Babylonian paper was finally published by the Royal Asiatic Society in London and was later described as 'one of the great adventures in the history of science'.[41] It included not only his translations and the list of 246 signs that had been printed and circulated several months previously, but also an analysis of the text, followed by a 'memoir' on Babylonian and Assyrian inscriptions. Rawlinson had been unable to amend the first part of his paper, but the second part incorporated his more recent ideas. The analysis was a detailed line-by-line study of the inscription, presented in 104 pages, in which he discussed aspects of the signs, vocabulary and grammar. In line five, for example, he explained the word for Egypt: 'The name of Egypt, which in the Persian is *Mudaráya*, and in the Median *Mutsariya*, is here written ⟨𒋾 𒌋𒂖 *Miṣir*, exactly equivalent to the Arabic مصر, and the original form of the Heb. dual מִצְרַיִם. In Assyrian, the usual orthography is 𒈬 𒋩 𒊑 *Muṣuri*, or 𒈬 𒊼𒊑 *Muṣri*.'[42]

At the end of the discussion for each paragraph, Rawlinson gave an English translation, which replaced his earlier Latin ones. Illegible parts of the Babylonian inscription were restored by referring to the Old Persian version, but he highlighted these areas in square brackets. For paragraph six (lines four to six), for example, his translation was: 'Says Darius the king: these [are the provinces which have come into my possession: by the grace of Ormazd] I am now king of them: Persis, Susiana, Babylonia, Assyria, Arabia, Egypt, the Archipelago, Saparda, Ionia, [Media, Armenia, Cappadocia, Parthia, Zarangia,] Aria, Chorasmia, Bactria, Sogdiana, Gandara,(?) the Cimmerians or Scythians, Sattagydia, [Arachotia, and Mecia; in all 23 provinces].'[43] A modern translation, made over a century later, is: 'King Darius states: These are the lands which obey me. Under the protection of Ahura Mazda I became their king. Persia, Elam, Babylonia, Assyria, Arabia, Egypt, (those) on the sea, Sardis, Ionia, Media, Urartu, Cappadocia, Parthia, Drangiana, Aria, Chorasmia, Bactira, Sogdiana, Paruparaesanna, Scythia, Sattagydia, Arachosia, Maka – a total of 23 lands.'[44]

Not all his translations were so accurate, but the similarity between these two versions shows the astonishing progress Rawlinson had made. Where he appeared to make mistaken identifications, his deeper analysis of the name often shows this to be far from true. For 'Gandara', he wrote that this 'must be pronounced *Paruparaesanna*, and as it answers to the name of *Gandara* in the Persian, corresponding with the Γανδάριοι of Herodotus, the natural inference is, that we have here the true orthography of a name which the Greeks rendered Παροπάνισος and applied to the mountains above *Sindhu Gandhára*'.[45] Rawlinson decided to stick to Gandara, simply because, 'I cannot pretend that the "prima facie" explanation of *Paruparaesanna* which I have hazarded, is at all satisfactory'.[46]

This analysis was intended to supersede the first part of his report, as Rawlinson made clear in a note written just before he left England: I wish it . . . to be understood, that in all cases of disagreement, a preference must be given to the text, rendering, and translation, as they appear in the Analysis.'[47] He went on to say that with the advance of knowledge, his latest explanations should be embraced and earlier ones discarded. He was especially vexed that Julius Oppert, now working in France, was about to publish an analysis of the Old Persian inscription at Bisitun using Rawlinson's earlier theories and not taking into account his published revisions: 'This is, I think, to say the least of it, uncandid; and as I should be sorry to see the present Papers subjected to a similar scrutiny, I have thought it necessary formally, at the outset, to protest against such a system of criticism.'[48] Rawlinson's revised analysis dealt only with the first thirty-seven lines of the Babylonian inscription, however, not the entire 112 lines. The pages of the analysis were numbered i to civ, whereas the memoir that followed was numbered 1 to 16. This was done, as the editor explained, to enable the rest of the analysis to be added in its correct numerical order, but it was never finished.

The sixteen-page memoir, on Babylonian and Assyrian inscriptions, was likewise published in an unfinished state, but it is uncertain whether only a few words or many pages were left unpublished by the Royal Asiatic Society, because both the text and the footnotes on the final page finish mid-sentence, just like the previous report on Old Persian vocabulary. These sixteen pages were intended to be the first of several chapters, beginning with the 'alphabet', which Rawlinson now knew full well was not an alphabet in the literal sense, but a collection of syllables. This chapter was intended to be a detailed discussion of every individual Akkadian cuneiform sign known to Rawlinson, but it only discussed the first two signs from his list of 246, and he never did publish what would have been a massive undertaking in the years to come.

Although Rawlinson was incredibly advanced in reading Akkadian, he was daunted by the task ahead, 'for the more that I have extended my investigations,' he explained in the memoir, '– the more that I have sought to verify previous conclusions, by testing their general applicability – the more reason have I found to mistrust that which before seemed plain; the more alive, indeed, have I become to the sad conviction that in the present stage of the inquiry, as regards materials, no amount of labour will suffice for the complete resolution of difficulties; no ingenuity, however boldly or happily exerted, can furnish readings of such exactitude as to lead at once to positive results. There are certain inherent difficulties in the construction of the Assyrian alphabet, which meet us on the very threshold of the inquiry, and envelope all our subsequent labours in obscurity and doubt.'[49]

A significant aspect of the memoir was his discussion of polyphones, signs that have more than one value. This discovery was originally revealed by Hincks to the Royal Irish Academy in 1849, but Rawlinson greatly extended the argument. 'It can be shown beyond all possibility of dispute', he declared, 'that a very large proportion of the Assyrian signs are Polyphones – that is, they represent more than one sound; and strange as this irregularity may at first sight appear, it does not, I think, defy explanation.'[50] He went on to explain correctly that he thought cuneiform signs may have originally been 'mere pictures, rude representatives of natural objects',[51] with a gradual transition from picture writing to a phonetic system leading to signs having more than one value as they came to represent ideas and then sounds. That the reasons were even more complex, owing to the Sumerian origins of Assyrian and Babylonian, was still not realized.

Just before Rawlinson left England, he gave Edwin Norris permission to publish the Elamite portion of the Bisitun monument. To copy the 260 lines of the inscription had cost Rawlinson much effort and nearly his life when his ladder bridge collapsed as he tried to reach the inscription. He finally realized, though, that he would never have time to publish a report. It took Norris nine months to complete the work using Rawlinson's material, but the paper was not published for a further three years. At the end of it, Norris wrote: 'I have nothing further to remark than the small fragment, a fac-simile of which is engraved on the eighth plate. It is made from a paper cast which I found among those left at my disposal by Colonel Rawlinson, and it appears to be the bottom left hand corner of a large inscription. The especial interest of this bit is, that it proves to be part of a literal copy of the great inscription, a duplicate in fact, a sort of second edition which was made for some purpose or other.'[52] This paper cast had been done by Rawlinson in 1847 from the original Elamite inscription, when he discovered that it was poorly preserved but definitely Elamite. Norris, like Rawlinson, did not realize that Darius the Great had ordered a copy of the original Elamite inscription to be carved so as to allow the relief sculptures to be extended: 'I cannot understand why two copies should have been made upon the same rock: unless perhaps the first was found to be ill done, or upon too friable a surface, or too high to be visible; in which case the obliterated inscription is the original, and the one we have is the duplicate.'[53]

Norris had effectively completed the work on the Bisitun inscription that Rawlinson had embarked upon while training Kurdish troops in 1836, when only a handful of Old Persian signs were understood. If Rawlinson had not possessed the physical and intellectual skill and the stubborn perseverance to tackle Bisitun, the decipherment of cuneiform could not have progressed with such enormous strides in under two decades, and Layard may not have concentrated so much on inscriptions at Nimrud and Nineveh. The genius of Hincks would have ensured the progress of decipherment, but the lack of lengthy trilingual inscriptions would have been a serious impediment.

It was on Easter Monday, 13 April 1903, that the next person to climb Bisitun for over half a century approached the mountain. He was Abraham Valentine Williams Jackson, the American Professor of Indo-Iranian languages at Columbia University, and he observed that Bisitun was visible for miles around. Despite all he had read and heard about it, he admitted: 'I had not the faintest conception of the Gibraltar-like impressiveness of this rugged crag until I came into its Titan presence and felt the grandeur of its sombre shadow and towering frame.'[54] He went on to say: 'From the descriptions I had read, or perhaps from the mental picture I had previously formed of the scene, I had always fancied that the inscriptions and sculptures were carved nearer the middle of the mountain, whose general contour on this side runs from northeast to southwest. Not so. They are cut high in the side of a steep gorge or craggy gully that makes a deep gash in the face of the rock and extends three hundred feet downward to the plain beneath.'[55]

Jackson found that it was impossible to copy the inscriptions using a telescope, because the projecting ledge formed an obstruction, while it was equally impossible to climb the opposite rock face to undertake photography. He had hoped to be let down from above, but this also proved impossible, so instead six Persians hauled him up with ropes: 'The ascent of the first huge fissure in the side of the couloir, the clamber with torn hands and clothes along the brink of a precipitous crag, the tugging ropes that helped up the steep incline of the second rock, the scramble past the thorn bush that barred the way farther up, and the final tug and spring that brought [me] to the edge of the ledge, together with *khailīkhūb*, "very good," and the encouraging word of the guides, "no fear now, the danger is over" – will not readily be forgotten . . . On the first day it took a while to get somewhat used to the giddy height.'[56]

After five days, 'I begged the guides to let me use the ladder,' Jackson wrote, 'in order to examine some of the less certain readings in the upper part of the inscription. This they stoutly refused to do on account of the extreme danger from the high wind blowing at the time.'[57] Even so, he was glad he had managed to examine doubtful passages of the Old Persian inscription, and 'to prove in general the wonderful accuracy of Rawlinson's transcript'.[58] In fact, the professor was in awe of Rawlinson's achievement: 'Only when one has stood on the narrow ledge by the side of the inscriptions and looked out over the magnificent plain far beneath, and listened to the dull murmur of the stream below, as it bursts from the mountain's base, does one know how to appreciate Rawlinson's work. It may interest others, as it did me, to learn that he has carved his name in the stone, a few inches below the very inscriptions which he first made known to the modern world. This he was entitled to do, and one is almost inclined to append after his simple 'H.C. Rawlinson, 1844' the words of ancient India's homage – *namo namah* [homage to the venerable teacher].'[59]

Eighteen: Magic at Borsippa

Rawlinson could spare little time from his political duties in Baghdad to oversee archaeological excavations, and so he began to recruit agents. Initially he asked for the release of Loftus from the Turco-Persian Frontier Commission, because 'a sum of £500 had been voted by Parliament, and placed at his disposal, for the purpose of making further researches at Susa'.[1] After finishing his excavations at Warka, Loftus had turned to Susa, an extensive mound across the border in Persia that was once an Elamite city and later still the summer capital of King Darius the Great. Loftus had spent a month excavating this site and discovered the palace of Darius, which was reminiscent of Persepolis. Early in January 1852 he travelled to Baghdad to receive new instructions from Rawlinson and resumed operations at Susa the month after.

At Nineveh, Rawlinson continued to use Christian Rassam to organize the workmen, and in late February Rawlinson, Felix Jones and Dr Hyslop set off on an overland journey to the excavations, because the East India Company had agreed to them compiling the first ever detailed maps of Nineveh and Nimrud. At Mosul they stayed with Mrs Rassam, but after three days of incessant rain, they could delay their work no longer and pitched their camp 'in the swamp at the foot of the Koiyunjik mound'.[2] Over the next few days, interrupted by several fierce storms, Jones and Hyslop surveyed Nineveh while Rawlinson spent many hours copying inscriptions and taking casts of the relief sculptures that had been excavated by Layard. Rawlinson was disappointed to find that the artist Charles Doswell Hodder had not yet arrived from England as a replacement for the drowned Bell, and when he did appear in early April, he also seemed too young and inexperienced.

The Nineveh mound, Jones discovered, was an irregular oval, and its 'surface, in general flat, now exposes numerous mounds of loose earth, thrown up above its south-west extreme, and is dotted also with them in other parts'.[3] These mounds of soil were from the excavation of the palace, and Jones described a typical scene: 'We ascend the pile, and find these hillocks being daily added to by the excavated soil from deep trenches, which yawn in every direction beneath and around. A closer inspection shows man is the labourer; and, busy in his vocation, we see him in the bowels of the mound, running to and fro with the pick, the shovel, and the basket, endeavouring to rescue from oblivion the long-lost labour, and even the lost history of fellow-man; for among the operations we discern an eminent palaeographer, regardless of mud below and rain above him, transcribing from the lapidary tablets which face the chambers and galleries excavated by the indefatigable Layard.'[4]

The eminent palaeographer was of course Rawlinson, and Jones commented further on how he worked: 'Colonel Rawlinson was daily thus employed in a most inclement season: book in hand, sometimes seated in a swamp, sometimes protected only by an umbrella from the torrents coursing down from above, he persevered and succeeded in obtaining copies of all the legible tablets uncovered within the mounds both of Nineveh and Nimrud. It was ludicrous and interesting, indeed, to witness the shifts he was occasionally put to obtain a glimpse of light upon a defaced and uncertain character of the inscriptions. His activity of mind and body, in the pursuit of his favourite study in every situation, is certainly deserving of the success which the public and his numerous friends most cordially wish him.'[5]

The party moved on to Nimrud for three weeks and afterwards surveyed other mounds, including Khorsabad, where the French Consul Victor Place was excavating. Back in Baghdad, Jones and

Hyslop drew up three maps, which were highly praised – one was dedicated to Rawlinson and one to Layard. In a report to the Royal Asiatic Society the following year, Jones discussed why Nineveh's fate was possibly due to a prophecy. On the map, ancient dams could be seen near the city walls, and if torrential rainwater had caused their collapse, 'the prophecy, that "Nineveh could never be taken by force till the river became the city's enemy," would be easily filled . . . The panic-stricken king, under the conviction that the oracle had been accomplished, must have at once abandoned his empire and his life.'[6] Such was Jones's high regard for Rawlinson that he continued: ' "Their memorial had perished with them," indeed, had not the literary acumen of Rawlinson been at hand to develop the wonderful discoveries of Layard. To the former [Rawlinson], in anticipation of the approval of Government, we have inscribed the map of Nineveh. Though but a small tribute, it is one of admiration for the physical and mental energy which, in the fields of cuneiform and geographical inquiry, he has perseveringly displayed, and which we have been an eye-witness to for many years past.'[7]

In England, Layard was busy writing another book, *Discoveries in the Ruins of Nineveh and Babylon*, about his final excavations in Mesopotamia, and he had contacted Hincks to propose cooperation on the inscriptions. By now Hincks was desperate to find some way of financing his continued work on Akkadian cuneiform, as his clerical income was shrinking because of a reorganization of how the clergy in Ireland were funded, and so Layard made renewed efforts for him to obtain a pension. Though beset by financial worries, Hincks completed a major paper on phonetic cuneiform signs that was read to the Royal Irish Academy in May and published at the end of the year. In it he admitted that his previous talk to the Academy three years ago had contained errors, which Rawlinson had pointed out. 'I must observe, however,' Hincks commented, 'in justice to myself, that the Colonel admits . . . that my reading of the name Babylon is correct, contrary to his previous statements.'[8] In fact, both Hincks and Rawlinson were guilty of disputing what were often accurate discoveries.

Their growing obsession with proving each other wrong did little credit to either party, but did appear to stimulate their rapid progress in understanding inscriptions.

In this paper, Hincks revealed his jealousy and bitterness towards Rawlinson and his supporters, declaring that he was about to give up cuneiform: 'Having neither leisure nor opportunity to pursue the investigation as I could wish, I should probably have left it in the hands of those to whom public patronage has assigned it, if I did not entertain the most complete conviction, that other labourers in the field have assumed false principles as true, and that they are pursuing a method which can never lead to accurate knowledge. I wish, therefore, before I finally quit the field, to point out the mode of proceeding which must sooner or later be adopted.'[9] Hincks had been stirred into anger by 'a new aspect of the controversy between Colonel RAWLINSON and myself'.[10] Five months earlier, Rawlinson had published his extensive report on the Babylonian inscription at Bisitun, including a list of 246 signs, which infuriated Hincks as he was not acknowledged as the source of some of the signs and as the person who, he believed, had persuaded Rawlinson to adopt the idea that phonetic signs represented syllables, not a mixture of syllables and alphabetical letters. Hincks wrote acerbically: 'For this substitution of truth for error, I of course cannot blame him; but I think I have a right to complain that he has omitted all mention of my priority in asserting that truth which he has so recently embraced.'[11]

The intention of Hincks's new paper was to establish what he asserted were his own discoveries and what belonged to Rawlinson and other scholars, and his discussion of 252 cuneiform signs demonstrated considerable progress over Rawlinson's list. Hincks annotated each sign H.49 if it was identified in his 1849 paper (published in 1850), H.50 if it was in the lithograph he circulated at the British Association's Edinburgh conference, or H.52 if he was presenting it now. The letter R marked those values he had adopted from Rawlinson. Towards the end of his paper, he commented: 'It may be deemed satisfactory that I should compare

the results at which I have arrived with those announced by
Colonel RAWLINSON in his Memoir. To the above 252 characters
I have given 344 phonetic values; as to 177 of which I agree
with Colonel RAWLINSON; I differ from him as to 49; but in many
instances the difference only consists in my giving to the terminat-
ing vowel the value *e* or *o*, which he ignores, and for which he
substitutes either *i* or *u*. The remaining 118 values are new, being
omitted by him altogether. Of the 177 values which we have in
common, 100 were first published by me in my former paper, and
in the lithograph which I circulated at the Meeting of the British
Association in 1850. For the remaining 77 I have acknowledged
my obligations to him.'[12]

The failure of individual cuneiform scholars to acknowledge
previous work would not have been an issue if successive papers
had been regarded as ongoing progress, and not as attempts at
usurpation. The problem with Hincks was that his Irish publications were not widely available in England, still less abroad, and
he assumed that anyone reading Rawlinson's publications might
overlook his own work. Hincks was a victim of circumstances, a
brilliant scholar who had chosen to forgo a university path in
favour of the Church. He had limited financial resources, little
social standing, an unwillingness to join learned societies, and
lacked the diplomatic flair of Rawlinson. He himself told Layard
that he was convinced of prejudice towards him because he was
Irish.

From this point much of the focus of Hincks's and Rawlinson's
work was not only to advance the understanding of the Akkadian
script and language (especially at the expense of each other),
but to find out the historical events and their precise dating in
Mesopotamia by using the inscriptions, often with unnerving and
sophisticated accuracy. This was possible because many Babylonian and Assyrian kings ensured their genealogy and the events
of their reigns were recorded, such as on the Black Obelisk or on
the colossal bulls that gave Rawlinson his first names from the
Bible. These rulers also perpetuated the memory of their achievements by burying inscriptions in the foundations of buildings.

Such foundation records were inscribed on stone slabs, on hollow clay cylinders and on six-, eight- or ten-sided clay prisms (which Hincks and Rawlinson also termed cylinders).

During the summer of 1852 Rawlinson informed the British Museum that he wanted Loftus to take over excavations in Assyria and that Hormuzd Rassam should not be sent from England. Loftus had abandoned Susa at the end of April, after uncovering the palace of Darius the Great and discovering trilingual cuneiform inscriptions on stone columns and alabaster vases. Before the mound was excavated to any depth, he ran out of money. Expecting the British Museum to agree, Rawlinson appointed Loftus to the post in Assyria, once he had completed further work with the Frontier Commission in northern Persia, not realizing that Rassam had already left England. Quite by chance, in early October, Rassam met up with Loftus as they both headed towards Mosul to take up the same appointment. They visited Nineveh together, after which Loftus went to see Rawlinson in Baghdad.

Loftus decided he would rather return to England than resume work for Rawlinson in Babylonia. Many years later, Rawlinson recorded a story for his two young sons that is a strange echo of his uncle's skinning of the hanged criminal in Bristol. Loftus, Rawlinson related, 'was very anxious to obtain the skin of an Iguana Lizard before leaving Baghdad. We tried for some weeks in vain to produce one from the desert, but succeeded at last – the Arabs bringing in a fine specimen, young and healthy and nearly 2 feet long. Dr Hyslop the resident surgeon commenced operations in the evening in my presence with a view of killing the animal preparatory to skinning him: but as I forewarned them all, ordinary means of extinguishing life completely failed. They tried acupunctation, that is piercing the vertebrae of the back with a sharp needle, but he seemed insensible to pain or rather enjoyed it by shaking his head and showing more activity than usual. They then tried various deadly poisons such as prussic acid and strychnine, but he seemed to regard them as agreeable stimulants, and at the end of the sceance was certainly more lively than at the commencement. At Dr Hyslop's suggestion it was then decided to boil him! And he was accordingly curled up in a large copper vessel used in the kitchen, which was placed on the fire and kept boiling all night.'[13]

Rawlinson described that, early the next morning, 'I took my usual walk along the bank of the Tigris and on my return found the two savants standing beside an operating table at the edge of the water with the lizard laid out on the table for dissection, and some sharp knives placed ready at hand. The animal was apparently quite dead, and his skin was quite loose, so they set to work at once to disburthen him of his outer integument. Laying him on his back Dr Hyslop made an incision from his chin downwards, and I began to peel him, turning out the paws, drawing the skin over his head, and gradually down his back, so that the unfortunate reptile was displayed upon the table very much like a raw leg of mutton. As the skin however was being drawn down the back, I thought I perceived a convulsive movement. "Bless me doctor," I said. "The creature is not dead yet!" "Too late," said the Doctor, "We must go on." And another inch or two was peeled from off his back. As the scalping knife proceeded downwards, the animal showed unmistakable signs of vitality, raising his head and turning round on his paws. "Be sharp," said I to the Doctor, "I can't stand this much longer." With one vigorous effort he drew the skin clean off from the tail and at the same time, to the great astonishment of the Doctor, Mr Loftus and myself, the big skinless lizard threw himself off the table and scuttled away into the river, where doubtless in the course of a few months he grew a new skin, which for ought I know may have been filched from him by another operator to adorn some other Museum in England or India!'[14] By mid-December 1852 Loftus was back in England, and, as Rawlinson related, 'the skin to which this story relates is I believe now preserved in the Museum of Natural History at Newcastle Upon Tyne – to which it was presented by Mr Loftus'.[15] The skin was probably from an agama, not an iguana, and no longer survives.

Once Rassam took over the excavations, he embarked on work

at Nimrud, afraid that the French Consul Victor Place might stake a claim there, and he also continued excavations at Nineveh, keeping clear of the area reserved for the French. Towards the end of the year he sent parties to investigate many other mounds over an extensive area, as did Place while continuing his own work at Khorsabad. A period of intense rivalry and recriminations ensued between the competing digging parties, although Rawlinson and Place remained on good terms. At the beginning of 1853 Rassam dug for three weeks at Qalah Shergat, the site of ancient Ashur. As he and his workmen approached the mound, it became a race with the French, and he sent the artist Hodder and his overseer ahead to claim possession: 'An hour after Mr Hodder and Mahmood Alfaraj left', related Rassam, 'we were delighted to see the longed-for signal hoisted on the highest peak . . . We had not gone half the distance before we heard the sound of the war-cry and a great hubbub coming from the mound, which convinced us that our men had come into collision with those of the French. The Arabs who were with me at once took to their heels to help their comrades in the struggle. I tried all I could to quiet them, but to no purpose, as they said they were certain that their fellow-laborers were being beaten and slaughtered.'[16] Rassam managed to prevent any serious fighting and came to an agreement with the French about division of territory at Ashur, and although he uncovered remnants of walls and colossal statues, his major discovery was a clay prism of King Tiglath-Pileser I, who ruled in Assyrian from 1115 to 1077 BC. Tiglath-Pileser was the first king to record his exploits on clay prisms, and this particular prism would in a few years' time feature in a landmark test of cuneiform decipherment.

In late May it was reported to the Royal Asiatic Society that the 'last letter just received from Colonel Rawlinson, informs us that after preparing, with great pains, a full account of his recent labours and discoveries, intended to be read at this annual meeting, he had dispatched it by the mail, which unfortunately had been plundered on its way by the Anezeh Arabs, and the whole of the Foreign Correspondence distributed among those

marauders, who are said to be now wearing the unknown Babylonian characters as amulets'.[17] Rawlinson did manage a hurried
follow-up note, reporting Rassam's discovery of the Tiglath-Pileser
prism, 'a splendid relic, containing 800 lines of beautiful writing,
at least 100 years older than the oldest monument hitherto discovered. It was, when found, broken into a hundred fragments,
and in some parts, even reduced to powder; but the whole was
now carefully joined together, and barely a dozen lines lost.'[18]

Rawlinson also reported that he had been examining the clay
tablets that were still being discovered in the library at Nineveh.
Just a few months earlier Hincks had given a hint about the
potential of these inscriptions, when he recognized what was
written on a clay tablet fragment that Layard showed him. He
explained that it 'contains parts of four columns, each of which
is divided by ruled lines into three series. That in the middle
contains the characters to be valued; that on the left contains the
values; and that on the right contains the plural form, or the
value which the character would have if the plural sign were
added.'[19] Hincks had realized that this was an original Assyrian
syllabary, a dictionary of cuneiform signs, which proved beyond
doubt that they were syllables. Lists and texts of all kinds were
inscribed on clay tablets, to maintain a permanent record of scientific and literary knowledge and, very importantly, to train scribes.

The astounding potential of the clay tablets was now revealed
to the meeting by Rawlinson: 'I now turn to the real treasure
house of discovery . . . I have found fragments of alphabets, syllabaria, and explanations of ideographic signs. In one place, a table
of notation, giving the phonetic readings of all the signs, and
shewing that the Assyrians counted by sixties, as well as by hundreds . . . The numbers are completely Semitic, and of great interest. Among the tablets there are also elaborate dissections of the
Pantheon; geographical dissertations explaining the ideographic
signs for countries and cities, designating their products, and
describing their position; the same with the principal Asiatic
rivers and mountains. Again, there are treatises on weights and
measures, divisions of time, points of the compass, &c. &c. There

is an almanack for twelve years ... I find, indeed, that all the old annals are numbered according to this cycle, each year having a particular name ... Again, we have lists of stone, metals, and trees; also astronomical and astrological formula without end. I suspect, likewise, there are veritable *grammars* and *dictionaries*.'[20]

'The whole collection is in fragments,' Rawlinson continued, 'but it gives us a most curious insight into the state of Assyrian science whilst Greece was still sunk in barbarism ... The tablets upon which I have been engaged form, it must be remembered, the lower stratum, – the debris, in fact, of the Royal library, while Layard's collection, which was first found, and formed the upper layer, is, of course, in much better preservation ... Altogether, I am delighted at the splendid field now opening out. The labour of carrying through a complete analysis will be immense; but the results will be brilliant.'[21]

When Hincks heard of the prism of Tiglath-Pileser I, he realized that it was similar to one in the British Museum where he was then working, and wrote to *The Athenaeum* in July suggesting a date for it, but adding that Rawlinson's prism did not seem 'so interesting, as much of the chronological matter appeared to be wanting on it, – or, at all events, had not been noticed by Col. Rawlinson'.[22] Through the intervention of Layard, the British Museum had agreed earlier in the year that Hincks could do some work for them. Initially, he spent around ten days in February and March studying the Black Obelisk and Sennacherib bull inscriptions, then it was agreed to employ him for a year from June, two months in London and the rest at Killyleagh, although in fact their fee barely covered his expenses.

Rawlinson had only just seen the attack on him by Hincks in the Royal Irish Academy publication and had also heard that in his newly published book, Layard chose to adopt the side of Hincks, not himself. This was a substantial, popular book of nearly seven hundred pages, in which Layard took up the cause of Hincks and invariably followed, not always wisely, his translations, saying: 'I must here remind the reader that any new discoveries in the cuneiform inscriptions referred to in the text are to be attributed to Dr Hincks.'[23] He wrote to Hincks: 'I think ... my work will excite considerable attention on account of the connexion of the inscriptions and sculptures with Biblical History. It will have a considerable sale, and between ourselves Murray has already disposed of nearly the whole 8000 copies he is printing, when the public will be ... more alive to the great value and importance of your discoveries.'[24] The name of Hincks undoubtedly became better known, but Layard merely deepened the dissension between Hincks and Rawlinson by presenting their differing translations as cause for controversy.

The unhappy outcome was that Rawlinson vehemently opposed Hincks working for the British Museum and made his position known to the Trustees. He wrote to Layard: 'I have not yet seen your book, but ... am assured that the main drift of the antiquarian part is to exalt Hincks at my expense. You are of course at liberty to take any view you please of what the Irishman calls our "controversy" – but the result of being thus run down is that it forces me to take up the cudgels – and this I shall do forthwith.'[25] In the same letter he complained: 'You talk a great deal of Hincks's difficulties but is Baghdad "a bed of roses"? My constitution is ruined by this infernal climate and after 18 years laborious study on the Cuneiform Inscriptions I should like to know what single reward or encouragement I have personally received from the British Govt?'[26] In London, Hincks felt that the Museum was deliberately obstructive towards him, becoming increasingly aggrieved when they failed to publish his research. In October he did publish a new and more accurate translation of the Black Obelisk inscription in the *Dublin University Magazine* – the only translation of a cuneiform inscription he ever published. Where Rawlinson was far more interested in the translation of texts, for the wealth of historical and geographical information they contained, Hincks was especially absorbed by the intricacies of the language and signs.

In November 1853, Rassam took a large workforce back to Qalah Shergat, but again results were poor, the most noteworthy being another clay prism of Tiglath-Pileser I. Norris at a Royal Asiatic Society meeting reported that Rawlinson had described the prism as 'in a shocking state of mutilation; and, very provokingly, the line which would contain the date read by Dr Hincks on the copy in the British Museum is all in minute fragments, which he is almost in despair of ever joining together, though resolved to make the attempt as soon as he can find leisure. We have seen success accompanying the efforts of Col. Rawlinson so frequently, that we do not despair.'[27] Norris added: 'The Colonel spoke of his further gratification at the success of his photographical apparatus, with which he was making excellent copies of the bricks and tablets found.'[28] This was almost the earliest instance of photography in Mesopotamia – it had begun to be used the year before at Khorsabad, because Place was employing a photographer, Gabriel Tranchard, who took the very first calotype images. Earlier still the artist Bell had intended using a calotype camera on Layard's excavations, but had drowned before any pictures were taken. The calotype photographic technique, invented by William Henry Fox Talbot, was the first to create negative images on paper.

No photography was being used in the excavations at Nimrud and Nineveh, and when the artist Hodder became too sick to work, he was sent to Baghdad to be cared for by Dr Hyslop. Although without an artist to record important discoveries, Rassam was extremely anxious to test the northern part of Nineveh before he returned to England, but Rawlinson had agreed that it should be reserved for Place, even though the owner of that part of the mound had never given permission to the French. 'My difficulty', Rassam explained, 'was how to do this without getting into hot water with M. Place. I feared if I did so, and failed, I might displease Colonel Rawlinson, and get into trouble with the trustees of the British Museum.'[29] His solution was to undertake covert operations by night, but the first night, 20 December 1853, was unpromising. The second night's work produced a marble wall and relief sculptures, but these petered out, much to Rassam's dismay. He had in his enthusiasm already informed the British

Museum and Rawlinson that he had discovered a new palace and was desperate to find evidence that his theory was correct. The third night fortunately proved his instinct right, as a relief sculpture in perfect condition was found. Because news of his activities had become known in Mosul, he continued the excavation throughout the next day, 'because it was an established rule that whenever one discovered a new palace, no one else could meddle with it, and thus, in my position as the agent of the British Museum, I had secured it for England'.[30]

Once Victor Place at Khorsabad heard about the discovery, he came to Nineveh to complain, but, Rassam noted, 'on my explaining matters, and telling him that Sir Henry Rawlinson had no power to give away ground which did not belong to him, and that it was evident, as the owner of the mound was indemnified by us, it was but right that the British nation should benefit by any discovery made in it, he seemed to be quite satisfied with my reasoning, and before we parted he congratulated me on my good fortune'.[31] In the south-west part of the mound, much of the palace of King Sennacherib with its library had already been excavated. Sennacherib had rebuilt Nineveh to replace the new capital that his father Sargon II had built at Khorsabad, which itself replaced an earlier capital at Nimrud. On Sennacherib's death in 681 BC, murdered by two sons, the younger son Esarhaddon took over, who in turn was succeeded by Ashurbanipal. Rassam was now free to excavate the palace built by Ashurbanipal, ruler of Assyria from 668 to 627 BC.

In a single day Rassam completely cleared a room lined with relief sculptures of a royal lion hunt. In the centre of the room he made what is regarded as the most important discovery in all the excavations of Mesopotamia – another immense library of clay tablets. 'In the center of the same saloon,' Rassam later wrote, 'I discovered the library of Assur-bani-pal, consisting of inscribed terra-cotta tablets of all shapes and sizes; the largest of these, which happened to be in better order, were mostly stamped with seals, and some inscribed with hieroglyphic and Phoenician characters.'[32] The library owed its existence to Ashurbanipal, who had ordered his scribes to search for and copy all known examples of cuneiform literature. Among the clay tablets was an early version of the Biblical flood story, which, when translated nearly twenty years later, would cause a sensation.

Rawlinson was too involved in political issues to do much archaeological work himself, as relations between Turkey and Russia and Britain and Persia were at a low ebb. Now forty-three years old, he had held his post at Baghdad since the end of the Afghan War. He was hoping to be appointed as British Envoy at Tehran on the retirement of Lieutenant-Colonel Justin Sheil, who had replaced Sir John McNeill over ten years previously. Rawlinson applied for the job and was widely considered the most suitable person.

In February 1854, Rawlinson managed to visit Nineveh, and because the artist Hodder was still sick, he copied inscriptions at Rassam's newly discovered palace, hampered by dreadful storms. Because Rassam remained sceptical that cuneiform inscriptions could be read, he tested Rawlinson with one inscription, then later tried out the same inscription on Oppert. Apart from Place's excavations, a French mission headed by the Arabic scholar Fulgence Fresnel and Julius Oppert was excavating in Babylonia. Of the inscription, Rassam recorded: 'I was curious to know what rendering other reputed Assyrian scholars would give it. It happened that at that time the learned French savant, M. Oppert, visited Mossul on his way to Europe from Baghdad, and, of course, he was very much interested in seeing what had been found; and while I was showing him over the Susiana chamber in the palace of Assur-bani-pal, I asked him to tell me what the inscription meant. To my surprise and satisfaction he gave it the same meaning as Sir Henry Rawlinson.'[33]

The British Museum could no longer cope with the influx of new Assyrian monuments, so Rawlinson selected a few relief sculptures and, disastrously as it happened, let the French take many others from the new palace at Nineveh, even though few were ever drawn. Just over a year later, these and nearly all the French finds from Khorsabad and elsewhere in Mesopotamia were lost when the rafts transporting them to Basra sank to the bottom of the Tigris.

After visiting Nimrud and Ashur, Rawlinson returned to Baghdad, and during the journey he 'ran a very narrow risk of his life. He had obtained the usual Arab escort, and was descending the Tigris on a raft, when fire was opened upon him and his escort from the bank by some Arabs, who, it appeared, had revolted from the chief under whose protection he was travelling. The head-man of the escort was shot and died of his wound. He [Rawlinson] himself happened to be writing, and holding the ink-bottle in his left hand, when a bullet struck it from between his fingers. The firing did not cease till he caused the raft to draw to shore and landed with a few men, when the assailants took to their heels, and no more was seen or heard of them.'[34]

The following month Rawlinson went to Basra to oversee the loading of over one hundred cases of antiquities from Rassam's excavations. Hodder, much recovered but far from well, sailed with the frigate to Bombay, loaded with material given to him by Rawlinson to take back to England. Rawlinson was himself expecting to return there very soon, as his health was increasingly affected by the climate of Baghdad, and the East India Company had granted him a period of sick leave. The unstable political situation, with war having recently broken out between Turkey and Russia, caused him to write for advice to Canning in Constantinople, who tried to persuade him to stay. Rumours had already reached England that Rawlinson was on his way home, and at their meeting in May, the Royal Asiatic Society's council reported that they 'had hoped to have seen in this room and on the present occasion their valued friend Colonel Rawlinson, and they had intended in that case to propose him as a member of their body, but they hear with regret that political events will not permit him to return to England for some time; this he himself laments, as he had hoped to be enabled to dedicate himself for some long period to the work of arranging and bringing out the results of his labours. For this purpose he had already dispatched to England, under care of Mr Hodder, all the tablets, cylinders, vocabularies, syllabaria, &c., for the British Museum . . . He consoles himself, however, with the prospect of the important work which he may still achieve, for he observes in a late communication, 'the vast mass of Chaldaean legends, which come pouring in from all quarters, will find me in ample occupation during the few hours which political business, and the withering climate of Baghdad, will leave at my disposal during the summer.'[35]

More details from Rawlinson were read out, including a 'further very curious discovery . . . that the employment of the Babylonian cuneiform writing was continued down at least. . . [to] the time of Macedonian dominion in Asia, the commencement of the 3rd century, B.C. This appears to be ascertained from a hasty examination of some tablets found at Warka by Mr Loftus, which reached Colonel Rawlinson a couple of days before he sent off his last letter. These are merely notices of benefactions to the temples at Warka, but the royal names upon the tablets . . . are unmistakeably those of Seleucus and Antiochus . . . we are so accustomed to look upon the Assyrian writing as a thing of antiquity, beyond the reach of Greek history, that its appearance on the monuments of the successors of Alexander is somewhat startling.'[36] Loftus had returned to Warka to work for the recently formed Assyrian Excavation Fund, and, to his astonishment, Rawlinson had discovered on clay tablets from the site that cuneiform continued in use beyond the conquest of Alexander the Great.

With the outbreak of the Crimean War against Russia, Rawlinson again wrote to Canning for advice on his course of action. Canning replied in early August: 'Nothing can be more natural than the perplexity which you feel as to the conflicting claims upon your sense of public duty . . . If I did not write sooner in reply to the communication on the subject, the delay was owing to my wish to obtain a clearer insight into eastern probabilities before I undertook to assist you in coming to a decision.'[37] Although there were grave threats from Russia, Canning thought that Persia would probably not want to risk a quarrel with England, in which case Rawlinson was free to go, but if the reverse was true then Rawlinson should not go 'unless you can satisfy your mind that in plain reality Captain Jones would do the work at Bagdad as well as Colonel Rawlinson. That he would do it *well* I have no doubt; but that he would do it *so* well as *you* is a question of experiment from which conjecture recoils. On personal grounds you have to consider your health, and the chances of promotion . . . I should be glad to see you in Persia, but interference on my part would be misplaced.'[38] Throughout the summer, Rawlinson was involved in drafting suggestions for the Foreign Office on the political situation, then, to everyone's surprise, Charles Murray, formerly Consul in Egypt, was given the post of Envoy at Tehran, even though he had never set foot in Persia.

In late October 1854, Rawlinson went to Babylon with Dr Hyslop and camped beneath the ruins of Nebuchadnezzar's palace. While there, he wrote to Norris, who in turn reported to the Royal Asiatic Society that Rawlinson 'had been engaged in tracing the course of the old river through the ruins, and had succeeded by the aid of bricks and slabs with inscriptions, – all found where they were originally deposited, – in identifying most of the buildings of the city, and in tracing the wall . . . The terrific heat (110° in the tent) had, however, stopped all out-door work, and the Colonel had passed the time in his tent in making a literal translation of the great slab found on the Euphrates, brought home by Sir Harford Jones . . . and deposited in the East India House'[39] – the East India House inscription of Nebuchadnezzar. Rawlinson reported that the inscription was a record of the king's building works at Babylon, including the repair of temples, rebuilding of the defensive walls, the adorning of the gates that gave the city its name, and the building of the palace where they had set up their camp.

After ten days, they moved south-west to the neighbouring mound of Birs Nimrud, a city known in ancient times as Borsippa. Over the last three months Rawlinson had instructed one of his agents, Joseph Tonietti, to investigate a prominent tower-like structure on the summit that early travellers had identified with Babylon's legendary Tower of Babel. From the accounts of the ancient Greek historian Herodotus, it was believed Babylon covered a vast area that could have included Borsippa. The feature was a ruined mud-brick ziggurat, although another huge ziggurat in Babylon itself known as Etemenanki ('Foundation of Heaven and Earth') most likely gave rise to the Tower of Babel legend.

Tonietti carried out Rawlinson's instructions 'with care and judgment',[40] but had no surveying instruments. From Rassam's discoveries at Ashur, Rawlinson knew that clay prisms or cylinders would have been buried as foundation deposits at the corners of the building: 'On reaching the ruins I placed a gang at work upon each of the exposed angles of the third stage, directing them to remove the bricks forming the corner, carefully, one after the other, and when they had reached a certain level to pause until I came to inspect the further demolition of the wall. In the meantime I proceeded with flag staffs, compass, and measuring tape, to do what I could in taking sections and elevations. After half an hour I was summoned to the southern corner where the workmen had reached the tenth layer of brick above the plinth at the base, which was the limit I had marked out for their preliminary work. The bricks had been easily displaced, being laid in a mere bed of red earth of no tenacity whatever.'[41]

Rawlinson went on to say: 'The workmen eyed my proceedings with some curiosity, but as they had been already digging for above two months at various points of the mound without finding any thing, and as the demolition of a solid wall seemed to the last degree unpromising, and had at its commencement yielded no results, they were evidently dispirited and incredulous. On reaching the spot I was first occupied for a few minutes in adjusting a prismatic compass on the lowest brick now remaining of the original angle, which fortunately projected a little, so as to afford a good point for obtaining the exact magnetic bearing of the two sides, and I then ordered the work to be resumed. No sooner had the next layer of bricks been removed than the workmen called out there was a *Khazeneh*, or "treasure hole;" that is, in the corner at the distance of two bricks from the exterior surface, there was

a vacant space filled half up with loose reddish sand. "Clear away
the sand," I said, "and bring out the cylinder;" and as I spoke
the words, the Arab, groping with his hand among the débris
in the hole, seized and held up in triumph a fine cylinder of baked
clay, in as perfect a condition as when it was deposited in the
artificial cavity above twenty-four centuries ago. The workmen
were perfectly bewildered. They could be heard whispering to each
other that it was *sihr*, or "magic," while the grey-beard of the
party significantly observed to his companion that the *compass*,
which, as I have mentioned. I had just before been using, and
had accidentally placed immediately above the cylinder, was certainly "*a wonderful instrument*".'[42]

The Arab workmen thought it magic, and Rawlinson was
equally impressed by this clay cylinder that commemorated the
repair and rebuilding of the temple by Nebuchadnezzar, King of
Babylon: 'I sat down for a few minutes on the ruins of the wall
to run over the inscription on the cylinder, devouring its content
with that deep delight which antiquaries only know – such, I
presume, as German scholars have sometimes felt when a Palimp-
sest yields up its treasures, and the historic doubts of ages are
resolved in each succeeding line – and I then moved my station
to the other angle of the stage, that is, to the eastern corner, in
order to direct the search for a second cylinder. Here the discovery
was not accomplished with the same certainty and celerity as in
the first instance; the immediate angle of the wall was gradually
demolished to the very base, and although I fully expected, as
each layer of bricks was removed, that the cavity containing the
cylinder would appear, I was doomed to disappointment. I then
directed the bricks to be removed to a certain distance from the
corner on each face, but the search was still unsuccessful; and I
had just observed to my fellow-travellers that I feared that there
had been foul play in carrying out His Majesty's orders, when a
shout of joy arose from the workmen and another fine cylinder
came forth from its hiding place in the wall. As I knew the inscription would prove to be a mere duplicate of the other, I did not
peruse it with the same absorbing interest, but still it was very

satisfactory to have at least a double copy of the primitive auto-
graphic record.'[43] Later, at Baghdad, Rawlinson recorded: 'The
news of this discovery of the cylinders at the Birs seems to have
flown far and wide on the wings of fame, for since my return to
Baghdad I have been besieged by applications to employ "the
magic compass" in extracting treasures which are believed to be
buried in the court yards or concealed in the walls of the houses;
often in the very "boudoirs" of the ladies.'[44]

Although Rawlinson had done surveying and copied inscriptions on sites, Borsippa was the only place where he became
involved in the actual excavation. Appropriately, it was the cult
centre of the god Nabu, and the ziggurat temple had been restored
by Nebuchadnezzar, whose name means 'Nabu protect the heir'.
Nabu was the god of scribes, patron of writing and the divine
scribe of destinies. He was worshipped throughout Mesopotamia
for over two millennia – he and his father Marduk, patron god of
Babylon, eventually became the principal gods of Babylonia.
Nabu's symbol was a vertical or horizontal wedge-shaped object,
possibly representing a writing stylus.

At the very end of the year, Rawlinson received from William
Vaux, an Assistant Keeper at the British Museum, several pages
of notes and translations done by Hincks while employed by the
museum, but which remained unpublished. Vaux, who was himself the author of a highly popular book on Mesopotamia based
largely on the work of Layard, had covertly copied Hincks's
material at the behest of Rawlinson. It arrived too late, because
other events eclipsed cuneiform for some time. At the beginning
of 1855 Rawlinson recorded that 'Charles Murray and his Mission
reached Baghdad, on their way to Teheran – which was rather
a disappointment to me as I had hoped to have been nominated
to this post myself.'[45] In the end Murray proved a disastrous
choice. He very soon incurred the hostility of the Shah and his
Prime Minister, diplomatic relations between Britain and Persia
were broken a few months later, Murray and his staff withdrew
to Baghdad for nearly two years, and war broke out between
Britain and Persia in 1858. All this occurred after Rawlinson had

returned to England, but it is most likely that war would have been averted if he had obtained the post.

Just before Murray's visit, Rawlinson fell from his horse while hunting wild boar along the east bank of the Tigris and broke the same collar-bone as ten years previously. His recovery was extremely slow and painful, and by late February 1855 he was still unable to ride and could not walk far: 'Being now a good deal out of health, I determined to go home, taking preparatory leave to Bombay with a view to being sent to England on sick certificate.'[46] He resigned his post and left Baghdad for good in March, travelling by steamer down the Tigris and then by sea to Bombay, where he spent a fortnight as a guest of the Governor, Lord Elphinstone. By then he was sufficiently recovered to travel home, his journey taking him to Aden, Egypt, Trieste, Vienna, Prague, Dresden and Leipzig, 'arriving in London early in May, as the London "season" was commencing'.[47]

There was enormous anticipation at the Royal Asiatic Society, who a few days before his return announced: 'COLONEL RAWLINSON is daily expected in England, having quitted Baghdad in early March. He has closed his diplomatic career, and intends to devote himself wholly to the inscribed monuments of Assyria and Babylon, of which he brings with him a very numerous collection. We cherish the confident expectation that these lettered monuments, and the stores already deposited in our national Museum, will yield up all their hidden meaning to the steadily continued investigation of our learned member, whose past labours, although much interrupted by engrossing official duties, and frequently by severe indisposition, have produced a copious harvest of results, invaluable to students in history, palaeology, languages, and scientific research.'[48]

Nineteen: The Final Test

Rawlinson retired from the East India Company on the full pension of a Lieutenant-Colonel at £365 per year, having achieved twenty-eight years' service, including his remaining entitlement to leave. From the summer of 1855 he lived at Langham Place in London and in February the following year he accepted a knighthood. Over the next few years he received numerous other honours from learned societies and institutions, both from within England and far afield. In early 1854 Hincks had also finally obtained a pension, though the annual £100 did not solve his financial problems. Two years later, contrary to his wishes, the Royal Asiatic Society made Hincks an honorary member.

The two rivals continued their research and publications, attended conferences and maintained their disagreements. A few months after his return, Rawlinson revealed the existence of Sumerian, a predecessor of Akkadian cuneiform. He and Hincks had already suspected that Akkadian – Babylonian and Assyrian – must have its origins in an earlier language, possibly Egyptian, but examples of Sumerian had never been seen. Towards the end of Rawlinson's time in Baghdad, Sumerian sites in southern Babylonia, such as Warka, began to be excavated by his agents. At the end of 1852, Rawlinson wrote to the Royal Asiatic Society about his first impressions of Sumerian, and his letter was read out at a meeting in February 1853. This was a totally new discovery, and Rawlinson was very much in the dark. Rather than

Sumerian, he chose the term Scythic and assumed a link with the later Elamite language. *The Athenaeum* made public his letter, which included his recognition of 'a large number of inscriptions in real, *bonâ fide* Scythian languages, allied more or less with the so-called Median [Elamite] languages of the Achaemenian Inscriptions . . . These inscriptions are all more ancient than those of the Achaemenian kings, and generally, even, than the dynasty of Nebuchadnezzar. He finds that all the inscriptions from the southern part of the Persian empire, preceding the time of Nebuchadnezzar, including the bricks and tablets of Niffer, Senkereh, Warka, Susa, and Elymais, were in such Scythian languages . . . The discovery of this primaeval Scythism has induced the learned officer to draw up a paper on the subject.'[1]

In a lengthy talk to the society on 1 December 1855, Rawlinson presented his latest ideas on what would later be termed Sumerian, noting that 'the primitive inhabitants of Babylonia . . . were of the Scythic, and not of the Semitic family'.[2] He was correct in supposing that Sumerian was not a Semitic language and also observed: 'The Babylonian Scyths, whose ethnic name is *Akkad*, may be assumed to have invented the cuneiform writing – forming rude pictures of objects in the first place, and afterwards, when these pictures were fashioned into letters, giving to such letters a phonetic power, corresponding with the name of the original object.'[3] That Rawlinson recognized this more primitive type of writing in Babylonia and could formulate theories was, as he explained, due to his discovery at Nineveh of many bilingual clay tablets, with texts and lists written in Sumerian and Assyrian.

Twenty months later, at a meeting in Dublin of the British Association for the Advancement of Science, Hincks presented the first discussion of grammar of this 'Accadian' language. Because the name Accad (or Akkad) occurred in Genesis as one of the earliest cities and also in Assyrian inscriptions, Hincks concluded: 'It has therefore been chosen with great propriety by Sir H. Rawlinson to represent the people who invented the Assyrian mode of writing. The language of the people may be called Accadian.'[4] The choice of Akkad was actually regrettable, as this was the area north of Sumer, and Rawlinson had also recognized the name Shumir – Sumer. It was Julius Oppert in France in 1869 who first suggested the use of Sumerian, and Akkadian then came to be used for Assyrian and Babylonian.

Hincks was corresponding frequently with scholars over his grievances about priority of discovery and about the British Museum not publishing his translations. One of his correspondents was William Talbot of Lacock Abbey, the inventor of calotype photography and a scholar and mathematician. Recently he had become fascinated by cuneiform and had just published a translation of a clay cylinder that was in the British Museum, not realizing that Hincks had already translated it. Talbot urged Hincks to persuade the Museum's Trustees to publish it as a comparison with his own version, because considerable doubt existed that cuneiform texts could be translated: 'Now, nothing is so convincing an argument to [the] minds of most people as the agreement between two independent translators . . . As I know several of the Trustees personally I should have great pleasure in aiding your request.'[5]

In reply, Hincks poured out his resentment towards the British Museum and Rawlinson, commenting on Talbot's suggestion that 'I am not prepared to undertake it on my own account; but I think that, for the reasons you mention, it would be well that portions of the translations should be published (and perhaps in parallel columns) along with other translations made independently of them, either by yourself or by Sir H. Rawlinson.'[6] By now, Rawlinson was preparing cuneiform texts for publication at the British Museum, and Hincks was angry that the lithographs of the inscriptions were not being published until the accompanying translations were ready. He was afraid that Rawlinson would include ludicrous errors in the translations, or at least 'may make many minor mistakes; but what then? The *public* will fare worse; but the *individual* will have more credit . . . It is not my present intention to meddle with it. I may have a laugh in private over any mistakes that I notice; but I will not enlighten the public in respect to them. The public has given its choice in favour of Sir

Henry's exclusiveness, and if it be deceived in consequence thereof, let it be so!'[7]

A few months later, Talbot received from the British Museum a copy of the first inscription to be lithographed – that of Tiglath-Pileser I on the duplicate clay prisms that had been found by Rassam at Ashur. He embarked on a translation, but continued to worry about the prevailing scepticism over decipherment. It seemed to many that a translation of an inscription was nothing short of invention. 'The public at large', reported *The Athenaeum*, '. . . have been content to look on with incredulous wonder, and when they have found Assyrian or Chaldaean [Babylonian] records at variance with their own preconceived historical views, they have too often taken refuge in absolute disbelief. In fact, at the present day the French Academy, the first critical tribunal in the world, ignores the whole question of Cuneiform decipherment, and treats the so-called translations from the Assyrian as pure empiricism.'[8]

Even the Royal Asiatic Society had admitted three years earlier that they needed to address a popular question: 'how are we to be satisfied that the readings of the cuneatic inscriptions, and consequently, the results deduced from them can be relied on?'[9] There was one simple answer, the society said, which was that no single person had worked on the problem, 'but that kindred spirits of energy, knowledge, and zeal, from Grotefend to Rawlinson and Hincks, have been sedulously engaged in the same task during a succession of years, and in places wide apart; and that the conclusions at which they have arrived, in the progressive stages of research, by their separate and independent operations, are generally accordant and corroborative of each other . . . It may be added, that no human ingenuity could devise any system, by which consistent results should be obtained from any number of documents, however large, unless such system were true.'[10]

This explanation was not sufficient to quell the unease, and so Talbot sent his Tiglath-Pileser translation to the Royal Asiatic Society on 17 March 1857, suggesting it could be compared with Rawlinson's work: 'Many persons have hitherto refused to believe in the truth of the system by which Dr Hincks and Sir H. Rawlinson have interpreted the Assyrian writings, because it contains many things entirely contrary to their preconceived opinions. For example, each Cuneiform group represents a syllable, but not always the same syllable; sometimes one, and sometimes another. To which it is replied, that such a licence would open the door to all manner of uncertainty; that the ancient Assyrians themselves, the natives of the country, could never have read such a kind of writing, and that, therefore, the system cannot be true, and the interpretations based upon it must be fallacious.'[11] Talbot then declared: 'Experience, however, shows that the uncertainty arising from this source is not so great as might easily be imagined. Many of the Cuneiform groups have only one value, and others have always the same value in the same word or phrase, so that the remaining difficulties and uncertainties of reading are reduced within moderate limits. Practically speaking, and considering the newness of the study, there is a fair amount of agreement between different interpreters in their versions of the Assyrian historical writings of average difficulty. It is with the hope of showing that such agreement exists, that I have ventured to offer this translation to the Society.'[12] He concluded: 'I have annexed to my translation a transcription of the whole into Roman characters, with a nearly literal version of each line, disposed in opposite columns. I am in hopes that this arrangement will prove of some use to the students of the Assyrian language. In conclusion, I have to request, for obvious reasons, that the packet containing this MS. translation may not be opened previously to the publication of the volume of the lithographs of the British Museum.'[13]

At a meeting of the Royal Asiatic Society four days later, it was reported that: 'A sealed packet was laid on the table from Henry Fox Talbot, Esq., containing a translation of the inscription on the large cylinder [actually a prism] of Tiglath Pileser the First, in the British Museum, – a copy of which, prepared by Sir Henry Rawlinson, had been furnished to him by the Trustees of the British Museum, with the concurrence of that gentleman . . . the object of Mr Talbot's version now sent was, that those persons who doubted the reality of the decipherment of these ancient monuments might be furnished with two versions of the same inscription, made in entire independence of each other . . . For this purpose, it was important that the seals should not be broken until Sir Henry Rawlinson's translation was published. The Secretary engaged to keep the sealed packet in safe custody for this desirable object.'[14] Oppert was attending the meeting and asked to take part: 'Dr Julius Oppert . . . stated that he was now engaged upon the cylinder of Tiglath Pileser, and requested that he might be allowed to deposit his version, when completed, with the Secretary of the Society, for the object of more fully carrying out the views of Mr Talbot, by affording three independent versions of the same document. This was assented to.'[15]

Rather than wait for the British Museum's publication, the Royal Asiatic Society held the competition straightaway, and Rawlinson, Oppert and later Hincks were invited to submit translations by 20 May. Hincks was aggrieved not to have been included from the outset: 'Sir Henry Rawlinson had a copy of the inscription years before the 21st March; Mr Fox Talbot obtained a copy so long before that date, that he had his translation then prepared. Dr Offert [sic] undertook the translation on the day when Mr Fox Talbot gave in his, – the 21st of March; but he had previously made great progress in the study of the inscription. No copy, however, was placed in *my* hands, nor had I any intimation that such a trial of skill . . . was in contemplation, until the other three translations were in the hands of the Secretary of the Royal Asiatic Society. The copy of the inscription sent me did not reach me till the 26th of April; and I had little more than a fortnight allowed me for a translation, to execute which in a proper manner would require at least two months. I gave in a hasty translation of about half the inscription, selecting those parts which appeared to me of most importance.'[16]

A committee 'of scholars, whose names it was thought would command general respect'[17] was set up. Their function was 'to open the envelopes on an appointed day, and to compare the translations with each other – not with a view, however, of testing or deciding on the merits of the respective translations . . . but in order to satisfy themselves of the agreement, or otherwise, of the independent versions, and to be thus in a position to give a critical opinion on the validity of the system of interpretation. If the translations were discrepant it would be evident that the decipherers must employ different methods of interpretation, and that one only of such methods could be right. In fact, the experiment would show that the decipherment had broken down, and that no confidence was to be placed in the translations: whereas, if the results were identical, or nearly identical, there would be the strongest reason for believing in the correctness of the system of interpretation and in the truth of the translations, because it would be against calculation that three or four independent inquiriers could possibly read and understand a long inscription of 1,000 lines in the same way, unless they were working in the right path.'[18]

The 'literary inquest'[19] to prove whether or not cuneiform decipherment was valid took place at a special meeting in the society's rooms in New Burlington Street on Wednesday 20 May 1857: 'Dean Milman [of St Paul's] presided, and Dr Whewell, Mr Grote and Sir Gardner Wilkinson were in attendance . . . The sealed envelopes were opened and the four versions were examined and compared, the result being . . . that the translations of Sir Henry Rawlinson, of Dr Hincks and of Mr Fox Talbot were found to be identical in sense, and very generally in words also, whilst it appeared to be merely owing to Dr Oppert's very imperfect acquaintance with the English language that a difficulty was found in bringing his version into unison with the others . . . The Committee have not yet given in their verdict . . . but of the fact of the general, if not the exact, coincidence of the three independent versions of the inscription, they are . . . thoroughly satisfied.'[20]

The official reports were presented on 6 June: 'Of the four translations submitted, those of Mr Fox Talbot and Sir Henry Rawlinson are entire; that of Dr Hincks comprises twenty-eight of the fifty-four paragraphs into which the inscription may be divided, the copy in his possession having been received rather too late to allow of a more extended version. Dr Oppert's contains twenty-one paragraphs, being translated from an imperfect copy, taken by himself, from a single cylinder, and that, apparently, defective. In both instances, however, although the translation of the whole has not been effected, yet there is quite enough to enable a conclusion to be drawn as to the amount of agreement or disagreement between the several translators, and the result is, upon the whole, a very remarkable coincidence.'[21] The examiners added: 'It is to be regretted also that Dr Oppert did not translate into French, in which language his version would have been more clear and more precise, and might have been compared with equal facility.'[22]

The examiners next remarked: 'By all the translators, the inscriptions were understood to relate to King Tiglath Pileser, to his campaigns, building and consecration of temples, and other royal acts; campaigns against nations bearing names mostly analagous to those known from the sacred writings, and from other ancient authorities; temples to deities with appellations bearing the same resemblance to those found in other quarters. There was a constant recurrence of these words, names, and titles, yet a sufficient variety of words to test, to a certain degree, the extent of the knowledge claimed by the translators of the sound of the words, and of the language to which the words are supposed to belong. It is right, perhaps, to add, that the closest coincidence was found between the versions of Colonel Rawlinson and Dr Hincks, who are understood to have prosecuted the study for the longest time and with the greatest assiduity.'[23]

In retrospect, this was a decisive moment in the decipherment process, when all those closely involved had their work vindicated, but the test failed to achieve its aim. The doubters remained unconvinced, and it was only through the revelations of translations of cuneiform texts in the years to come that scholars and the public alike were finally persuaded that the decipherment of cuneiform was not merely a delusion. Years later, it was said of Rawlinson's Royal Asiatic Society publications that 'tourists abroad found that a copy of the Journal, unfolding the wonderful Cuneiform discoveries, was the most acceptable present in the scientific world at foreign Capitals'.[24]

By now Rawlinson was a Crown Director of the East India Company and often attended their meetings at India House in Leadenhall Street. His ambition was to stand for Parliament, and in February 1857 he had unsuccessfully contested the seat for Reigate, but gained it a few months later in a by-election. His maiden speech supported the India Bill that proposed the abolition of the dual government of India by the Crown and the East India Company. His parliamentary career was short-lived, because in September 1858 he resigned his seat to become a Member of the new India Council following the passage through Parliament of the India Bill. That position was itself short-lived, because on the retirement of Sir Charles Murray as Envoy to Persia, Rawlinson was finally offered the prestigious post, which he accepted on condition that it was under the control of the India Office.

On 18 August 1859 Rawlinson set out from London for Tehran, with the local rank of Major-General, on a 4,000-mile journey that took him to Paris, Lyons, Marseilles, Malta and then Athens, which he had never before visited and found delightful. From here he travelled to Constantinople, where he was presented to the Sultan, then sailed to the eastern side of the Black Sea, and travelled overland to Yerevan, Tabriz and on to Tehran. It was now late December, and a few miles from Tehran he was met by an escort of honour composed of dignitaries from many nations, who accompanied him into the city. One Constantinople newspaper reported that Rawlinson, 'on arriving at the residence of the British Embassy, received complimentary visits from all the great officers of State, and on the Saturday following, all the members of the Mission were received by the Shah. His Majesty deigned to accord to the Ambassador a most friendly reception. Sir Henry responded by a speech in the Persian language which produced a great impression on all who heard it; after which he offered for his Majesty's acceptance some magnificent presents from her Majesty the Queen of England. In a word, the arrival of Sir Henry Rawlinson was the occasion of a general *fête* in the capital of Persia, and his reception was of the most flattering kind.'[25]

In late February 1860, Rawlinson was informed that his post

was being transferred to the Foreign Office, a move that to him was disastrous, as it changed totally his relations with the Court of Persia, not least, he explained, 'in regard to presents and contingent expenditure, which, in deference to Oriental usage, is sanctioned for all other diplomatic establishments in the East'.[26] He immediately resigned, but continued working until early May, when his journal recorded: 'The English Mail came in early this morning, bringing me the intelligence that my resignation was accepted . . . The news fell on Teheran like a thunderbolt, being totally unexpected by any one.'[27] Twelve days later he left Tehran: 'All the dependents of the British Embassy, all the Russian, French, and Prussian *attachés*, and a considerable number of the other European residents, anxious to do him honour, swelled the crowd which followed him, and made his departure from the city almost as magnificent as his entrance into it had been.'[28]

In England rumours that Rawlinson had been recalled in disgrace were quelled when Henry Danby Seymour, Member of Parliament for Poole, raised the matter in the House of Commons. When he himself was in Persia in 1846, he said that he had heard so much about Rawlinson that 'he was led to ride all the way to Bagdad for the purpose of visiting this wonderful man, and the beginning of a friendship was then laid which he was happy to say had lasted to the present time'[29] – he was now surprised by events and referred to the disastrous period when Murray was Envoy. After Rawlinson's arrival in Tehran, Seymour observed that 'in a very brief space of time England began to be as much respected as ever in Persia; the favour in which Sir H. Rawlinson was held being so great that the Shah jocularly called him his Prime Minister'.[30]

At the end of July 1860, Rawlinson arrived back in London, where he lived in Hill Street. No longer publicly employed, he devoted himself to cuneiform, especially the production of volumes of inscriptions for the British Museum. For over three years he spent many hours in study at the Museum and also wrote pieces for journals and literary magazines. One significant discovery was part of the Assyrian King List on a broken clay tablet from Nineveh, a list that included each king's name, length of reign and key events. It was compiled by scribes in the late seventh century BC and extended far back to before 2000 BC. Even though the list is now known to be not entirely trustworthy, it was an exciting discovery, which Rawlinson announced in a long letter to *The Athenaeum* in May 1862: 'amid the many thousand crumbling tablets of "terra cotta" rescued from the *débris* of the Royal Library at Nineveh, and now in the British Museum, there were a considerable number of fragments bearing lists of names and having the appearance of official documents . . . I found that the majority of the names were merely those of officers of the Assyrian crown, and my interest in the discovery abated'[31] – these were the officials who gave their names to individual years in the absence of a numerical system for identifying years (such as AD 1805). 'The fragments, too, proved, on examination,' Rawlinson continued, 'to be so minute and heterogeneous that, after expending much time and labour in a fruitless attempt to arrange them, I gave up, in despair, the hope of extracting from them any chronological or historical information of value. Lately I have resumed the work, and this time my patience has been amply rewarded. I have found, indeed, that the fragments belong to four different tablets . . . , No one copy is complete or nearly complete; but still, by a careful collation of the several sets of fragments . . . the order and duration of at least thirteen reigns have been ascertained without the possibility of any considerable amount of error.'[32] *The Athenaeum* added a note that Rawlinson's communication 'will be read by every one interested in classical and Jewish history. It contains the announcement of a great discovery, all the consequences of which may not be seen at once. It is certain, however, that the data recovered . . . will not only fill up some gaps in Assyrian History, but will disturb a good many existing theories as to Scriptural Chronology.'[33]

The translation of cuneiform texts on the clay tablets was not only the key to reconstructing thousands of years of forgotten ancient history; it also furnished a vast amount of information about the beliefs, everyday life and state of knowledge of these earliest civilizations, in far more detail than could be derived from studying the relief sculptures that had already made such an impression. Rawlinson was starting to discover that the clay tablets included lists of place-names and gods, rituals, incantations, omens, magical spells and prayers, texts on medicine, language, astronomy and astrology, mathematical tables, accounts, records on taxation, marriage, slaves and property, letters on affairs of state, and literature, including the earliest known epics. The Epic of Gilgamesh with its story of the flood, older than the Bible, would soon be major news.

Although the Assyrian King List had been an immense discovery, Rawlinson found that after a twenty-five-year quest, his work on cuneiform was losing its excitement, and he confessed in his journal for 1862 that 'I am very desirous of doing something definite with regard to Cuneiforms, but find the work sadly irksome'.[34] On Tuesday 2 September, at the age of fifty-two, he 'At last got married and done for!'[35] His marriage was to Louisa Caroline Harcourt Seymour, the twenty-nine-year-old sister of Henry Danby Seymour, at St George's Church, Hanover Square, where his parents had married over six decades earlier. The ceremony was performed by his brother George, then Camden Professor of Ancient History at Oxford. The couple travelled throughout Italy and returned home in December to their newly purchased house near his previous lodgings in Hill Street.

Rawlinson resumed his cuneiform studies, spending several hours each day at the British Museum, and also dined out five or six times a week, afterwards attending one or two evening parties and meeting all manner of eminent men. He and Louisa spent each summer and autumn in the country, often renting a house and letting out their London property. On 20 February 1864 their first son, Henry Seymour Rawlinson, known as Harry or Sennacherib, was born at Louisa's family home of Trent Manor in Dorset. That summer Rawlinson's mother died.

After all his years abroad, Rawlinson began to find his way of life dull and tedious and longed for a return to active employment. In July 1865 he was elected Member of Parliament for Frome in

Somerset, defeating the Conservatives in a bitter contest. 'A great victory has been gained by the Liberal party,' Rawlinson proclaimed in a letter to the *Frome Times*, 'a victory the more remarkable as it has been achieved against a deservedly most popular townsman, in the face of the most determined opposition, and in spite of every obstacle which intimidation, temptation, and the abuse of influence could unite to throw in our way.'[36] In Parliament, he mainly occupied himself with matters connected with India, as well as bringing to public notice what he believed were the increasingly dangerous designs and intentions of Russia towards Persia, Afghanistan and India. Remaining distrustful of Russia, a few years later he published *England and Russia in the East*, a collection of essays on central Asia and the Russian threat.

In Ireland, Hincks continued to feel embittered that he was overlooked, even though the cuneiform contest in 1857 had shown that he was Rawlinson's equal in translation. His publications continued to be in various obscure journals, and on Christmas Day 1854, Max Müller, a professor of languages at Oxford, complained: 'I wish you would publish a collection of your papers ... [from] the *Transactions* of your [Royal Irish] Academy. It is impossible to get at them now without going to a Library, which is a great inconvenience.'[37] In letters to scholars in England and France, Hincks constantly asserted his own claims to priority and in 1862 engaged in somewhat irascible correspondence with Oppert over such issues – Oppert sharply rebuked him: 'You protest against Sir Henry ... I made, after your claim, a cross-examination, and saw, that in very numerous instances, the discoveries belong to Rawlinson and not only to you ... You never composed a great systematical work, never edited an Assyrian text with transcript, translation and commentary, never wrote a paper intelligible to other than Assyriologists, and able to provoke the criticism of oriental scholars. And therefore, the public in England looks upon these studies with a mistrusting eye, and does not believe in your discoveries ... Who, dear doctor, can have here [in France] the *Journal for Sacred Literature*? ... And ignoring all researches of continental and even British students, *you* proclaim *yourself* (as I hear from English friends of Rawlinson's and mine) to be at the head of Assyrian decypherment, when never you explained an Assyrian text.'[38]

The following year, 1863, Hincks proposed to Norris that they should work on an Assyrian dictionary together, but he refused Norris's invitation to submit a paper on Assyrian verbs to the Royal Asiatic Society, apparently because Rawlinson was now Director of the society. Norris responded in late September: 'I am sorry you have made up your mind not to send any papers to our *Journal*, for *this* among other reasons that we should get it done better than elsewhere, having a full fount of types . . . I wish I could destroy the impression you have received of Rawlinson. I know that his manner, contracted by long command of inferior Turks, Arabs, Persians, &c. may be deceptive, but I know also *that he has not* the feeling towards you which you suppose.'[39]

On Christmas Eve 1863, Hincks fell seriously ill with jaundice, but recovered after a long convalescence the following year. He resumed his studies and concentrated on an Assyrian grammar. His last journal entry was on 30 November 1866: 'Unwell. To bed at 9.15.'[40] He died suddenly at Killyleagh three days later, on 3 December, at the age of seventy-four. Other key figures of the era of decipherment and discovery had died before him, including the fifty-one-year-old Burnouf in 1852, Grotefend two years later, Fresnel in 1855, and Loftus, only thirty-seven years old, in 1858. In its obituary of Hincks, *The Athenaeum* commented poignantly: 'Living in a remote country village, with very limited means at his command, he had to contend with great difficulties. In London, beside the British Museum, he would have accomplished more than he did . . . This profound and original philologist, whose name will ever be associated with the names of Rawlinson and Oppert, was highly esteemed on the Continent, especially in Germany, where his judgment, caution and conscientiousness in deciphering inscriptions were duly appreciated . . . This is not the place to mention his opinions on ecclesiastical matters or the question of national education – subjects on which he wrote with a courage and independence that hindered his promotion in the Church.'[41]

Although Hincks had been unable to realize his potential, *The Athenaeum* predicted that his achievements would be long recognized: 'With all his attainments, he was simple-hearted, good, upright, honourable, and kind; a man loved, as well as admired, by those who knew him. Ireland may well mourn his loss. As she reckons up her scholars, the name of Edward Hincks cannot be forgotten as long as learning, genius and goodness live in their influence upon future generations.'[42] Yet only a few years after the death of Hincks, Max Müller wrote that he was 'the first to lay the solid foundation for a grammatical study of the Assyrian language. His labours, scattered about in different journals, are now in danger of being almost forgotten; and it would be but a just tribute to his memory if the Irish Academy or some of his surviving friends and admirers were to publish a collected edition of his numerous though not voluminous contributions to the study of the cuneiform inscriptions.'[43] This task was never done, and Müller's prediction came true.

In the year that Hincks died, George Smith began to study inscriptions at the British Museum. Born in Chelsea in March 1840, he was apprenticed to learn banknote engraving, but became inspired to read everything about Assyria and constantly visited the British Museum, as he explained: 'Everyone has some bent or inclination which, if fostered by favourable circumstances, will colour the rest of his life. My own taste has always been for Oriental studies, and from my youth I have taken a great interest in Eastern explorations and discoveries, particularly in the great work in which Layard and Rawlinson were engaged ... in 1866, seeing the unsatisfactory state of our knowledge of those parts of Assyrian history which bore upon the history of the Bible, I felt anxious to do something towards settling a few of the questions involved.'[44]

Smith wrote to Rawlinson to ask if he could see relevant inscriptions. 'Sir Henry Rawlinson,' he commented, 'with whom I had corresponded before, took a generous interest in any investigations likely to throw light on the studies in which he held so distinguished a place, and he at once accorded me permission to examine the large store of paper casts in his work-room at the British Museum. This work I found ... of considerable difficulty, as the casts were most of them very fragmentary, and I was quite inexperienced, and had little time at my disposal.'[45] Smith was inexperienced, but he was a brilliant scholar – self-taught, as so many decipherers (including Rawlinson), seem to have been. He soon recognized an inscription that could be linked to the Black Obelisk: one that mentioned Jehu, and thus enabled him to date the events of the obelisk. He published this discovery in a short account in *The Athenaeum*, 'and being encouraged in my researches by Sir Henry Rawlinson and Dr Birch, the keeper of the Oriental department of the British Museum, I next set to work on the cylinders containing the history of Assurbanipal ... by comparing the various copies, I soon obtained a fair text of the earlier part of these inscriptions, and Sir Henry Rawlinson proposed that I should be engaged by the trustees of the British Museum to assist him in the work of preparing a new volume of 'Cuneiform Inscriptions.' Thus, in the beginning of 1867, I entered into official life, and regularly prosecuted the study of the cuneiform texts. I owed my first step to Sir Henry Rawlinson, whose assistance has been to me the greatest value throughout my work.'[46]

On 17 January 1867, Rawlinson's second son, Alfred, known as Toby, was born. For financial reasons Rawlinson decided to leave Parliament and join the India Council once again, accepting one of the last permanent posts on offer. This became his main occupation and increased his salary to a substantial £1,500 per year. He now settled into a routine, on most days driving to the India Office in his carriage at about eleven in the morning and returning five or six hours later. In 1869 he and his wife sold their property at Hill Street and moved to 21 Charles Street, with stables and coachhouses in the adjacent Hay's Mews. From this point in his life, the time he spent on researching cuneiform dropped dramatically, though he continued to publish new ideas and discoveries and oversee George Smith's work at the British

Museum. In late 1870, the Society of Biblical Archaeology was formed, and Rawlinson became its Vice-President. Less than two years later, Smith made an outstanding discovery at the British Museum on a large clay tablet fragment from Nineveh – a version of the flood story that was earlier than the one in the Bible: 'The first fragment I discovered contained about half of the account: it was the largest single fragment of these legends. As soon as I recognized this, I began a search among the fragments of the Assyrian library to find the remainder of the story. This library was first discovered by Mr Layard, who sent home many boxes full of fragments of terracotta tablets, and after the close of Mr Layard's work, Mr Hormuzd Rassam and Mr Loftus recovered much more of this collection. The fragments of clay tablets were of all sizes, from half an inch to a foot long, and were thickly coated with dirt, so that they had to be cleaned before anything could be seen on the surface.'[47]

Smith described his search for other fragments: 'Whenever I found anything of interest, it was my practice to examine the most likely parts of this collection, and pick out all the fragments that would join, or throw light on the new subject. My search for fragments of the Deluge story was soon rewarded by some good finds, and I then ascertained that this tablet, of which I obtained three copies, was the eleventh in a series of tablets giving the history of an unknown hero, named Izdubar; and I subsequently ascertained that this series contained in all twelve tablets. These tablets were full of remarkable interest, and a notice of them being published, they at once attracted a considerable amount of attention, both in England and abroad. I arranged to give the public, as soon as possible, a translation and account of these fragments in a lecture before the Biblical Archaeological Society, and this was delivered on the 3rd of December, 1872.'[48]

The unknown hero was in fact Gilgamesh, who seems to have been a Sumerian king of Uruk (Warka) around 2600 BC and who came to be worshipped as a god. Legends grew up around him, and he was the subject of five narrative poems, the most famous being the Epic of Gilgamesh. This lengthy poem, repeatedly copied by scribes from clay tablet to clay tablet, was first written down around 2000 BC, but probably had much earlier origins. It recounted the friendship between Gilgamesh, the tyrannical ruler of Uruk, and Enkidu, who was raised by wild animals, with descriptions of their exploits together and Gilgamesh's unsuccessful quest for immortality. The eleventh of the twelve tablets is a version of the flood story written at least 1,500 years before the Biblical version, but similar in many ways. In order to find the secret of immortality, Gilgamesh tracked down Utnapishtim, who related to him an account of the flood in which he built a boat or ark to survive. After the flood, Utnapishtim was granted immortality, though not eternal youth, but he offered Gilgamesh immortality if he stayed awake for six days and seven nights – which Gilgamesh failed to do.

The Times reported Smith's lecture in detail, saying that many distinguished people attended, including William Gladstone, the Prime Minister. Presiding over the packed meeting, Rawlinson declared that it demonstrated 'the great public interest which was taken in the subject to be brought forward that evening. Some 15 years ago, he explained, during the excavations of the site of the old palace of Nineveh, the *débris* of the Royal Library was found. In ancient days books were merely inscribed on clay tablets, and a great many of these were discovered among the ruins in as perfect a state of preservation as they had been 2,500 years previously. They were deposited in the British Museum, and had since furnished a perfect mine of resource to all Assyrian scholars, of whom Mr Smith was the first of the day.'[49] In introducing the lecturer, Rawlinson 'pledged his reputation and authority that the translation of the inscription which they would hear from Mr Smith would be as generally perfect as could possibly be. Mr SMITH, who was received with cheers, then read his paper.'[50]

After the lecture, a lively discussion took place, following which Gladstone rose to loud applause and gave a vote of thanks, ending on a note of caution: 'I feel, as has been well said, that above all things we must be on our guard against travelling too fast in these matters, and that it is a very slow and laborious process in which we are engaged. We are like children with an enormous pattern-map broken into a thousand pieces, in which, through the ingenuity and learning of men like your president and vice-president and the gentlemen whom we have heard tonight, we are gradually ascertaining the proper spot for this or that particular fragment, then, by care, adding another to the first, and so we go on from point to point until at length I believe we shall be permitted to know a great deal more than our forefathers in respect of the early history of mankind – perhaps the most interesting and most important of all the portions of the varied history of our race, with reference to the weighty interests that are involved either as regards science or religion.'[51]

Smith's discovery was incredible news, because it showed that the Hebrew Old Testament version was not unique, and the *Daily Telegraph* offered 1,000 guineas to resume excavations and find more inscriptions. Smith arranged for six months' leave of absence from the British Museum and departed for Assyria in January 1873. He dug first at Nimrud and then at Nineveh, including the area of the libraries in the two palaces. He recorded that in mid-May he 'sat down to examine the store of fragments of cuneiform inscriptions from the day's digging, taking out and brushing off the earth from the fragments to read their contents. On cleaning one of them I found to my surprise and gratification that it contained the greater portion of seventeen lines of inscription belonging to the first column of the Chaldean account of the Deluge, and fitting into the only place where there was a serious blank in the story.'[52] Telegraphing the news to the *Daily Telegraph*, his latest discovery was published on 21 May, and soon after Smith returned to England.

In the first part of 1874, Smith was again at Nineveh, this time on behalf of the British Museum, and so important were his discoveries that in October 1875 he was sent on another expedition, but plague at Baghdad and the unsettled state of the country made his work impossible. In a state of utter exhaustion he attempted to return home, but died in the consulate at Aleppo in August 1876, only thirty-six years old, and leaving 'a wife and a large family of young children, the youngest of whom was born but a short time before his departure from England'.[53]

The Times reported that on the day of Smith's death and at almost the precise hour, a 'young German Assyriologist of the highest promise, Dr. Friedrich Delitzsch . . . was on his way to the house of Mr William St Chad Boscawen, who is also a rising Assyriologist, and has been Mr Smith's substitute at the British Museum ever since that gentleman started on his third expedition to the East. Mr Boscawen resides in Victoria-road, Kentish-town, and in passing the end of Crogsland-road, in which Mr George Smith lived, and within a stone's throw of the house, his [Smith's] German friend and translator says he suddenly heard a most piercing cry, which thrilled him to the marrow . . . Dr. Delitzsch, who strongly disavows any superstitious leanings, was ashamed to mention the circumstance to Mr Boscawen on reaching that gentleman's house, although on his return home he owns that his nervous apprehensions of some mournful event in his own family found relief in tears, and that he recorded all the facts in his note-book that same night.'[54] *The Times* considered this a most striking coincidence that was worth reporting, but declined to make any comment.

The discovery of texts that were far earlier than similar stories in the Bible – including the very first story of the creation of the world – sent shock waves through the western world, but to younger scholars everything that had been discovered was becoming accepted wisdom. Two decades later it was said of Rawlinson's cuneiform work: 'All the romance of these discoveries has become mere History now to the younger generation, but the secret, concealed so many years, was unrolled before the very eyes of the few older survivors of the old generation: the world knows the secret now, which the Greek and Roman never knew.'[55]

Rawlinson himself had become increasingly involved with the Royal Geographical Society. As its President for two years from 1871, he was embroiled in the expedition to rescue the explorer and missionary David Livingstone in Africa and in the controversy surrounding Henry Morton Stanley. The society was initially reluctant to acknowledge the achievements of Stanley, whose story about finding Livingstone was doubted on his return to England, but in September 1872 Rawlinson in his capacity as President travelled to Dunrobin Castle in Scotland to present Stanley to Queen Victoria. In 1874 Rawlinson was again President, retiring two years later, with the explanation: 'I have been for thirty-two years a member of this Society; for twenty years, with very few breaks, I have served upon your Council, and I have now presided five times at your Anniversary Meetings. The greater part of my spare time since I returned from the East has thus been devoted to your service, and I am proud to state that my most agreeable memories are associated with the growing prosperity, and what I may now call the assured success, of the Geographical Society. But time steals on. I am not as active in mind or body as I was; and, as I find the continued direction of your affairs to be hardly compatible with the discharge of other duties connected with my public office, I am obliged to tender my resignation of the post of President.'[56] He took on further duties elsewhere, though, because in 1878 he became President of the Royal Asiatic Society and a Trustee of the British Museum.

On 31 October 1889, Rawlinson's wife Louisa died suddenly, at the age of fifty-six. Layard wrote in sympathy from Venice: 'I have learnt with the sincerest grief the irreparable loss that you have sustained. I trust that you will not think me intruding upon your sorrow, if, as a very old friend and one who has ever felt the deepest interest in your career, I venture to offer you my sincerest sympathy. I know how little such sympathy can tend to afford relief in such heavy affliction; but it may still be some consolation to you to know that you have friends who feel truly for you.'[57]

Twenty years earlier, at the age of fifty-two, Layard had married Enid, the twenty-five-year-old daughter of his cousin Charlotte Guest, at whose house of Canford Manor he had written his bestselling book. That same year he became Ambassador in Madrid, where he and his wife spent the next seven years until in 1877 he was appointed Ambassador in Constantinople, where his career had begun. He retired to Venice with Enid seven years later and died on 5 July 1894 at the age of seventy-seven. Many others involved in Rawlinson's life had already died: Botta in 1870, Edwin Norris in 1872, his older brother Abram in 1875, Lassen and Mohl in 1876, Talbot in 1877, Westergaard and Felix Jones in 1878, and Canning in 1880.

Rawlinson was made a baronet in 1891, when he was eighty-one years old, and his brother George commented that few people meeting him for the first time would have guessed his true age: 'He moved with firmness and vigour; his eyes were bright with intelligence; he held himself erect as he stood or walked; his hair alone, which was almost wholly white, proclaimed him an old man'[58] – he was by this time, though, slightly deaf. His wife's death affected him deeply, and he 'lost much of that prevailing cheerfulness, and even sparkle, which had previously been characteristic of him, and had rendered him so delightful an associate. He became comparatively grave and serious in his demeanour, rarely indulged in laughter, and not much in light conversation.'[59] His sons, Harry and Toby, had joined the army, and George noted that Rawlinson's 'own athletic vigour and sporting tastes had descended to both sons, for, while the elder was an adventurous hunter of the pig, the younger was by general consent allowed to be the best polo player in India!'[60] In order to be with his beloved father, Harry and his wife took over 21 Charles Street as their home on their marriage in 1890.

On Tuesday 26 February 1895, Rawlinson attended the weekly meeting of the India Council, but the next day he complained of a headache, and on Thursday took to his bed. On Friday his temperature rose rapidly, causing great loss of strength, which possibly marked the onset of influenza, as the country was in the grip of an epidemic. Although he rallied somewhat during the following day, there was a further rise in his temperature at mid-day on Sunday, coupled with bronchial congestion of the right lung. He sank gradually until twenty minutes to six on the morning of Tuesday 5 March, when he died. The barometer was already falling, and by the time of his funeral five days later at the cemetery of the London Necropolis Company, the rain was incessant. This cemetery, opened in 1854 at Brookwood near Woking, 20 miles south-west of London, had been intended as a permanent solution to the insanitary and horrific conditions of London's overcrowded burial grounds. Up to then, previous burials were constantly desecrated in order to cram in new ones, tons of human bones were removed and crushed each year for use as fertilizer, old coffins were reused or sold as firewood, and water supplies were contaminated by decomposing bodies. Set in 500 acres of Surrey heathland purchased from Lord Onslow, the new cemetery was served by a private railway that conveyed coffins and mourners from the York Street Necropolis Station at Waterloo in London to Brookwood. All social classes and religions were catered for, and even the special hearse vans had separate compartments, so that the coffins travelled first, second or third class, with Nonconformist and Anglican mourners also being segregated.

The train with Rawlinson's coffin and mourners, travelling first class, arrived at Brookwood's south station at around one o'clock in the afternoon, a journey of just over an hour. After a short interval, the coffin, covered in flowers, was taken from the train and into the nearby Anglican chapel, where the greater part of the service was read by the chaplain of the Surrey County Asylum. Few were in attendance, because of the dreadful weather and also because a memorial service was being held simultaneously at St George's Church in Hanover Square. *The Times* of London reported that 'the mourners were Mr Henry Rawlinson [his older son], who succeeds to the title, and Mrs Rawlinson [his daughter-in-law], Mr Alfred Rawlinson [his younger son], Mr Henry Bouverie and Miss Bouverie, Mr Creswicke Rawlinson, Mr and Mrs Henry Thornton, Captain Cecil Rawlinson, Lord Methuen, and Mr Asheford Sanford. Among the personal friends ... who followed in the procession to the graveside were Lord Roberts, Sir Owen Burne and Sir Charles Turner, his colleagues at the India Office, and Lieutenant-Colonel Godwin-Austen (Shelford-house), who was closely associated with him in the Royal Geographical Society ... There were a large number of beautiful wreaths and other floral emblems.'[61]

Overcoming injuries and ill-health, including repeated bouts of malaria, Henry Rawlinson had survived to the age of eighty-four and outlived many of his contemporaries, but his death was greatly lamented. The Royal Geographical Society remarked: 'Sir Henry Rawlinson, notwithstanding an occasional *brusquerie* of manner and reserve, was a kindly, genial, and sincere adviser and friend. His hospitality as President of the Geographical Society or Asiatic Society, or as a mere mover in London society, was large; and at his dinner and receptions, in Lady Rawlinson's lifetime, were met together the most noted of travellers, *savants*, and diplomatists of our own country or from abroad.'[62] *The Athenaeum* also made reference to his intimidating style, yet discussed at length his achievements and honours in its fulsome obituary, noting that: 'There was nothing wanting to the long list of honours by which he was rewarded for sterling and successful work. Nor could any one who knew him well grudge him a tittle of his fame or a ribbon of his decorations; he had earned them all and wore them worthily. Strangers, indeed, found him somewhat imperious and gruffly abrupt in manner, after the old Anglo-Indian style; but his friends admired and reverenced a great heart no less than a clear and commanding intellect. He represented a grand tradition, and it will be impossible to fill his place.'[63]

In its obituary, the Royal Asiatic Society recorded that Rawlinson 'attracted to the study of Oriental Languages and Archaeology a fashion and popularity; he was at home in the Camp, the Court, the Council Chamber, and the Senate, as well as the Public Library, the British Museum, and amidst his books and notes in his own study . . . in conversation Sir Henry Rawlinson, when he found himself amidst kindred spirits, passed readily, and gaily, and instructively, from a discussion on the policy of the Shah of Persia, or the Amir of Afghanistan, or from some geographical detail regarding the region of the River Oxus, to the intricacy of the translation of a Cuneiform word or sentence, whether Semitic, or Old-Persian, or Akkadian, or the probable date and affinity of a new variety of Alphabetic Script lately discovered in Arabia. This was a great and special gift almost peculiar to himself, which rendered his society so delightful and profitable ... it is an honour, a profit, and a joy, to have known him.'[64]

Digging Down to Babylon

Three years after Rawlinson's death, his brother George published his biography, a loyal memoir in which he barely mentioned Edward Hincks. George Rawlinson died suddenly on 6 October 1902 at the age of eighty-nine and was buried in the now overgrown cemetery of Holywell in Oxford.

The East India Company's army was distinguished by many officers who displayed immense proficiency in languages and an interest in history, but none possessed Rawlinson's remarkable combination of qualities: the physical prowess, bravery, intellect, self-motivation, consummate diplomacy and above all luck in defying death from disease and war. He also seized opportunities to fulfil his obsession with the ancient past and satisfy his ambition to make a name for himself in the field of literature, even though he sacrificed his career prospects for his love of learning. In its obituary of Rawlinson, *The Athenaeum* commented that he 'belonged to a fine old school, fast disappearing from our midst. "John Company" had a knack of turning out a splendid class of scholarly soldiers and civilians – men who seemed equal to any sort of task, of war, of administration, or of research, that chanced to come in their road; but there were few who were more eminently successful in every department than Henry Rawlinson. He enjoyed the best of opportunities, and he made the most of any chance.'[1]

Rawlinson's long journey to India in 1827 as a young, self-conscious cadet had been one of torment. Although accustomed to boarding school, he was dreadfully homesick, realizing that Company regulations would not permit him to return to England for at least ten years. His misery was compounded by the failure of his family to write to him, but before too long he reluctantly admitted that he was beginning to enjoy himself. His full social life at times approached what he considered to be dissipation, and to assuage his guilt he applied himself ever harder to his studies of local languages and history, for which he had a genuine passion and talent. His knowledge of Persian was instrumental in him being one of the handful of officers chosen for a military mission to Persia, a fortuitous decision that changed Rawlinson's life when he came face-to-face with ancient cuneiform inscriptions, most notably the immense rock-carved inscription at Bisitun.

When Rawlinson embarked on the decipherment of cuneiform, very few texts had ever been found, and most were known only from the more visible monuments in Persia. Cuneiform inscriptions from Mesopotamia were extremely rare, and information about its history was scanty. Nineveh had been destroyed in 612 BC, and Biblical prophets writing soon afterwards rejoiced in its fate. Over two hundred years later, in 401 BC, the Greek soldier and historian Xenophon marched past the site with an army of mercenaries who had been attempting to help Cyrus the Younger seize the Persian throne from his older brother Artaxerxes II. As they retreated after being defeated in the battle of Cunaxa near Babylon, Xenophon observed the ruins of the once great city, whose name was already forgotten. By the time Rawlinson retired from his post at Baghdad and returned to England in 1855, the situation had changed dramatically. The excavation of cities, temples and palaces in Sumer, Assyria and Babylonia, and the decipherment of their numerous cuneiform texts, had led to the discovery of several empires that had disappeared from view long before the ascendance of the ancient Greeks and Romans. While these achievements were profound and unimaginable, Rawlinson was also fortunate over the next forty years in witnessing the advances made by younger scholars across Europe and America.

Following Rawlinson's departure from Baghdad in 1855, nearly two decades passed before excavations were revived in Mesopotamia, initially by George Smith in his search for further evidence of the story of the Flood. After Smith's tragic death, Hormuzd Rassam was once again appointed by the British Museum to undertake excavations at Nineveh, with particular instructions to search for more clay tablets. He started his work in late 1877, but did not restrict himself to Nineveh, and his most significant discovery was a pair of huge cedarwood gates over 20 feet high with decorated bronze fittings. These came from a palace at Balawat, near Nimrud, that belonged to King Shalmaneser III, the ruler of Assyria from 858 to 824 BC who had erected the Black Obelisk. The wood had long since rotted, but lifesize replicas of these gates now form an imposing exhibit in the British Museum.

Rassam returned to England for good in 1882, leaving guards to watch over the sites he had been excavating. Five years earlier, just before he had resumed work at Nineveh, Ernest de Sarzec was appointed French Vice-Consul at Basra in the far south, and he pioneered the excavation of the mud-brick structures of an ancient mound, uncovering a substantial temple at Telloh, which produced the very first examples of Sumerian art. Having sold his initial batch of finds to the Louvre in Paris, word spread of the immense monetary value of what was being dug up, and so dealers of antiquities began to operate at Baghdad. As with Rassam's excavations, de Sarzec's supervision of the digging at Telloh was minimal, and when in 1894 his workmen uncovered a chamber with 30,000–40,000 clay tablets, many thousands were stolen and illicitly sold.

At the end of 1887, Wallis Budge of the British Museum was sent to Baghdad by the Trustees to investigate the circumstances of clay tablets being offered for sale, because of suspicions that the Museum was buying from dealers tablets it had already paid to excavate. On his way, Budge stopped in Egypt, because he had heard that cuneiform tablets were also being offered for sale there. That year, a woman digging for ancient mud brick to use as fertilizer (or possibly for antiquities to sell) at Tel el-Amarna in Upper Egypt had discovered hundreds of clay tablet fragments

inscribed in cuneiform, many of which had found their way on
to the antiquities market. Known today as the Amarna Letters,
they were found in what would later be recognized as the Palace
Records Office of Amarna, a new city founded by the heretic
pharaoh Akhenaten as his capital. Because the local dealers in
antiquities were unfamiliar with cuneiform writing, many tablets
were lost or destroyed in the belief that they were forgeries, but
nearly four hundred survived, virtually all of which are diplomatic
correspondence to the court of Egypt from the rulers of neighbouring independent and vassal states, such as Babylonia, Assyria,
Anatolia, Cyprus, Palestine and Syria. The topics contained in the
letters included the description of exchanges of gifts, complaints
about their quality, diplomatic marriages, trade agreements and
requests for help from the Egyptian pharaoh in local conflicts.

This sensational discovery showed for the first time the widespread use of cuneiform and the relationships between far-flung
states. The diplomatic correspondence between them was not written in Egyptian hieroglyphs, but was largely in cuneiform in the
Babylonian language, the lingua franca of the time. The Amarna
Letters date mainly to the reign of Akhenaten (1352–1336 BC),
as well as that of his father Amenhotep III and the first year
of the reign of his successor Tutankhamun, who subsequently
abandoned Amarna as the capital city. Realizing that the clay
tablets were genuine, Wallis Budge purchased some for the British
Museum, then made his way to Baghdad to consult with the
British Consul-General, Colonel William Tweedie, on what to do
about the huge number of clay tablets that were flooding the
market there. He discovered that the watchmen appointed by
Rassam to guard various sites were the same as those offering
tablets for sale, and he was also horrified to see the damage being
done by illicit digging to ancient cities such as Babylon and Borsippa, with thousands of tablets and bricks being plundered and
the sites wrecked. He accused Rassam of negligence if not com-
plicity in allowing all these objects to be plundered and sold, but
a few years later Budge was successfully sued for libel by Rassam.

At the Residency, Budge met Tweedie's confidential clerk, a

small, elderly man by the name of Ya'qub. On discovering that Budge had letters from Rawlinson, the clerk overwhelmed him with a barrage of questions: 'How was he? When did I see him last? Was it true that he was married and had sons? And so on as fast as he could speak. In answer to my questions he told me that he had been employed in the Residency all his life, and that of all the Consuls-General whom he had served he respected and loved and admired Rawlinson most of all. In knowledge and learning he was, he said, "like God," as a horseman he was like Antar [an Arab hero], as a king he was like Nimrod, and when he spoke at the Mijlis (*i.e.*, Town Council) of Baghdâd the heart of the Wâlî Pâshâ melted, and the knees of his councillors gave way under them.'[2]

Ya'qub related to Budge numerous stories of Rawlinson. Each year, he said, his power in the country became stronger, and 'towards the end of his time here had he taken one dog, and put his English hat on his head and sent him to the Serai, all the people in the bazâr would have made way for him, and bowed to him, and the soldiers would have stood still and presented arms to him as he passed, and the officials in the Serai would have embraced him; and if he had sent another dog with another of his hats across the river to Kâzimên, the Shi'ites and Sunnites would have stopped fighting each other, and would have asked him to drink coffee with them.'[3]

Not long after Budge left Baghdad, the first American excavations began in Mesopotamia, conducted by the University of Pennsylvania at Nippur, a mound explored by Rawlinson over four decades earlier. The systematic excavations produced remarkable results, including the discovery of the temple library of over 20,000 mainly Sumerian cuneiform tablets. Equally systematic were German excavations that began at Babylon and Ashur from the very end of the nineteenth century, all heralding an era of scientific excavation.

Results from excavations such as these would finally lay to rest the controversy surrounding Sumerian that had erupted. It had been thrilling yet highly disturbing to learn that particular elements of the Bible, such as the story of the Creation or the Flood, were derived from much earlier accounts. Traditionally, it was believed that the Hebrew Bible (the Old Testament) was the word of God, and that its authors, most notably Moses, were divinely inspired, but discoveries of earlier cuneiform texts threw such theories into doubt. For centuries there had been speculation about the origins of language and whether there was one source or several. One widely held belief was that at the time of Creation the Semitic language of Hebrew was spoken in the Garden of Eden, and although the etymology of the Hebrew word Eden is disputed, there was a Sumerian word *edin*, meaning plain, from which it may have been derived. The Garden of Eden may therefore have referred to the cultivated plain of Mesopotamia. Whatever its derivation, the discovery in the cuneiform texts of the existence of the earlier Semitic language of Akkadian proved that Hebrew had an earlier ancestry, which was an interesting but not controversial discovery, because Akkadian could be considered merely the earliest form of Hebrew. The greatest controversy of all surrounded Sumerian.

Languages such as French, Italian and English obviously had roots in Latin, but in the late eighteenth century it was realized that Sanskrit, the classical language of India, also had many similarities to these European languages, which were therefore termed Indo-European or Indo-Germanic. The theory developed that they were first spoken by Aryans (the Sanskrit word for 'noble'), who had migrated from Asia to Europe, and from these people true civilization and a superior white race developed. The discovery that Sumerian, the first language written in cuneiform, was even earlier and was used by a non-Aryan and non-Semitic society that had all the trappings of civilization upset many partisan beliefs.

Only two years after Oppert had suggested the name Sumerian for the language that Rawlinson and Hincks had identified, the foundations of the Sumerian language were set out in a paper published in 1871 by Archibald Henry Sayce, a Fellow at Oxford University who became its first Professor of Assyriology twenty years later. In 1873 François Lenormant in Paris published the principles of Sumerian in an extensive and systematic form, though he and Sayce still used the obsolete term Akkadian – a name nowadays transferred to the language previously called Assyrio-Babylonian. Lenormant's work led to disagreements that persisted for over three decades, because a Semitic scholar at Paris, Joseph Halévy, refuted the existence of the Sumerian language and people. He claimed that Sumerian was purely a secret code invented by the Semitic Babylonians for sacred purposes, and that civilization and writing in Mesopotamia had Semitic origins. Over the years he gained supporters to his cause, while others such as Oppert and Lenormant vigorously opposed him. With more and more discoveries at Sumerian sites such as Telloh and Nippur undermining his theories, Halévy merely shifted his stance, even though in 1889 the German scholar Carl Bezold published the text of a clay tablet proving that the Babylonians had a word for the Sumerian language.

By the end of the nineteenth century, Halévy's views were gradually abandoned, yet as late as 1902 one writer commented that 'M. Halévy disputed the very existence of the Sumerian race and language, and the controversy he excited has not even yet wholly died away. Others cannot reconcile themselves to the subordinate position of the Semite to the Sumerian in laying the foundations of all modern culture, and they still endeavour to show that the two races were at least contemporary workers from the earliest times, and contributed equally to the great result. All this is perhaps symptomatic only of a passing phase of irritation, for the evidence on the other side seems too overwhelming to be long withstood.'[4]

Five years later in 1907 Sayce severely condemned those apparently racist scholars who had been unable to accept the new discoveries: 'Among the first results of the decipherment of the Assyrian cuneiform inscriptions was one which was so unexpected and revolutionary, that it was received with incredulity and employed to pour discredit on the fact of decipherment itself. European scholars had long been nursing the comfortable belief that the white race primarily, and the natives of Europe secondly, were *ipso facto* superior to the rest of mankind, and that to them belonged of right the origin and development of civilization. The discovery of the common parentage of the Indo-European languages had come to strengthen the belief; the notion grew up that in Sanskrit we had found, if not the primeval language, at all events a language that was very near to it, and idyllic pictures were painted of the primitive Aryan community living in its Asiatic home and already possessed of the elements of its later culture. Outside and beyond it were the barbarians, races yellow and brown and black, with oblique eyes and narrow foreheads, whose intelligence was not much above that of the brute beasts. Such culture as some of them may have had was derived from the white race, and perhaps spoilt in the borrowing. The idea of the rise of a civilization outside the limits of the white race was regarded as a paradox.'[5]

Sayce went on to describe the effect that decipherment had on old prejudices: 'It was just this paradox to which the first decipherers of Assyrian cuneiform found themselves forced. And another paradox was added to it. Not only had the civilization of the Euphrates and Tigris originated amongst a race that spoke an agglutinative language [Sumerian], and therefore was neither Aryan nor Semitic, the civilization of the Semitic Babylonians and Assyrians was borrowed from this older civilization along with the cuneiform system of writing. It seemed impossible that so revolutionary a doctrine could be true, and Semitic philologists naturally denounced it. For centuries Hebrew had been supposed to have been the language of Paradise, and the old belief which made the Semitic Adam the first civilized man still unconsciously affected the Semitic scholars of the nineteenth century. It was hard to part with the prejudices of early education, especially when they were called upon to do so by a small group of men whose method of decipherment was an enigma to the ordinary grammarian, and who were introducing new and dangerous principles into the study of the extinct Semitic tongues. The method of decipherment was nevertheless a sound one, and the result, which seemed so incredible and impossible when first announced, is now one of the assured facts of science.'[6]

To emphasize his argument, Sayce added that it was impossible for Semite people to have adopted Sumerian from later conquerors: 'The first civilized occupants of the alluvial plain of Babylonia were neither Semites nor Aryans, but the speakers of an agglutinative language, and to them were due all the elements of the Babylonian culture of later days . . . This, then, was the great archaeological fact which resulted from the decipherment of the Assyro-Babylonian texts. The earliest civilized inhabitants of Babylonia did not speak a Semitic language, and therefore presumably they were not Semites. It is perfectly true that language and race are not synonymous terms, and that we are seldom justified in arguing from the one to the other. But the Sumerian language is one of the exceptions which proves the rule. Those who spoke it were the first civilizers of Western Asia, the inventors and perfecters of a system of writing which was destined to be one of the chief humanizing agents of the ancient world.'[7]

One sign of a civilized society is a system of laws and justice, and an extremely important discovery was made at the mound of Susa, which Jacques de Morgan, a French geologist and engineer, had been excavating with spectacular results since 1897, in stark contrast to the disappointing results of Loftus nearly five decades before. At the end of 1901, de Morgan dug up one of the most important monuments in Mesopotamia, which is now on display in the Louvre – the law code of Hammurabi, engraved in over 3,500 lines of cuneiform on a black basalt stele 7 feet 4 inches tall. Hammurabi was king of Babylon from 1792 to 1750 BC, and he greatly enlarged his empire so that he became sole ruler of all Mesopotamia. It was not a law code in the modern sense, since it was not a codification of all law. Instead, it was a series of cases that not only give information about ideas of justice, but illuminate everyday life. It was realized with astonishment that these laws were centuries older than law codes in the Bible, and yet they contain many striking similarities.

The laws covered a range of issues, such as property ('If a man have stolen the goods of a god or palace, that man shall be put to death'),[8] business ('If a man be in debt, and sell his wife, his son, or his daughter for the money, or has handed them over to service, for three years they shall work in the house of their purchaser or exploiter; in the fourth year they shall be set at liberty'),[9] women ('If a man's wife causes her husband to be killed for the sake of another man, they shall impale that woman'),[10] assault ('If a man have knocked out the tooth of a man of his own rank, they shall knock out his tooth'),[11] services ('If a doctor have operated, with a bronze lancet, on a man for a severe wound, and have caused the man's death, or have removed a cataract, with a bronze lancet, and have destroyed the man's eye, they shall cut off his hand')[12] and agriculture ('If a man have hired an ox or an ass, and a lion kill it in the field, it is the owner's loss').[13]

At the top of the stele is a carved sculpture representing King Hammurabi standing before Shamash, god of the sun and of justice, whose religious centre was at Sippar, situated on the banks of the Euphrates, 20 miles south-west of Baghdad. The stele had been erected by Hammurabi at Sippar, but it had been looted by Elamite raiders and taken back to the city of Susa, where it was discovered by de Morgan. Several years before the discovery of this stele, Rassam had excavated the mound of Sippar, including part of the temple to Shamash, as well as some 150 rooms surrounding the ziggurat. He found thousands of clay tablets and cylinders, and a century later excavations in the same part of the site revealed a library of hundreds of clay tablets that were still filed in pigeonholes.

Also at Sippar, Rassam found a cylinder of Nabonidus that produced evidence for this king being the earliest archaeologist in Mesopotamia. The son of a nobleman and of a priestess of the moon god Sin at Harran in south-eastern Turkey, Nabonidus became the last Babylonian king, ruling from 555 BC after apparently murdering the legitimate heir to the throne. Nabonidus tried to make Sin the chief deity of his empire in place of Marduk, the patron god of Babylon, and this caused great disquiet. He had temples of different cults rebuilt, including the temple of Sin at

Harran, and made sure that the early foundations were exposed so that he could read the inscriptions deposited by his predecessors. The cylinder of Nabonidus from Sippar related that when he dug down to the original foundations of the temple of Shamash, he found 'the foundation stone of Naram-Sin, which no king had found for 3,200 years'.[14]

For unknown reasons, Nabonidus turned his back on his capital city of Babylon and spent much of his reign at the oasis town of Tayma in the Arabian desert, leaving his son Belshazzar to rule Babylonia. He returned in about 543 BC, but by then it was too late to face up to the threat in the east: the advance of the Persian Empire under its king Cyrus the Great. In 539 BC Cyrus marched into Babylonia and defeated Belshazzar. Sippar surrendered, and Babylon was taken without a struggle.

In excavations at Babylon, Rassam had also discovered what became known as the Cyrus Cylinder. Its cuneiform inscription described how Marduk, patron god of the city, had called on Cyrus for help against Nabonidus: 'To his city Babylon he [Marduk] caused him [Cyrus] to go, he made him take the road to Babylon, going as a friend and companion at his side . . . Without battle and conflict he permitted him to enter Babylon. He spared his city Babylon a calamity. Nabonidus, who did not fear him, he delivered into his hand.'[15] The second part of the cylinder related events from the point of view of the Persian king: 'I am Cyrus, king of the world, the great king, the powerful king, king of Babylon, king of Sumer, king of the four quarters of the world.'[16] It went on to relate that Cyrus had captured Babylon peacefully, restored the worship of Marduk, returned to their shrines images of gods that had been brought into Babylon by Nabonidus and allowed deported peoples to return to their homes – 'All their inhabitants I collected and restored them to their dwelling places'[17] – a reference that included the return to Jerusalem of the Jews who had been captured by Nebuchadnezzar nearly fifty years earlier.

Cyrus continued the expansion of the Persian Empire, but was killed in battle nine years after his capture of Babylon. His son Cambyses II became king, but he in turn died in 522 BC when hurrying back from the newly conquered Egypt to suppress Gaumata, who had usurped the throne in his absence. Darius the Great then became king, and after his many ruthless victories over the rebel leaders throughout the Persian Empire, he had the trilingual cuneiform inscription carved at Bisitun – the inscription that was to survive for over two thousand years, shape the life of Henry Rawlinson, and provide the catalyst for discoveries that would change our perception of history and the very roots of civilization itself.

Notes

Abbreviations
Add mss: Additional manuscripts (in the British Library)
BL: British Library
Excursion from Baghdad 1847: RGS Rawlinson archives, number 10
Journal of an exile: in RAS archives, written from 6 July 1827
JRAS: Journal of the Royal Asiatic Society
JRGS: Journal of the Royal Geographical Society
Personal adventures: in RGS archives, number 15
RAS archives: Rawlinson archives in the Royal Asiatic Society
RGS archives: Rawlinson archives in the Royal Geographical Society
Rough annuary: in RAS archives, a black leather notebook 'Rough annuary of Sir Henry Creswicke Rawlinson begun Oct 31 21 Charles St, finished Dec 1884' – a year-by-year summary of his life, with annotations by one of his sons, probably Harry

One: Into India
1 G. Rawlinson 1898, p 4
2 Ibid.
3 RAS archives: Journal for 12 December 1827
4 RAS archives: Rough annuary
5 Ibid.
6 *The Times*, 12 August 1890, p 7
7 G. Rawlinson 1898, p 12
8 Ibid., p 16
9 Ibid., p 15
10 RAS archives: Rough annuary
11 RAS archives: Journal of an exile
12–15 Ibid.
16 Cary 1820, p 15
17 RAS archives: Journal of an exile
18–27 Ibid.
28 Cary 1820, p 16

29 RGS archives: Personal adventures
30 RAS archives: Journal of an exile
31 Ibid.
32 RGS archives: Personal adventures
33 RAS archives: Journal of an exile

Two: From Poona to Panwell

1 RAS archives: Journal for 2 December 1827
2–4 Ibid.
5 Ibid., 3 December 1827
6–7 Ibid.
8 Ibid., 4 December 1827
9 Ibid., 5 December 1827
10 Ibid., 9 December 1827
11–12 Ibid.
13 Ibid., 11 December 1827
14 Ibid., 14 December 1827
15 Ibid.
16 Ibid., 16 December 1827
17 Ibid., 17 December 1827
18 Ibid., 18 December 1827
19 Ibid., 22 December 1827
20 Ibid., 23 December 1827
21 Ibid., 24 December 1827
22 Ibid., 25 December 1827
23 Ibid., 24–28 January 1828
24 Ibid., 16 February 1828
25–26 Ibid.
27 Ibid., 16 February, 11 March 1828
28–30 Ibid., 11 March 1828
31 RGS archives: Personal adventures

32 RAS archives: Journal for 5 February 1828
33 Ibid., 16 February 1828
34 Ibid.
35 Ibid., mid-March 1828 [no specific date given]
36 Ibid., 2 May 1828
37 Ibid., 23 November 1828
38 RGS archives: Personal adventures
39 RAS archives: Journal for 6 July 1828
40 Ibid., 23 November 1828
41 Ibid., 21 October 1828
42 Ibid., 24 October 1828
43 Ibid., 25 October 1828
44 Ibid., 29 October 1828
45 Ibid., 31 October 1828
46 Ibid., 11 November 1828
47 RGS archives: Personal adventures
48 RAS archives: Rough annuary
49 RAS archives: Journal for 10 December 1828
50 RAS archives: Rough annuary
51 Ibid.
52 RGS archives: Journal for 11 April 1831
53 RAS archives: Rough annuary for 1830
54 G. Rawlinson 1898, p 27
55 RGS archives: Personal adventures
56 G. Rawlinson 1898, p 28

57 RGS archives: Personal adventures
58 RAS archives: Rough annuary

Three: In the Service of the Shah
1 G. Rawlinson 1898, p 36
2 Ibid.
3 RGS archives: Personal adventures
4–9 Ibid. (similar account in G. Rawlinson 1898, pp 37–9)
10 G. Rawlinson 1898, p 39
11 RGS archives: Personal adventures
12 The Saturday Magazine, 14 March 1840, pp 99–100
13 RGS archives: Personal adventures
14 G. Rawlinson 1898, p 40
15 Ibid., p 42
16 Ibid., p 43
17 Ibid., p 44
18 G. Rawlinson 1875, p 262 note 1 by Henry Rawlinson
19 G. Rawlinson 1898, p 47
20 RGS archives: Journal for 18 October 1834
21 Kaye 1874, vol. 1, p 141
22 G. Rawlinson 1898, p 48
23–24 Ibid., p 51
25–26 Ibid., p 53
27 RGS archives: Journal for 1831, overwritten on 11 April 1835
28 Rawlinson 1846–47, p 5

Four: The Cuneiform Conundrum
1 Genesis 9, verse 1
2 Ibid., 11, verses 3–9
3 Ibid., 11, verse 7

Five: Discovering Darius
1 Booth 1902, p 15
2 Ibid., p 19
3 Ibid., p 28 (Budge 1925, p 15, quotes the original Italian version)
4 Ibid., p 28 (ibid., p 16, quotes the original Italian version)
5 JRAS 15, 1855, Annual report for May 1854, pp ix–x (report by a former pupil)
6 Layard 1887, vol 1, pp 224–5
7 RAS archives: Rough annuary
8 G. Rawlinson 1898, p 57
9 RAS archives: Rough annuary
10 Ibid.
11 RGS archives: Personal adventures
12 RAS archives: Rough annuary
13 Ross 1902, p 34 fn 1, added to a letter of Henry Ross by his wife Janet
14 RAS archives: Rough annuary
15 Rawlinson 1839, p 28
16 Jones 1857, p 159
17 Rawlinson 1839, pp 33–4
18 Ibid., p 31

19 Ibid., pp 37–8
20 Jones 1857, p 159
21 Rawlinson 1839, p 50
22–23 Ibid., p 52
24 Ibid., p 68
25 Ibid., pp 68–9
26 Ibid., p 69
27 G. Rawlinson 1898, p 63
28 Rawlinson 1839, p 71
29 Ibid., p 73
30 Ibid., p 79
31 Ibid., p 104
32 Ibid., p 105
33 G. Rawlinson 1898, p 63
34 Ibid., pp 63–4
35–36 Ibid., p 64
37 Ibid., p 62
38 Ibid., pp 62–3
39 Rawlinson 1839, p 100

Six: Bewitched by Bisitun

1 Rawlinson 1852, p 74
2 Porter 1822, p 154
3 Ibid., p 154
4 Ibid., pp 157–8
5 Ibid., p 158
6 Flandin 1851, pp 418, 421, 448
7 Ibid., pp 448, 450
8 Ibid., pp 450–1
9 Ibid., pp 451–2
10 Rawlinson 1852, p 74
11 Rawlinson 1846–47, p 6
12 RAS archive, unlocated; published in Borger 1975–78, p 1, but wrongly as 1835
13 Ibid.
14 RGS archives: Personal adventures

15 Rawlinson 1846–47, p 7
16 Ibid.
17 RGS archives: Journal for 1831, overwritten on 11 April 1837
18–19 Ibid.
20 RGS archives: Personal adventures

Seven: Royal Societies

1 Kaye 1874, vol 1, pp 193–4 fn quoting a private letter from Rawlinson
2 Ibid., p 194
3 RGS archives: letter of 10 January 1838
4 Ibid., 16 February 1838
5 Rawlinson 1846–47, p 7
6 RAS archives: letter of 1 January 1838
7 G. Rawlinson 1898, p 311
8 Ibid.
9 Ibid., p 312
10 *JRAS* 5, 1839, Annual report for May 1838, p ix
11 Ibid., pp ix–x
12 Ibid., p x
13 Burnouf 1836, p 2
14 Rawlinson 1846–47, p 8
15 RAS archives: letter of 30 July 1838
16 Ibid.
17 Rawlinson 1846–47, p 8
18 RGS archives: Personal adventures
19 G. Rawlinson 1898, p 68
20 Rawlinson 1841, pp 5–6
21–22 Ibid., p 9
23 Ibid., pp 16–17

24–26 Ibid., p 20
27 Ibid., p 21
28 Ibid., pp 20–1
29 Ibid., p 21
30 Ibid., p 24
31 Ibid., pp 27–8
32 Ibid., p 43
33 Ibid., p 53
34 Ibid., p 55
35–36 Ibid., p 56
37 *The Times*, 2 June 1860, p 6
38 Rawlinson 1846–47, p 14
39 G. Rawlinson 1898, p 317
40 Rawlinson 1846–47, p 10
41 Ibid., p 11
42 Ibid., p 10–11
43 *JRGS* 10, 1841, The President's address on presenting medals on 25 May 1840, p xiii
44 RAS archives: letter of 25 July 1839
45–46 Ibid., 21 August 1839
47 Rawlinson 1846–47, p 14

Eight: An Afghan Adventure

1 RGS archives: Journal for 2 January 1840
2 Neill 1845, p 3
3 Mitford 1884, vol 2, pp 113–14
4 *The Saturday Magazine*, 21 September 1839, p 111
5 Kaye 1878, p 9
6 Ibid., p 71
7 Neill 1845, pp 144–5
8 Ibid., p 145
9 G. Rawlinson 1898, p 77

10 Kaye 1878, p 103
11 Stocqueler 1854, vol 1, p 165
12 Ibid., pp 256–7
13–14 Ibid., p 227
15 Ibid., p 158
16 Mitford 1884, vol 2, pp 102, 103, 104
17 Ibid., pp 102–3
18 Mitford 1884, vol 1, p vii
19 Rawlinson 1843, p 112
20 Ibid., pp 113, 114
21 Kaye 1878, p 123
22 Ibid., pp 125–6, 127
23 G. Rawlinson 1898, p 82
24 Ibid., pp 88–9
25 Ibid., p 83
26 Kaye 1874, vol 3, pp 125–6
27 G. Rawlinson 1898, p 86
28 Neill 1845, p 151
29 Ibid., p 331
30 RGS archives: Personal adventures
31 Ibid.
32 Neill 1845, p 166
33 RGS archives: Political journal for 17 February 1842
34 Neill 1845, p 188
35 Kaye 1874, vol 3, p 153
36 G. Rawlinson 1898, p 107
37 RGS archives: Journal for 1831, overwritten on 11 April 1842
38 Ibid.
39 Kaye 1874, vol 3, pp 203–4
40 RGS archives: Political journal for 7 August 1842

41 Kaye 1874, vol 3, p 337
42 Ibid., p 338 from Rawlinson's journal
43 Ibid., pp 343–4 from Rawlinson's journal
44 *The Saturday Magazine*, 21 September 1839, p 111
45 Kaye 1874, vol 3, p 346, Rawlinson's journal of 14 September 1842
46 Ibid., p 348, letter from Nott to Pollock, 17 September 1842
47 Ibid., p 369 from Rawlinson's journal
48 Neill 1845, p 273
49 *Leisure Hour* 26 1877, p 522

Nine: Back to Baghdad
 1 G. Rawlinson 1898, p 136
 2 RAS archives: Rough annuary
 3 G. Rawlinson 1898, p 137
 4 Ibid.
 5 RAS archives: Rough annuary
 6 *The Athenaeum*, 8 November 1884, p 593
 7 Mitford 1884, vol 1, p 309
 8 Ibid., p 310
 9 G. Rawlinson 1898, p 140
10 Jones 1857, p 339
11 Ibid., p 311
12 Layard 1903, vol 1, pp 327, 342–3
13 Ibid., p 341
14 Ibid., p 328
15 Ibid., p 341
16 G. Rawlinson 1898, p 142

17 Ross 1902, p 34
18 G. Rawlinson 1898, pp 142–3
19 Rawlinson 1846–47, pp 14–15
20 Ibid., p 14
21 BL Add mss 47658, f 5–8 (grammar altered slightly)
22–23 Ibid.
24 Rawlinson 1846–47, p 15
25 Jones 1857, p 137
26 Ibid., p 137
27 Ibid., p 145
28 Ibid., p 152
29 Ibid., p 155
30 Ibid., p 158
31 Ibid., p 159
32 Ibid., pp 176, 178
33–34 Ibid., p 176
35 Ibid., p 184
36 Rawlinson 1852, p 74
37 Jones 1857, p 177
38 Rawlinson 1852, pp 74–5
39 Ibid., pp 74–5
40 Ibid., p 75
41 Ibid., p 76
42 Jones 1857, p 179
43 Rawlinson 1846–47, pp 192–3
44 Jones 1857, p 180
45 Rawlinson 1846–47, p 193
46 Jones 1857, p 184
47 Mitford 1884, vol 1, p 353
48 Jones 1857, p 184
49 Ibid., p 177
50 Ibid., p 188

Ten: Introduction to Layard
 1 Jones 1857, p 189

2 Ibid., p 189
3 Ibid., p 197
4 Ibid., p 198
5–8 Ibid., p 200
9 Ibid., pp 201–2
10 Ibid., pp 202–3
11 Ibid., p 204
12 Ibid., p 209
13 Ibid., p 212
14 RAS archives: Rough
    annuary
15 RGS archives: Personal
    adventures
16 Ross 1902, p 34
17 Ibid., p 34
18 Ibid., pp 34–5
19 Ibid., p 36
20 Rawlinson 1846–47, p lxi
21 Ibid., p 16
22 Layard 1903, vol 1, p 12
23 Ibid., p 14
24 Ibid., p 13
25 Ibid., p 15
26 Ibid., p 24
27 Ibid., pp 26–7
28 Ibid., p 38
29 Ibid., p 39
30 Ibid., p 40
31–32 Ibid., p 39
33 Ibid., p 40
34 Ibid., p 44
35 Ibid., p 45
36 Ibid., p 94
37 Ibid., p 103
38 Ibid., p 107
39 Ibid., pp 108–9
40 Ibid., p 153
41 Ibid., p 156
42 Ibid., p 209

43 Ibid., pp 245–6
44 Ibid., p 263
45 Layard 1894, p 18
46 Layard 1903, vol 1, pp 305,
    309
47 Mitford 1884, vol 1, p 280
48–49 Layard 1903, vol 1,
    p 309
50 Ibid., p 305
51 Ibid., p 306
52 Ibid., pp 306–7
53 Ibid., p 320
54 Ibid., p 311
55 Ibid., pp 313–14
56–57 Ibid., p 325
58 Ibid., pp 349–50
59 Ibid., p 350
60–61 Ibid., p 351
62 Mitford 1884, vol 1, p 352
63 Ibid., pp 352–3
64 Layard 1887, vol 1, p 227
65 Ibid., p 228
66 Ibid., p 229
67 Mitford 1884, vol 1, p 348
68 Ibid., pp 349–50
69 Layard 1887, vol 1, p 242
70 Mitford 1884, vol 1, p 367
71 Layard 1887, vol 1, p 272
72 Layard 1903, vol 2, p 5
73 Layard 1894, p 385
74 Layard 1887, vol 2, p 369
75 Layard 1903, vol 2,
    pp 107–8
76–77 Ibid., p 108
78 Ibid., p 103
79 BL Add mss 38976, f 141–2
80 BL Add mss 38976, f 158–9
81 Ibid.

Eleven: Old Persian Published

1 RGS archives: Journal for
    1831, overwritten on 11
    April 1845
2–4 Ibid.
5 BL Add mss 38976, f 158–9
6 Cust 1895, pp 684–5
7 BL Add mss 38976, f 158–9
8 BL Add mss 38976, f 182–5
9 BL Add mss 38976, f 158–9
10 BL Add mss 38976, f 182–5
11 BL Add mss 38976,
    f 188–90
12 Ibid.
13 *JRAS* 8, 1846, Annual
    report for June 1845, p x
14 BL Add mss 38976, f 195–6
15 BL Add mss 38976,
    f 211–14
16 Ibid.
17 BL Add mss 38976, f 220–1
18–20 Ibid.
21 BL Add mss 38976,
    f 227–8
22 Layard 1849, vol 2,
    pp 193–4 fn
23 Rawlinson 1846–47, p xl
24 Ibid., p liii
25 Ibid., p liv
26 Ibid., p lvi
27 Ibid., pp lvi–lvii
28 Ibid., p lxvii
29 Ibid., pp lxix–lxx
30–32 Ibid., p 18
33 Ibid., p 19
34 Ibid., p 20
35 BL Add mss 38976, f 227–8
36 Rawlinson 1846–47, p 29
37 Ibid., p 29

38 Ibid., p 33
39 BL Add mss 38976, f 147–8
40 Ibid.
41 BL Add mss 38976, f 170–1
42 Layard 1903, vol 2,
    pp 152–3
43 Layard 1849, vol 1, pp 21–2
44 Ross 1902, p 41
45 Layard 1849, vol 1, p 25
46 Layard 1903, vol 2,
    pp 158–9
47 BL Add mss 38976, f 240–2
48 Ibid.
49 Layard 1849, vol 1, p 26
50 Ibid., pp 26–7
51 Ibid., p 27
52 Layard 1903, vol 2, p 158
53 Layard 1849, vol 1, p 33
54 Ibid., p 40
55 Layard 1903, vol 2,
    pp 160–1; BL Add mss
    58149, f 207
56 Layard 1849, vol 1, pp 44–5
57 Layard 1903, vol 2, p 161;
    BL Add mss 58149, f 207
58 Layard 1903, vol 2, p 161
59 BL Add mss 38976, f 255–6
60 Ibid.
61 RAS archives: letter of 27
    November 1845
62 BL Add mss 38976, f 255–6
63 Ibid.
64 BL Add mss 38976, f 274–6
65 Ibid.
66 *Genesis* 10, verses 8–12
67 Layard 1903, vol 2, p 159
68 *Genesis* 10, verses 11–12
69 BL Add mss 38976, f 274–6
70 Ibid.

71 Layard 1849, vol 1,
    pp 49–50

Twelve: Nimrud, Niffer and Nineveh

 1 BL Add mss 58149, f 211–
   12
 2 Ibid.
 3 Layard 1849, vol 1, p 53
 4 Ibid., p 55
 5 BL Add mss 38976, f 294–5
 6 Layard 1849, vol 1, p 65
 7 Ibid., p 66
 8 Ibid., pp 66–7
 9 Ibid., p 69
10 Layard 1903, vol 2, p 162
11 RGS archives: Personal
   adventures
12–15 Ibid.
16 BL Add mss 38976, f 324–7
17 Layard 1849, vol 1, pp 77–8
18 Ibid., pp 69–70
19 Layard 1903, vol 2, p 164
20 BL Add mss 38976,
   f 339–40
21 Ibid.
22 Lane-Poole 1888, pp 148–9
23 Layard 1903, vol 2,
   pp 155–6
24 BL Add mss 38976, f 335–6
25 BL Add mss 38976, f 339–
   40
26 Layard 1849, vol 1, p 139
27 RAS archives: letter of 27
   March 1846
28 Rawlinson 1846–47, p 188
29 *JRAS* 9, 1848, Annual
   report for June 1846, p xiv
30 Rawlinson 1846–47, p 194

31 Ibid., p 206
32 Ibid., p 258
33 Ibid., p 261
34–35 Ibid., p 262
36 Ibid., pp 228–9
37 Ibid., p 219
38 Ibid., pp 265–8 [there are no
   pages numbered 266–7]
39–40 Ibid., p 269
41 Ibid., p 349
42 BL Add mss 38976, f 351–2
43 Layard 1849, vol 1,
   pp 123–4
44 Ibid., p 129
45 Ibid., p 130
46 Ibid., p 131
47 Layard 1903, vol 2, p 169
48 Ibid., pp 169–70
49 BL Add mss 38976, f 362–4
50 Ibid.
51 Layard 1903, vol 2, p 172

Thirteen: An Irish Intruder

 1 Layard 1903, vol 2,
   p 173
 2 BL Add mss 38976,
   f 362–4
 3 BL Add mss 38976,
   f 395–400
 4 Ibid.
 5 BL Add mss 38977, f 5–6
 6 BL Add mss 38977, f 13–15
 7 Layard 1903, vol 2, p 173
 8 Layard 1849, vol 1, p 140
 9 Ibid., p 142
10 Layard 1903, vol 2,
   pp 172–3
11 BL Add mss 38977, f 18–19
12 BL Add mss 38977, f 25–7

13 Rawlinson 1846–47, p 185
14 Layard 1867, p 112
15 BL Add mss 38977, f 33–6
16 BL Add mss 38977, f 54–9
17 Ibid.
18 Layard 1849, vol 1,
    pp 325–6
19 Ibid., pp 326–7
20 BL Add mss 38977, f 54–9
21 *Literary Gazette*, 27 June
    1846, p 579
22 *JRAS* 9, 1848 report of
    meeting of 16 May 1846,
    noted in the annual report
    for June 1846, p xvii
23 Davidson 1933, p 136
24 *Literary Gazette*, 25 July
    1846, p 667
25 Davidson 1933, p 137
26 Ibid.
27 BL Add mss 38977, f 68–9
28–29 Ibid.
30 Davidson 1933, p 137
31 Ibid., pp 137–8
32 *The Athenaeum*, 19 December
    1846, p 1302
33 *The Athenaeum*, 15 November
    1884, p 624
34 Ibid.
35 *The Athenaeum*, 22 November
    1884, p 659
36 RAS archives: letter of 14
    October 1846
37 Ibid.
38 Davidson 1933, p 138
39 Layard 1867, p 228
40 Ibid., p 229
41 Layard 1849, vol 1, p 350
42 Ibid., pp 345–7
43 Ibid., pp 363–4
44 BL Add mss 38977, f 88–91
45 Layard 1849, vol 1, p 371

Fourteen: Battling with Babylonian

 1 BL Add mss 38977, f 153–5
 2 BL Add mss 38977, f 161–4
 3 Ibid.
 4 Davidson 1933, p 138
 5 Hincks 1848a, pp 241–2
 6 Ibid., p 244
 7 Davidson 1933, p 138
 8 Ibid., pp 138–9
 9–11 Ibid., p 139
12 Layard 1849, vol 2, p 47
13 Ibid., p 54
14 BL Add mss 38977, f 192–4
15–16 Ibid.
17 Davidson 1933, pp 140–1
18 Hincks 1848b, p 249
19 Ibid., p 249
20 Ibid., p 250
21 Davidson 1933, p 141
22–23 Ibid., p 141
24 Ibid., p 142
25 Layard 1867, p 316
26 Layard 1903, vol 2,
    pp 177–8
27 BL Add mss 38977, f 201–2
28 BL Add mss 38977,
    f 208–10
29 Ibid.
30 BL Add mss 38977,
    f 219–24
31–32 Ibid.
33 *Dublin University Magazine*,
    1847, p 16
34 Ibid., p 18

35 Ibid., p 19
36 Ibid., p 21
37 Ibid., pp 21–2
38 BL Add mss 38977,
    f 219–24
39 RGS archives: Journal for
    1831, overwritten on 11
    April 1847
40–42 Ibid.
43 BL Add mss 38977,
    f 219–24
44 Layard 1867, p 322
45 Ibid., pp 326–7
46 Ibid., p 290
47 Ibid., p 343
48 Ross 1902, p 48
49 Layard 1867, p 346
50 Ibid., pp 357–8
51 Layard 1849, vol 2, p 124
52 Layard 1867, p 374
53 RGS archives: Excursion
    from Baghdad
54–59 Ibid.
60 RAS archives: letter of 20
    July 1847
61–67 Ibid.
68 RGS archives: Excursion
    from Baghdad
69–72 Ibid.
73 RAS archives: letter of 20
    September 1847
74 Rawlinson 1852, p 75
75 Ibid., p 76
76 Ibid., p 75
77 BL Add mss 38977, f 334–7
78 RAS archives: letter of 20
    September 1847
79 BL Add mss 38977, f 334–7
80 Rawlinson 1852, pp 75–6

81 BL Add mss 38977, f 334–7
82 RAS archives: letter of 20
    September 1847
83–84 Ibid.
85 BL Add mss 38977, f 334–7
86 Ibid.
87 RAS archives: Rough
    annuary

Fifteen: A Brief Encounter

1 Davidson 1933, p 143
2 Ibid.
3 Layard 1903, vol 2,
   p 185
4 Ross 1902, p 144
5 Ibid., p 151
6 Davidson 1933, pp 146–7
7 Ibid., p 148
8 BL Add mss 38978, f 23–6
9–10 Ibid.
11 *JRAS* 9, 1848, Annual
    report 13 May 1848, p viii
12–13 Ibid.
14 BL Add mss 38978, f 53–4
15 Ibid.
16 BL Add mss 38978, f 90–2
17 Layard 1903, vol 2, p 189
18 Hincks 1848c, p 432
19 Ross 1902, p 155
20 Ibid.
21 BL Add mss 38978,
    f 115–16
22 BL Add mss 38978, f 193–5
23–24 Ibid.
25 BL Add mss 38978, f 228–9
26 BL Add mss 38978,
    f 239–40
27 BL Add mss 38978, f 263–4
28 BL Add mss 38978, f 77–9

29 RAS archives: letter of 15
    January 1849
30 BL Add mss 38978, f 252–3
31 Ibid.
32 BL Add mss 38978, f 263–4
33 Davidson 1933, p 153
34 *Dublin University Magazine*,
    1849, pp 427–8
35 RGS archives: Journal for
    1831, overwritten on 11
    April 1849
36–37 Ibid.
38 Loftus 1857, p 7
39 Ibid., pp 7–8
40 Ibid., p 8
41 BL Add mss 38978, f 347–9
42 Loftus 1857, p 9
43 Davidson 1933, p 150
44 *Literary Gazette*, 11 August
    1849, p 590
45 Davidson 1933, p 142
46–48 *Literary Gazette*, 11
    August 1849, p 590
49 Hincks 1850, p 6
50 Ibid., p 19
51 BL Add mss 38978, f 347–9
52–53 Ibid.
54 BL Add mss 38978,
    f 357–60
55 Ibid.
56 BL Add mss 38978, f 369
57 Layard 1853, p 474
58 BL Add mss 38979, f 10–13
59 *JRAS* 11, 1849, Annual
    report for May 1849, p viii
60 Rawlinson 1849, p 192
61 Layard 1853, p 69
62 Ibid., p 75
63 Ibid., p 98

64 Ibid., p 100
65 BL Add mss 47660
66 BL Add mss 39096
67 BL Add mss 47660
68–69 Ibid.
70 BL Add mss 39096
71 Layard 1853, p 100
72 Davidson 1933, p 152
73 Ibid., p 153
74–75 Ibid., p 152
76 Ibid., p 154
77 RAS archives: Rough
    annuary
78 Ibid.

Sixteen: Celebrity

1 G. Rawlinson 1898,
   pp 162–3
2 Ibid., pp 161–2
3 Davidson 1933, p 20
4 RGS archives: Personal
   adventures
5 *Literary Gazette*, 26 January
   1850, p 63
6 *Literary Gazette*, 23 February
   1850, p 145
7 Ibid.
8 Rawlinson 1850a, p 408
9 Ibid., p 409
10 Ibid., pp 403–4
11 Ibid., p 404
12–13 Ibid., p 431
14 Ibid., p 447
15 Ibid., p 483
16 Ibid., p 401
17 Ibid., p 401
18 Ibid., p 402
19 Davidson 1933, p 155
20 Rawlinson 1852, p 73

21 BL Add mss 38979, f 159–60

22 Ibid.

23 BL Add mss 38979, f 157–8

24 Ibid.

25 BL Add mss 38979, f 215–16

26 Rawlinson 1850b, p I

27 Ibid., p XIX

28 BL Add mss 38979, f 157–8

29 Layard 1903, vol 2, p 191

30 Ibid., pp 191–2

31 Ibid., p 191

32 Davidson 1933, p 155

33 Ibid., p 156

34 Ibid., pp 157–8

35 Ibid., pp 156–7

36 G. Rawlinson 1898, pp 165–6

37 Ibid., pp 166–7

38 BL Add mss 38979, f 215–16

39 Ibid.

40 *JRAS* 13, 1852, Annual report for May 1850, p viii

41–42 Ibid., p xx

43 *The Athenaeum*, May 1850, p 555

44 Ibid.

45 Davidson 1933, pp 158–9

46 Ibid., p 159

47 *Literary Gazette*, 8 June 1850, p 394

48 G. Rawlinson 1898, p 167

49 Ibid., pp 168–9

50 Ibid., p 169

51 Layard 1853, p 205

52 Ibid., pp 345–6

53 Walpole 1851, p 21

54 *JRAS* 13, 1852, Annual report for May 1850, p viii

Seventeen: Rivals

1 Davidson 1933, p 46

2 Ibid., p 46

3–6 Ibid., p 160

7 *Literary Gazette*, 17 August 1850, p 584

8–9 Ibid.

10 *The Athenaeum*, 24 August 1850, p 908

11–12 Ibid.

13 *Literary Gazette*, 17 August 1850, p 585

14–15 Ibid.

16 Loftus 1857, p 203

17 *Literary Gazette*, 17 August 1850, p 585

18 Davidson 1933, p 161

19–20 Ibid.

21 BL Add mss 38979, f 283–5

22–24 Ibid.

25 Layard 1853, p 473

26 Ibid., pp 475–6

27 Ibid., p 485

28 BL Add mss 38979, f 404–5

29 RAS archives: Rough annuary

30 BL Add mss 38979, f 404–5

31 Layard 1853, p 527

32 Ibid., p 568

33 *JRAS* 13, 1852, Annual report for May 1851, pp vi–vii

34 *The Athenaeum*, 13 September 1851, p 977

35–36 Davidson 1933, p 49

37 Ibid., p 49–50
38 Ibid., p 167
39 *The Athenaeum*, 27 December 1851, p 1384
40 *The Athenaeum*, 23 August 1851, p 903
41 Pallis 1956, p 157
42 Rawlinson 1851, p xviii
43 Ibid., p xxii
44 Voigtlander 1978, p 54
45–46 Rawlinson 1851, p xx
47–48 Ibid., unpaginated 'Note by Colonel Rawlinson'
49 Ibid., p 1
50–51 Ibid., p 2
52 Norris 1855, p 163
53 Ibid.
54 Jackson 1906, p 187
55 Ibid., p 187
56 Ibid., p 192
57–58 Ibid., p 195
59 Ibid., p 192

Eighteen: Magic at Borsippa

1 Loftus 1857, p 356
2 Jones 1857, p 459
3–5 Ibid., p 431
6–7 Ibid., p 439
8 Hincks 1852, p 295
9 Ibid., p 295
10 Ibid., p 305
11 Ibid., p 307
12 Ibid., p 363
13 RGS archives: Personal adventures
14 Ibid.
15 Ibid; L. Jessop personal communication
16 Rassam 1897, p 16

17 *JRAS* 15, 1855, Annual report for May 1853, p xvi
18 Ibid.
19 Hincks 1852, p 352
20 *JRAS* 15, 1855, Annual report for May 1853, p xviii
21 Ibid., p xix
22 *The Athenaeum*, 23 July 1853, p 893
23 Layard 1853, p 139
24 Davidson 1933, p 53
25 BL Add mss 38981, f 299–302
26 Ibid.
27 *The Athenaeum*, 18 February 1854, p 215
28 Ibid., p 216
29 Rassam 1897, p 23
30 Ibid., p 26
31 Ibid., p 27
32 Ibid., p 31
33 Ibid., p 33
34 G. Rawlinson 1898, p 173
35 *JRAS* 15, 1855, annual report for May 1854, pp x–xi
36 Ibid., p xv
37 RAS archives: letter of 9 August 1854
38 Ibid.
39 *The Athenaeum*, 16 December 1854, p 1529
40 Rawlinson 1861, p 4
41 Ibid., p 2
42 Ibid., pp 2–3
43–44 Ibid., p 3
45 RAS archives: Rough annuary
46 Ibid.
47 G Rawlinson 1898, p 199

48 *JRAS* 16, 1856, Annual report for May 1855, pp ii–iii

Nineteen: The Final Test

1 *The Athenaeum*, 19 February 1853, p 228
2 *The Athenaeum*, 8 December 1855, p 1438
3 Ibid., referred to by Hincks 1859, p 44 in a footnote incorrectly dated 1852
4 Hincks 1858, p 137
5 Davidson 1933, p 205
6 Ibid., pp 205–6
7 Ibid., p 206
8 *The Athenaeum* 23 May 1857, p 663
9 *JRAS* 15, 1855, Annual report for May 1854, p xvi
10 Ibid.
11 Talbot et al. 1861, p 150
12 Ibid., pp 150–1
13 Ibid., p 151
14 *The Athenaeum*, 4 April 1857, p 440
15 Ibid.
16 *The Athenaeum*, 27 June 1857, p 822
17 *The Athenaeum*, 23 May 1857, p 663
18–20 Ibid.
21 Talbot et al. 1861, pp 155–6
22–23 Ibid., p 153
24 Cust 1895, p 689
25 G. Rawlinson 1898, p 222
26 Ibid., pp 224–5
27 RGS archives: Journal for 5 May 1860
28 G. Rawlinson 1898, p 232

29 *The Times*, 2 June 1860, p 6
30 Ibid.
31–2 *The Athenaeum*, 31 May 1862, p 724
33 Ibid., p 728
34 G. Rawlinson 1898, p 242
35 RAS archives: Rough annuary
36 *Frome Times*, 19 July 1865, p 1
37 Davidson 1933, p 189
38 Ibid., p 238
39 Ibid., p 249
40 Ibid., p 28
41 *The Athenaeum*, 22 December 1866, p 839
42 Ibid.
43 Müller 1878, p 12
44 Smith 1875, p 9
45 Ibid., p 10
46 Ibid., p 11
47 Ibid., p 13
48 Ibid., pp 13–14
49 *The Times*, 4 December 1872, p 7
50–51 Ibid.
52 Smith 1875, p 97
53 Letter to *The Times* by A. H. Sayce, 13 September 1876, p 10
54 *The Times*, 11 September 1876, p 11
55 Cust 1895, p 685
56 G. Rawlinson 1898, pp 265–6
57 RAS archives: letter of 4 November 1889
58 G. Rawlinson 1898, p 291

59–60   Ibid., p 292
61 *The Times*, 6 March 1895,
    p 6
62 Goldsmid 1895, p 497
63 *The Athenaeum*, 9 March
    1895, p 314
64 Cust 1895, pp 689–90

Digging Down to Babylon
1 *The Athenaeum*, 9 March
    1895, p 313
2 Budge 1920, pp 231–2
3 Ibid., p 232
4 Booth 1902, pp xvi–xvii (he
    uses the term Turanian
    rather than Sumerian)

5 Sayce 1907, pp 67–8
6 Ibid., p 68
7 Ibid., pp 68, 70
8 Rogers 1912,
    p 404
9 Ibid., p 425
10 Ibid., p 433
11 Ibid., p 445
12 Ibid., p 448
13 Ibid., p 452
14 Rogers 1901, p 318
15 Rogers 1912, p 381
16 Ibid., p 382
17 Ibid., p 383

Afterword and Acknowledgements

My intention in this book has been to present the story of how Henry Rawlinson came to be involved in the decipherment of cuneiform and the study of ancient history and geography. I have chosen to concentrate much more on his early life, when decipherment and discovery were at such a pioneering stage, and when his activities had the greatest impact on recovering the lost history of Mesopotamia and Persia. Because he lived to the age of eighty-four and his life had so many strands and changes of direction, a full biography was not feasible without it being immensely long or superficial. I have not attempted to describe the decipherment process in intricate detail, but rather to tell the story of the progress of decipherment.

By and large, I have retained the spelling that was used in the nineteenth century, such as Bombay and Poona, rather than Mumbai and Pune, but elsewhere I have preferred more modern usage, such as Kabul rather than Cabool and Ghazni rather than Ghuznee. In other cases, where spelling seems inconsistent, I have used what is most common today, such as Muhammed Shah and Dost Mohammed. Spelling of proper names was universally inconsistent, so that Rawlinson, for example, used both Bisitun and Behistun.

When quoting from archives, I have not changed the content, but to clarify the meaning I have at times introduced a little more punctuation and expanded a few of the abbreviations. Rawlinson's own handwriting is a challenge, and previously published material has at times understandably misquoted what he wrote (such as Hester for Hector). I hope that I myself have not introduced too many new errors.

I have attempted to trace all copyright holders, and would especially like to thank the British Library, Royal Asiatic Society and Royal Geographical Society for giving me access to their archives. I would like to extend sincere thanks to all those who so willingly provided assistance and granted permission to use material: Revd Mark Abrey (The Chase Benefice), Professor A.D.H. Bivar (School of Oriental and African Studies), David Bromwich and Will Deckner (Somerset Studies Library), Corpus Inscriptionum Iranicarum, Masters, Fellows and Scholars of Christ's College, Paul Cox (National Portrait Gallery), Dr John Curtis and Christopher Walker (Department of the Ancient Near East, British Museum), the Trustees of the British Museum, Stuart Davison and Claire Jeffrey, Robin Francis (Heinz Archive & Library, National Portrait Gallery), Rex Geissler (of http://arcimaging.org), Mr S.J. Hobbs (Chadlington), Adrian James (Society of Antiquaries of London Library), Leslie Jessop (Hancock Museum), Mogens Trolle Larsen (Carsten Niebuhr Institute), Janet Law, Richard Martin (Canford School), the Mathias family of the Manor House at Chadlington, Susan and Robin Mitra, University College Oxford, Michael Pollock and S. Preetha Nair (Royal Asiatic Society), Kate Pool (Society of Authors), Professor D.T. Potts (University of Sydney), Nora Rawlinson, Elizabeth Ross (of www.bloodlines.net), Kevin Smith, Sarah Strong (Royal Geographical Society), Peter Tyrrell, Eric Williams and Patrick Walsh of Conville and Walsh Ltd. In addition, I would like to thank all the staff in the British Library reading rooms (Manuscripts, OIOC, Humanities, Rare Books), Bristol Zoo Gardens, Brookwood cemetery, Centre for Oxfordshire Studies, Chipping Norton Museum of Local History, Devon Library Services (notably St Thomas Library), the London Library, Devon and Exeter Institution, Exeter University library, University of Bristol library, the Office of Who's Who, John D. Wood & Co.

(Oxford) and everyone at HarperCollins involved in this book, in particular Mary Ore and Louise Tucker.

My greatest thanks must be to Michael Fishwick for his steadfast support and to Roy Adkins for much typing, photography, compiling the illustrations, taking on numerous chores, criticism, etc etc.

List of Illustrations

Recommended Reading

The following books and other published references are suggested for pursuing further particular topics – full references are given in the Bibliography.

Henry Creswicke Rawlinson

Rawlinson 1898: biography of Henry Rawlinson written by his brother George. Henry Rawlinson's main academic papers are Rawlinson 1846–47, 1849, 1850a and b, 1851, 1852 and 1861, his two papers on exploration are Rawlinson 1839 and 1841, and his book on Russia in central Asia is Rawlinson 1875.

Other Rawlinsons

Cunliffe 1978: detailed account of the Lancashire Rawlinsons; Foster 1873: family tree; Payne 1935: summary of Chadlington; Tashjian 1990: accounts of Richard Rawlinson the antiquary, the sale of his brother Thomas's book collection, and Daniel Rawlinson, friend of Samuel Pepys.

Austen Henry Layard

Fales and Hickey (eds) 1987: conference papers, with mentions of Rawlinson and Hincks; Gadd 1936: catalogue of all the known stone sculptures from Assyria, with a description of their discovery, excavated mainly by Layard; Larsen 1996: detailed and readable account of Layard's work in Mesopotamia, with a discussion of other people, such as Rawlinson and Hincks; Russell 1997: Layard and the Assyrian sculptures at Canford; Waterfield 1963: useful biography. Layard's own main books are: 1849 (two-volume account of his early excavations, mainly at Nimrud); 1853 (his later excavations); 1887 and 1894 (his early travels); and 1903 (a two-volume autobiography).

Others

Budge 1925: short accounts of numerous Assyriologists; Cathcart (ed.) 1994: papers on Hincks and his role in decipherment; Davidson 1933: biography of Hincks; Fontan (ed.) 1994: essays on Khorsabad, including Botta, in French; Harbottle 1973: paper on Loftus; Jones 1857: personal account of his survey work; Lloyd 1980: early exploration in Mesopotamia, including Layard and Rawlinson; Loftus 1857: account of his own excavations and travels; Mitford 1884: account of his travels with Layard; Rassam 1897: his excavations in Mesopotamia; Ross (ed.) 1902: letters of Henry Ross; Smith 1875: his first two expeditions; Stocqueler 1854: biography of Nott. Hincks's main academic papers are 1848a–c, 1850, 1852, 1858 and 1859.

East India Company and India

James 1997: introduction to India's history from 1740; Keay 1991: early history of the Company; Keay 2000: history of India from earliest times; Lawson 1993: clear explanation of the Company's history to 1857.

Cuneiform

There is a desperate need for basic and intermediate books about cuneiform. Many of the following are out-of-print or very difficult to obtain: *Assyrian Dictionary of the Oriental Institute of Chicago*: a multi-volume work, all in transliteration (no cuneiform signs); Bermant and Weitzman 1979: contains a very useful chapter on decipherment; Black et al. (eds) 2000: essential dictionary of Akkadian, all in transliteration (no cuneiform signs); Booth 1902: discovery and decipherment of trilingual inscriptions from the late fifteenth century; Caplice 1980: a typescript manual of Akkadian with exercises for students; Daniels and Bright (eds) 1996: includes discussions of numerous types of cuneiform and decipherment – a good, general introduction; Driver 1948: includes a detailed account of how clay tablets and styli were used; Gadd 1924: invaluable and straightforward introduction to Sumerian, but long out-of-print; Kent 1953: essential guide to Old Persian; Labat and Malbran-Labat 1999: detailed textbook on Akkadian, mostly a handwritten typescript, in French; Lecoq 1997: good introduction to Old Persian, in French; *Naissance de l'écriture* 1982: substantial illustrated exhibition catalogue on hieroglyphs and cuneiform; Pallis 1956: enormous and wonderful book on ancient Iraq, with much devoted to the decipherment and discovery of cuneiform inscriptions; Pope 1999: includes decipherment of Sasanian and Old Persian cuneiform, but only a limited discussion of Akkadian; Robinson 1995: highly illustrated introduction to early scripts, including cuneiform; Snell 1979: useful typescript manual of exercises (with answers) for students learning Akkadian cuneiform signs; Thomsen 1984: textbook on Sumerian, all in transliteration (no cuneiform signs); Walker 1990: illustrated introduction to cuneiform.

Bisitun

Greenfield and Porten 1982: Aramaic version of Bisitun; King and Thompson 1907: detailed account of the monument after a new survey, with inscriptions given in cuneiform and translation; Schmitt 1991: Old Persian version of the inscription (all in transliteration), with detailed discussion; Voigtlander 1978: Babylonian version of the inscription (all in transliteration).

Persia and Mesopotamia

Bienkowski and Millard (eds) 2000: dictionary of the ancient Near East; Black and Green 1998: dictionary of religion in Mesopotamia; Collon 1990: cylinder seals; Crawford 1991: textbook on Sumer; Curtis 2000: introduction to ancient Persia; Curtis and Reade (eds) 1995: illustrated exhibition catalogue of numerous Assyrian objects; Dalley (ed.) 1998: impact of Mesopotamia on other civilizations, including Victorian Britain; Fontan (ed.) 1994: essays relating to Khorsabad, in French; Frye 1975: Persia from Sasanian times; Frye 1976 and 1983: pre-Islamic history of Persia; Leick 1999: dictionary of people in ancient Mesopotamia; Matheson 1972: guidebook to archaeological sites of Iran; Meyers (ed.) 1997: five-volume encyclopedia on many aspects of the ancient Near East; Moorey 1994: textbook of the archaeological evidence for Mesopotamian technology; Pollock 1999: introduction to early Mesopotamia; Postgate 1992: readable account of early Mesopotamia, including a section on cuneiform; Potts 1999: detailed and readable textbook on Elam, from earliest times to the Sasanian period; Reade 2000: introduction to Mesopotamia; Saggs 1984: introduction to Assyria; Wiesehöfer 1996; pre-Islamic Persia; Wright 1977: the English in Persia from 1787.

Afghanistan

Allchin and Hammond 1978: textbook of the archaeology of Afghanistan; Ball 1982: detailed gazetteer of the archaeology of Afghanistan; Ewans 2001: readable history of Afghanistan; Hopkirk 1990: incidents in the Great Game, including Rawlinson; Kaye 1874, Macrory 1966 and Norris 1967: First Afghan War.

Noah's Ark and Biblical Archaeology

Corbin (ed.) 1999: numerous essays on Mount Ararat; Parrot 1845: account of his ascent of Mount Ararat.

Bibliography

Allchin, F. R. and Hammond, N. 1978 *The archaeology of Afghanistan from earliest times to the Timurid period* (London)

The Assyrian Dictionary of the Oriental Institute of the University of Chicago (1961 onwards) – multi-volume work (Chicago)

Ball, W. 1982 *Archaeological gazetteer of Afghanistan, vols 1 and 2* (Paris)

Bermant, C. and Weitzman, M. 1979 *Ebla: an archaeological enigma* (London)

Bienkowski, P. and Millard, A. (eds) 2000 *British Museum dictionary of the ancient Near East* (London)

Black, J. and Green, A. 1998 (2nd edn) *Gods, demons and symbols of ancient Mesopotamia: an illustrated dictionary* (London)

Black, J., George, A. and Postgate, N. (eds) 2000 *A concise dictionary of Akkadian* (Wiesbaden)

Booth, A. J. 1902 *The discovery and decipherment of the trilingual cuneiform inscriptions* (London, New York and Bombay)

Borger, R. 1975–78 'Dokumente zur Entzifferung der altpersischen Keilschrift durch H.C. Rawlinson', *Persica* 7, pp 1–5

Budge, E.A. Wallis 1920 *By Nile and Tigris. A narrative of journeys in Egypt and Mesopotamia on behalf of the British Museum between the years 1886 and 1913. Vol 1* (London)

——1925 *The rise and progress of Assyriology* (London)

Burnouf, E. 1836 *Mémoire sur deux inscriptions cunéiformes trouvées près d'Hamadan* (Paris)

Caplice, R. 1980 *Introduction to Akkadian* (Rome)

Cary, H.V. [probable author] 1820 *The cadet's guide to India; containing information and advice to young men about to enter the army of the Hon. East India Company* (London)

Cathcart, K.J. (ed.) 1994 *The Edward Hincks bicentenary lectures* (Dublin)

Collon, D. 1990 *Near Eastern seals* (London)

Corbin, B.J. (ed.) 1999 *The explorers of Ararat and the search for Noah's Ark* (Long Beach)

Crawford, H. 1991 *Sumer and the Sumerians* (Cambridge)

Cunliffe, L. 1978 *The Rawlinsons of Furness, being an account and the pedigree of an old Lancashire family* (Kendal)

Curtis, J.E. 2000 (2nd edn) *Ancient Persia* (London)

Curtis, J.E. and Reade, J.E. (eds) 1995 *Art and Empire: treasures from Assyria in the British Museum* (London)

Cust, R. 1895 Obituary notice, *Journal of the Royal Asiatic Society*, pp 681–90

Dalley, S. (ed) 1998 *The legacy of Mesopotamia* (Oxford)

Daniels, P.T. and Bright, W. (eds) 1996 *The world's writing systems* (New York/Oxford)

Davidson, E.F. 1933 *Edward Hincks. A selection from his correspondence with a memoir* (London)

Driver, G.R. 1948 *Semitic writing from pictograph to alphabet* (London)

Ewans, M. 2001 *Afghanistan: a new history* (Richmond)

Fales, F.M. and Hickey, B.J. 1987 (eds) *Austen Henry Layard. Tra L'Oriente e Venezia 26–28 ottobre 1983* (Rome)

Flandin, E. 1851 *Voyage en Perse de MM. Eugène Flandin, peintre, et Pascal Coste, architecte, attachés à l'ambassade de France en Perse pendant les années 1840 et 1841 entrepris par ordre de M. le ministre de l'intérieur. Vol 1 Relation du voyage* (Paris)

Fontan, E. (ed.) 1994 *De Khorsabad à Paris. La découverte des Assyriens* (Paris)

Foster, J. 1873 *Pedigrees of the county families of England compiled by Joseph Foster and authenticated by members of each family. Vol 1 Lancashire* (London)

Frye, R.N. 1975 *The Golden Age of Persia. The Arabs in the East* (London/New York)

——1976 (2nd edn) *The heritage of Persia* (London)

——1983 *The history of ancient Iran* (Munich)

Gadd, C.J. 1924 *A Sumerian reading-book* (Oxford)

——1936 *The stones of Assyria: the surviving remains of Assyrian sculpture, their recovery and their original positions* (London)

Goldsmid, F.J. 1895 Obituary notice, Major-General Sir Henry Creswicke Rawlinson, Bart., G.C.B. etc, *Geographical Journal* 5, pp 490–7

Greenfield, J.C. and Porten, B. 1982 *Corpus Inscriptionum Iranicarum. Part I Inscriptions of ancient Iran. Vol 5 The Aramaic versions of the Achaemenian inscriptions etc. Texts I. The Bisitun inscription of Darius the Great, Aramaic version* (London)

Harbottle, S. 1973 'W.K. Loftus: an archaeologist from Newcastle', *Archaeologia Aeliana* 1, 5th series, pp 195–217

Hincks, E. 1848a 'On the three kinds of Persepolitan writing and on the Babylonian lapidary characters', *Transactions of the Royal Irish Academy* 21, pp 233–48

——1848b 'On the third Persepolitan writing, and on the mode of expressing numerals in cuneatic characters', *Transactions of the Royal Irish Academy* 21, pp 249–56

——1848c 'On the inscriptions at Van', *Journal of the Royal Asiatic Society* 9, pp 387–49

——1850 'On the Khorsabad inscriptions', *Transactions of the Royal Irish Academy* 22, pp 3–72

——1852 'On the Assyrio-Babylonian phonetic characters', *Transactions of the Royal Irish Academy* 22, pp 293–370

——1858 'On the relation between the newly-discovered Accadian language and the Indo-European, Semitic, and Egyptian languages; with remarks on the original values of certain Semitic letters, and on the state of the Greek alphabet at different periods', *Report on the twenty-seventh meeting of the British Association for the Advancement of Science; held at Dublin in August and September 1857*, pp 134–43

——1859 'On a tablet in the British Museum, recording, in cuneatic characters, an astronomical observation; with incidental remarks on the Assyrian numerals, divisions of time, and measures of length', *Transactions of the Royal Irish Academy* 23, pp 31–57

Hopkirk, P. 1990 *The Great Game: on secret service in High Asia* (Oxford)

Jackson, A.V.W. 1906 *Persia past and present: a book of travel and research* (New York and London)

James, L. 1997 *Raj: the making and unmaking of British India* (London)

Jones, James Felix 1857 *Memoirs by Commander James Felix Jones, I.N.* (Bombay)

Kaye, J.W. 1874 (3rd edn) *History of the War in Afghanistan. Vols 1–3* (London)

——1878 (4th edn) *History of the War in Afghanistan. Vol 2* (London)

Keay, J. 1991 *The Honourable Company. A history of the English East India Company* (London)

——2000 *India: a history* (London)

Kent, R.G. 1953 (2nd edn) *Old Persian: grammar, texts, lexicon* (New Haven)

King, L.W. and Thompson, R. Campbell 1907 *The sculptures and inscription of Darius the Great on the rock at Behistûn in Persia. A new collation of the Persian, Susian, and Babylonian texts, with English translations, etc* (London)

Labat, R. and Malbran-Labat, F. 1999 (6th edn) *Manuel d'épigraphie akkadienne: signes, syllabaire, idéogrammes* (Paris)

Lane-Poole, S. 1888 *The life of the Right Honourable Stratford Canning. Vol 2* (London)

Larsen, M.T. 1996 *The conquest of Assyria: excavations in an antique land* (London)

Lawson, P. 1993 *The East India Company: a history* (London and New York)

Layard, A.H. 1849 *Nineveh and its remains: with an account of a visit to the Chaldaean Christians of Kurdistan, and the Yezidis, or devil-worshippers; and an enquiry into the manners and arts of the ancient Assyrians. Vols 1 and 2* (London)

——1853 *Discoveries in the ruins of Nineveh and Babylon; with travels in Armenia, Kurdistan and the desert: being the result of a second expedition undertaken for the Trustees of the British Museum* (London)

——1867 *Nineveh and its remains: a narrative of an expedition to Assyria during the years of 1845, 1846, & 1847* (London)

——1887 *Early adventures in Persia, Susiana, and Babylonia including a residence among the Bakhtiyari and other wild tribes before the discovery of Nineveh. Vols 1 and 2* (London)

——1894 (new edn) *Early adventures in Persia, Susiana, and Babylonia including a residence among the Bakhtiyari and other wild tribes before the discovery of Nineveh* (London)

——1903 *Autobiography and letters from his childhood until his appointment as H.M. Ambassador at Madrid. Vols 1 and 2* (London)

Lecoq, P. 1997 *Les inscriptions de la Perse achéménide. Traduit du vieux perse, de l'élamite, du babylonien et de l'araméen* (Paris)

Leick, G. 1999 *Who's Who in the ancient Near East* (London)

Lloyd, S. 1980 (rev edn) *Foundations in the dust: the story of Mesopotamian exploration* (London)

Loftus, W.K. 1857 *Travels and researches in Chaldaea and Susiana* (London)

Macrory, P. 1966 *Kabul catastrophe: the invasion and retreat, 1839–1842* (London)

Matheson, S.A. 1972 *Persia: an archaeological guide* (London)

Meyers, E.M. (ed.) 1997 *The Oxford encyclopedia of archaeology in the Near East. Vols 1–5* (Oxford)

Mitford, E.L. 1884 *A land march from England to Ceylon forty years ago, through Dalmatia, Montenegro, Turkey, Asia Minor, Syria, Palestine, Assyria, Persia, Afghanistan, Scinde, and India, of which 7000 miles on horseback. Vols 1 and 2* (London)

Moorey, P.S. 1994 *Ancient Mesopotamian materials and industries: the archaeological evidence* (Oxford)

Müller, F.M. 1878 'Julius Mohl', *Contemporary Review* 33, pp 1–21

Naissance de l'écriture, cunéiformes et hiéroglyphes 1982 (Paris)

Neill, J.M.B. 1845 *Recollections of four years' service in the East with H.M. Fortieth regiment* (London)

Norris, E. 1855 'Memoir on the Scythic version of the Behistun inscription', *Journal of the Royal Asiatic Society* 15, pp 1–163

Norris, J.A. 1967 *The First Afghan War 1838–1842* (Cambridge)

Pallis, S.A. 1956 *The antiquity of Iraq: a handbook of Assyriology* (Copenhagen)

Parrot, F. 1845 *Journey to Ararat* (trans W.D. Cooley, London)

Payne, J.D. 1935 *Notes on the history of the parish of Charlbury with Chadlington and Shorthampton Oxon* (Oxford)

Pollock, S. 1999 *Ancient Mesopotamia: the Eden that never was* (Cambridge)

Pope, M. 1999 (rev edn) *The story of decipherment, from Egyptian hieroglyphs to Maya script* (London)

Porter, R.K. 1822 *Travels in Georgia, Persia, Armenia, ancient Babylonia. Vol 2* (London)

Postgate, J.N. 1992 *Early Mesopotamia: society and economy at the dawn of history* (London)

Potts, D.T. 1999 *The archaeology of Elam: formation and transformation of an ancient Iranian state* (Cambridge)

Rassam, H. 1897 *Asshur and the land of Nimrod being an account of the discoveries made in the ancient ruins of Nineveh, Asshur, Sepharvaim, Calah, Babylon, Borsippa, Cuthah, and Van, including a narrative of different journeys in Mesopotamia, Assyria, Asia Minor, and Koordistan* (New York Cincinatti)

Rawlinson, G. 1875 (3rd edn) *History of Herodotus, Vol 1* (London)

——1898 *A memoir of Major-General Sir Henry Creswicke Rawlinson* (London/New York/Bombay)

Rawlinson, H.C. 1839 'Notes on a march from Zoháb, at the foot of Zagros, along the mountains of Khúzistán (Susiana), and from thence through the province of Luristan to Kirmánsháh in the year 1836', *Journal of the Royal Geographical Society* 9, pp 26–116

——1841 'Notes on a journey from Tabríz, through Persian Kurdistán, to the ruins of Takhti-Soleïmán, and from thence by Zenján and Tárom, to Gílán, in October and November, 1838; with a Memoir on the site of Atropatenian Ecbatana', *Journal of the Royal Geographical Society* 10, pp 1–158

——1843 'Comparative geography of Afghanistan', *Journal of the Royal Geographical Society* 12, pp 112–14

——1846–47 'The Persian cuneiform inscription at Behistun, decyphered and translated; with a memoir on Persian cuneiform inscriptions in general, and on that of Behistun in particular' *Journal of the Royal Asiatic Society* 10, pp i–lxxi, 1–349

——1849 'The Persian cuneiform inscription at Behistun, decyphered and translated; with a memoir', *Journal of the Royal Asiatic Society* 11, pp 1–192

——1850a 'On the inscriptions of Assyria and Babylonia', *Journal of the Royal Asiatic Society* 12, pp 401–83

——1850b 'Note on the Persian inscriptions at Behistun', *Journal of the Royal Asiatic Society* 12, pp i–xxi

——1851 'Memoir on the Babylonian and Assyrian inscriptions', *Journal of the Royal Asiatic Society* 14, pp i–civ, 1–16

——1852 'Notes on some paper casts of cuneiform inscriptions upon the sculptured rock at Behistun exhibited to the Society of Antiquaries', *Archaeologia* 34, pp 73–6

——1861 'On the Birs Nimrud, or the Great Temple of Borsippa', *Journal of the Royal Asiatic Society* 18, pp 1–34

——1875 *England and Russia in the East: a series of papers on the political and geographical condition of central Asia* (London)

Reade, J. 2000 (2nd edn) *Mesopotamia* (London)

Robinson, A. 1995 *The story of writing. Alphabets, hieroglyphs & pictograms* (London)

Rogers, R.W. 1901 *A history of Babylonia and Assyria, Vol 1* (London)

——1912 *Cuneiform parallels to the Old Testament* (London Toronto Melbourne Bombay)

Ross, J. (ed.) 1902 *Letters from the East by Henry James Ross 1837–1857* (London)

Russell, J.M. 1997 *From Nineveh to New York: the strange story of the Assyrian reliefs in the Metropolitan Museum and the hidden masterpiece at Canford School* (New Haven London)

Saggs, H.W.F. 1984 *The might that was Assyria* (London)

Sayce, A.H. 1907 *The archaeology of the cuneiform inscriptions* (Brighton New York)

Schmitt, R. 1991 *Corpus Inscriptionum Iranicarum. Part I Inscriptions of ancient Iran. Vol I The Old Persian inscriptions. Texts I. The Bisitun inscriptions of Darius the Great: Old Persian text* (London)

Smith, G. 1875 *Assyrian discoveries; an account of explorations and discoveries on the site of Nineveh during 1873 and 1874* (London)

Snell, D.C. 1979 *A workbook of cuneiform signs* (Malibu)

Stocqueler, J.H. 1854 *Memoirs and correspondence of Major-General Sir William Nott, G.C.B., Vols 1 and 2* (London)

Talbot, W.H.F. Hincks, E. Oppert, J. and Rawlinson, H.C. 1861 'Comparative translations of the inscription of Tiglath Pileser I', *Journal of the Royal Asiatic Society* 18, pp 150–219

Tashjian, G.R. and D.R. 1990 *Richard Rawlinson, a tercentenary memorial* (Michigan)

Thompson, R.C. (no date) 'Behistun', pp 554–61 in J.A. Hammerton (ed.), *Wonders of the Past, Vol 2* (London)

Thomsen, M.-L. 1984 *The Sumerian language: an introduction to its history and grammatical structure* (Copenhagen)

Voigtlander, E.N. von 1978 *The Bisitun inscription of Darius the Great: Babylonian version* (London)

Walker, C.B.F. 1990 'Cuneiform', pp 14–73 in J.T. Hooker, *Reading the past. Ancient writing from cuneiform to the alphabet* (London)

Walpole, F. 1851 *The Ansayrii, and the assassins, with travels in the further east, in 1850–51 including a visit to Nineveh. Vol 2* (London)

Waterfield, G. 1963 *Layard of Nineveh* (London)

Wieshöfer, J. 1996 *Ancient Persia from 550 BC to 650 AD* (London New York)

Wright, D. 1977 *The English amongst the Persians* (London)

Index

P.S.

Ideas,
interviews
& features ...

About the author

About the book

Read on

Portrait
Tom Cochrane talks to Lesley Adkins

LESLEY ADKINS IS a difficult person to track down. Her house in the heart of Devon is perched on a hillside with stunning views across the valley to Dartmoor, and as she sat at her desk opposite a huge picture window opening on to this wonderful panorama, I suggested this would be a terrible distraction for any author. 'When I am writing, I am totally focused,' she explained, 'and I can work for an hour or so at a stretch without even noticing who or what surrounds me; but when I need a break, it is so refreshing to look out at the landscape or go for a walk. I lived in London for some years, but found the lack of colour depressing – here the colours change day by day, and there is always something fresh to see.'

In her career so far, Lesley has led a nomadic life, although always living in Britain and only going abroad for research expeditions and holidays. Having studied archaeology, ancient history and Latin at the University of Bristol, she started out working as a field archaeologist at Milton Keynes ('it was just one huge building site then'), and there she met her husband Roy, who is also an author. 'We have worked together ever since,' comments Lesley, 'and many people who only see their partners at breakfast, in the evening and at weekends find that strange.' Having signed the contract for their first jointly written book just months before they were married, they moved to London ('in field archaeology, you have to go where the work is'), and even there they lived in several places.

'Archaeology is a very poorly paid profession, and the first home we could afford to buy was a derelict semi-detached in Croydon, where we had to reinstall the water and electric supplies and build a bathroom. While we were renovating it, we were writing books together, I was finishing the thesis for my Masters degree, and we were also out all day working as field archaeologists – it was anything but a nine-to-five routine. Looking back, I really appreciate the tranquillity we have here now.'

From London, Lesley eventually moved to Somerset. 'A dramatic change in archaeology was taking place then,' she observes, 'which effectively turned field archaeologists from local government employees to freelancers competing for work. We set up our archaeological consultancy business in Somerset, and after surviving the deep recession, we moved to Devon. We still work as archaeologists occasionally, but most of our time now is taken up with writing.' Having written many books and articles together, Lesley and her husband decided it was time to write independently. 'It was *The Keys of Egypt*, which HarperCollins published in 2000, that made us take the plunge,' Lesley explains. 'Working together on the research was stimulating and great fun, and it was not just the dusty library and archive work to unravel how Egyptian hieroglyphs came to be rediscovered and deciphered – our research trips to Egypt and France to track the movements of Champollion (who ▶

> 6 We still work as archaeologists occasionally, but most of our time now is taken up with writing. 9

3

Portrait *(continued)*

◀ finally deciphered hieroglyphs) were just wonderful, but the actual writing presented problems. Even though the historical facts determined the general course of the narrative, where there was any leeway we found we were pulling in different directions. Paradoxically, this may have strengthened the narrative, as every digression was discussed and sometimes argued over, but it took the edge off the pleasure of writing, and so we decided to write individually.'

Empires of the Plain is Lesley's début book as sole author, and she admits she found writing it a completely different experience. 'Roy and I still help each other with research for our individual projects and discuss problems that arise, but it felt strange at first, having total control.' Lesley chose the subject in the time-honoured tradition of finding a gap on the bookshelves. 'While writing *The Keys of Egypt,* which was all about hieroglyphs, I looked in detail at cuneiform writing for the first time and realized what a colourful character Rawlinson was. He not only bore the brunt of the decipherment, but he led a startlingly adventurous life that spanned most of the nineteenth century. It is one of the real joys of non-fiction writing when you can describe incredible events that actually took place – events that any editor might be tempted to cut from a novel or short story for stretching the credulity of the reader too far. For me, the most important part of the book was piecing together the details of Rawlinson's life and those around him, discovering information for the very first time. Nobody had ever looked in detail at the archives held by the Royal Geographical Society, so it was an absolute thrill, for example, to discover Rawlinson's almost illegible journal giving the previously unknown account of his final visit to the momentous mountain of Bisitun.'

Rawlinson was certainly an adventurer, but hardly a role model for the politically correct modern world. 'He was a man of his century,' agrees Lesley, 'and yet he had some qualities that would shine in any age. He was much more tolerant and understanding of foreign peoples and foreign cultures than many of his contemporaries, and his outstanding success as a diplomat was largely due to his empathy with the people and his ability to judge the state of affairs around him. He knew, for example, that they were heading for disaster in Afghanistan, but his superiors brushed aside his fears. As a soldier, he could be tough and even ruthless, yet he was one of the few officers not disgraced by incompetence during that First Afghan War. For me he epitomizes the early period of archaeological exploration that looks so romantic when viewed from the safety and comfort of the twenty-first century, when pioneer archaeologists all too often had to record their finds with a loaded pistol at the ready in case of trouble.'

Asked what it was like to write about areas such as Afghanistan and Iraq that are so much in the news today, Lesley explained that this was not the case when she started out on the research for the book: 'Many of the places were really very obscure, but all that changed after 11 September. ▶

> 6 Rawlinson was certainly an adventurer, but hardly a role model for the politically correct modern world. 9

I rarely, if ever, read a
book more than once, as
I always want to get on to
the next one. I tend to
alternate between reading
fiction and history or
historical biography.
The fiction is for pure
relaxation, and my
preference is for thrillers
and detective novels,
with favourite authors
including Jeffrey Deaver,
James Lee Burke, Kathy
Reichs, Patricia Cornwell,
Paul Eddy, Michael
Dibdin, Donna Leon,
Lee Child and Janet
Evanovich. As for non-
fiction, I have most
recently read and
thoroughly enjoyed
Peter Ackroyd's *London:
The Biography*, Richard
Holmes's *Redcoat* and
Claire Tomalin's *Samuel
Pepys*. But my favourite
history book has got to be
*Trafalgar: The Biography of
a Battle* by Roy Adkins.

Portrait *(continued)*

◄ Wonderful remote places such as
Kandahar seemed overnight to become
public property, in the news all the time! It
has been very strange.'

When asked about her future plans,
Lesley sighs. 'What needs seeing to most of all
is our house. We fell in love with it because of
the views and the enormous, wild garden, but
the house itself is far from perfect. Perhaps
this year we'll gradually renovate it.' As to
her future writing plans, Lesley would not
be drawn. 'What I love doing most of all is
bringing the stories of history alive and
telling the adventures of the past in an
accessible way. That's what I'll be looking to
do in my next book.' ■

A Critical Eye

IN *EMPIRES OF THE PLAIN*, Lesley Adkins really impressed the reviewers with her exploration of the life of Henry Rawlinson, described by the *Daily Telegraph* as 'a Victorian Indiana Jones' whose life story was 'like a *Boy's Own* adventure story'. Several reviewers particularly enjoyed the blend of archaeological investigation with real-life drama, with the *Sunday Times* summing it up as 'a colourful account of a fascinating and little-known story' that combined 'scholarship with high adventure, and is enlivened by the larger-than-life character of Henry Rawlinson'.

Scotland on Sunday commented on the parallels between the Middle East in Rawlinson's day and the present situation, noting that the 'story is resonant now, as again warring empires clash in Mesopotamia', but did not miss the fact that Lesley 'tells the tale with verve'. *The Times* took a more academic view, observing that '*Empires of the Plain* is a welcome addition to history writing on the archaeological exploration of the Near East'. It was the *Sunday Telegraph*, however, that really got to the heart of the matter: 'the real value of this book is that it not only tells the story of Rawlinson's life and work, but also introduces the reader to the whole range of 19th-century breakthroughs that opened up modern knowledge of the "Empires of the Plain" – the linguistic and archaeological discoveries that illuminated ancient Babylon, Assyria and Sumer.' ■

Henry Rawlinson:
A Life in Brief

TO DO HENRY RAWLINSON justice, a two- or three-volume book would be needed. He led such a full and eventful life that not every detail can be covered in one book, so Lesley decided she would concentrate on the earlier years of Rawlinson as an adventurer and explorer and not on his later life when he retired to England. She was determined that this should not be an unreadable academic analysis, but, in the manner of her previous book *The Keys of Egypt*, that it should open up the world of ancient Persia and Mesopotamia to a wide readership, at the same time giving an entertaining account of the life and adventures of this fascinating man.

Henry Rawlinson was born in 1810 in the manor house in the village of Chadlington in north Oxfordshire, close to the town of Chipping Norton; here he spent much of his childhood on an idyllic estate of several hundred acres. The manor house still exists, next to the church, but much of Wychwood Forest to the south has been cleared, so the view from the house has changed greatly. There are reminders today of the Rawlinson family in Chadlington. Set in the west wall of the manor house is a plaque commemorating the life of Henry Rawlinson, while Coronation Cottage nearby celebrates the astounding win his father had at the Derby with a horse by the name of Coronation. In West Chadlington, the modern Rawlinson Close keeps the family name alive, while in the church a stained-glass window commemorates Henry's father Abram and his mother.

As a young boy, Henry also spent much time at Bristol, where he lived with his aunt and uncle in Park Street on what was then the very edge of the city. Henry's aunt, Anna Smith, was part of a large literary circle in Bristol, many of whom were also involved in the movement to abolish slavery. At the age of eleven, Henry began to spend less and less time at Chadlington and Bristol when he was sent away to various boarding schools, the last being at Ealing, then a village near London and not, as today, part of the urban sprawl.

In 1827 Rawlinson went to India as a military cadet in the East India Company's army, based initially at Bombay. Military duties were not onerous and left him plenty of time to engage in his passions of horse racing and game hunting. Unusually for a young man, he also had other passions: history, languages and buying books. He was so good at languages that he became an interpreter in his regiment and in 1833 was chosen to go to Persia because of his excellent knowledge of Persian. It was in Persia (today's Iran) that he became obsessed with ancient cuneiform writing.

Cuneiform literally means 'of wedge-shaped form' and is probably the earliest writing in the world, first invented by accountants to keep track of produce entering and leaving the palaces of Mesopotamia. It may have been 'picture writing' at a very early date, but most ▶

❝ He was so good at languages that he became an interpreter in his regiment ❞

Henry Rawlinson (continued)

◄ cuneiform writing that we see on monuments, clay tablets, relief sculptures and so on resembles abstract strokes and arrows. The Persian king Darius the Great unwittingly helped the decipherment of cuneiform enormously, because he actually invented a simplified form that could be used to write down the language of Old Persian.

When Rawlinson first went to Persia, cuneiform was barely understood, although the German scholar Georg Grotefend had made a useful attempt to work out the meaning of the signs. As well as being gifted in languages, both ancient and modern, Rawlinson had the good fortune to be posted to Kermanshah, a remote town in the west of Iran in the Zagros mountains, just a few miles from a rock-cut monument at Bisitun that turned out to be far more significant than Egypt's Rosetta Stone. Cuneiform was a writing system, not a language. This is rather like Roman letters today, which are used to write down many languages, such as English, German, French, Swedish, Spanish and so on.

On the rock face of the Bisitun mountain, the Persian king Darius the Great had ordered a huge inscription to be carved, with the same message written in three different languages, all carved in cuneiform writing. One of those languages was Old Persian, carved in Darius's newly invented cuneiform, and the other two languages were Babylonian and Elamite. Rather fortunately, after the monument was completed, Darius ordered all access to it to be quarried away, so nobody could

❝ Cuneiform literally means 'of wedge-shaped form' and is probably the earliest writing in the world, first invented by accountants to keep track of produce entering and leaving the palaces of Mesopotamia. ❞

reach it and deface it. It was far too difficult for anyone to climb, until the intrepid Rawlinson came along. With nerves of steel, he constantly climbed up to the monument, copying at his peril the enormous inscription, which in the end gave him the key to deciphering two of the languages, Babylonian and Old Persian, and greatly helped with the third, Elamite.

All did not go smoothly, however, as Rawlinson's dangerous work was halted and he was sent to Afghanistan, where he became embroiled in the First Anglo-Afghan War. He was based for around two years as the political agent (diplomat) in Kandahar, a city that has appeared in the news often following the events of 11 September 2001. While much of the British Army perished, Rawlinson survived and subsequently accepted a posting to Baghdad, where he remained for twelve years. Apart from his diplomatic duties, he made two expeditions back into Persia to copy more of the Bisitun monument, and also continued his cuneiform decipherment work, making many discoveries while based in the British Residency at Baghdad by the River Tigris. Also in Baghdad he made the acquaintance of Austen Henry Layard, who began to excavate the huge ancient mounds of Nineveh and Nimrud, with astounding and unsuspected results. When Layard finally gave up his work, Rawlinson became much more involved in the excavation of Iraq's ancient cities.

Even when he retired to England, Rawlinson continued his work at the ▶

6 Cuneiform was a writing system, not a language. This is rather like Roman letters today, which are used to write down many languages, such as English, German, French, Swedish, Spanish and so on. 9

Henry Rawlinson *(continued)*

◀ British Museum, helping other students, including George Smith, who became so proficient that he was taken on as an employee of the museum. Smith made the astounding discovery on one clay tablet that there was a story of the flood similar to that in the Old Testament, but much earlier in date. This was exciting, yet disturbing news, and resulted in the *Daily Telegraph* sponsoring Smith to undertake further excavations at Nineveh.

Rawlinson married late in life, as did Layard. He had two sons, but his wife died tragically early. He himself kept busy right to his death at the age of 84, most notably as a Member of Parliament, with the Royal Asiatic Society, Royal Geographical Society, as a Trustee of the British Museum and as a Director of the East India Company. ■

Have You Read?

The following is a selection of other books written by Lesley Adkins and her husband Roy:

The Keys of Egypt: The Race to Read the Hieroglyphs
The fascinating and at times tragic story of Jean-François Champollion, his obsession with Egyptian hieroglyphs, and his struggle to succeed in the dangerous political climate of Napoleonic France.

The Little Book of Egyptian Hieroglyphs
A light-hearted and basic introduction, for complete beginners, to Egyptian hieroglyphs.

Introduction to the Romans
A beginner's guide to the world of the Romans, with numerous colour photographs.

Introduction to Archaeology
A beginner's guide to the meaning of archaeology and what it can achieve. Illustrated throughout with colour photographs.

Abandoned Places
An exploration of places that have been completely abandoned, for instance through natural disasters, warfare or climate change. Illustrated throughout with colour photographs. ∎

If You Loved This,
You'll Like . . .

Persia in the Great Game: Sir Percy Sykes –
Explorer, Consul, Soldier, Spy
Antony Wynn
A fascinating biography of Britain's
colourful point-man in pre-First World War
Persia. Combining rollicking adventure with
serious historical scholarship, Wynn has
written a thoroughly engaging story with
startlingly relevant themes.

....

A Book of Lands and Peoples
Eric Newby
Compiled by the legendary travel writer Eric
Newby, this massive book is a treasure trove
of bizarre, intriguing and profound writings
from several centuries and seven continents.
From Herodotus to Paul Theroux, from
Marco Polo to Christopher Columbus, the
cream of the travel writing crop has finally
been collected in one volume.

If You Loved This *(continued)*

The Sword and the Cross
Fergus Fleming
This is the enthralling story of two fanatical
adventurers who sought to conquer the
Sahara for France, sacrificing everything in
their pursuit of personal obsessions that
only the unforgiving desert could satisfy.

The Age of Kali: Travels and Encounters in India
William Dalrymple
An enchanting collection of Dalrymple's
essays about life in modern India. From
the badlands of Bihar to the cosmopolitan
scene of Bombay, Dalrymple reveals
the fascinating range of places and
characters that make up this most
intriguing country. ■

Find Out More

WEBSITES

www.adkinsarchaeology.com
The webpage of Lesley Adkins and her
husband and fellow archaeologist and
writer, Roy. Contains a wealth of
information about both of their books,
including photos, summaries, excerpts
and more.

www.cdli.ucla.edu
The homepage of the Cuneiform Digital
Library, whose curators are in the process of
assembling an online archive of virtually
every cuneiform text currently housed in
museums across the world.

**www.smm.org/research/Anthropology/
cuneiform/cuneiform.php**
Fantastic interactive website maintained by
the Science Museum of Minnesota. A
complete digital photographic library of all
of the Museum's cuneiform tablets,
including histories, translations and
commentary on each.

PLACES

**The British Museum, Great Russell Street,
London WC1**
This amazing museum has a large collection
of artefacts from Mesopotamia, ranging
from cuneiform tablets to the Black Obelisk
and the colossal human-headed bulls and
lions, many of which were excavated by
Layard and Rawlinson. Visit their website
www.thebritishmuseum.ac.uk. ∎